RESILIENCY IN AFRICAN-AMERICAN FAMILIES

RESILIENCY IN FAMILIES SERIES
Hamilton I. McCubbin, *Series Editor*

Volumes in This Series

Stress, Coping, and Health in Families: Sense of Coherence and Resiliency
Edited by Hamilton I. McCubbin, Elizabeth A. Thompson, Anne I. Thompson, and Julie E. Fromer

Resiliency in Native American and Immigrant Families
Edited by Hamilton I. McCubbin, Elizabeth A. Thompson, Anne I. Thompson, and Julie E. Fromer

Resiliency in African-American Families
Edited by Hamilton I. McCubbin, Elizabeth A. Thompson, Anne I. Thompson, and Jo A. Futrell

Dedication

This book is dedicated to special friends and family who represent to us what is important about resiliency and ethnicity past and future:

Dr. Marie F. Peters
&
Dr. John L. McAdoo

whose leadership on behalf of people and families of color in the National Council on Family Relations and whose contributions to the body of knowledge on African-American families will always be appreciated and valued, and to

Jessica Emily Whitesell McCubbin
Rachel Stephanie Whitesell McCubbin
Joseph Armando Thompson
&
Lane Berdelle Thompson

who represent our futures, which we anticipate will include a greater respect for and appreciation of ethnic diversity.

RESILIENCY IN AFRICAN-AMERICAN FAMILIES

EDITORS

HAMILTON I. McCUBBIN

ELIZABETH A. THOMPSON

ANNE I. THOMPSON

JO A. FUTRELL

RESILIENCY IN FAMILIES SERIES

SAGE Publications
International Educational and Professional Publisher
Thousand Oaks   London   New Delhi

For information:

SAGE Publications, Inc.
2455 Teller Road
Thousand Oaks, California 91320
E-mail: order@sagepub.com

SAGE Publications Ltd.
6 Bonhill Street
London EC2A 4PU
United Kingdom

SAGE Publications India Pvt. Ltd.
M-32 Market
Greater Kailash I
New Delhi 110 048 India

Printed in the United States of America

Library of Congress Cataloging-in-Publication Data

Main entry under title:
    Resiliency in African-American families / edited by Hamilton I.
    McCubbin ... [et al.].
    p. cm. -- (Resiliency in families series ; v. 3)

    ISBN 0-7619-1392-0 (acid-free paper)
    ISBN 0-7619-1393-9 (pbk. : acid-free paper)
    1. Afro-American families. I. McCubbin, Hamilton I. II. Series:
    Resiliency in families series (Thousand Oaks, Calif.) ; v. 3
    E185.86 .R46 1998
    306.85'089'96073--ddc21
                        98-9024

This book is printed on acid-free paper.

98 99 00 01 02 03 04 10 9 8 7 6 5 4 3 2 1

Contents

I. Families and Communities

Contributors

William D. Allen
Department of Family Social Science
University of Minnesota
St. Paul, MN

Cherie A. Bagley
Department of Family Practice
University of Iowa
Iowa City, IA

Marilyn L. Cantwell
School of Human Ecology
Louisiana State University
Baton Rouge, LA

Juanitaelizabeth Carroll
Grant African Methodist Episcopal
    Church
Chicago, IL

Ana Mari Cauce
Department of Psychology
University of Washington
Seattle, WA

Michael E. Connor
California State University,
    Long Beach
Long Beach, CA

William J. Doherty
Department of Family Social Science
University of Minnesota
St. Paul, MN

Kelly M. Elver
School of Human Ecology
University of Wisconsin–Madison
Madison, WI

Wm. Michael Fleming
School of Human Ecology
University of Wisconsin–Madison
Madison, WI

Jo A. Futrell
Center for Excellence in
    Family Studies
University of Wisconsin–Madison
Madison, WI

Nancy P. Genero
Department of Psychology
Wellesley College
Wellesley, MA

Nancy A. Gonzales
Department of Psychology
Arizona State University
Tempe, AZ

Yumi Hiraga
Department of Psychology
University of Washington
Seattle, WA

Carol Sue Holtz
Department of Nursing
Kennesaw State College
Marietta, GA

Dorothy I. Jenkins
School of Human Ecology
Louisiana State University
Baton Rouge, LA

Alex Kotlowitz
Author & Journalist
Oak Park, IL

Harriette Pipes McAdoo
Department of Family and Child
    Ecology
Michigan State University
East Lansing, MI

Hamilton I. McCubbin
School of Human Ecology
University of Wisconsin–Madison
Madison, WI

Marilyn A. McCubbin
School of Nursing
University of Wisconsin–Madison
Madison, WI

Velma McBride Murry
Department of Child & Family
    Development
University of Georgia–Athens
Athens, GA

Paul Neitman
Boysville of Michigan
Clinton, MI

Su An Arnn Phipps
College of Nursing
University of Oklahoma–Tulsa
Tulsa, OK

Sue Ann Savas
Boysville of Michigan
Clinton, MI

Anne I. Thompson
School of Human Ecology
University of Wisconsin–Madison
Madison, WI

Elizabeth A. Thompson
School of Human Ecology
University of Wisconsin–Madison
Madison, WI

Michael C. Thornton
Department of Afro-American Studies
University of Wisconsin–Madison
Madison, WI

Series Preface

Families at Their Best

The scholarly work of Aaron Antonovsky on *salutogenesis* brings our current emphasis in Resiliency in Families into sharper focus by underscoring the importance of the *sense of coherence* as a vital dispositional world view that expresses the individual's and the family's shared dynamic feeling of confidence that the world is comprehensible, manageable, and meaningful. The construct of sense of coherence fits within the broader rubric of *resiliency*, the positive behavioral patterns and functional competence individuals and families demonstrate under stressful or adverse circumstances.

It was more than coincidence that the Center for Excellence in Family Studies at the University of Wisconsin–Madison would launch its initial lecture and publication series, Resiliency in Families, by inviting Professor Antonovsky to present and discuss his current work and efforts with colleagues who have studied and examined his theories, propositions, and hypotheses. At the core of salutogenesis and the sense of coherence is the fundamental belief that individuals and families have dispositional qualities that serve to promote their health and well-being. The search for knowledge about these central concepts, incorporating a cross-cultural perspective, will shed light on why some families manage life events with relative ease and recover from adversity with renewed strength, harmony, and purpose. The invitational conference laid the foundation for the special publication entitled *Stress, Coping, and Health in Families: Sense of Coherence and Resiliency,* the first publication in the Resiliency in Families Series.

The Center for Excellence in Family Studies, approved and established by the Board of Regents of the University of Wisconsin System, has also created for itself a research focus and agenda that would best be stated in this inaugural publication. The theme of Resiliency in Families places the creation, integration, application, and dissemination of knowledge about the *power of families* of all forms, structures, ethnic groups, and cultures to recover from adversity as the highest priority in the Center's agenda. In its efforts

to advance research on resiliency in families, the Center will draw
from and foster the advancement of research that:

- searches for family resources (e.g., financial well-
  being, management skills) that will buffer the family
  from the disabling effects of stressors, promote the
  family's recovery in the face of adversity, and promote adaptation.

- searches for family member strengths and capabilities (e.g., the sense of coherence, personality) that
  will buffer the family from the disabling effects of
  stressors, promote the family's recovery in the face
  of adversity, and promote adaptation.

- searches for established patterns of family functioning (e.g., family traditions and routines) that will
  buffer the family from the disabling effects of stressors, promote the family's recovery in the face of
  adversity, and promote adaptation.

- searches for new and instituted patterns of functioning (e.g., effective utilization of health care and mental health services) that families create to facilitate
  the family's recovery from adversity and that promote adaptation.

- searches for family dispositional traits and competencies (e.g., the sense of coherence, hardiness) that families develop over time that will buffer the family
  from the disabling effects of stressors, promote the
  family's recovery in the face of adversity, and promote adaptation.

- searches for family processes of appraisal (e.g., schema,
  paradigms) that will buffer the family from the disabling effects of stressors, promote the family's recovery in the face of adversity, and promote
  adaptation.

- searches for family patterns of unproductive coping
  and adaptations (e.g., avoidance, denial), which have
  the short-term value of promoting adaptation but

which, if adopted as an established pattern, have adverse maladaptative outcomes.

- searches for family patterns of productive coping and adaptations (e.g., problem-solving behavior, social support), which have both short- and long-term positive adaptive outcomes.

- searches for family-oriented intervention programs and public policies that have the value of promoting the resistance resources in families under stress and fostering the resiliency in families faced with crises and adversity.

- searches for dysfunctional patterns in families that increase the family's vulnerability to stressors and that curtail the family's recovery from adversity.

Out of the ten strategic agendas of resiliency in families research, only one focuses upon the study of dysfunctional families. Consistent with the salutogenic framework, research on the resiliency in families underscores the importance of understanding the natural resistance resources in families and the capabilities and patterns of functioning that families call upon to manage the ebb and flow of life and all its hardships. From this salutogenic and resiliency orientation, the well-being of families can be best understood by studying the natural capabilities of families to endure, survive, and even thrive in the face of crises. While helpful, the theories and methodologies flowing from the study of dysfunctional families may limit and skew our search for the productive responses and capabilities of families. The resiliency in families may have the greatest potential of coming to light through theories and research that focus on why families succeed and endure in spite of adversities and crises. With this perspective in mind, this publication is offered to continue our search for knowledge about families at their best.

HAMILTON I. MCCUBBIN
Editor, Resiliency in Families Series

Preface

Resiliency in African-American Families is the second volume in a unique two-volume collection devoted to issues facing racial and ethnic minority families. In a field dominated by deficiency and deviance models for minority families, these chapters are the product of an innovative conference held on the University of Wisconsin–Madison campus, which focused on the strengths and resources of minority families. In focusing on the issue of resiliency, the positive behavioral patterns and functional competence individuals and families demonstrate under stressful or adverse circumstances, particular attention was given to the role that culture and ethnicity play in the families' development of coping strategies and the meaning given to stressful life events.

To link the two volumes, the final chapter of this book was created by the editors as a review of the major themes presented here and in *Resiliency in Native American and Immigrant Families*. This book is divided into two parts:

Part I. *Families and Communities* addresses issues related to the context in which the family unit lives, and the effects of community and cultural resources on the family's resilient adaptation to stressful life events. The authors in this part explore the realities of urban and community life for African-American families as well as employing a resiliency framework to investigate how African-American families mobilize extended family resources, racial socialization strategies, health care, religious supports, and caregiving supports available within their communities.

Part II. *Family Relationships* focuses on issues of resiliency within the context of the family. These chapters explore the resilient strategies of coping and adaptation employed by African-American families in addressing marital relations and parent-child relations, as well as the challenges associated with adolescent pregnancy and parenthood.

Far too frequently, the social science literature on African-American families has measured African-American families using the norms constructed for Caucasian families. By employing a resiliency perspective in research on African-American families, we may begin to understand and appreciate the unique strengths and capabilities of these families. Through the recognition of the strengths in the African-American community, we can add a vital and positive picture of African-American family life that has long been missing from the family science literature.

HAMILTON I. McCUBBIN
ELIZABETH A. THOMPSON
ANNE I. THOMPSON
JO A. FUTRELL
Editors

Acknowledgments

This second volume on resiliency in ethnic families also reflects the work of many whose support and contributions cannot be overstated. We are deeply grateful to Dean Ayse Somersan and Dr. Ellen Fitzsimmons of the Cooperative Extension Service, who saw the value of this unique effort, made a personal and special contribution to the conference's success, and offered support for this publication. When combined with the vision and support of Director Winston Van Horne and Associate Director Thomas Tonnesen of the Institute on Race and Ethnicity, we found a special team working together with a common goal. We are deeply grateful for this opportunity to work together with prominent units of the University of Wisconsin System, the Cooperative Extension Service, and the Institute on Race and Ethnicity to place ethnic families in the forefront of our teaching, research, and service.

Our team continues to work together to make wonderful things happen. We are grateful for the contributions of Mr. George Fisher, Ms. Christine Davenport, Ms. Diane Sosa, and Ms. Gloria McCord, as well as our new supporters of this effort, Assistant Dean Anthony Johnson and Ms. Cherlynn Stevens, Director of our Minority programs. Their efforts are combined with our continued support from the leaders within the University of Wisconsin Foundation—President Andrew Wilcox, Senior Vice President Tim Reilley, John Feldt, and Martha Taylor, Vice President Marion Brown, and our Development Officer Nancy Gibson. Our partnerships in these efforts have made ideas come to life and serve to support the mission of the University of Wisconsin–Madison.

Our hats are off to Mr. Wade Masshardt and Ms. Kelly Elver, who have provided us with quality work and analyses, contributing both to the content and overall quality of the publication. Mr. Masshardt's collaboration with Mr. Hjalmer (Jim) Harried of Extension Duplicating has produced wonders of which we are very proud.

We are reminded that this publication, and others to follow in the Resiliency in Families Series, flow from the wisdom and visionary thinking of two important women who have been leaders on behalf of the School of Human Ecology. We will forever be grateful for the gifts from Professor Emeritus Ruth Dickie, which established the Institute for the Study of Resiliency in Families, and the gift of Mrs. Jean Manchester-Biddick, President of the Bascom Hill Society, who endowed the Center for Excellence in Family Studies. All proceeds from this publication are returned to the Institute to continue the support of this publication series.

I. Families and Communities

Chapter 1

Breaking the Silence

Growing Up in Today's Inner City[1]

Alex Kotlowitz[2]

Editors' note: This chapter is adapted from a keynote address given by Alex Kotlowitz as part of the "Resiliency in Families: Racial and Ethnic Minority Families in America" conference, held at the University of Wisconsin–Madison, May 31-June 2, 1994.

Thanks for having me. I have strong competition with this wonderful sunset over here. I hope I can compete well.

I wanted to start off tonight by recounting the first episode in my book. For those of you not familiar with *There Are No Children Here*, it follows two young brothers, Lafeyette and Pharoah Rivers, through two years in their lives. The two boys, who at the time were twelve and nine years old, respectively, lived in the Henry Horner Homes, a public housing complex on the near west side of Chicago. Many of you may be familiar with the complex because it sits just a couple of blocks north of the Chicago Stadium where the Chicago Bulls and Chicago Blackhawks play.

The book opens on a June afternoon in 1987, and the two brothers have decided that they want to hunt for garter snakes. Being urban kids—and I was once one myself so I certainly identify with them—they didn't have the foggiest idea where to look. So with no better place in mind they decided to walk to the nearby railroad tracks just a couple of blocks north of where they lived. They took with them six friends and four crowbars figuring they would use them to dig for these snakes. While they burrowed through the dirt, a suburban commuter train began to wend its way from downtown Chicago to the western suburbs.

I had and still have many friends who ride that train, and they would tell me that as that train passed through Chicago's the temperature approaches 85 degrees. Having said all this, the thing that is most notable about a community like Henry Horner is not so much what is there, but what isn't there.

First of all, there are few, if any, jobs. The unemployment rate at Henry Horner is estimated to be between 70 and 80 percent, which means that 7 to 8 of every ten adults are without work. There are no banks, just currency exchanges. There are no movie theaters, libraries, bowling alleys or skating rinks for the children. The only outsiders who spend any time there are the police and teachers. Welfare caseworkers no longer make home visits. Truant officers, if in fact there are any, will only make rounds in pairs. Stores and pizza places refuse to make deliveries. Taxicabs turn down rides. And I will also concede that my profession, fellow journalists, rarely venture into these neighborhoods as well.

One of the first things that surprised me as I spent time working on my book was what I saw as a collapse or breakdown in community. I had expected, perhaps somewhat naively, to find a very strong sense of community, a very strong sense of neighborhood. In fact, I had heard stories, perhaps somewhat apocryphal, of families turning down opportunities to leave neighborhoods like Henry Horner because of strong ties to friends and to family. But what I found instead was not only a community that distrusted outsiders like myself, which I expected to find, but also a community in which neighbors distrusted neighbors. I can remember in 1987, when I first began to spend time with Lafeyette, who was all of 12 years old, and I asked Lafeyette if he would introduce me to some of his friends. Lafeyette said to me, "I don't have friends. I just have associates. Friends you trust." This was a 12-year-old boy speaking. I found a community in which there were very weak institutions: a fractured political organization, disconnected churches and few social service agencies. In fact, in the 1970s there were 13 social service agencies at Henry Horner, and today there are only three, and that's if you include a soup kitchen run by four sisters from Mother Teresa's order. In fact, the only institution that seems somewhat stable and functional are the gangs. Of course, the gangs—while providing a source of family and income to some youth—have only further destabilized these communities.

This unraveling of community can create enormous divisions in loyalties. I can remember one Saturday afternoon shortly after I had finished my reporting for the book and was in the process of writing, I had gone over to Henry Horner to ask Lafeyette if he would join me for lunch. He had with him a new friend named

Isaac, and he asked whether Isaac could join us. I said sure, but I asked Isaac to go home and get permission from his mother. Well, Isaac left and a couple of minutes later there was a knock on the door. Lafeyette and I went to answer the door and were greeted by two uniformed police officers, a man and a woman. They had with them a picture of Isaac, and they asked Lafeyette and they asked me whether we had seen this boy. Lafeyette lied. He said he hadn't seen Isaac in three days. I said absolutely nothing. I can assure you that if this incident had happened just a year and a half or two years earlier, there is no question in my mind that I would have asked the police why they were looking for Isaac, and assuming that there was some credible or legitimate reason, would have informed them that not only had we just seen Isaac, but that if they waited around a few minutes, he'd undoubtedly be back. Instead, I found that in the short time I had spent at Henry Horner my own loyalties had become divided: my loyalty to the police, whom I had been brought up to trust and respect, my loyalty to this boy Isaac, whom I hardly knew, my loyalty to my dear friend, Lafeyette, who clearly did not want the police to know of Isaac's whereabouts, and most importantly, the loyalty to myself, to my own instincts, to what I knew was best. And as I thought about it later, I realize how divided the loyalties of this 12-year-old boy Lafeyette must be, and how these children with such split loyalties become kind of spiritual nomads with no one to turn to, often—and I emphasize this—often not even themselves. As a footnote, it turned out the police were looking for Isaac because he had run away from home. When we eventually learned that, we brought Isaac back to his mom. But I came away from that with an indelible lesson: the collapse of community eats away at the human psyche, the ability to not only trust others, but also the ability to trust oneself.

Related to this issue of community is the violence. I expected to hear about shootings and stabbings, but was unprepared for the intensity and relentless nature of the brutality.

During the two years I spent with Lafeyette and Pharoah, they lost three friends, all 19 years of age and younger, in very violent ways. And after I had finished reporting the book and was in the process of writing, Lafeyette watched as a friend of his stumbled out of a high-rise after being shot in the stomach. Pharoah watched as a young friend of his was shot in the back of the neck. And both boys watched as an older friend was wheeled out of a nearby restaurant after a holdup attack. These are children nine to fourteen years of age, children who have seen more than most of us will see in a lifetime.

Not too long ago, I went to speak about my book to a seventh grade class at the Brown Elementary School which serves that same community. I asked what has become a fairly familiar reportorial question of inner-city children: "How many of you have seen somebody shot or stabbed?" All but two or three hands in the class went up. But I was struck by the response to my next question. I asked them how many people they thought I had seen shot or stabbed in my 39 years. The estimates ranged from four to seven people. I had to tell them that in my 39 years I have never seen anybody shot or stabbed, and that my experience is assuredly more typical than theirs. It made me realize how much the violence has become an integral part of their daily lives.

What I saw in these children who have witnessed the violent death of friends and relatives is the very same kind of post-traumatic-stress disorder we saw in veterans returning from combat in Vietnam. I have seen children who are more aggressive, who tend to act out conflict in violent ways. I've seen children who are hyperactive. Elementary school teachers frequently complain of children virtually bouncing off the walls. Hyperactivity is a direct consequence of experiencing such trauma. I've seen children who are depressed. It is not at all uncommon in a community like this to find young boys with dark circles under their eyes, children who clearly have trouble sleeping. I saw children who had flashbacks. There is a boy in my book, Rickey, who at the age of 12 watched as his 15-year-old cousin was shot and killed on the lawn outside of his high-rise. Rickey had a terrible temper and would tell me that whenever he would get angry he would relive the death of his cousin up until the very moment when his cousin actually died. This same boy, Rickey, a year later at the age of 13, said to me, "I wish I was eight years old again." Here is a child wishing for his childhood back. I've seen children who have physiological problems. Lafeyette got regular stomach aches. Pharoah would suffer from frequent headaches, particularly when the gunfire would become more regular.

I think we have just begun to break the surface in understanding the effect of the violence on these children. One singular act of violence is—for most children—the defining moment in their lives, the event around which everything else revolves. We have yet to fully understand what the consequences are for them and for their families. One obvious result—and this relates to the issue of community—is that it is very difficult for many of these children to build any kind of meaningful relationships in their lives. I remind you what Lafeyette said to me at the age of twelve. "I don't have friends. I just have associates. Friends you trust." If you go into most classrooms in communities like Henry Horner you will hear children talking about associates instead of friends. There is also a very strong foreboding among many of the children that they will not make it to adulthood. There is little sense of future. I remember when I first met Lafeyette, which was during the summer of 1985. I was working on a magazine piece on children growing up in poverty in Chicago and had all of two hours to spend with Lafeyette. I asked what was a fairly typical question to ask of a ten-year-old boy and that was: What do you want to be when you grow up? Lafeyette said to me, "If I grow up, I want to be a bus driver." "If," not "when."

As I've said, I don't think we fully understand yet the effect of the violence on the psyche of these children. Nor do we understand what this violence does to undermine the internal strength of the family. I strongly feel that we must deal with this issue of violence as an issue of public health, and while we don't yet fully understand the long-term effects of the violence on the children, I believe there is no question as to what we do know: it has a deep and lasting impact on them. The scars, I suspect, run deep.

Let me give you a quick sense of what I mean by suggesting that we treat violence as an issue of public health. If somebody attempts to do harm to themselves, attempts to commit suicide, they are in all likelihood wheeled into an emergency room and sewn up. They are then sent for counseling out of fear that if they don't receive some sort of nurturing or assistance they will in all likelihood attempt to kill themselves again. Yet, when a teen who is the victim of a beating, stabbing or shooting is wheeled into the emergency room, they are sewn up and then sent right back to the streets where in all likelihood they will seek revenge, harming either themselves or someone else. We must begin to deal with the violence as a public health concern. There is an intriguing program in New Haven in which the police, whenever they respond to a violent crime, are instructed to refer all the children who are at all involved, whether as witnesses or as family members, to the Yale School of Psychiatry for counseling. We need to look at programs like New Haven's, programs which attempt to deal directly with the impact of the violence.

Finally, I want to talk about silence. There are two kinds of silences that I want to address: One which will be fairly obvious and the other which is perhaps more subtle but no less important.

The obvious kind of silence—and I think that if my book has a theme it is this—the institutional silence that surrounds the lives of children like Lafeyette and Pharoah. I am talking about the silence of the institutions like the Department of Public Aid, the schools, the juvenile courts, the police, the public housing authority and so on. This is not to suggest that there are not individuals, and in some cases many individuals in these institutions with a great deal of compassion and commitment. Nor is it to suggest that there are not individuals at the helms of these institutions with a comparable amount of compassion and commitment. But I am talking about a kind of institutional silence. Let me give you a quick example of what I am talking about because I suspect this will be fairly apparent to those of you who work with children. About halfway through my book there is an episode where a nine-year-old boy, Alonzo Campbell, a friend of Lafeyette's and Pharoah's, was caught in crossfire while walking into his building at Henry Horner. He was accidentally shot in the back of his head. This happened on a Saturday morning. I will get back to Alonzo in a minute, but I want to back up, if I could, to that previous Thursday when a psychotic woman named Laurie Dann—and many of you may remember reading about this in the newspapers—in the tony suburb of Winnetka, just north of Chicago, stormed into the Hubbard Elementary School, shooting seven children, killing one of them, an eight-year-old boy named Nicholas Corwin. What struck me was how quickly, ably, and appropriately that community mobilized around that crisis. They brought in crisis teams of psychiatrists and social workers, not only to counsel the children, but also to counsel the adults in their lives, the teachers and their parents. The teachers received instructions on how to deal with the children over the coming months. The governor called for increased school security. There were cries for tighter gun control legislation.

Now let me fast forward three days to when Alonzo Campbell was shot. Alonzo thankfully lived, but nobody counseled Alonzo. Nobody counseled Lafeyette and Pharoah. In fact, if anything, the children in that community were discouraged from talking about the shooting out of fear that if they did they would somehow be held culpable for the crime. That is the kind of institutional silence I am talking about. We must get back to a point where the institutions that are there presumably to serve the children and their families are responding to what has become a weekly, if not daily crisis in these communities.

The other kind of silence I want to talk about is, as I said, not so obvious. It is the kind of silence that frankly I did not come to terms with until after my book was published: a kind of self-imposed silence on the part of people living in neighborhoods like the one I spent time in. I remember it was a couple of weeks after my book was published; I was on tour promoting the book and was being interviewed in Seattle by a black reporter a few years younger than myself. I was talking to him about the institutional silence, and I looked up and saw that there were tears in his eyes. He said to me: "I grew up in public housing in Detroit, and I have never spoken to my wife of those years." I thought about that afterwards and realized that during the two years I spent working on the book I found it virtually impossible to talk to even the closest of friends or family about all that I had seen and all that I had heard. Part of it was because emotionally I didn't know what to do with it all, but as I thought back upon it, I realize in large part I feared that even if I told the closest of friends and family all that I had seen and all that I had heard, they might not believe me.

This raises something I think is very critical, particularly for those of us who deal with families in our inner cities: the issue of believability. I will tell you that I have come across this time and time again since my book has come out. I remember getting a phone call from the director of the Boys and Girls Club at Henry Horner who told me that he had just received a phone call from one of the administrators downtown, who having just finished my book called to say that he couldn't believe all of that took place over the course of two years. In fact, Jerome, the Boys and Girls Club director, had to get another staff member on the phone to convince the downtown administrator that, if anything, my book understated all that had occurred during that period of time. I remember the sage advice I received from a police officer when I started reporting the book; he said to me, "Alex, whatever you do, you are going to have to understate all that goes on here because otherwise people won't believe you." I also remember the very first time I met Lafeyette, which as I said was in the summer of 1985 when Lafeyette was ten years old and I was doing the text for a photo essay on children growing up in poverty in Chicago. I had all of two hours to spend with Lafeyette. It was my first time in public housing in Chicago. In those two hours this ten-year-old boy told me of a young girl who just a couple of weeks earlier had been shot in the leg, caught in the crossfire while skipping rope outside his high-rise—and of an older boy who just a few weeks prior to that incident had been shot in a gang war and died on the stairway outside of his apartment. Lafeyette, I should say, showed very little affect, very little emotion. In fact, I found it hard to believe all that I was hearing. Lafeyette must have sensed that because he literally grabbed me by the arm and dragged me out to the stairwell to show me the bloodstains. And as I think back upon that afternoon, all he wanted me to do was believe.

I'm reminded of another incident in which the issue of believability arose. I was fortunate enough to sell the book as a made-for-TV movie, which some of you may have seen. Oprah Winfrey produced and starred in it. When the screenwriter first came out to Chicago a couple of years ago, I was to be a kind of tour guide for a few days, to introduce him to the people I wrote about, and to the neighborhood. He was a quiet, soft-spoken, gentle man, and as we spent time together, I began to get this uneasy feeling that he didn't believe all that I had written. So, I took him to the worst high-rises and pointed out the big-time drug dealers and gang leaders. On the last day, he and I and two friends of mine who live and work at the neighboring housing complex went to lunch at a restaurant on the west side. While we were sitting in our booth, a young boy, maybe 14 or 15 years old, ran into the restaurant and ducked behind the heating grill. As he ducked, a group of boys walked by. One of them pulled a pistol out of a brown paper bag and started shooting. As you can imagine we were all scared for our lives; we ducked under our table. I can remember as we lay there, all I could think to myself was "now he's going to believe me." This self-imposed silence is the most painful and destructive kind of silence there is. It is the kind of silence that will slowly strangle the life out of an otherwise spirited people. And what it says to me is something very, very simple. We have stopped listening. We have stopped believing.

So where do we start? Where do we go from here? I think we need to start listening. Listening to the voices in communities like Henry Horner, particularly to those of the children. Listening to their aspirations, their dreams, their anxieties, and their fears. I emphasize the need to listen *closely* to the children. With kids, adults have a tendency to hear what they want to hear. Not to probe. Not to get beyond the bravado of youth. I'll give you just one quick example. When I was at Brown Elementary School's seventh grade class, I talked to them about the violence I witnessed and heard about while working on my book. And I said to them "I'm sure you must know what it is like to be afraid." This young boy sitting in the first row started shaking his head. He couldn't or wouldn't admit he might at times be afraid. I said to him: "But you must know what it is like when the gangs start shooting. You must be incredibly fearful." He said, "No, I'm not afraid." He was full of bravado. I asked him, "What happens when people start shooting?" He said, "Well, I run." I said, "How do you feel?" He said, "Well I run and run and run. My heart just be beating so fast." And that is all he had to say. Without conceding to me or his peers his vulnerability, he was telling me of his fears. We must listen to children very closely.

Although listening is the first step, what we need to do ultimately is to find a way to rebuild a sense of community, both physically and spiritually. I feel very strongly about this. If we are to strengthen the family, if we are to provide a sense of future for these children, the first thing we must do is provide a sense of community. I have become convinced over time that the place we must begin is in the schools, particularly with the elementary school, which is one of the few institutions remaining with any semblance of respect and dignity. We must use these schools as a kind of building block, a foundation for community. Keep these schools open in the afternoon and evening as a place where children can go for recreation, a place for them to do homework or perhaps a place where they and their parents can receive counseling, or where the adults can go in the evening for adult education classes.

It's also very important as we think about rebuilding community that we not look at all the problems as vertically compartmentalized, to retreat from seeing the problems of law enforcement, health care, housing as separate issues. Let me give you just one example of what I mean by that. Rockwell Gardens is a housing complex just west of Henry Horner. As bad as Henry Horner is, Rockwell Gardens is worse. When Vince Lane, who has been the head of the Chicago Housing Authority for seven years, first took over, one of the first things he did was to go into Rockwell Gardens and reclaim that complex from the gangs. So for a year and a half, the violence in that community diminished considerably. During that time the test scores of the children at Ulysses S. Grant Elementary rose quite dramatically. There was no magic, no new teachers, no new programs. The children, though, finally felt safe going to and from school. They were finally able to focus and concentrate while in class. That for me said so much about how related these problems are. We are mistaken if we think that we can take even the best equipped school with the most experienced teachers and put it in a neighborhood like Henry Horner and expect it to make a difference. It will make no difference in the lives of the children if we don't also rebuild community, if we don't address the other forces at work on the lives of the children.

are growing fewer in number and older on the average, while persons of color are becoming the younger workers who will be supportive of the now dominant group. As we move toward a period of time in which people of color will become a distinct majority, it is imperative that resources are provided to these families. Our society will need the resources of all persons in order to survive.

An ecological framework shows the linkages that exist between the society in which families exist and the cultural and historical context of the lives of young children (McAdoo, 1993b). We will need to understand the dynamics of families and children and realize the consequences for the entire society if these resources are not provided.

An area that was not highlighted in the original work of Myrdal has come to be almost central to the examination of African Americans today: the coping strategies of black families within our communities. This chapter will explore the following issues as we examine this important element of American life:

1. The changing faces of families in all groups; change that is particularly more radical in families of color, specifically in families of African Americans;

2. The structures of families and the causes for these structures;

3. The divergent economic conditions and the related presence of poverty in these homes.

Family Changes in All Groups

All groups in society are now facing changes in their families. Babies in all groups are being conceived outside of marriage; divorce is rampant; unemployment of parents is becoming a factor that hits all segments of our society; drugs are flowing in rural, urban, and suburban areas; and senseless violence is increasing all over. Change has occurred in all ethnic, racial, and socioeconomic groups in America, but more radically for persons of color, particularly African Americans. Never before has it been more obvious that there is not just one reality of the black experience. The growing diversity of experiences, both economic and social, is increasing every day. Despite attempts by the media and journals to mold our experiences into one social class, usually a lower class, it is important to understand that the common element of being of African descent does not determine exactly what the life patterns of individuals will be. It has just become more difficult to excel in the present environment.

These changes come at the same time as the free flow of drugs into the black community, increases in AIDS and other destructive illnesses, and the increase in gang-like behavior of our youth. These may or may not be coincidental. Regardless, the sum experience for families of the next generation has been more negative than positive. The crises that are faced by that portion of our community are probably as great as those faced during enslavement.

There have been demographic changes for all ethnic and economic groups: longer periods of time before young people get married; more divorces; more births out of wedlock; increases in step-families and blended families being formed; and all families have been under great economic pressures, especially in the younger years of child rearing. Changes in these statistics have been exaggerated for persons of color and African Americans, and their overall condition in general has become worse.

As we look at the development of African-American families over the past three to four hundred years, we are increasingly faced with growing problems among these families: isolation from the economic mainstream, public schools that are becoming even more unsuccessful, violence that abounds in our communities, and more children being raised in families by women alone. It is very tempting to move into a problem-oriented focus when one looks at African-American families, for the problems that we face are life threatening and overwhelming. Yet one must avoid this orientation as much as possible, for it will force us to focus on the disproportionate representation of families who are in trouble. We need to examine families who are resilient and who have overcome many of the hurdles present in their environment. We will otherwise overlook the families who are making it everyday, although under less than ideal conditions. They are rearing their children to be competent adults who do not resort to violence, some of whom are even excelling.

Again, these changes have occurred in all families, but the implications of the changes are more serious for those of color. Those of us who are studying families will have to expand our conceptualizations of the family to include the interactions of more diverse family groupings. Many of these elements are in uncharted waters and will require the attention of researchers, policy analysts, and practitioners who come from a variety of fields of study.

Changes in African-American Families

As some individuals have had difficulties maintaining their families, others have prospered. We must keep the diversity and resiliency of African-American families in mind as we study the statistics that too often rely only on mean scores and on negative events. Researchers tend not to desegregate their statistics in order to present a more realistic view of all families. When we were working on the Status of Black America for the National Academy of Science (Jaynes & Williams, 1989), we were unable to find Census data, such as marriage rates, number of children, and residential location, that could be desegregated for African Americans in terms of their social class or educational levels. This simple process was rendered impossible by a little quirk in the way the data were stored. Thus, we were not able to desegregate the experiences of families of different backgrounds and had to use only African Americans as a group. Yet many of us know that there are several different groups within our communities. When you relate only to median statistics, the wide diversity of family experiences gets lost. This is an area we need to explore in more depth in future endeavors and attempts to understand our family experiences.

A prediction, based on Census projections, has been made by Marable (1993) and others that by the year 2050, non-Latino white families will become a distinct minority in our country. Persons of color will be a numerical majority. These changes will occur because of two factors related to families. Persons of color are younger on average than mainstream families. They have larger families because of cultural patterns and religious guidelines. African Americans have increased by 26% from 1980 to 1990 and will increase even more in the near future (Frey, 1994).

The role of African-American men and women in the labor market will become more important in the future as we move toward a society that is more multicultural and divergent. It is predicted that white males will become a minority among workers in the labor market, although these same men will still be in charge of the corporate sector. Between 1980 and 2005, white men will move from 51% of the work force to 44% (Galen & Palmer, 1994). Persons of color will be 26% of the work force (Galen & Palmer, 1987).

Demographic Picture of
African-American Families

African Americans now comprise 12.1% of all Americans. There have been many changes in the location of Blacks in our country. The largest numbers of African Americans live in the four most populous states: California, New York, Texas, and Florida. The growth spots for Blacks are the outer-ring suburbs of central cities. These places are also the national focus of overall population growth ("Black American," 1991). Yet some metropolitan areas are disproportionately Black.

The counties with the highest proportion of Blacks remain in the southern region, the "Black Belt or Bible Belt." The share of Blacks in the South has fallen steadily for most of the 20th century, and this has now shifted. More Blacks have moved into the South than have moved out. In the 1980s, the southern Black population rose for the first time since the turn of the last century or since the period of enslavement (Robinson, 1992). Now 53% of Blacks live in the South, and the share in the Midwest is decreasing. Blacks who are moving South are generally younger, better educated and at the point in life when many are starting families ("Marriage," 1992).

Now there are other changes. There have been shifts in attitudes among African Americans, toward themselves and toward others. For example, in a recent poll African Americans were asked what name they would prefer their race to be called. African American was preferred by 26% in 1989, but rose to 53% by February 1994; Black was preferred by 61% in 1989, and dropped to 36% in 1994 ("Chronicles," 1994).

Family Patterns

We need to look at the cultural patterns that are found in African-American families. Family researchers and social service practitioners have found growing evidence of families' identification with their descent groups from all over the world. There are cultural patterns and lifestyles that have been brought to America. Some have been developed in the United States as minority families were not allowed access to the resources of communities.

When we look at these family patterns, we find there are similarities that cut across specific religious beliefs, and across ethnicities, whether the patterns are from the Caribbean, Africa, or were the result of enslavement within the United States. When one analyzes these groups for commonalities, one finds strong similarities. There are very similar family patterns in other groups of color, such as Mexican Americans and Native Americans. As an example, the "familism" of Latinos and "extended families" of Blacks mean practically the same thing, but they are never discussed as common elements. It is almost as if the dominant groups prefer to divide and conquer rather than focus on similarities. All of these groups have culturally evolved in unique ways that reflect the country, the terrain, and the culture of their particular group, yet they are very similar in the manner that family patterns are played out.

The common cultural patterns that have contributed to the resiliency of African-American families are: supportive social networks; flexible relationships within the family unit; a strong sense of religiosity; extensive use of extended family helping arrangements; the adoption of fictive kin who become as family; and strong identification with their racial group (Stack, 1974; Boyd-Franklin, 1989; McAdoo, 1993a; Allen, 1993).

It is easy to get caught up in stereotypes, but we must be aware of the diversities that exist in all groups. Many groups across the world have similar patterns, but people of color are more often likely to have a greater concentration of these patterns, patterns that concentrate more on the collective action of families, rather than on the more individualistic emphases that are found in many mainstream families. Some of these patterns that have existed for hundreds of years are now being eroded, because of financial difficulties. Even the extended family members have found themselves stretched beyond the stretching point and are often close to the breaking point because of economic survival issues. But the patterns of resiliency have continued to provide protective cover for entire families and communities.

Marital Structures of Families

Many pressures have led to modifications in the living arrangements of families. African Americans have always had diverse family forms, even during the period of enslavement. Marriage between enslaved Africans was not legal because owners wanted to be able to sell them without regard for family ties. Despite this obstacle, there were many long-term relations that for all practical purposes were "marriages." Couples made their relationships official immediately after the end of enslavement, when they went to the county courthouses and recorded the relationships to become officially married. Some persons traveled for long distances in attempts to reunite with their partners who had been sold away (Franklin, 1988). Families were formed around married unions and their relatives. A few families had one-parent forms, usually as a result of the death of the fathers. The mother and child could not survive alone and therefore attached themselves to a larger family unit. Many extended families composed of relatives and non-relatives existed. The cultural pattern of collectiveness is a continuation of African and Caribbean family forms (McAdoo, 1991).

There were many varieties of family structures because of the hardships that families faced. The vast majority of families had two parents, though they often had extended family members residing with them. Over 75% of families maintained two-parent structures until the 1970s, when a series of depressions heralded the acceleration of economic decline (Glick, 1988). Simple causal explanations have not been supported by hard data. Many hypotheses have been presented about these family situations. Simple economic incentives cannot explain the changes in African-American family structures (Ellwood & Crane, 1990).

Marriage rates have fallen for men who are employed and for those who are unemployed. These findings question Wilson's contention that the number of unemployed men was the cause of marriage decline (Ellwood, 1990). In fact marriage rates fell more for the employed between 1970 and 1988 (Ellwood & Crane, 1990). Overall the earnings of men and the weaker employment of men can explain at most only 10 to 20% of the decline in marriage.

There were drops in marriages at all levels of education between 1960 and 1988, with more of a decline for those with lower educational attainment, although the differences are small and not the overall trend. Welfare has also been rejected by empirical studies as a reason for the decline (Wilson, 1987). These changes in family structures are the result of the interaction of many factors, the sum of many forces in effect.

There are clear signs of growing changes in the marital status of black parents. Marriage is becoming a minority lifestyle for black parents. African Americans are delaying marriage until their late 20s. Marriage among African Americans is declining; only 44% of adults were married in 1991, compared with 64% in 1970, according to the Census Bureau (Ellwood & Crane, 1990). This 20% decline is double the 10% decline experienced by the population as a whole. This is a result of the delay of marriage until couples are older and high levels of divorce. Those who have divorced represented 11%; those who have never married increased to 23%. Of those who have never been married 43% were black women and 44% were black men ("Marital Status," 1991). The level of marriage is important because two parents may command a higher income than other patterns of households.

The fertility of black and white women have followed similar patterns. Fertility for both has increased, although black fertility levels have been at a higher level (Ahlburg & DeVita, 1992). Blacks report that they intend to have 2.9 children, lower than Hispanics (3.1) and higher than Whites (2.3). Present family arrangements are the result of many factors.

Sex-Ratios of African Americans

The sex-ratio imbalance is one of the reasons for the decline in marriages. Among Blacks there is an inadequate supply of marriageable males to marriageable females. This fact has been noted since DuBois' work in 1908 and has consistently been addressed over the years by other writers (Cox, 1940; Jackson, 1971; Tucker & Mitchell-Kernan, 1985; Darity & Myers, 1991).

Darity and Myers (1991) stated that there are four sex-ratio indicators: (1) the ratio of men to women of marriageable age, 14 years and older; (2) the ratio of unmarried males to unmarried females; (3) the ratio of employed males to females (Wilson & Neckerman, 1986); and (4) the ratio of unmarried males in the labor force, or in school, to unmarried females.

The first of these ratios relates to the mortality level since birth for males and females: the actual number who are still alive. There were approximately the same number of girls born as there were boys. The third ratio treats all women as eligible for marriage, regardless of their present marital status. All men must be employed to be potential husbands. The fourth ratio restricts the population only to unmarried who are employed or in school. All unmarried women are seen as potential wives.

Using the fourth and most restrictive of the ratios, Darity and Myers have estimated that there are approximately 32 men for every 100 women in the marriage pool. As education of the woman moves up, the number of possible mates decreases. This imbalance is caused by the high death rate in the teen years experienced by black boys, the high incarceration rate, poor health conditions, and the insecurities of the labor market. The imbalance of the male-to-female ratio prevents young marriage unions from forming. All of these are seen as contributing to the further marginalization of the roles of black males. These statistics contribute to the stresses that result in a high level of divorce in these families. The excess of women over men also leads to the sexual exploitation of women and the lessening of a commitment to long-term relationships in favor of more short-term liaisons (McAdoo, 1992).

It is important to explore the environment in which children are reared. The changes that have occurred in family structures are the result of many strongly interacting forces. However, the economic situations have become so difficult that former family arrangements are not as effective as they have been in the past. Many grandparents have become primary parents for young children because of the AIDS epidemic, drug use, and the high incarceration rate of parents (Hernandez, 1993). They have become a source of resiliency for the children, but often at the expense of their own health and financial needs.

All of these factors have contributed to the substantial increase in the number of children who are developing in mother-only families with limited access to resources. The high divorce rate and the delay of marriages, even after the birth of children, have resulted in more families being composed of step-parents and many types of blended families.

Children in Single-Parent Homes

The major problem the African-American family faces is related to children who must grow up without the resources and love that are often found with more than one parent. Bronfenbrenner has stated that children need the resources of unconditional love from one or two persons who are dedicated to the child (Bronfenbrenner, 1979). This person may be a parent, grandparent, or other relative. Blacks have traditionally formed families that have included many persons in the parenting role.

Some children live with single parents, step-parents, or other relatives. More and more children are spending important parts of their lives with single parents or in alternative parent arrangements. In 1980, 80% of African-American children had spent part of their life with less than two parents by the age of 17 years, in contrast with 46% of white children (Hernandez, 1993).

The divorce level for African-American women is twice the level of other women. Over 80% of the women do get married, but there are difficulties in remaining married. Surprisingly enough, when one looks at the research literature on divorce, little attention is paid to the divorces in these families. Also, little attention is paid to the children who were born in marriages that later dissolved. It is almost as if the researchers make the assumption that African-American single mothers are the result of adolescent pregnancies, while white mothers are single because of divorce. This is another area where public opinion and reality do not accurately match.

The level of unwed births is very high for African-American women. However the distribution does not match the perception of many policy analysts, who seem to believe that the children are born mostly to adolescents. According to the Children's Defense Fund data the majority of out-of-wedlock births are not to adolescents, but to adult women over the age of 20 (McAdoo, 1991). Two-thirds of these children are born to older women and one-third are born to adolescents (Edelman, 1987). The overall level of birth to unwed mothers is 46.6% (Usdansky, 1994). Two-thirds of all black children born in 1990 had unmarried mothers (DeParle, 1994). The services that now only target adolescent mothers should be extended to older mothers, to those who have been previously married and are now single, and to those older women who have never been married.

The rearing of children is such an expensive proposition that poverty comes with single parenting. This is not a concern for just African Americans, for only half of America's 32.2 million children live in traditional two-parent families. Those who live in families with both biological parents now include 56.4% for Whites, 37.8% for Latinos, and 25.9% for African Americans (Whitmire, 1994).

Young girls who have children are the most destitute and vulnerable group of mothers. They tend to have the lowest education and the highest levels of poverty for their entire lives. The birth rate of young black girls, 15 to 19 years old, is twice the rate of other groups. Yet, again contrary to public opinion, the rate for teenage childbearing is rising faster among Whites (19%) than among Blacks (13%) between 1986 and 1991 (Usdansky, 1994).

The non-marital birth rate for black teens has varied. In 1970 the level was 97 births per 1,000; 86 per 1,000 in 1980; and up to 110 in 1990 ("Monthly Vital Statistics," 1993). The teen birth rates varied by ethnicity and race for girls 15-19 years. The number of births per 1,000 was: 116.2 for Blacks; 100.3 for Hispanics, 81.1 for Native Americans; 42.5 for Whites; and 26.4 for Asian and Pacific Islanders (Moore, Snyder, & Halla, 1993).

Researchers have empirically found that these pregnancies are unplanned. These teens are not attempting to "have someone to
love," though the media often gives this as the reason why teens
get pregnant (Usdansky, 1994).

Family and Child Poverty

There are many challenges to family resiliency, and poverty in
black families is paramount. Poverty has continued to be a concern of persons who are serious about the welfare of all children.
The Carnegie Corporation of New York released a summary of the
plight of all of America's children (Chira, 1994). The report stated
that young children with certain characteristics were at risk to
suffer neurological effects that can be irreversible. They may never
be able to reach their full potential.

This is because the most vulnerable are at high risk: those
who are born to unmarried mothers (28%); who live with only one
parent (27%); and, when they are under six, their mothers are in
the labor force. If it is a concern for all children in general, it is a
very serious concern for African-American families; their levels in
all of these characteristics are double the rate for other American
children. If the levels stated in the report lead to alarm, then the
risk for black children is at an untenable level.

Poverty levels for African-American children did decrease
after 1949, when the level of poverty in black families was almost
75%. By 1969 it had fallen to 34%, in 1973 it was 31%, and by
1991 the level was 29% (Danziger, 1993). But since that time
things have deteriorated and for all of these characteristics
African-American children have fallen into even greater despair.
They now are at greater risk because of their reliance on parents
who are in even more tenuous situations. Their educational systems are for the most part inferior and they do not receive
adequate health care.

However, to end on a more positive note, there has been a
significant decline in the black infant death rate, according to a
press release by the Centers for Disease Control (1994).

> The rate of black infant deaths dropped nearly 21% from
> 1980 to 1991, growing from 22.2% to 17.6% per 1,000 births.
> It is still higher than the white rate, which went from
> 10.9% to 7.3% in the same time period. The differ-
> ences are due to inequities in housing, income, and stress
> factors.

In summary, all of these facts direct us to issues that must be seriously addressed. We cannot simply have a great conference, produce a good book, and go on as if this is just another report. The issues are too profound to dismiss lightly. We need to become advocates for African-American children.

As Marian Wright Edelman of the Children's Defense Fund has stated, we must formulate an action agenda for our children (Edelman, 1988). The future for all of us will be determined, to a great extent, by our ability to take action and improve the situations of African-American children. As we move into a period of time when there will be more persons of color in the labor market, and when they will in fact form the majority of persons in this country, we are all dependent upon the futures of these families and children. They will need to draw even more on the traditional sources of support that have been found to be successful in the past, sources of support that have provided resiliency for our families.

Note

1. This chapter is adapted from a keynote address given by Dr. Harriette Pipes McAdoo as part of the "Resiliency in Families: Racial and Ethnic Minority Families in America" conference, held at the University of Wisconsin–Madison, May 31-June 2, 1994.

References

Ahlburg, D., & DeVita, C. (1992). New realities of the American family. *Population Bulletin, 47,* 18–19.

Allen, W. (1993). Black families: Protectors of the realm. *Morehouse Research Institute Bulletin, 93,* 1–3.

Banks, J. (1994). *The construction and the deconstruction of race: Theoretical transformation.* Paper presented at Colloquium, Michigan State University, April 19, 1994.

Black American. (1991). *American Demographic Desk Reference,* No. 1, 8–10.

Boyd-Franklin, N. (1989). *Black families in therapy.* New York: Guilford Press.

Bronfenbrenner, U. (1979). *The ecology of human development: Experiments by nature and design.* Cambridge, MA: Harvard University Press.

Centers for Disease Control and Prevention. (1994). Infant mortality gap. *Lansing State Journal*, April 30, 4A.

Chira, S. (1994, April 12). Study confirms worst fears on U.S. children. Review of "Starting points: Meeting the needs of our youngest children." Carnegie Corporation of New York. *New York Times*, A1, A11.

Chronicles: Which would you prefer as a name for your race? (1994, April 4). *Time.*

Cox, O. (1940). Sex ratio and marital status among Negroes. *American Sociological Review, 5,* 937–947.

Danziger, S. (1993). Presented in a lecture on Family Poverty at the Institute for Children, Youth, and Families, Michigan State University, July 17.

Darity, W., & Myers, S. (1991). *Sex ratios, marriageability, and the marginalization of Black males.* Paper presented at the biennial meeting of the Society for Research in Child Development, Seattle, WA, May.

DeParle, J. (1994, March 22). Clinton target: Teenage pregnancy. *New York Times, CXLI(49),* A10.

Edelman, M. (1987). *Families in peril.* Cambridge, MA: Harvard University Press.

Edelman, M. (1988). An advocacy agenda for Black families and children. In H. McAdoo (Ed.), *Black families* (2nd ed.). Newbury Park, CA: Sage.

Ellwood, D. (1990). Men and marriage in the Black community. *Research Bulletin: Malcolm Wiener Center for Social Policy.* John F. Kennedy School of Government. Cambridge, MA: Harvard University, 1-5.

Ellwood, D., & Crane, J. (1990). Family change among Black Americans: What do we know? *Journal of Economic Perspectives, 4(4),* 65-84.

Franklin, J. (1988). A historical note on black families. In H. McAdoo (Ed.), *Black families* (2nd ed., pp. 23–26). Newbury Park, CA: Sage.

Frey, W. (1994, April). The new white flight. *American Demographics,* 40-48.

Galen, M., & Palmer, T. (1987). *Workforce 2000: Work and workers for the 21st century.* Indianapolis, IN: Hoover Institute.

Galen, M., & Palmer, T. (1994, Jan. 31). White, male, and worried. *Business Week,* 50–55.

Glick, P. (1988). Demographic pictures of black families. In H. McAdoo (Ed.), *Black families* (2nd ed., pp. 107–132). Newbury Park, CA: Sage.

Hernandez, D. (1993). *America's children, resources from family, government and the economy.* New York: Russell Sage Foundation.

Jackson, J. (1971). But where are all the men? *Black Scholar, 3,* 34–41.

Jaynes, G., & Williams, R. (1989). *A common destiny: Blacks and American society.* Committee on the Status of Black Americans. Washington, DC: National Academy Press.

Marable, M. (1993). Racism and multicultural democracy. *Poverty and race. Poverty and Race Research Action Council 2(5),* Sept./Oct. 1–4, 12–13.

Marital status and living arrangements. (1991, March). *Current Population Reports,* Series P-20, No. 461.

Marriage, homeownership, and other recent Census releases. (1992, Sept. 16). *American Demographics*.

McAdoo, H. (1991). A portrait of African American families in the United States: A status report. In S. Rix (Ed.), *The American woman 1990-1991: A status report* (pp. 71-93). New York: W. W. Norton.

McAdoo, H. (1992). Reaffirming African American families and our identities. *Psych Discourse, 23*, 6–7.

McAdoo, H. (1993a). Family equality and ethnic diversity. In K. Altergott (Ed.), *One world, many families*. Minneapolis, MN: National Council on Family Relations, 52–55.

McAdoo, H. (1993b). The social cultural contexts of ecological developmental family models. In P. Boss, W. Doherty, & W. Schyumm (Eds.), *Sourcebook of family theories and methods: A contextual approach* (pp. 298-301). New York: Plenum.

Monthly Vital Statistics Report. (1993). *Advance Report of Final Natality Statistics, 1990, 41*. Table 11 and 12. National Center for Health Statistics, Public Health Service.

Moore, K., Snyder, A., & Halla, C. (1993). Facts at a glance. Unpublished data from the National Center for Health Statistics, Department of Health and Human Services; forthcoming in *Vital Statistics of the United States, 1990, 1*. Natality, 1–6.

Myrdal, G. (1944). *An American dilemma: The Negro problem and modern democracy* (2 vols.). New York: Harper & Bros.

Peters, M. (1988). Parenting in black families with young children: A historical perspective. In H. McAdoo (Ed.), *Black families* (pp. 228–241). Newbury Park, CA: Sage.

Robinson, I. (1992). Blacks move back to the South. *black Americans*. Ithaca, NY: American Demographics. Reprint Package #318-A, 10–12.

Stack, C. (1974). *All our kin: Strategies for survival in a black community*. New York: Harper & Row.

Tucker, B., & Mitchell-Kernan, C. (1985). Sex ratio imbalance among Afro-Americans: Conceptual and methodological issues. In R. Jones (Ed.), *Advances in black psychology, Vol. 1*. Berkeley, CA: Cobb & Henry.

Usdansky, M. (1994, Feb. 22). One in three born out of wedlock. *USA Today*, 2A.

Whitmire, R. (1994, Aug. 30). Just half of kids in traditional homes. *Lansing State Journal*, 5A.

Wilson, W. (1987). *The truly disadvantaged: The inner city, the underclass, and public policy*. Chicago, IL: University of Chicago Press.

Wilson, W., & Neckerman, K. (1986). Poverty and family structure: The widening gap between evidence and public policy issues. In S. Danziger & D. Weinberg (Eds.), *Fighting poverty*. Cambridge, MA: Harvard University Press.

Chapter 3

Culture, Resiliency, and Mutual Psychological Development[1]

Nancy P. Genero

Advancing the understanding of resiliency in racial and ethnic minority families is a formidable task. Some look for the vital signs of resiliency in personality traits, temperament, or dispositions (Kobasa & Pucetti, 1983). Others search for social competencies and developmental accomplishments in the midst of adversities (Jessor, 1993; McLoyd, 1990; Rutter, 1979; Werner & Smith, 1992). Yet others look to the ongoing process of making sense of life's ironies and unpredictable events (Antonovsky, 1994; Antonovsky & Sagy, 1986; Grossman & Moore, 1984). Whether measuring traits, developmental milestones, or mentalistic adaptive processes, there are complex substantive and methodological questions to be considered and political and ethical concerns to be weighed. For example, is resiliency a culturally specific or universal concept, and, depending on one's perspective, which research methods are likely to generate the most reliable data? Should researchers entrench themselves into the hearts of the communities that they study, or should they maintain a safe distance to protect their science as well as the people they study? And, from a political standpoint, what should be expected from those who study racial and ethnic minority families?

Moreover, the study of resiliency in minority families also involves coming to grips with the social inequities of racism. The public health and social welfare statistics on poverty, homicide, AIDS, teen pregnancy, and homelessness hang like a thick dark cloud. Some families are literally living in a state of siege. Within their communities, devastating acts of violence are commonplace and highly unpredictable. In Boston, for example, an elderly

African-American minister died of a heart attack when police mis-
takenly raided his home in search of illegal drugs. Even among
families who are financially secure and whose neighborhoods are
relatively safe, explicit and covert forms of racism and discrimination can lead to what some psychotherapists now refer to as "cultural depression" (Meltz, 1994).

Notwithstanding these negative realities, most minority families go on with the ordinary business of everyday living: raising
and educating their children and grandchildren, caring for the elderly and infirm, celebrating birthdays and anniversaries, attending family reunions, and finding ways to make ends meet. As a
deeper understanding of resiliency is sought, perhaps a closer look
at the ordinary might be instructive. For many racial and ethnic
minority families, the ability to do the "ordinary" is in itself an
extraordinary achievement. Daily functioning amidst negative realities requires a high level of motivation, commitment, tenacity,
and creativity. The following story is a case in point.

Hindsabout (1994) recently described how a group of African-
American families living in a public housing project in southwest
Philadelphia organized a community farmer's market. One of the
residents, a woman who is now an organizer, was quoted as saying, "I used to go to the Italian market in South Philadelphia, but
it's about 20 blocks away, and it's hard for large families to take all
the kids and carry all the bags" (p. 8). For the 2,500 women, men,
and children living in Tasker Homes in southwest Philadelphia,
lack of basic services is a way of life. As Gilkes (1994) points out,
families of color do not typically benefit from mainstream institutional and ideological supports.

However, through their sustained collaborative relationships,
these Philadelphia families are now able to do what other families
in cities and towns all over America ordinarily do—go to a market
in their own neighborhood. By doing so, they are redefining themselves from victims of poverty to agents of social change. To coin a
phrase from Jean Baker Miller (1976), these families are engaging
in "action through interaction." Emerging work on community
activism and leadership suggests that collaborative efforts can lead
to a sense of personal discovery and transformation (Gilkes, 1994).
What can researchers learn about resiliency from the extraordinary measures that minority families must take to lead ordinary
lives? This particular story about the Tasker Homes community
speaks to the possibilities of growth and adaptation through a
willingness to risk involvement (Jordan, 1992). Thus, minority
families may develop and maintain a sense of resiliency by engag-

ing in "... diverse modes of social interaction that facilitate participation in and growth through relationships" (Genero, Miller, Surrey, & Baldwin, 1992, p. 37). Consequently, a relational rather
than an individualistic mode of adaptation is key to understanding
resiliency (Jordan, 1992; Miller, 1988; Surrey, 1985).

A relational perspective assumes the centrality of relationships in human development. That is, psychological growth is
viewed as a process of differentiation and elaboration *in* relationships rather than disengagement and separation *from* relationships (Surrey, 1985). Although the literature on relational processes
includes a wide range of variables, such as reciprocity (Antonucci
& Jackson, 1989; Rook, 1987; Walster, Bercheid, & Walster, 1973),
interdependence (Kelley et al., 1983), shared meaning (Duck, 1994),
and relationship awareness (Acitelli, 1992), current research on
perceptions of mutuality in close relationships may be highly relevant to the study of resiliency.

The term mutuality does not simply refer to that which one
has in common with others, but rather to the bidirectional movement of feelings, thoughts, and activity between persons (Genero
et al., 1992). According to Jordan (1986), the process of mutuality
involves "openness to influence, emotional availability, and a constantly changing pattern of responding to and affecting the other's
state" (p. 1). Clinical observations of dyadic interactions suggest
that individuals are enhanced by mutual interchanges in at least
five ways. Both members of the dyad experience an increased
sense of vitality or zest by virtue of feeling connected to one another, feel empowered or more able to take action on behalf of
oneself and others, acquire an increased sense of knowledge of self
and other, gain a greater sense of self-worth and validation, and
desire more connection with others beyond the immediate interaction (Miller, 1988). Considering these outcomes, mutuality is said
to lead to the growth of the participants in the relationship. The
relationship itself is enhanced due to the increased sense of connection between individuals. The term *mutual psychological development* explicitly refers to the salutary gains derived from joint
participation in relationships over time (Miller, 1988). Depending
on the interrelatedness of relationships and the interdependence of
goals, benefits derived in connection with others may be experienced at the group level as well. Thus, a relational approach to
resiliency facilitates the study of processes and outcomes associated with *mutual* adaptive functioning and development.

To explore mutuality in close relationships, the Mutual Psychological Development Questionnaire (MPDQ) was developed,

based on the elements of empathy, engagement, authenticity, zest, diversity, and empowerment (Genero et al., 1992). These six conceptual elements were defined accordingly:

> Empathy refers to the shared flow of thoughts and feelings between individuals. Engagement is the focusing on one another in a meaningful way. Authenticity describes a process of coming closer to knowing and sharing each other's experiences, recognizing the other for who she or he is, and being recognized for who one is. Zest refers to the energy-releasing quality of relationships, and diversity is the process of expressing and working through different perspectives and feelings. Empowerment describes a capacity for action whereby each person can have an impact on the other and the relationship (Genero et al., 1992, p. 38).

These elements were operationalized in 22 items, which were subdivided into the two subsets presented in Table 1.

Table 1
Item Subsets

Subset 1	Subset 2
Be receptive	Pick up feelings
Get impatient	Feel like we're not getting anywhere
Try to understand	Show an interest
Feel moved	Get frustrated
Avoid being honest	Change the subject
Get discouraged	Share similar experiences
Have difficulty listening	Keep feelings inside
Get involved	Respect point of view
Feel energized	See the humor in things
Get bored	Feel down
Keep an open mind	Express an opinion clearly

From Genero, Miller, Surrey, & Baldwin, 1992, p. 41.

The questionnaire is structured so as to encourage respondents to contemplate both sides of the relationship. That is, for each of the items respondents are asked what they would do in a given situation in response to another, and what they think the other person in the relationship would do in response to them. Methodologically speaking, this kind of perspective-taking is not typically incorporated into standardized questionnaires. Although this particular approach and the mutuality elements being explored do not represent the definitive solution to measuring mutuality, documenting such processes can begin to illuminate the association between perceived mutuality and other psychological dimensions that may be predictive of resiliency.

For example, in the validation study of the MPDQ (Genero et al., 1992), perceptions of mutuality in close relationships, such as spouse/partner and friends, were explored. As hypothesized, findings indicated that adequacy of social support, relationship satisfaction, and relationship cohesion were significantly predictive of mutuality in spouse or partner relationships. In addition, low spouse or partner mutuality was found to be predictive of significant depressive symptoms in women but not in men. The friendship data also revealed a significant pattern of gender differences. That is, men who reported having a close male friend had on average lower mutuality scores than women in same-sex friendships or men in cross-sex friendships. On the basis of these findings, it seems that perceptions of mutuality in conjunction with social network and other relationship characteristics are predictive of psychological outcomes. Further, due to differences in socialization, women may be more vulnerable than men to negative outcomes in the absence of mutuality. The application of these findings in exploring the benefits of same-sex friendships between women has proven to be quite helpful. For example, in a study of peer support among high-risk mothers of young children (Genero, Miller, Surrey, & Angiolillo, 1991), findings suggest that participants who perceive their relationships with peers as being mutual are more likely to report a significant reduction in depressive symptoms over time than their study counterparts who view their peer relations as being less mutual. The MPDQ is also currently being used to evaluate the connection between mutuality and psychological outcomes in a variety of relationships, including heterosexual couples, mothers and adult daughters, chronically ill patients, and racial and ethnic minority adolescents. As the cumulative findings of these studies and their implications are considered, how might the conceptual understanding of resiliency in racial and ethnic minority families expand?

First, it is proposed *that mutual participation in relationships facilitates and gives meaning to the adaptive processes that arise in response to environmental demands and challenges over time.* Differences in culture, family structure, and class determine the unique ways in which patterns of adaptation may occur. As

McCubbin, Thompson, Thompson, McCubbin, and Kaston (1993) have suggested, the adaptive responses of racial and ethnic minority families can be highly variable and depend in large measure on the "fundamental convictions and values shaped and adopted by the family system" (p. 1064). One might ask, how do sociocultural influences foster or hinder mutual participation in relationships? Do minority families have access to different types of relationships? If sociocultural influences limit participation or access to a wide range of relationships, in what ways are adaptive responses subsequently affected? Moreover, what specific costs do minority families incur in forming and maintaining mutually empowering relationships? And what interpersonal strategies do minority families use to minimize these risks? With respect to the challenges of connection, Jordan (1992) pointed out that "one must be willing to risk the vulnerability of emotional responsiveness. Since we do not want to open ourselves to unnecessary risk, we must learn how to judge when our trust and confidence in the other person is warranted and when it is not" (p. 3).

For racial and ethnic minority families, marginalization and socioeconomic barriers pose clear and serious threats to mutual connection. Negative realities and social inequities all too often place family and other relationships in jeopardy through uncertainties, conflict, and loss. Within this context, staying in connection with others necessitates a highly developed capacity to gauge and manage the risk of involvement. As in the case of the Tasker residents in southwest Philadelphia, community involvement occurs within a context of few external positive social reinforcers. Managing the risk of involvement is part of a creative interactive process directed toward understanding others' motives and behaviors. In the absence of external social indicators, much can be learned from minority families about how they maximize adaptive outcomes within a context of mistrust and violations. For example, what roles do family members play in estimating the risks of involvement, and to what extent are internal cues important in judging others and novel situations?

Secondly, *meaning derived through mutual relationships is a critical source of validation.* The concepts of meaning and validation are linked to culture and are, therefore, socially defined. That is, cultural values, beliefs, and customs impart meaning to what is and what is not valid within a given social context. Thus, it is proposed that the family, as the most basic and perhaps most meaningful unit of culture, is *the* primary source of validation. For racial and ethnic minorities who are continuously colliding with external devaluing messages, the family represents the touchstone of validation. Within the context of mutual psychological development, validating experiences lead to authenticity—the process of being recognized for who one is and recognizing the other for who she or he is. As Jordan (1992) suggested, inauthenticity precludes the possibility of real mutuality.

By valuing individual strengths, promoting community cohesion, and providing a protective but permeable boundary between cultures, families help to maximize authenticity and minimize the risk of involvement. Previous research on resiliency has drawn attention to the synergy between family relationships and adaptive functioning. For example, studies of family schemas and paradigms on coping with chronic illness in children (McCubbin, Thompson, Thompson, McCubbin, & Kaston, 1993), the role of families and extended kin as protective shields against racism (McAdoo, 1993; Tatum, 1987), perceptions of family solidarity and supportive transactions (Hatchett & Jackson, 1993), and coping with teenage parenting (García Coll, Escobar, Cebollero, & Valcárcel, 1989; Williams, 1991) suggest that minorities actively utilize their familial bonds and cultural values to cope with environmental demands and challenges. Further, these studies suggest that transactions among racial and ethnic minority families are not limited to the give and take of emotional support and material aid. Mutual interchanges among family members may serve as reality checks— a way to validate one's personal sense of meaning and social identity against the pressures of racism and acculturation.

A growing number of studies on biculturalism and identity development in minority children demonstrate the extent to which minority families must cope with the problems of validation (Barnes, 1980; Tatum, 1987). For example, in her research of black families living in predominantly white communities, Tatum (1987) explored the nature of conflicting developmental tasks and their impact on racial identity. Tatum pointed out that these tasks conflict because ". . . racism of those societal views the children are struggling to internalize is intended to prevent them from reaching the limits of their potential" (p. 14). Thus, for minority children to develop a healthy sense of personal and group identity requires that adult family members cultivate in them the ability to discern instances of inauthenticity and to connect with others with whom they can move toward greater authenticity. To do so, adult family members must be able to attune empathically to their children's needs. As children develop into young adults, their abilities to attune empathically to others' needs would be expected to increase.

Further, research on childrearing practices that place a heavy emphasis on authoritarianism suggests that reliance on "power-over" practices are not compatible with mutuality (Martinez, 1993).

In more recent work, Tatum (1993) has begun to explore the relational dimensions of racial identity development in black women. She described the process of identity development as movement from "internalized racism to a position of empowerment based on a positively affirmed sense of racial identity" (p. 1). In addressing the role of similar others in affirming one's identity, Tatum (1993) stated that the "validation of one's own experience by others who have shared aspects of that experience is empowering and contributes to the positive redefinition of racial identity" (p. 5). Thus, families are critical in promoting shared understandings and providing a supportive network where feelings of anger and self-doubt can be expressed without fear of isolation. Tatum further suggested that during developmental phases where immersion in one's own racial or ethnic peer group is important, families can play a key role in constructing opportunities for their children to access peer relationships. Further research describing how mutual psychological development promotes racial and ethnic identity is clearly needed. Study into the ways in which intergenerational family relationships promote authenticity and other culture-specific elements associated with mutuality is warranted. Moreover, questions raised by Tatum (1993) regarding the processes of forming and maintaining enhancing connections outside of the boundaries of one's own racial and ethnic group and the role that racism plays in hindering the growth of such relationships require further exploration.

In cases where there are few opportunities for validation, there is a tendency to submerge one's feelings and thoughts and stay out of connection with others. Although disconnection from *non-mutual* relationships can be a protective strategy (Jordan, 1991), persistent relationship impasses and disconnections over time can lead to a diminished sense of self-worth and isolation. To explore the processes and outcomes associated with developmental transitions that can cause persistent and damaging disconnections, the author and her colleagues are currently conducting the Mothers' Project, a study of peer support in high-risk mothers of young children.

The Project's goals are twofold. First, the researchers seek to understand the relational experiences of a diverse group of women as they relate to the developmental tasks of motherhood and their perceptions of well-being. Second, a preventive intervention program is being evaluated, intended to reduce the risk of depression by enhancing access to peer support. The Mothers' Project builds on previous gender-specific research that suggests that culture influences the kinds of relationships that people form and the ways in which they are likely to participate in those relationships. That is, mounting evidence now suggests that the socialization of women predisposes them to participate in relationships in specific ways. For instance, women tend to prefer confiding relationships for the provision of support (Cohen & Wills, 1985; Heller & Lakey, 1985; Stokes & Wilson, 1984). Moreover, they tend to be empathic (Davis & Oathout, 1987) and aware of the nature, benefits, and conflicts in their relationships (Acitelli, 1988). Norms and expectations surrounding family structures and childrearing responsibilities are also culturally rooted, and these norms exert an inordinate influence on the way in which women understand motherhood (Urwin, 1985). In most contemporary societies, for example, women continue to be the designated caretakers and hold primary responsibility for the rearing of children (Phoenix, Woollett, & Lloyd, 1991; Sudarkasa, 1993; Williams, 1991). One might ask, why a peer support model as a preventive intervention for high-risk mothers of young children?

Recent work points to the role of interpersonal factors in explaining the greater prevalence of depression among women. Epidemiological studies of psychiatric disorders have shown that the absence of intimate social relationships may increase women's susceptibility to depression (Brown & Harris, 1978; Brown, Bhrolchrain, & Harris, 1975; Hall, Schaefer, & Greenberg, 1987; Koeske & Koeske, 1990). Some researchers have suggested that even the absence of casual, less intimate friends is highly predictive of elevated symptom levels of psychological and physical distress in women (Miller & Ingham, 1976). These findings have been found to be relatively robust and have been found to be applicable to minority women as well. Vega, Kolody, and Valle (1986), for example, suggested that the absence of confiding relationships may be particularly problematic among Hispanic women, where strong cultural norms surround interpersonal relationships.

The demands and strains of parenting can also leave mothers of young children feeling depleted and socially isolated (Hall, 1990). It has been argued (Antonucci & Mikus, 1988) that, as a major developmental transition, motherhood often involves the renegotiation of existing relationships with spouse, family, and friends and perhaps the search for new personal relationships as they begin to expand their own sense of identity through the experiences of motherhood. For many women, these relational tasks may provoke interpersonal friction, and feelings of anger, guilt, inadequacy, and shame. And, in the absence of *mutual* relationships, the "cost of caring," as Belle (1982) has suggested, may be excessive and detrimental to their efforts to connect with others. There is also a growing body of literature that suggests that maternal satisfaction and positive affect can be significantly enhanced by peer contact—that is, contact with others outside of one's immediate family with whom mothers can share similar experiences and concerns. According to Crnic and Greenberg (1990), there are significant interactive effects between friendship support and daily hassles of parenting on measures of maternal affect and gratification. Moreover, the relatively low cost of a peer program versus formal group support services was also an important and practical consideration.

To promote confiding peer relationships, the six-month Mothers' Project intervention focused on validating relational strengths, such as mutual empathy, engagement, expressiveness, and empowerment. The intervention included structured group meetings as well as unstructured contact between paired "program partners." The most active part of the intervention was intended to be the regular, informal contact or check-ins that program partners maintained with each other by phone or in person over the six-month period. Focus groups were conducted during the initial planning stages of the program in which diverse groups of women met to discuss the intervention and implementation issues. Questions regarding the development of trust and comfort were repeatedly raised. The criteria and logistics for pairing the women were never completely resolved to everyone's satisfaction. Mothers were ultimately paired by geographic proximity and age. Facilitators underwent an intensive three-month didactic and experiential training. As part of their training, they were randomly paired with another facilitator with whom they maintained regular contact for three months. By experiencing the peer intervention firsthand, facilitators were better prepared to communicate the goals and potential problems and benefits to the program participants.

The study was conducted in two stages. To identify a pool of program participants a risk assessment of approximately 800 women between the ages of 20 and 47 living in the Boston area was conducted. The sample was drawn from a regional health maintenance organization. The risk status of study participants was determined via a pencil-and-paper survey using the ten criteria listed in Table 2.

Table 2
Depression Risk Factors

Risk Factor
SES—employment, marital status, level of education
Relational distress
Life maintenance stress, including financial worries
Role dissatisfaction
Low self-esteem
Major relationship life event in the past six months
Frequent moves before age 16
Death of a parent before age 11
Low social support
Absence of a confiding spouse or partner

To be included in the pool of potential intervention recruits, respondents were required to have children between the ages of one and six and at least three of the ten risk criteria. Because of the preventive focus of the intervention women were excluded from the subject pool if they were:

Presently in therapy;

Experiencing a serious medical illness;

Diagnosed with a serious psychiatric illness within the past year;

Currently taking psychotropic medications;

Abusing drugs or alcohol.

Women who met risk and eligibility criteria and who agreed to participate in the intervention phase of the study were randomly assigned to an experimental or control group. In the experimental group, women were paired with another mother. Each pair was encouraged to schedule regular check-ins and to attend a series of meetings where their relational strengths and challenges could be openly discussed. A majority of the women were in contact with their program partners at least one to three times per week throughout the six-month program. Although check-ins could take place by phone or in person, mothers typically contacted each other by phone and conversations tended to be at least 15 minutes in duration. Controls received a modified intervention, in which they were interviewed twice by phone regarding parenting hassles over the same six-month period. All participants were consistently acknowledged for their involvement in the study.

The analysis of the risk data indicates that relational distress in mothers of young children is a highly significant predictor of depression above and beyond the explanatory power of other predictor variables. Depressive symptoms were measured using the 20-item Center for Epidemiological Studies Depression Scale (CES-D) (Radloff, 1977). A CES-D score of 16 or greater is indicative of serious depressive symptoms. Respondents with a score of 16 or greater must have had at least 6 of the 20 CES-D symptoms for most of the previous week or a majority of the symptoms for a shorter duration of time. However, a score of 16 or greater is not the same as a diagnosis of major depressive disorder.

Thus, through research on the interpersonal aspects of depression, findings suggest that the developmental shift to motherhood clearly has serious implications for well-being. And, in certain cases, the consequences may be highly adverse. For example, the depression data for never-married mothers seem to suggest that the toll appears to be significantly higher among them, and especially great among Latinas in comparison to African-American and white women. Although the differences in ratings may be a function of Latinas' idiosyncratic responses to depression questionnaires in general, the investigators have speculated that for never-married Latina mothers, the Hispanic values surrounding motherhood, marriage, and the male as head of household may prevent them from connecting authentically with others within their group. Consequently, problems of disconnection may drive their depression ratings upward. Because of demographic and acculturation factors, accessing meaningful relationships outside of their immediate families may prove to be especially difficult. The net result may be a sense of condemned isolation and a downward spiral toward depression (Jordan, Kaplan, Miller, Stiver, & Surrey, 1991). As Jordan pointed out, it is "when we feel most separate from others and from the flow of life that we are at most risk" (1992, p. 5).

In evaluating the intervention, preliminary findings suggest that the most significant reduction in depressive symptoms occurred among women who perceived their peer relationships as being mutual. It's difficult to generalize about the nature of their relationships because there was such a great deal of diversity in their needs and life experiences. There were pairs who were highly educated and pairs who were not. Some minority women asked to be paired with women from similar racial and ethnic backgrounds, while others explicitly requested to be paired with someone very different from themselves. Some women found it easy to stay in touch with their partners, whereas others experienced a great deal of difficulty. For one pair in particular, where one women was living in a shelter, keeping in touch often involved phoning relatives and others who might convey a message. However, many mothers reported consistently that they valued talking with someone who was not judgmental and who understood what they were going through. It is suspected that women who were experiencing a significant degree of relational distress in their lives may have found it difficult to establish a mutual connection with a program partner. A number of women found it difficult to engage mutually. For example, some women expected concrete expert advice about parenting, and were frustrated by the idea of working through a shared understanding with their partner about parenting experiences more generally.

Follow-up data indicate that a significant number of relationships have continued voluntarily beyond the six-month intervention period. In exit interviews, it has been learned that in some instances peer contact between a pair of women has grown into contact between pairs of families. In those instances where the peer relationship was not considered to be mutual, there were unexpected gains as well. One women said that although things hadn't worked out with her partner, she had recognized her need for friendships with other women. At the time she was interviewed she had made a firm decision to become actively involved in her neighborhood PTA. In fact, when asked what she thought the program was about, one mother confidently stated that it was about building community. In response to the question "What did you like about being paired with another mother?" statements regarding the benefits of personalized contact with a partner as well as group participation were often mentioned. In response to questions regarding the drawbacks of being paired, the lack of involvement in the relationship by one of the partners proved to be problematic for some. Analysis of the Mothers' Project data continues to explore the role of mutual psychological development in reducing the risk of depression in women.

Although the understanding of the effects of mutual peer support on reducing the risk of depression remains incomplete, relational models of intervention may provide yet another piece of the story of resiliency among minorities. Bringing people into connection with each other in meaningful ways may require challenging existing structural barriers and articulating cultural norms regarding relationships. In the process of recruiting eligible minority women to participate in the study, the Project was most successful in attracting white and African-American women and least successful with Latina and Asian women. The pattern of response to recruitment among white and African-American women seemed surprisingly similar. Although it is possible that Latina and Asian women may have been struggling with realities that may have prevented them from making a commitment to the study, it is also possible that the idea of participating in a "women's program," which in some ways may have excluded existing meaningful relationships, may have violated some of their own ideas about what it means to be relational. If culture influences the kinds of relationships that people form and the ways in which they are likely to participate in those relationships, the study of mutual psychological development and resiliency should clearly reflect this diversity. Research on the cultural meanings of relationships will help to make future relational interventions more workable and effective.

This chapter opened with a description of the collaborative efforts of the residents of southwest Philadelphia and their willingness to risk involvement. In ending with the Mothers' Project, the discussion is essentially where it started—exploring the benefits and risks of mutual psychological development. The parallels between the two are striking—people taking extraordinary measures to move out of isolation and toward connection. Whether interpersonal disconnections arise out of poverty, racial barriers, or the lack of understanding and conflict associated with major life events, the end result is one of debilitation and diminished self-worth. By most standards, organizing a neighborhood farmer's market or women talking to other women about their children, families, work, and everyday ups and downs doesn't appear to be out of the ordinary. Closer examination, however, highlights the many creative ways in which people overcome the barriers to connection. That deliberate movement out of isolation tells us a great deal about resiliency.

Reframing the concept of resiliency from an individualistic to a relational one allows alternative methodological avenues of inquiry to be explored. It may be that participation in relationships and resiliency may be best studied using naturalistic, prospective longitudinal designs to study dyadic relationships, families, and communities. Further, the use of in-depth case studies and narratives about past, current, and hopes for future relationships could make a vital and innovative contribution to this area. In studying resiliency within a context of relationships, variables such as class, gender, sexuality, and culture cannot be relegated to a background status. Nor can differences in the conceptual meaning of relationships, family, and cultural groups be ignored. Within a relational context, the use of broader social indicators such as quality of neighborhood, community organizations, and workplace assume greater importance and make a great deal of sense. Although the use of both qualitative and quantitative data-gathering techniques may be desirable, it seems that an interdisciplinary, multi-method approach may generate the most exciting data. In any case, documenting the diverse ways in which minority families experience resiliency through mutual psychological development will provide a repository of information of scientific, cultural, and historical significance.

Note

1. This research is supported by grant MCJ–250608 from the Maternal and Child Health Bureau (Title V, Social Security Act), Health Resource and Services of Administration, Department of Health and Human Services, and funding from Stone Center for Developmental Services and Studies at Wellesley College. The author would like to thank Jean Baker Miller, Lauren Goldstein, Roberta Unger, and Mark Genero for their valuable comments on an earlier draft of this chapter. To the many project staff members, research assistants, and collaborators at Wellesley College and the Harvard Community Health Plan, my deepest gratitude for helping to keep the study on track.

References

Acitelli, L. K. (1988). When spouses talk to each other about their relationship. *Journal of Social and Personal Relationships, 5*, 185–199.

Acitelli, L.K. (1992). Gender differences in relationship awareness and marital satisfaction among young married couples. *Personality and Social Psychology Bulletin, 18*, 102–110.

Antonovsky, A. (1994). The sense of coherence: An historical and future perspective. In H. I. McCubbin, E. A. Thompson, A. I. Thompson, & J. E. Fromer (Eds.), *Sense of coherence and resiliency: Stress, coping, and health* (pp. 3–20). Madison, WI: The University of Wisconsin System.

Antonovsky, A., & Sagy, S. (1986). The development of a sense of coherence and its impact on responses to stress situations. *Journal of Social Psychology, 126*, 213–225.

Antonucci, T. C., & Jackson, J. S. (1989). Successful aging and life course reciprocity. In A. Warnes (Ed.), *Human aging and later life: Multidisciplinary perspectives* (pp. 83–95). London: Hodder & Stoughton.

Antonucci, T. C., & Mikus, K. (1988). The power of parenthood: Personality and attitudinal changes during the transition to parenthood. In G. Y. Michaels & W. A. Goldberg (Eds.), *The transition to parenthood: Current theory and research* (pp. 62–84). Cambridge, England: Cambridge University Press.

Barnes, E. (1980). The black community as the source of positive self-concept for black children: A theoretical perspective. In R. Jones (Ed.), *Black psychology* (2nd ed., pp. 106–130). New York: Harper and Row.

Belle, D, (1982). The stress of caring: Women as providers of social support. In L. Goldberger & S. Brenitz (Eds.), *Handbook of stress: Theoretical and clinical aspects* (pp. 496–505). New York: Free Press.

Brown, G. W., Bhrolchrain, M. N., & Harris, T. O. (1975). Social class and psychiatric disturbance among women in an urban population. *Sociology, 9,* 225–254.

Brown, G. W., & Harris, T. O. (1978). *Social origins of depression.* London: Tavistock.

Cohen, S., & Wills, T. A. (1985). Stress, social support, and the buffering hypothesis. *Psychological Bulletin, 98,* 310–357.

Crnic, K. A., & Greenberg, M. T. (1990). Minor parenting stresses with young children. *Child Development, 61,* 1628–1637.

Davis, M. H., & Oathout, H. A. (1987). Maintenance of satisfaction in romantic relationships: Empathy and relational competence. *Journal of Personality and Social Psychology, 53,* 397–410.

Duck, S. (1994). *Meaningful relationships: Talking, sense, and relating.* Newbury Park, CA: Sage.

García Coll, C. T., Escobar, M., Cebollero, P., & Valcárcel, M. (1989). Adolescent pregnancy and childbearing: Psychosocial consequences during the postpartum period. In C. T. García Coll & M. de Lourdes Mattei (Eds.), *The psychosocial development of Puerto Rican women* (pp. 84–114). New York: Praeger.

Genero, N. P., Miller, J. B., Surrey, J., & Angiolillo, D. (1991). *Peer support in high risk mothers of young children.* [Grant proposal MCJ–250698 awarded by the Maternal and Child Health Program] (Available from Nancy P. Genero, Psychology Department, Wellesley College, 106 Central Street, Wellesley, MA 02181).

Genero, N. P., Miller, J. B., Surrey, J., & Baldwin, L. M. (1992). Measuring perceived mutuality in close relationships: Validation of the Mutual Psychological Development Questionnaire. *Journal of Family Psychology, 6,* 36–48.

Gilkes, C. T. (1994). "If it wasn't for the women ..": African-American women, community, work, & social change. In M. B. Zinn & B. T. Dill (Eds.), *Women of color in U.S. society* (pp. 229–246). Philadelphia: University Press.

Grossman, F. K., & Moore, R. P. (1994). Against the odds: Resiliency in an adult survivor of childhood sexual abuse. In C. Franz & A. Stewart (Eds.), *Women creating lives: Identities, resilience, and resistance* (pp. 71–82). Boulder, CO: Westview.

Hall, L. A. (1990). Prevalence and correlates of depressive symptoms in mothers of young children. *Public Health Nursing, 7,* 71–79.

Hall, L. A., Schaefer, E. S., & Greenberg, R. S. (1987). Quality and quantity of social support as correlates of psychosomatic symptoms in mothers with young children. *Research in Nursing & Health, 10,* 287–298.

Hatchett, S. J., & Jackson, J. S. (1993). African-American extended kin systems: An assessment. In H. P. McAdoo (Ed.), *Family ethnicity: Strength in diversity* (pp. 90–108). Newbury Park, CA: Sage.

Heller, K., & Lakey, B. (1985). Perceived support and social interaction among friends and confidants. In I. G. Sarason & B. R. Sarason (Eds.), *Social support: Theory, research, and applications* (pp. 287–300). Dordrecht, the Netherlands: Martinus Nijoff.

Hindsabout, M. deC. (1994, May 14). Inner city market blossoms. *New York Times,* p. 8.

Jessor, R. (1993). Successful adolescent development among youth in high-risk settings. *American Psychologist, 48(2),* 117–126.

Jordan, J. (1986). *The meaning of mutuality* (Work in Progress, No. 23). Wellesley, MA: Stone Center, Wellesley College.

Jordan, J. (1991). The movement of mutuality and power (Work in Progress, No. 53). Wellesley, MA: Stone Center, Wellesley College.

Jordan, J. (1992). *Relational resilience* (Work in Progress, No. 57). Wellesley, MA: Stone Center, Wellesley College.

Jordan, J., Kaplan, A., Miller, J. B., Stiver, I., & Surrey, J. (1991). *Women's growth in connection.* New York: Guilford.

Kelley, H. H., Bercheid, E., Christensen, A., Harvey, J. H., Huston, T. L., Levinger, G., McClintock, E., Peplau, L.A., & Perterson, D. R. (1983). *Close relationships.* New York: Freeman.

Kobasa, S. C., & Pucetti, M. C. (1983). Personality and social resources in stress resistance. *Journal of Personality and Social Psychology, 45,* 839-850.

Koeske, G. F., & Koeske, R. D. (1990). The buffering effect of social support on parental stress. *American Journal of Orthopsychiatry, 60,* 440–451.

Martinez, E. A. (1993). Parenting young children in Mexican-American/ Chicano families. In H. P. McAdoo (Ed.), *Family ethnicity: Strength in diversity* (pp.184–198). Newbury Park, CA: Sage.

McAdoo, H. P. (1993). *Family ethnicity: Strength in diversity.* Newbury Park, CA: Sage.

McCubbin, H. I., Thompson, E. A., Thompson, A. I., McCubbin, M. A., & Kaston, A. J. (1993). Culture, ethnicity, and the family critical factors in childhood chronic illnesses and disabilities. *Pediatrics, 91,* 1063–1070.

McLoyd, V. (1990). The impact of economic hardship on black families and children: Psychological distress, parenting, and socio-emotional development. *Child Development, 61,* 311–346.

Meltz, B. F. (1994, January 13). Bringing up black sons poses special challenges. *Boston Globe,* p. A4.

Miller, P. M., & Ingham, J. G. (1976). Friends, confidants, and symptoms. *Social Psychiatry, 11,* 51–58.

Miller, J. B. (1976). *Toward a new psychology of women.* Boston: Beacon.

Miller, J. B. (1988). *Connections, disconnections, & violations* (Work in Progress, No. 33). Wellesley, MA: Stone Center, Wellesley College.

Phoenix, A., Woollett, A., & Lloyd, E. (1991). *Motherhood: Meanings, practices, and ideologies.* Newbury Park, CA: Sage.

Radloff, L. S. (1977). Sex differences in depression: The effects of occupation and marital status. *Sex Roles, 1*, 249–265.

Rook, K. S. (1987). Reciprocity of social exchange and social satisfaction among older women. *Journal of Personality and Social Psychology, 52*, 143–154.

Rutter, M. (1979). Protective factors in children's responses to stress and disadvantage. In M. W. Kent & J. E. Rolf (Eds.), *Primary prevention of psychopathology, Vol. 3, Social competence in children.* (pp. 49–74). Hanover, NH: University Press of New England.

Stokes, J. P., & Wilson, D. G. (1984). The inventory of socially supportive behaviors: Dimensionality, prediction, and gender differences. *American Journal of Community Psychology, 12*, 53–69.

Sudarkasa, N. (1993). Female-headed African-American households: Some neglected dimensions. In H. P. McAdoo (Ed.) *Family ethnicity: Strength in diversity* (pp. 81–89). Newbury Park, CA: Sage.

Surrey, J. (1985). *The "self-in-relation": A theory of women's development* (Work in Progress, No. 13). Wellesley, MA: Stone Center, Wellesley College.

Tatum, B. D. (1987). *Assimilation blues: Black families in white communities.* Northampton: Hazel-Maxwell.

Tatum, B. D. (1993). *Racial identity development and relational theory: The case of black women in white communities* (Work in Progress, No. 63). Wellesley, MA: Stone Center, Wellesley College.

Urwin, C. (1985). Constructing motherhood: The persuasion of normal development. In C. Steedman, C. Urwin, & V. Walkerdine (Eds.), *Language, gender, and childhood* (pp. 165–202). London: Routledge & Kegan Paul.

Vega, W. A., Kolody, B., & Valle, J. R. (1986). The relationship of marital status, confidant support, and depression among Mexican immigrant women. *Journal of Marriage and the Family, 48*, 597–605.

Walster, E. H., Bercheid, E., & Walster, G. W. (1973). New directions in equity research. *Journal of Personality and Social Psychology, 25*, 151–176.

Werner, E. E., & Smith, R. S. (1992). *Overcoming the odds: High risk children from birth to adulthood.* Ithaca: Cornell University Press.

Williams, C. W. (1991). *Black teenage mothers: Pregnancy and child rearing from their perspective.* Lexington, MA: Lexington Books.

Chapter 4

Indigenous Resources and Strategies of Resistance

Informal Caregiving and Racial Socialization in Black Communities

Michael C. Thornton

The deviant family has become part of American cultural mythology. Blacks, Asian Americans, Native peoples, and Hispanics have been portrayed in the popular literature and by social scientists as if their family forms were deficient. Black families in particular have become synonymous with family instability and disorganization. In this prevailing view, the family is itself a social problem.

The stereotype of black families as inherently deficient and unstable is predicated on the belief that slavery destroyed traditions and familial ties among Blacks. This characterization, based on an historical artifact, is used to explain contemporary assertions about lack of family values among African Americans. In contrast, those who believe social structure is the key attribute family deficiencies to severe economic and racial oppression that continues to create havoc within black communities and among individuals. Interestingly, while these views point to different sources of "the Black problem," both have one underlying assumption in common: Black families are passive beings in this process. Those who see slavery as a legacy hold black passivity culpable for their current plight. For structuralists, the nature of the oppression encountered by Blacks is deterministic of a debilitated population; Blacks remain victims of forces outside of their control.

The history of black life in America is one in which families face increasing pressures to sustain viable units. Indeed, the measure of the resiliency and strength of black communities is that the family has survived in the face of so much racial hostility and discrimination. By now it should be a truism that no human group can exist in isolation from the institutions in its environment. Another axiom little appreciated in research on black families is that they have adapted to adverse conditions, and, given the circumstances, with remarkable completeness. The resources emanating from within black communities, the power that these individuals possess, even in dire circumstances, deserves more attention by researchers. In this revisionist version, black families underline the strengths and the backbone, not the weaknesses, of black communities.

Like many emerging works, this chapter begins with the assumption that communities and families possess resources that, while remaining unappreciated, contribute immensely to survival, to the abilities to counteract oppressive forces. These resources are left unexplored because they are often manifest in day-to-day activities. These mundane struggles of life that form the foundation of the overall effort of resistance are unspectacular, they are average. Nevertheless, placing these average life events at the center of analysis reveals empowered individuals within structures of domination. Investigating forms of power by historically marginalized groups is a way to rethink social change and the politics of empowerment.

This alternative to the model of disorganized and pathological families presumes that neighborhoods and families—even those in so-called urban ghettos—are communities that have constructive legacies that are more influential than slavery. Part of this organizational heritage is related directly to family and its cultural/experiential foundation. Cultural heritage provides a repertoire of resources, familial lifestyles, and culturally influenced patterns of social involvement (Holzberg, 1982). This chapter accents the role culture plays in influencing patterns of familial support and resistance. Ethnic heritage creates a "community tradition" of mutual aid strategies influencing the nature of family life (Mindel & Wright, 1988). This, in turn, reflects norms and values of prescribed behavior by which families operate, including how family members identify, define, and attempt to solve problems. One of the most significant ways ethnic culture is expressed is through family activities.

The key to understanding how Blacks have forged powerful family ties lies in the adaptive capacities they have constructed from culture and experience. They have not simply reacted to the abuses of the institutions in their lives or lay down to await their inevitable fate. Instead, they make choices from several possible ways of responding. The elements of adaptation, culture, and choice are important in understanding how Blacks resist oppression. Foremost has been the development of a kinship system that has persisted even against great adversity.

This resistance is contoured by the wider social environment. More specifically, resistance involves an interaction between how the larger social context affects everyday experiences and the way in which day-to-day activities help shape the larger social contexts. Agency is how micro-level activities influence the macro level and vice versa. Agency concerns events of which an individual is a perpetrator. As defined by Giddens (1993), action or agency is "the stream of actual or causal interventions of corporeal beings in the ongoing process of events-in-the-world." This action occurs despite other options, the individual "could have done otherwise." These actions are often intentional and purposive because "the agent knows (believes) [the act] can be expected to manifest a particular quality or outcome, and in which this knowledge is made use of by the actor in order to produce this quality or outcome." (p. 83). While the effects of this act may not be predicted (or predictable), agency implies that people are not simply passive bystanders in their own lives, for they make choices and act to change their world. Agency is about what happens that would not have happened if the individual had not intervened. How black families make things happen despite the larger social context is the focus of this chapter.

To highlight agency, which lies at the heart of resiliency, this chapter will examine two subjects based on the author's research: First, discussion will focus on the extent of the support black communities, via families, provide to frail elderly; and second, another vital issue will then be explored—the responsibility of preparing children for life as black Americans. Parents make choices of how and/or if this is done based on their assessment of the nature of the social forces that surround them. In this case, what strategy they choose to socialize their children is based largely on their appraisal of the role race and discrimination will play in their children's lives.

Informal Caregiving: Family and Assistance to Frail Elders

Minority elderly have particularly limited access to formal medical care. Low socioeconomic status, culturally homogeneous services, and discrimination have led to low utilization of and discontinuous access to formal market-supplied medical services among black elderly (Petchers & Milligan, 1988). Although access to Medicare and Medicaid leads to increased usage (Davis et al., 1989), many poor and minority elderly face difficulty meeting medical expenses because they cannot afford private medical health insurance supplements. When formal services are used at all, they are more typically outpatient facilities and emergency rooms (White-Means & Thornton, 1989a, 1989b).

Over the past decade, access to formal services has been restricted further because of the federal government's attempt to reduce its share of hospital and nursing home costs. Filling the vacuum created by these cost-cutting efforts, informal home health care services are now touted as the "rediscovered alternative to institutional care" (Scheier, 1987, p. 1). Informal providers (e.g., family, friends, and other unpaid help) bear the responsibility for providing a range of services for elders. Thus, these providers intrinsically determine the quality of home health services and family life. However, little is known about this type of informal care among Blacks. Furthermore, while seen as a key factor in caregiving, it is unclear how ethnicity serves as an intervening influence on and an indigenous characteristic of long-term health care for the elderly.

Over the last few years, a research project has examined networks of informal home health caregivers of frail elderly among Black, English, German, and Irish Americans (White-Means & Thornton, 1990a, 1990b; Thornton, White-Means, & Choi, 1993). The data from which these sets of studies were drawn are two surveys that form the 1982 National Long Term Care Survey (NLTCS), sponsored by the U.S. Department of Health and Human Services and conducted by the Bureau of the Census (Gayer, 1982). The NLTCS of frail persons contains a representative sample of noninstitutionalized persons in the U.S., 65 years of age or over, who received assistance with activities of daily living. A supplementary survey was conducted in 1983 on the subgroup of informal helpers who were identified by the Long Term caregiver survey respondents. The data set contains 1,617 active caregivers who were at least 14 years of age and provided assistance to an elderly respondent with limitations in one of six activities. For a more in-depth discussion of sampling procedures and methodology, refer to Phillips, Stephens, and Cerf (1986) and to the studies cited above.

The analysis described here used an ethnic subsample of the above data sets. Ethnic background was generated by asking respondents to examine a list of national and ethnic categories and answering the following question: "What is your ethnic origin or descent?" Seventeen distinct ethnic groups were identified. Included in the analysis were those groups with the largest numbers: English, Irish, German, and African Americans (see White-Means & Thornton, 1990b, for a more detailed discussion).

Several patterns stand out when examining the extent of the support provided to elders. First, while home health care was found to be generally time-consuming, it was especially time-consuming for Blacks. Of the four groups, Blacks spent much more time in caring for elders—over 29 hours in an average week. The white ethnics provided care for anywhere from 17 to 21 hours per week. Thus Blacks spent about 4 hours a day in care, often in addition to working outside the home.

Secondly, and consistent with the wider literature, caregiving duties were most often assumed by females. Nevertheless, there was some variation by sex. Giving the most time to this endeavor, black women spent approximately 32 hours a week in care, a figure 9 to 12 hours more than that for white ethnic women. Black males gave 20 hours per week to care, ranking them after black and English-American women, and Irish-American males. This pattern shows that black men were more involved in direct caregiving than some groups of women, particularly German- and Irish-American females.

The extent of involvement among black caregivers also emerges in an examination of the role of substitutes. Substitutes are individuals who are available to give respite to those who provide care. One would expect that those with substitutes would put less time into caregiving than those who are without them. This assumption was supported for white ethnics. Among Blacks, those without substitutes spent 29 hours a week in caring for the elder. In contrast, those caregivers with substitutes actually spent more time, 30 hours a week, in caregiving activities. Why this pattern exists only for Blacks is unclear. Generally, black elderly are more physically deteriorated than their white counterparts. Black elderly suffer more illnesses, see a doctor less often, and are more likely to have heart disease, strokes, and high blood pressure (Edmonds, 1993). This trend is in part related to a delay in blacks seeking medical care, which is associated with a host of reasons, such as financial limitations, child care problems and a fear of hospitals (White, 1979). Due to this fact, there are probably more things that black caregivers need to do for them than would their white ethnic counterparts. A number of these duties might conflict with primary tasks. When temporarily relieved of those responsibilities, perhaps the resultant "free" time is used to perform neglected caregiving obligations.

In part, reflecting the cultural tradition of extended families, an interesting pattern is observed when contrasting the time spent in caring for immediate (e.g., spouse, siblings, children, or grandparents) versus nonimmediate (e.g., distant kin, friends, neighbors) elders. Black caregivers to immediate family members spent on average 28 hours a week with their duties. This figure rose by 2 hours more a week when they cared for nonimmediate members. The greater hours spent with nonimmediate family members may be related to time spent in traveling to and from this care situation. Devotion to elders is extensive regardless of the kinship, legal or extralegal.

The literature on extended family households recognizes the important economic benefits of these arrangements; they are often viewed as an effective mechanism for pooling limited resources. The emotional support provided by this structure is also emerging in recent work (see Taylor et al., 1990). The presence of nonnuclear adults within the household is associated with the reallocation of employment and domestic responsibilities. Another adult in the household who assists with duties may help alleviate the burden associated with caring for an impaired family member (Hogan, Hao, & Parish, 1990). In comparison to direct cash transfers, having an extended household is generally a less expensive method of providing for needy relatives. Angel and Tienda (1982) found that among Blacks the relative contribution of a wife, adult children, and nonnuclear relatives constituted a greater portion of the total family income than is the case for Whites. Among lower income Blacks, lower earnings require supplemental income from others to achieve a desired standard of living or even to meet daily needs.

That Blacks remain attached to extended family in a way comparable to that for immediate family speaks volumes about the idea of community among Blacks. This bond cannot be assessed through conventional models of family and community life. Likewise, traditional models are not helpful in the development of policy that will utilize the devotion that black families give to elders in our communities. The direct result is that the extended family is not recognized as a resource by those who develop family policy. More ominously, social policy often works to punish black families for what they do best. Public policy is not typically based on a clear understanding of how family members work together and how existing family culture provides a background for cooperative efforts—these policies are therefore detrimental to black families. Factors generally included in formulas for designing cost-effective waiver programs include sex, age, marital status, and functional disabilities. The emphasis of most public policy has been on cost-effectiveness. Family cultural differences and other nonfinancial indigenous resources seldom function as policy criteria.

Many states are attempting to develop policies on family leaves of absence to care for elderly relatives (Wisensale & Allison, 1988). The issues of debate and concern among legislatures include questions about whether family leave should apply to the public sector, the private sector, or both. Other issues of discussion include whether family leave should be paid or unpaid, and whether family leave should be limited to children and spouses or include other members as well. Existing family-leave policy for caring for elders typically provides only the spouse with limited unpaid leave. Failing to incorporate existing systems of family care into family-leave policy would impose a disproportionate burden on black families, who often turn to family members outside of the immediate context. A policy incorporating this sensitivity to diverse definitions of family would benefit Blacks tremendously.

As is clear from research on families, women perform the bulk of caregiving tasks. Not appreciating cultural differences between groups in the level of support provided to elders has particular import for them. Ironically, the very culture of resistance created by black women to survive, that which provides the foundation to black family life, and that is essential to the struggle for group survival, is used by wider entities to further the oppression of black families and women by denying them resources (Collins, 1991).

Because their activities are not legitimated, the level of family members' commitment to each other is generally an unknown quantity in black communities. Many of the duties performed for black elders would be paid for with government assistance in other communities. Thus self-sufficiency is often thrust upon black families because they don't fit neatly into definitions of family used in the development of policy. Nevertheless, despite this tendency and a shrinking pool of outside financial resources, these communities and families adjust and utilize indigenous assets. Black culture has influenced the definition of family, and the lack of financial resources has meant that they must rely on themselves.

Clearly, agency lies at the heart of the black community's efforts to care for its elderly members. Indeed, for a number of reasons, this endeavor dwarfs that of other communities, especially when the contributions made by women are examined. Perhaps indicative of contemporary black America, the caregiving described above is merely the end point to a process of resistance that begins earlier in life. To enable Blacks to reach adulthood as mentally stable human beings, the foundation must be set in childhood. To prepare for a successful journey through life, most black parents believe that their children must appreciate the role race will play in their lives (Thornton et al., 1990; Billingsley, 1992).

Racial Socialization

Perhaps the earliest "intervention into the ongoing process of the events-of-the-world," as Giddens describes agency, occurs for Blacks when they have children. The process of explicit racial socialization is a distinctive childrearing activity that black parents engage in to prepare their children for life in America. Parents who incorporate race into the socialization process are not raising an American, but a Black or African American, whose experience is distinct from that of other Americans (Peters, 1985). Presuming that their children will encounter a hostile environment, these parents believe they must make their children comfortable with their blackness (Harrison, 1985; Daniel, 1975). The process of racial socialization is one means by which black families and parents address these concerns. Broadly defined, racial socialization includes specific messages and practices relevant to and providing information about the nature of race status as it relates to: (1) group and personal identity; (2) intergroup and interindividual associations; and (3) position in the social hierarchy. Specific forms of racial socialization may include verbal behaviors (direct statements regarding race), modeling of behaviors, and exposure to specific objects, contexts and environments (Thornton et al., 1990). Aside from these general tendencies, however, how parents prepare their children for this environment is not clearly understood.

Nevertheless, certain things appear clear. How race affects the socialization process is apparently influenced by several social factors. Certain sociodemographic influences are associated with imparting racial messages. Gender, marital status, and education are related to an increased likelihood of presenting racial messages (Bowman & Howard, 1985; Thornton, Chatters, Taylor, & Allen, 1990). Mothers more often than fathers socialize their children to race issues, which is in part related to greater maternal responsibilities for this sort of task (Lamb & Lamb, 1976). Never-married parents and less educated parents are less likely to make a special effort to instill the importance of race in their children than married or better educated parents (Thornton, Chatters, Taylor, & Allen, 1990). Why never-married parents are less likely to socialize their children to racial dictums is unclear. General research on the effects of marital status on socialization indicates that these parents provide less parental supervision than married couples (Dornbusch et al., 1985). Single female parents are often found to reduce the time involved in active childrearing because of excessive demands placed upon them by housekeeping and outside employment (McLanahan, 1985). Widowed men also may suffer emotional and social losses affecting their ability to fulfill many of the role obligations incumbent upon parents (Stroebe & Stroebe, 1983), including racial socialization.

While the delineation of structural effects on racial socialization is just now emerging, Boykin and Toms (1985) suggested that the socialization of black children involves an interplay between three major parental themes: (1) mainstream experience (i.e., influences of white, middle-class culture or so-called universals of family living); (2) minority experience (i.e., social, economic, and political forces impinging on racial minorities leading to a set of coping styles, social outlooks, and adaptive positions); and (3) cultural experience (i.e., styles, motifs, and patterns of behavior unique to Blacks).

The analysis reported here explores in greater detail the paradigm of socialization messages identified in Boykin and Toms (1985) and further explored in Thornton et al. (1990). This study examined the relationship between what parents chose as socialization strategies and how these choices were influenced by a set of sociodemographic and attitudinal measures. The sociodemographic measures include age, gender, marital status, region, and education. Among the attitude measures are negative and positive stereotypes of other Blacks, having white friends, feelings of closeness with Africans and Whites, and what respondents believe about how Whites feel about Blacks. For a more in-depth discussion of the analyses, refer to Thornton (1997).

The data used in this study come from the National Survey of Black Americans (1979–1980), a multistage area probability sample of the adult black population. This data set contains 2,107 respondents. The sample is the first nationally representative cross-section of the adult black population living in the continental United States. For a more complete description of the sample, see Neighbors and Jackson (1984).

Based on these analyses, there are four strategies utilized by parents to socialize their children to being black in America. The first strategy is illustrated by those parents who do nothing. As supported in other work, one-third of black parents report they do not convey racial socialization messages to their children (Bowman & Howard, 1985; Thornton et al., 1990). Many of these parents assert that if racial issues are important, their children will learn them on their own, or they will learn them as they grow up. Some of these parents accept negative images of Blacks perpetuated by society, while others simply downplay the importance of race and thus do not systematically address these images in their socialization approaches. Some researchers describe these families as populations at risk and researchers see the children from these families as manifesting problems of racial dissonance (e.g., Ogbu, 1983). In our analysis, these parents are most likely to be male, young, single and poorly educated.

The remaining three strategies are found among parents who do incorporate race into the socialization process. Most parents mentioned socialization goals corresponding to what Boykin and Toms (1985) called the "mainstream experience." These parents see their primary role as that of teaching life skills. Possessing personal qualities such as confidence, ambition, and respect is seen as most important. Teaching children about race and discrimination is perceived as much less critical for preparing for life as a Black in America. Thus, these parents tend to transcend issues of race in their socialization efforts, focusing instead on human values (Spencer, 1983) and highlighting hard work, achievement or moral virtues. This specific strategy stresses what researchers describe as personal self-esteem, a reference to how the individual feels about the comprehensive self (Porter & Washington, 1993).

On the surface these parents appear to be the most acculturated or anchored into American society, as they are among the better educated, and tend to have white friends. Parents with the mainstream view feel close to Africans but hold no special feelings toward Whites generally. The tendency to distance themselves from Whites, but to focus on qualities that are esteemed in "American" culture, suggests that mainstream parents identify with America but that this is unrelated to a special identification with Whites.

The parents in this category were more likely than those who do not socialize for race to hold a number of positive stereotypes about Blacks. Mainstream parents feel an affinity with other Blacks that may reflect their tie with an African-American belief system identified in the literature (e.g., Allen, Thornton, & Watkins, 1992). Among these acculturated parents, racial group membership remains an important part of their world view, even if not ostensibly in terms of explicit racial socialization messages.

Certain sociodemographic factors influence these patterns. Older parents are more likely than younger parents to advocate mainstream views. This relationship with age is perhaps associated with a different political socialization among older generations of parents. This particular socialization emphasized more strongly than that of today the ideas of good citizenship, self-image, and achievement, ideas implicit in the mainstream socialization dimension. Older parents grew up when bonds with other Blacks were vital to personal and group survival. A collective focus also signified a mutual reliance to uphold behavior that would reflect positively upon the community and enhance individual and group advancement (Smith & Thornton, 1993). The fact that older parents are also more likely to be the educational backbone of black communities (i.e., are at least high school graduates) may also be related to the stress placed on success and mainstream values.

Other important factors reflect functional realities of the parent's particular social qualities (Thornton et al., 1990). Fathers and single parents are less likely than married parents and mothers to socialize their children to mainstream perspectives. Nevertheless, these qualities were also related to all socialization strategies identified here. Single parents supervise their children less than married parents (Dornbusch et al., 1985), often reducing the time for childrearing because of the excessive demands of employment and housekeeping (McLanahan, 1985). Mothers usually have more responsibility for child care and tend to specialize in the intellectual and emotional aspects of socialization (Lamb & Lamb, 1976).

On the other hand, the second and third patterns we identified among parents who socialized for race—focusing on minority and cultural experiences—may stress what the wider literature calls group self-esteem, feelings about racial or ethnic group membership (Porter & Washington, 1993). Those who highlight the minority experience view the primary goal of racial socialization as preparing their offspring for an oppressive environment (Richardson,

1981; Tatum, 1987). These parents acknowledged the presence of racial restrictions (e.g., "Blacks don't have the opportunities that Whites have"), emphasized a general recognition of one's race (e.g., "accept your color"), or provided information that would help to develop appropriate psychological coping styles and perspectives regarding minority status. To prepare their children for this world, these parents believe they must instill in them self-respect and pride and teach them how to survive and cope with prejudice. They must also stress the importance of a good education and inform them that fair play, while important, will not be reciprocated by Whites (Peters, 1985).

In contrast to those who highlighted mainstream perspectives, our analysis showed that those who socialize for minority experience are more ambiguous about their place in American society, a perhaps predictable result of their stress on barriers in the larger society. These parents did not feel close to any group, and were no more likely to hold positive or negative stereotypes about other Blacks. However, antipathy is directed at Whites. Whites are seen as unsupportive of black efforts to gain equality (i.e., they don't want them to get a better break). This perception, of course, provides the broader context of what they believe children must prepare for. Antipathy is a component of socialization only for this group of parents.

Based on the sociodemographic variables important for minority socializers, these parents are among the most affected by racial restrictions. Besides the factors found for all groups (gender and marital status), poor education (0–11 grade), urban residence and region were associated with minority socialization. Those with little education and those living in urban areas are among the least economically successful of all the parents examined here.

The final socialization theme emphasizes black culture. When this view is stressed, parents recount historical events in their own family lives or speak of famous black historical figures (Spencer, 1983; Tatum, 1987). The messages conveyed reflect an emphasis on black heritage, history, and traditions (e.g., "I taught what happened in the past about how people coped") (Thornton et al., 1990; Spencer, 1983; Tatum, 1987). One might assume that parents stressing black culture make special efforts to teach children about their African and African-American heritage and historical traditions. On closer inspection, it appears that they don't feel a special bond to Africa. These parents are no more likely as a group to feel close to Africa than are parents who do not racially socialize their children. Apparently these parents highlight black American heritage in the socialization process.

In contrast to the previous strategy, parents accenting the culture approach seem more optimistic about various aspects of their lives. That cultural socialization is a tactic that attracts parents who hold many positive stereotypes about other Blacks is perhaps not surprising. One would expect that positive aspects of one's heritage would be highlighted. What is puzzling is that these parents are also more likely than those who do not socialize for race to trust that Whites support their efforts to better themselves.

Racial socialization is a complex process, mirroring important perceptions of the black experience in the United States. How one traverses the pitfalls provided by race in this society is probably the most significant challenge faced by black parents. Does one highlight restraints to cushion the pain or does one concentrate on the opportunities available? Clearly there are any number of strategies available. This process, however, remains an inherent part of the process of black life, even for those who may not appreciate its significance. Effective racial socialization should provide the resources necessary to resist and change the system. Without a committed identity, black communities would lose their vitality and their ability to respond to oppression.

Conclusion

Pauli Murray wrote: "A system of oppression draws much of its strength from the acquiescence of its victims, who have accepted the dominant image of themselves and are paralyzed by a sense of helplessness" (Murray, 1987, p. 106). Blacks are typically characterized as overwhelmed by racism or as using it as a cloak for a lack of personal initiative. These characterizations treat the people at the heart of the discussion as impotent objects. They are to be pitied or blamed for their plight, for they are resigned to their fate.

Despite these assertions, however, researchers are now beginning to appreciate what many in black communities have long known: Black families in their day-to-day living have not acquiesced to the oppression around them. What is also becoming clearer is that this struggle in large part has been due to family bonds and particularly to black female activism (Collins, 1991). Agency lies at the heart of both the effort to prepare black children for life in America and family efforts to help their elders adjust to later life.

While both black mothers and fathers play key roles in transmitting an Afrocentric world view to their children or in caring for elders, mothers remain the primary caretakers. Fannie Barrier Williams (1987, p. 151) argued that black women are not defenseless victims but strong-willed resisters: "As meanly as she is thought of, hindered as she is in all directions, she is always doing something of merit and credit that is not expected of her." In *Black Feminist Thought,* Patricia Hill Collins (1991) argued that this tradition of resistance highlights group survival and institutional transformation.

Black women enable their families to resist oppression by creating female spheres of influence within existing structures of oppression. Dodson and Gilkes (1987, p. 81) contended that "the ties that bind the black community together exist primarily because of the vigilant action of black women. Black women are the *something within* that shapes the culture of resistance, the patterns of consciousness and self-expression, and the social organizational framework of local and national expressions of community."

These internal family struggles, Collins noted, have traditionally meshed smoothly with activism outside the traditional definitions of family. Boundaries between biological mothers and other women who care for their children are fluid. These so-called bloodmothers and othermothers—women who share mothering responsibilities with bloodmothers—form a central tradition to the institution of families in black communities. While men have well-defined and culturally significant roles in the extended family and in the kin network, women-centered child care has always been the rule.

These networks of community-based child care extend beyond boundaries of biologically and legally related persons and are commonly known as fictive kin. Even when relationships do not involve kin or fictive kin, community norms traditionally have been such that neighbors cared for one another's children. The resiliency of these networks illustrates how cultural values help people cope with and resist oppression. Collins suggested that this system challenges one fundamental assumption underlying capitalism: that children are private property. Notions of child care, property, and gender differences in parenting style are embedded in the institutional arrangements of the economy. By seeing the larger community as responsible for children and by giving nonbiological parents rights in childrearing, black communities challenge prevailing property relations. It is in this sense that traditional kin and fictive kin relationships in women-centered networks are a key to undermining oppression. In this way black women work as cultural workers, and this experience is empowering. This culture is one of resistance, essential to the struggle for group survival; it also lies at the heart of agency.

In the best of times this is a trying endeavor. But in the worst of times, with growing numbers of women and children who must make it on their own, with growing numbers of black males incarcerated, unemployed, or underemployed, the family often buckles under the strain. Yet still they go on and persist despite the odds. The reasons for this are many, but are most often due to the cultural and experiential repertoire manifest in the nature of family relations. Expanding beyond the traditional family of common lore, black families are often described as dysfunctional because they do not fit the norm. Ironically, without the agency of caregivers from outside of nuclear families, many black elders would live significantly briefer and less comfortable lives. Without black parents attending to issues of race with their children many more of them would find the transition to adulthood all the more troubling.

Black people as a group have persistently fought oppression, sometimes in overt fashion, but most often covertly. Some of the most important social changes that have occurred in this country are directly attributed to black activism, the Civil Rights Movement perhaps the most obvious example. Blacks have never been powerless. The question is how do they identify and more effectively use the forms of power that exist within communities to hold back the flood gates that seem to persistently threaten their survival.

References

Allen, R., Thornton, M. C., & Watkins, S. (1992). An African-American racial belief system and social structural relationships: A test of invariance. *National Journal of Sociology, 6,* 157–186.

Angel, R., & Tienda, M. (1982). Determinants of extended household structure: Cultural pattern or economic model? *American Journal of Sociology, 87,* 1360–1383.

Billingsley, A. (1992). *Climbing Jacob's ladder.* New York: Simon & Schuster.

Bowman, P., & Howard, C. (1985). Race-related socialization, motivation, and academic achievement: A study of black youths in three-generation families. *Journal of the American Academy of Child Psychiatry, 24,* 131–141.

Boykin, A. W., & Toms, F. (1985). Black child socialization: A conceptual framework. In H. McAdoo & J. McAdoo (Eds.), *Black children* (pp. 33–51). Beverly Hills, CA: Sage.

Collins, P. (1991). *Black feminist thought.* New York: Routledge, Chapman, & Hall.

Daniel, J. (1975). A definition of fatherhood as expressed by black fathers. (Doctoral dissertation, University of Pittsburgh, 1975). *Dissertation Abstracts International, 36,* 2090A.

Davis, K., Lillie-Blanton, M., Lyons, B., Mullan, F., Powe, N., & Rowland, D. (1989). Health care for black Americans: The public sector role. In D. Willis, (Ed.), *Health policies and black Americans* (pp. 213–248). New Brunswick, NJ: Transaction Publishers.

Dodson, J., & Gilkes, C. (1987). Something within: Social change and collective endurance in the sacred world of black Christian women. In R. Reuther & R. Keller (Eds.), *Women and religion in America, Volume 3: 1900–1968* (pp. 80–130). New York: Harper and Row.

Dornbusch, S., Carlsmith, J., Bushwall, S., Ritter, P., Leiderman, H., Hastorf, A., & Gross, R. (1985). Single parents, extended households and the control of adolescents. *Child Development, 56,* 326–341.

Edmonds, M. (1993). Physical health. In J. Jackson, L. Chatters, & R. Taylor (Eds.), *Aging in black America* (pp.151–166). Newbury Park, CA: Sage.

Gayer, P. (1982). *Documentation for the National Long Term Care Survey/National Survey of Informal Caregivers—Report on methods and procedures used in the surveys,* Part II. Washington, DC: Office of the Assistant Secretary for Planning & Evaluation, Health Care Financing Administration, Office of Research.

Giddens, A. (1993). *New rules of sociological method* (2nd ed.). Cambridge: Polity Press.

Harrison, A. (1985). The black family's socializing environment. In H. McAdoo & J. McAdoo (Eds.), *Black children* (pp. 174–193). Beverly Hills, CA: Sage.

Hogan, D., Hao, L., & Parish, W. (1990). Race, kin networks, and assistance to mother-headed families. *Social Forces, 68,* 797–812.

Holzberg, C. (1982). Ethnicity and aging: Anthropological perspectives on more than just the minority elderly. *Gerontologist, 22,* 249–257.

Lamb, M., & Lamb, V. (1976). The nature and importance of the father-infant relationship. *Family Coordinator, 25,* 379–385.

McLanahan, S. (1985). Family structure and the reproduction of poverty. *American Journal of Sociology, 90,* 873–901.

Mindel, C., & Wright, R. (1988). Family lifestyles of America's ethnic minorities: An introduction. In C. Mindel, R. Habenstein, & R. Wright (Eds.), *Ethnic families in America* (3rd ed., pp. 1–14). New York: Elsevier.

Murray, P. (1987). *Song in a weary throat: An American pilgrimage.* New York: Harper and Row.

Neighbors, H., & Jackson, J. (1984). The use of informal and formal help: Four patterns of illness behavior in the black community. *American Journal of Community Psychology, 12,* 629–644.

Ogbu, J. (1983). Socialization: A cultural ecological approach. In K. Borman (Ed.), *The social life of children in a changing society* (pp. 253–267). Hillsdale, NJ: Erlbaum.

Petchers, M., & Milligan, S. (1988). Access to health care in a black urban elderly population. *Gerontologist, 28,* 213–217.

Peters, M. (1985). Racial socialization of young black children. In H. McAdoo & J. McAdoo (Eds.), *Black children* (pp. 159–173). Beverly Hills, CA: Sage.

Phillips, B., Stephens, S., & Cerf, J. (1986). *The evaluation of the National Long Term Care Demonstration: Survey data collection, design and procedure.* Princeton, NJ: Mathematica Policy Research.

Porter, J., & Washington, R. (1993). Minority identity and self-esteem. *Annual Review of Sociology, 19,* 139–161.

Richardson, B. (1981). Racism and child-rearing: A study of black mothers. (Doctoral dissertation, Claremont Graduate School, 1981). *Dissertation Abstracts International, 42,* 125A.

Scheier, R. (1987, February 13). Medicare home health reforms pinching low-income elderly. *American Medical News.*

Smith, R., & Thornton, M. C. (1993). Racial solidarity: Group identification and consciousness among older black Americans. In J. Jackson, L. Chatters, & R. Taylor (Eds.), *Aging in black America* (pp. 203–216). Newbury Park, CA: Sage.

Spencer, M. (1983). Children's cultural values and parental rearing strategies. *Developmental Review, 4,* 351–370.

Stroebe, M., & Stroebe, W. (1983). Who suffers more? Sex difference in health risks of the widowed. *Psychological Bulletin, 93,* 279–301.

Tatum, B. (1987). *Assimilation blues.* Westport, CT: Greenwood.

Taylor, R., Chatters, L., Tucker, M., & Lewis, E. (1990). Black families. *Journal of Marriage and the Family, 52,* 993–1014.

Thornton, M. C. (1997). Dimensions of racial socialization among black parents: Minority, mainstream and cultural components. In R. Taylor, L. Chatters, & J. Jackson, (Eds.), *Family life in black America.* Newbury Park, CA: Sage.

Thornton, M. C., Chatters, L., Taylor, R.J., & Allen, W. (1990). Sociodemographic and environmental correlates to racial socialization by black parents. *Child Development, 61,* 401–409.

Thornton, M. C., White-Means, S., & Choi, H. K. (1993). Sociodemographic correlates of the size and composition of informal care networks among frail ethnic elderly. *Journal of Comparative Family Studies, 24,* 235–250.

White, E. (1979). Giving health care to minority patients. *Nursing Clinics of North America, 12,* 27–40.

White-Means, S., & Thornton, M. C. (1989a). Nonemergency visits to hospital emergency rooms: A comparison of blacks and whites. *The Milbank Memorial Fund Quarterly, 67,* 33–57.

White-Means, S., & Thornton, M. C. (1989b). Sociodemographic and health factors influencing black and Hispanic use of the hospital emergency room. *Journal of the National Medical Association, 81,* 72–80.

White-Means, S., & Thornton, M. C. (1990a). Ethnic differences in the production of informal home health care. *Gerontologist, 30,* 758–768.

White-Means, S., & Thornton, M. C. (1990b). Labor market choices and home health care provision among employed ethnic caregivers. *Gerontologist, 30,* 769–775.

Williams, F. (1987). The colored girl. In M. Washington (Ed.), *Invented lives: Narratives of black women 1860–1960* (pp. 150–159). Garden City, NY: Anchor.

Wisensale, S., & Allison, M. (1988). An analysis of 1987 state family leave legislation: Implications for caregivers of the elderly. *Gerontologist, 28*, 779–785.

Chapter 5

Resiliency in African-American Families

Military Families in Foreign Environments[1]

Hamilton I. McCubbin[2]

Comprehensive reviews of family research indicate that much has been written about the impact of military service upon family life (McCubbin, Dahl, & Hunter, 1976; Hunter & Nice, 1978; Kaslow, 1993). Likewise, the effect of the family on the military organization (Orthner, 1980; Hunter, 1982) is well documented. Such reviews call attention to the ever-changing nature of military families in the context of a changing world and thus the changing role of the military in contemporary society. The increasing number of single-parent families, dual-career military families, and military families in which the "spouse" of the military member is male are clearly evident. Realizing that the majority of military family studies have been on "officers"—higher-ranking military members— analysts of military families point to and emphasize the need for penetrating research on enlisted soldiers and ethnic minority soldiers of lower rank and their families. Researchers have suggested that today's lower-ranking soldier is younger and very likely to be a member of an ethnic minority group. Furthermore, they are more likely to be married, and thus more vulnerable to the built-in stresses of military life (Brown, 1993). The investigation reported here attempted to advance research on resiliency in African-American enlisted soldiers and their families.

Refocusing Research: African-American Families, Enlisted Families, and Resiliency

Despite the proliferation of research on the military family, few studies have been conducted on ethnic minority military families or on families of enlisted personnel. With the exception of the broad-based surveys conducted by the Department of Defense on enlisted families (which included spouses and minorities) (Rakoff & Doherty, 1989) there is little evidence of a commitment to systematic research on these two important subgroups of families in the armed forces. A careful examination of the indices (which list the major topics of a publication) for two major reviews of the military family literature (McCubbin & Dahl, 1976; Hunter, 1982) revealed that African-American families and enlisted families are not referenced. Ethnic minorities were cited but the studies referred to were conducted on families with foreign-born wives. The relative absence of African-American family and enlisted family research gains added importance in view of the fact that an estimated one-fourth of the Army's soldiers are African Americans. Moreover, as all branches of the armed forces work toward improving the quality of community life and strengthening the family unit (Brown, 1993), research on both African-American and enlisted families will assist in the development of supportive family life programs and family-oriented policies (Nice, 1993; Kupchella, 1993). This study was designed to contribute to our understanding of resiliency in African-American enlisted families. The Department of Defense's commitment to these families through its programs and research will help build a stable foundation for future research on such families (Military Family Research Institute, 1995).

Previous research on military families has emphasized and documented the family's mental health, parenting style, and marital and financial problems, the personal cost of adopting and investing in the military lifestyle, as well as family considerations in the retention and combat readiness of military personnel and units. Studies on resiliency in African-American families have been limited. Only recently has a deliberate effort been made to examine families' resiliency in facing and overcoming the challenges and hardships of a military lifestyle. Following this line of positive reasoning, Peters and Massey (1983) pointed to new challenges for African-American family research. They recommended that researchers begin to understand the resiliency of African-American families and the various strategies that allow racism to be absorbed, deflected, combated, succumbed to, and/or overcome. They argued that by exploring the efficacy of personal and family coping in response to the "normal," mundane stresses of discrimination or personal humiliation (or the sudden eruption of racially based crisis situations), scholars can better understand the dynamics of the resilient and adaptive power of oppressed minorities. The research reported here places emphasis on the resiliency of African-American families.

African-American Families:
A Resiliency Model

When "at risk" military families in general, or "at risk" African-American military families in particular, are viewed in a social and ecological context, the level and success of family adaptation and resiliency is determined by the complex interplay of several critical factors as described in the Resiliency Model of Family Adjustment and Adaptation (McCubbin & McCubbin, 1993; McCubbin, McCubbin, Thompson, & Thompson, 1995).

> African-American military families at risk are characterized in part by imbalance and disharmony, a condition which is fostered by the inadequacy of the family's resources and capabilities to meet the demands and/or the problematic nature or inadequacy of the family's established patterns of functioning (T) in response to stressful situations (such as a relocation to a foreign country) and which places the family in a crisis situation (e.g. being vulnerable, but faced with an opportunity for constructive changes in its patterns of functioning). These families' situations are exacerbated by the concurrent pile-up of demands (AA) (e.g. other life changes and hardships such as prior strains, pre-relocation hassles or post-relocation stressors). By the family's own accord and will, and possibly with crisis oriented or transitional assistance or treatment, the family and its members may take on the challenge to regenerate itself, to change and improve upon its situation, to enter into a process of change, and thereby work to achieve a level of adaptation (XX). The goal of this process is the restoration of family harmony and balance in the family's interpersonal relations, the family's structure and function, the development, well-being, and spirituality of the family unit and its members as well as the family's relationship to the community and the natural environment. The family unit's structure and functioning may change but harmony and balance is achieved. The level of successful adaptation referred to as Bonadaptation (XX) is

determined by the interacting influence of newly instituted patterns of functioning (e.g., patterns of communication, rules, boundaries etc.) (T), the modification, maintenance or revitalization of already established patterns of functioning (e.g., traditions, celebrations, ethnic practices etc.), the family's own internal resources and capabilities (BB) (e.g., hardiness, coalitions, respect, support), the family's network of social support (e.g., extended family, neighborhood, church, community, friends, kinship etc.), the family's situational appraisal (CC). The family's situational appraisal (CC) is influenced by the families appraisal processes: Schema (CCCCC) (e.g., values, beliefs, ethnic orientation); the family's Sense of Coherence (CCCC) (e.g., dispositional view of the family's sense of order, trust, predictability and manageability); and Paradigms (CCC) (e.g., shared expectations as to how the family will function in areas of child rearing, discipline etc.). Finally, the instituted patterns of functioning, resources, and appraisal components of the family unit influence and are influenced by the family's problem-solving and coping abilities (PSC) (e.g., conflict resolution, family problem-solving, coping repertoires etc.). The family engages in a dynamic relational process over time introducing changes directed at restoring and maintaining family harmony and balance within the family system as well as in the family's relationship to the larger community and environment. The dynamic relational process involves a cyclical effort in such situations where the family's efforts at change prove to be unsuccessful and propel the family into a maladaptive outcome.

The Resiliency Model and its earlier formulations, which have been empirically tested (Lavee, McCubbin, & Patterson, 1985; McCubbin, Thompson, Thompson, Elver, & McCubbin, 1994; Thompson, McCubbin, Thompson, & Elver, 1995), emphasize the resiliency of African-American families in the face of the hardships of family life in the military (see Figure 1).

This investigation will focus on select dimensions of the resiliency model: (aA) the pile up of demands, (bB) family resources, and (cC) family appraisal in an effort to understand the dynamic properties of resiliency in African-American families and the nature of their adaptation to crisis situations.

African-American Family Adaptation (xX Factor)

How do African-American enlisted families face and adapt following the crisis of a transition to a foreign country and the related hardships of Army life in a way that fosters the growth and devel-

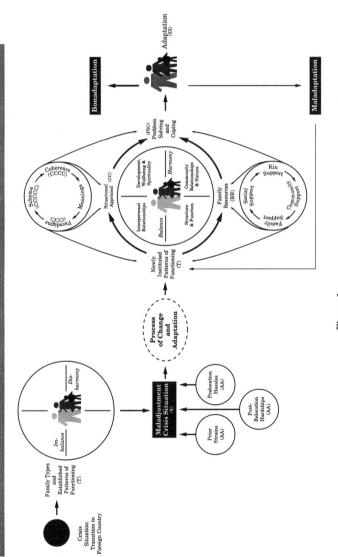

Figure 1
African-American Military Family At Risk: Modification of the Adaptation
Phase of the Resiliency Model of Family Stress, Adjustment and
Adaptation and the Relational Processes of Balance and Harmony

opment of individual members and the family unit as a whole? Adaptation (xX factor) is the central concept in the resiliency framework used to describe individual and family growth through balanced family functioning. There are three units of analysis to be considered in relation to adaptation: individual family members, the family unit, and the community. Each unit is characterized by both demands (stressors and strains) and capabilities (resources, supports, appraisals, and coping). Adaptation is achieved through reciprocal relationships where the demands of one unit are met by the capabilities of another, resulting in a "balance" in functioning (i.e., the military community's demands are met by the family's resources and capabilities). Families work to achieve balanced functioning (a) between individual family members and the family unit, (b) between the family unit and the local community, and (c) between the individual family members and the community. From the African-American military family's point of view, the central issue is the "fit" between the military member and his/her spouse

Military member-to-spouse fit is achieved through reciprocal relationships. Some needs are met by family capabilities (e.g., spouse and other family members provide encouragement for the military member's commitment to them). Some family needs are met by the military member (e.g., helping with home maintenance tasks and income or participating in shared family activities). The military member may experience stress or distress when his or her needs or expectations exceed the family's capability for meeting those demands, resulting in an imbalance.

Maladaptation	Bonadaptation
• Military Member Dissatisfaction and Alienation	• Military Member Satisfaction and Commitment
• Spouse Dissatisfaction and Alienation	• Spouse Satisfaction and Commitment
• Military Member Illness	• Military Member Wellness
• Spouse Illness	• Spouse Wellness
• Family Distress	• Family Eustress

A "fit" is also sought between the military family and the community through reciprocal relationships. The family's capabilities are used to meet the community demands (e.g., the family is called upon to prepare for a military career) and the Army community's capabilities are made available for the family's needs (e.g., a quality school system that meets the children's educational needs). Friendships and supportive relationships, important resources for family development, are part of the Army community's social network.

This discussion points to the complexity of African-American family adaptation. Often, the African-American family is required to balance conflicting demands, including racism and discrimination, with available capabilities. The African-American military person, spouse, and family members need to be attentive and responsive to the family unit and to the expectations of the Army community simultaneously. The concept of African-American family adaptation is used to describe a continuum of outcomes, from maladaptation to bonadaptation. Bonadaptation is characterized by minimal discrepancy between demands and capabilities. In bonadaptation, the growth and development of both individual members and the family unit is enhanced. Some of the critical indices of military member-to-family and African-American family-to-community fit are outlined below.

Pile-up of Demands
(aA Factor)

African-American families are rarely dealing with a single demand. Over time, they must contend with an ever-changing set of demands from the individual family members, the family unit, and the Army community. There are two types of demands—stressors and strains. Stressors are events that occur at a relatively distinct point in time and call for change, such as receiving orders for a foreign assignment (normative event) or being diagnosed with a major illness (nonnormative event). Strains are the unresolved hardships of prior stressors (e.g., prejudice, feelings of discrimination) or the inherent tensions of an ongoing role such as being African-American in a foreign country.

Adaptive Resources
(bB Factor)

The traits, characteristics, or abilities of individual family members, the family system, and the community can be used to meet the pile-up of demands. Over time, this repertoire of resources available to the family changes in response to the nature of demands. Some resources may be depleted from overuse (e.g., money or family patience in coping with family separations). Some resources are acquired in response to specific developmental needs (e.g., a spouse's need for a job to supplement the family's income).

Personal resources refer to the broad range of characteristics of individual family members that are potentially available to any family member in times of crisis. There are three basic components of personal resources: education, health, and knowledge.

Family system resources refer to the internal abilities of the family unit that protect it from the impact of stressors and serve to facilitate family adaptation during crises. Family cohesion and adaptability, income, family mutual support, and understanding appear to be some of the most important resources in the management of stress.

Community resources refer to the capabilities of people or institutions outside the family that the family can utilize in dealing with demands. Medical services and school programs are among such resources. One of the most important community resources for managing the pile-up of demands is social support. Both the availability of social networks (e.g., kinship groups, neighbors, and mutual self-help groups) and the ability of such networks to provide support vary greatly. But, in general, support from the community may serve as a protector against the effects of stressors and promotes recovery from distress or crises experienced by the family.

Family Appraisal (cC Factor)

The cC factor in the Resiliency Model refers to the family members' shared view of a crisis situation. A family's appraisal of a situation can vary from viewing circumstances positively as challenges and opportunities for growth to viewing situations negatively as hopeless, too hard, or unmanageable. Successful adaptation in a less-than-perfect world calls for family acceptance and understanding. Antonovsky (1979) described this orientation as "coherence," the pervasive, enduring, though dynamic feeling of confidence that environments are predictable; that things will work out as well as can be reasonably expected. Through the appraisal process and coherence, families are able to: (a) clarify issues, hardships, and tasks so as to render them more manageable and responsive to problem-solving efforts; (b) decrease the intensity of emotional burdens associated with stressors and strains; and (c) encourage the family unit to carry on with its fundamental task of promoting the social and emotional development of individual members (McCubbin, Thompson, Thompson, Elver, & McCubbin, 1994). Generally, family efforts to redefine a situation positively or to endow a situation with special meaning such as "believing that it is best for everyone" appear to facilitate African-American enlisted family coping and adaptation.

This modification of the Resiliency Model to focus on the resiliency of African-American families and their adaptation (Figure 1) is intended to underscore the complex array of individual, family system, and contextual community factors. In addition, it points to the interactional influences of such factors as African-American family development over time. The investigators attempted to examine one broadly stated question: Given the special mission of the Army to establish its forces on foreign soils, which elements of resiliency—personal strengths, family strengths, and community support—will facilitate the adaptation of African-American families to these stressful environments? Given the obvious fact that a soldier's morale and performance is affected by the family and its well-being, this question deserves special attention.

Methodology

Subjects

African-American families selected for this study emerged from a sampling plan designed to survey 1,000 Army families who experienced the stressor-crisis and transitional crisis of relocating from the United States to Western Europe. The sampling strategy was based on the premise that a representative sample of male "as military member" households from the U.S. Army could be obtained by selecting male soldiers and their families from three different Western Europe communities of various sizes and from four types of Army units. It was and remains a rare occurrence that an indepth study is conducted on a representative sample of military families with a focused emphasis on studying family functioning using standardized measures. All too often, for the sake of expedience, military family researchers have emphasized the use of single questions and single indexes to represent families and their functioning; thus limiting our insights into family life and reducing the generalizability of the findings. This study and analysis focuses on one segment of families in the Army, recognizing that in the contemporary military the number of dual career military (husband and wife in the Army) and single-parent military families are increasing in numbers and deserve separate consideration. The findings of this investigation are not intended to generalize to all military or Army families although they may, in fact, be relevant.

While this data of African-American families were collected slightly over a decade ago, these data and the observations remain valuable by virtue of the indepth nature of the study, the use of standardized measures of family functioning, and the study's focus on the strengths and capabilities in families. The data, now released into the public domain after being embroiled in controversy over alleged findings of racism and discrimination in the Army, and ultimately confiscated and manipulated to avoid analyses (see McCubbin, Olson, & Zimmerman, 1986), have much to offer family scientists studying resiliency. The data upon which this publication is based were released to the principal investigators before the data became the topic of controversy and subject of unique forms of data management.

To select a proportionate stratified sample, the researchers relied on command headquarters and personnel specialists to guide the final selections. The families who participated in the study were selected from combat, combat support, and combat service support units and military command headquarters. The three types of communities represented in the study were: a small community with a rural orientation; a moderate-sized community in a moderate-

Table 1
Units and Communities Selected for Study

Type of Military Unit	Type of Community
1. Armored Cavalry	Small community with primarily a rural orientation. The unit has a high-pressure border mission ($n = 189$ families).
2. Amored Cavalry Regiment	Small community in a rural German region. The unit has a high-pressure border mission ($n = 260$ families).
3. Infantry Brigade	Moderate-size community in the context of a moderate-size industrial town ($n = 160$ families).
4. Engineer Brigade	Moderate-size community but geographically close to an urban industrial German community ($n = 181$ families).
5. Headquarters Command	Large community surrounded by a German community environment ($n = 138$ families).
6. Personnel Command	Moderate-size military community in the context of a moderate-size but comfortable and attractive German city ($n = 132$ families).
7. Artillery Brigade	Small military community in the context of a moderate-size German city which supports both industry and agriculture ($n = 167$ families).

sized industrial town; and a large community in a major city. Participants were chosen by the command headquarters on the basis of their availability (i.e., not involved in priority missions and activities during the four weeks of data collection). Table 1 outlines the sampling distribution by military units and community types.

Military families in each unit selected for the study were briefed regarding its purpose. Prospective participants were informed that the study was designed to examine family strengths and involved collaborative support from the research staff. They were also informed that participation in the study was voluntary and that their questionnaires would remain anonymous. The military members selected for the survey were asked to explain its purpose to their spouses and request their participation. Participants were also asked to complete their questionnaire without consulting one another. In situations where a foreign-born spouse was not able to read the questionnaire (3% of the spouses surveyed could not read English) another spouse not in the same family or a friend was asked to assist. Questionnaires were to be returned to the research team within 24 hours. In those situations where the 24-hour return period created problems for families (e.g., the spouse out of town for a day; military member with night duty, etc.) the time period was extended to accommodate the family.

A total of 1,127 pairs (military member and spouse) of questionnaires were administered; and 1,052 pairs (86%) were returned. Of those returned, 1,036 pairs (98%) were usable. A total of 184 African-American families were among the usable surveys.

The sample selected was not only representative of accompanied (military members with spouses in Europe) officer and enlisted families, but also appeared to be representative of married personnel in the United States Army.

Profile of Enlisted African-American Families

The majority (76.8%) of the African-American soldiers were between 17 and 30 years of age, had achieved a high school or post-high school education (93.3%), were in the ranks E1 (Private) through E5 (non-commissioned officers) (63.2%), and were of either Protestant or Catholic religious preference (54.4%) (see Table 2). The majority of these soldiers (67.1%) had been in the Army from four to ten years. Nearly half (46.4%) were serving in Combat Arms units in Western Europe, and had been requested by the Army (73.1%) for overseas duty.

Table 2A
Military Member, Spouse, and Family Characteristics
of African-American Families in Contrast
to the Total Group of Enlisted Families

Characteristics	African-American Enlisted Families %	All Enlisted Families %
Military Member Characteristics		
Age		
17–25 years	34.5	34.6
26–30 years	42.3	29.7
31–50 years	23.2	35.7
Education level		
Less than high school	2.3	2.7
High school graduate	59.3	54.5
Some college/technical	34.0	37.6
College graduate	3.8	4.8
Graduate degree	.5	.4
Military rank		
Enlisted Personnel (E1–E5)	63.2	52.8
Enlisted Personnel (E6–E9)	36.8	47.2
Religious preference		
Protestant	48.6	46.6
Catholic	5.5	23.0
Other (Baptist, etc.)	45.9	30.4
Time in military service		
1–3 years	10.4	7.4
4–6 years	28.6	12.5
7–10 years	38.5	16.5
Over 10 years	22.5	63.6
Type of unit assignment		
Combat Army	46.4	44.2
Combat Support	28.5	28.2
Combat Service Support	7.8	6.5
Command Headquarters	17.3	21.1
Motivation: Volunteered for Overseas Assign.		
Yes, volunteered for overseas assignment	26.9	34.6
No, this overseas assignment was at the request of the Army.	73.1	65.4

Most spouses (79.7%) of African-American enlisted soldiers were between the ages of 17 and 30, had obtained a high school diploma (82.4%), and indicated a religious preference (51.8%) other than Protestant or Catholic. The majority (69%) of these spouses indicated that they had a record of paid employment (past or current). Nearly half (47%) were currently employed in Western Europe. Furthermore, the majority (69%) of the spouses of African-American enlisted soldiers were either on their second or third assignment in Western Europe.

Table 2B
Military Member, Spouse, and Family Characteristics
of African-American Families in Contrast
to the Total Group of Enlisted Familes

Characteristics	African-American Enlisted Families %	All Enlisted Families %
Spouse Characteristics		
Age		
17–25 years	51.7	43.0
26–30 years	28.0	28.1
31–40 years	18.1	24.1
41 + years	2.2	4.8
Education level		
Less than high school	11.5	19.8
High school graduate	82.4	42.8
Some college/technical	3.3	30.9
College graduate	.6	5.8
Graduate degree	2.2	.7
Religious preference		
Protestant	34.2	58.7
Catholic	14.0	29.3
Other (Baptist, etc.)	51.8	12.0
Employment status		
Employed now and before the relocation	29.9	28.7
Employed now but not before the relocation	17.1	15.0
Not employed now, but was employed before	22.0	16.2
Not employed now or before the relocation	31.0	40.1
Previous overseas experience		
First tour to Europe	32.9	49.6
Second tour to Europe	50.6	35.7
Third or more tour to Europe	16.5	14.7

The majority of African-American families (63.2%) had incomes (combined earnings of husband and wife) between $10,000 and $20,000 per year. However, nearly one-fourth (22%) of the African-American families had annual incomes of $10,000 or less. Most families had either one or two children (59.3%) and lived in permanent (military supported) housing either on or off the military base (62.4%). Moreover, the majority relocated to Europe without the official support of a military sponsor (61.1%) and thus had no formal forms of help with the transition to foreign assignments. Given the reality that African-American families may face the mundane stressor of discrimination (Peters & Massey, 1983) both within the military and in the European community, it is important to note that the majority (63.2%) lived in the European community rather than on a military base.

Table 2C
Military Member, Spouse, and Family Characteristics
of African-American Families in Contrast
to the Total Group of Enlisted Familes

Characteristics	African-American Enlisted Families %	All Enlisted Families %
Family Characteristics		
Income		
$10,000 or less	34.5	34.6
$10,001 – $20,000	42.3	29.7
$20,001 – $40,000	23.2	35.7
Number of children		
No children	2.3	2.7
One child	59.3	54.5
Two children	34.0	37.6
Three children	3.8	4.8
Four or more children	.5	.4
Family housing situtation		
Temporary housing	63.2	52.8
Permanent housing on military base	36.8	47.2

In general, when African-American enlisted families are compared to the profile of all enlisted families, a few differences were noted. As a group, African-American families tended to be younger and their levels of education were often lower. African-American enlisted soldiers were more likely to be of lower military rank, they had spent less time in the Army, and they were less likely to have volunteered for this overseas military assignment. There was also a greater chance that African-American soldiers would have been to Europe previously as part of their military career.

Measures of Vulnerability, Resiliency, and Adaptation

Adaptation (xX factor) was operationally defined as the composite index of five separate measures: (a) the military member's and (b) the wife's satisfaction with family life in the Army (e.g., mission, rules, etc.), (c) the military member's and (d) the spouse's report of their general well-being (e.g., energized, peppy, vital, cheerful, healthy, relaxed, calm, and happy), and (e) the family's level of distress (e.g., hospitalization, separation, economic difficulty, overuse of alcohol or drugs, and crime). Through factor analysis of these five indices, family factor scores were created and each family unit was given the appropriate score to represent the family system's index of adaptation.

The pile-up of family demands (aA factor) was measured with nine separate indices: (a) number of children in the family; (b) family life changes occurring before the family's relocation to the foreign assignment (the severity of family strain created by family life events, i.e., illness, death of relatives, conflict, drugs, alcohol, etc.); (c) pre-relocation hassles (severity of family strain associated with getting a passport, immunizations, and port call before relocation); (d) leaving others (severity of strain on the family created by leaving relatives and close friends behind); (e) strains related to leaving a home (severity of family strain created by losing a pet, selling the family home or automobiles before relocation); (f) losses (severity of family strain created by having to borrow money, leaving an educational program, interruption of medical care, leaving kids behind, and a family member getting a job before relocation); (g) post-arrival hassles (severity of family strain created by baggage delays, moving costs, late paychecks, delays in getting housing, major purchases, and temporary duty upon arrival); (h) foreign country hardships (severity of family strain created by the demands in a foreign country such as acquiring a driver's license, learning the language, using transportation, and using the telephone); and (i) military member and spouse's fear of war (i.e., the family getting caught in a war).

Personal strengths (bB factor) were measured with 15 indices: (a) rank in the Army; (b) status as a volunteer for overseas assignment as an index of commitment to duty; (c) prior tours of spouse and (d) prior tours of military member as an index of prior preparation and experience in these situations; (e) educational attainment of spouse and (f) educational attainment of military member as an index of personal abilities and learning potential in a foreign country; (g) spouse self-reliance and (h) military member's confidence in the spouse's capability to manage the children, finances, decisions, and to handle difficulties should they emerge; (i) military member's involvement in the community and (j) spouse's involvement in the community (as measured by the extent to which they are active and involved, feel useful and a part of everyday community activities); (k) military member's coping skills and (l) spouse's coping skills that facilitate their adaptation (i.e., knowing the language, driving in Europe, using the telephone, using public transportation, and shopping in the European economy); and (m) spouse's employment.

Family strengths (bB factor) were measured with 10 indices: (a) shared egalitarian roles, an agreement of the military member and spouse about sharing family roles and decision-making; (b) shared traditional roles, whether the military member and spouse "agree" on the performance of traditional roles (i.e., husband as breadwinner and wife as homemaker); (c) family emotional support to the military member and (d) the amount of caring and giving of love and affection in the context of the family unit; (e) family esteem support to the military member and (f) the amount of listening and understanding in the family unit to make members feel valued and respected; (g) family active recreation orientation, the degree of active family involvement in the community (e.g., camping, movies, education, recreation); (h) military member's assessment of family time together and (i) spouse's assessment of family time together (i.e., travel, enjoyment of family activities and appreciation of family togetherness).

The family appraisal of the situation (cC factor) was assessed through eight indices of coherence. Predictability was viewed as the degree to which the (a) military member and (b) spouse felt they could predict the immediate future in terms of work and family schedules, presence or absence of a family member, and planning for education and work. Commitment was seen as the degree to which the (c) military member and (d) spouse felt committed to the mission, priorities, and lifestyle of the Army, and the degree to which they felt that the Army was good for family life. Controllability was assessed as the degree to which the (e) military member and (f) spouse felt he or she could have some say about future military assignments and their ability to plan in advance for assignments. Family-Army fit was the degree to which

(g) military member and (h) spouse felt that they were a part of Army life in terms of feeling confident they could get help if needed, that they were being treated fairly and justly, and that the Army takes care of its families.

Community supports (bB Factor) were assessed through 12 measures. Community support was the extent to which the (a) military member and (b) spouse felt they could depend upon the community, felt secure and safe, and felt that they could depend upon help and support for their children. Friendship support was assessed as the extent to which the (c) military member and (d) spouse felt that they were part of an honest network of important friends who valued and cared for them. Quality of religious programs was the (e) military member's assessment of the Chaplain's programs and (f) church services and activities, in comparison to those available during their last assignment. Quality of neighborhood was the (g) military member's and (h) spouse's assessment of their housing and neighborhood, in comparison to those at their last assignment. Training, unit morale, and readiness (i) was compared by the military member to those of the last assignment. Overseas opportunity (j) was the spouse's assessment of the "compensations" for the hardships of an overseas tours (i.e., opportunities to travel). Assignment of a sponsor (k) measured whether the family had received an offer of support in the overseas transition, and sponsorship help (l) was the military member's assessment of the amount of assistance the family actually received from a sponsor (i.e., meeting the family, orienting the family to Europe, communicating with the family before their move, and giving the family practical advice).

Statistical analyses with zero-order correlations were obtained to identify the important independent variables—stressors, strengths, and supports associated with African-American family adaptation. The significant (zero-order) variables were entered into a stepwise regressional analysis, controlling for military rank, type of unit, and length of time in Europe. Finally, stepwise regression analyses were used to identify the important independent variables—stressors, strengths, and supports associated with each of the critical independent variables (identified in the stepwise regression analysis).

Results

The initial zero-order correlations (Table 3A) between African-American enlisted family stressors, strains, strengths, and sup-

Table 3A
Significant (Zero-Order Correlations) Military Member, Spouse, Family, and Community Factors Associated with African-American Enlisted Family Adaptation to Stressful Environments

Significant Factors Associated with African-American Enlisted Family Adaptation (xX)	r	$p \leq$
(aA) Pile-up of Stressors and Strains		
Spouse's fear of the impact of war (i.e., husband, family getting caught)	$-.15$	.05
Military member's fear of the impact of war (i.e., family getting caught)	$-.18$	.01
Pre-relocation hassles (e.g., passport, port call)	$-.18$	.01
Strains related to leaving a home (e.g., selling home, leaving pet)	$-.15$	.05
Losses (e.g., loss of job and medical care, borrowing money, leaving kids)	$-.16$	.05
Post-arrival hassles (e.g., delay in pay, delay in getting housing, delay in getting baggage, costs of moving)	$-.16$	.05
Foreign country hardships (e.g., language, telephone, transportation, driving)	$-.17$	.05
(bB) Military Member Strengths		
Rank	$+.20$	.001
Active involvement in the community by military member	$+.25$	.001
Coping skills (e.g., language, driving, telephone, shopping, eating out)	$+.24$	.001
Education, amount of	$+.22$	.01
(bB) Spouse Strengths		
Active involvement in the community by spouse	$+.20$	.01
Confidence in spouse self-reliance	$+.27$	.001
Spouse employment	$+.21$	.001
(bB) Family Strengths		
Military member and spouse agreement on traditional family roles	$+.16$	.05
Confidence in the Army Family Evacuation Plan (NEO) in case of armed "conflict"	$+.16$	.05
Family time together, as assessed by military member	$+.30$	.0001
Family time together, as assessed by spouse	$+.25$	.01
Family active recreation orientation (e.g., keeping active, involved)	$+.20$	.001

ports and the criterion index of family adaptation are statistically significant for several independent variables. Specifically, the pile-up of stressors and strains before relocation (pre-relocation hassles, strains of leaving a home, losses created by relocation), upon arrival (foreign country hardships, post-arrival hassles), and after the initial period in Western Europe (spouse's and military member's fear of the impact of war on the family) were negatively correlated with family adaptation.

Additionally, several family strengths were positively correlated with African-American enlisted family adaptation. Military member's strengths (rank, active involvement, coping skills, and education), spouse's strengths (active involvement in community, confidence in spouse self-reliance, and employment), family strengths (agreement on traditional family roles, confidence in Army family evacuation plan in case of armed conflict, military member's family time together, spouse's family time together, and family active recreation orientation), and community supports (military member's feeling of community support and security, spouse's feeling of community support and security, friendship support, and quality of community services) were positively related to family adaptation.

Furthermore, the military members' and spouses' independent appraisal of the total family situation were positively correlated with family adaptation. The military member's sense of coherence (family-Army fit, commitment to Army lifestyle, sense of

Table 3B
Significant (Zero-Order Correlations) Military Member,
Spouse, Family, and Community Factors Associated with African-
American Enlisted Family Adaptation to Stressful Environments

Significant Factors Associated with African-American Enlisted Family Adaptation (xX)	r	p ≤
(bB) Community Supports		
Community support and security for military member	+.34	.0001
Community support and security for spouse	+.18	.01
Friendship support for military member	+.23	.001
Quality of community services (e.g., Army community services, medical and dental care, clubs)	+.23	.001
(cC) Coherence		
Predictability of work-family situation, as assessed by military member	+.31	.0001
Family-Army "fit," as assessed by military member	+.39	.0001
Family-Army "fit," as assessed by spouse	+.21	.01
Commitment to Army lifestyle, as assessed by military member	+.26	.001
Commitment to Army lifestyle, as assessed by spouse	+.29	.0001
Controllability of future assignments, as assessed by military member	+.15	.05

control over future assignments, and predictability of work-family situation) was important to family adaptation. The spouse's sense of coherence (family-Army fit, commitment to Army lifestyle) was also positively correlated with African-American family adaptation.

Critical Resiliency Factors of African-American Family Adaptation

In an effort to isolate the most important independent variables of the pile-up of stressors and strains, strengths, supports, and appraisals, and recognizing that some of these variables are intercorrelated, a stepwise regression analysis was executed. The independent variables of military rank, type of military unit (combat versus others), length of time the family was in Europe, and the number of previous tours to Western Europe were forced as first predictors into the regression analysis (as control variables) in an effort to identify the most important independent variables that could explain the variance in African-American family adaptation when effects of the control variables were factored out. Even though rank was the only independent (control) variable correlated with adaptation in the zero-order correlations, it seemed reasonable to assume that type of unit, time in country, and previous experience in this type of situation, should be taken into consideration as control variables.

The findings presented in Table 4 reveal that only 4 of the 29 original vulnerability and resiliency variables emerged as being of critical importance in explaining 33% of the variance in the criterion index of African-American enlisted family adaptation. Specifically, after rank, military unit, time in Europe, and previous experience in Europe were considered (which explained only 3% of the variance) the military member's sense of coherence or the family's fit into the Army lifestyle emerged as the most important variable in explaining 19% of the variance in adaptation.

The second important variable, which explained an additional 5% of the variance in African-American family adaptation, was the military member's confidence in their spouse's self-reliance—to be able to manage her personal and family situation, if called upon to do so. The third important variable, which explained an additional 4% of the variance in African-American family adaptation was spouse's employment. If spouses were employed, the level of family adaptation was higher. Finally, the spouse's assessment of family time together in Europe emerged as the fourth

Table 4
**Stepwise Regression Analysis of Critical Stressors, Strengths, and
Supports in Explaining Variability in African-American Enlisted
Family Adaptation to Stressful Environments**

Critical Variables	Beta	R^2	F	$p =$
Control variables				
Enlisted rank	.14	.03	.12	.73
Military unit (combat)	.57	.03	.48	.49
Length of time in Germany	.34	.03	1.35	.25
Number of previous tours to West Germany	1.04	.03	2.13	.14
Predictor variables				
Family-Army "fit" (coherence)	.69	.22	21.05	.0001
Confidence in spouse self-reliance	.28	.27	9.36	.003
Spouse employment	2.21	.31	6.75	.01
Family time together	.55	.33	4.17	.04
Multiple correlation		.33	7.73	.0001

important factor in African-American enlisted adaptation, and this
variable explained an additional 2% of the variance.

Explaining Coherence, Self-Reliance, Employment, and Family Time

In an effort to shed light upon and improve our understanding of
these four independent variables, representing spouses' strengths,
family strengths, and the military members' appraisal/coherence,
the investigators examined the relationship of these important variables to the other indices of stressors and strains, strengths, supports, and appraisal/coherence. The stepwise regression analysis
of family-Army fit, summarized in Table 5, may be used to highlight the importance of community supports and the family's appraisal of the total situation. Specifically, over half (53%) of the
variance in the African-American soldier's sense of coherence—of
family-Army fit ($F=7.31$, $p=.0001$)—was explained by the soldier's
sense of support from the community (27%), by the predictability
of work and family schedules (11%), and the spouse's sense of
family-Army fit (8%), the military members' confidence in the Army's
evacuation plan for the family in case of war (4%), the military

Table 5
Stepwise Regression Analysis of Critical Stressors, Strengths, and
Supports in Explaining Variability in Family-Army "Fit"—Coherence

Critical Variables	Beta	R^2	F	p =
Military member's sense of community support	.24	.27	24.18	.0001
Predictability of work, family schedules, member presence or absence	.40	.38	18.94	.0001
Spouse's sense of family-Army "fit"	.25	.46	16.88	.0001
Military member's confidence in the Army's evacuation plan for family in case of war	1.02	.50	11.36	.001
Military member's sense of control over future jobs/assignments	.28	.52	5.42	.02
Family's active recreation orientation	.19	.53	4.58	.03
Multiple correlation		.53	7.31	.0001

members' sense of control over future assignments (2%), and the family's active recreation orientation (1%).

The second important variable, confidence in spouse self-reliance, was explained by military member strengths, military member and spouse's appraisal of the situation, and by family strengths. Specifically, one third (32%) of the variance in the military member's confidence in spouse self-reliance ($F=14.98$, $p=.003$), as summarized in Table 6, was explained by the military

Table 6
Stepwise Regression Analysis of Critical Stressors,
Strengths, and Supports in Explaining Variability
in Criterion—Confidence in Spouse Self-Reliance

Critical Variables	Beta	R^2	F	p =
Military member coping skills	.42	.17	24.44	.0001
Military member commitment to Army lifestyle	.42	.26	5.67	.02
Spouse and military member agreement on traditional family roles	.32	.29	7.22	.008
Spouse commitment to Army lifestyle	1.94	.32	5.18	.02
Multiple correlation		.32	14.98	.0001

member's coping skills (e.g., knowledge of the language, etc.) (17%), by the military member's commitment to the Army lifestyle (9%), by the spouses and military member's agreement on family functioning with traditional family roles (3%), and by the spouse's commitment to the Army lifestyle (3%).

Spouse's employment was the third important variable that explained a significant percentage of the variance in African-American enlisted family adaptation. The stepwise regression analysis of spouse employment, presented in Table 7, may be used to highlight the importance of spouse's personal strengths in explaining about one fourth (23%) of the variance in spouse employment ($F=12.67$, $p=.0001$). Specifically, spouse employment was partly explained by spouse involvement in community activities (11%), by the spouse's previous experience in Western Europe as reflected in the number of previous tours she participated in (6%), and the length of time she had been in Western Europe (6%).

Table 7
Stepwise Regression Analysis of Critical Stressors,
Strengths, and Supports in Explaining Variability
in Criterion—Spouse Employment

Critical Variables	Beta	R^2	F	$p =$
Spouse involvement in community life/activities	.10	.11	16.36	.0001
Spouse's number of prior tours to West Germany	.18	.17	9.50	.002
Spouse's length of time in West Germany	.08	.23	9.05	.003
Multiple correlation		.23	12.67	.0001

Family time together is an important variable that explains a significant portion of the variance in African-American enlisted family adaptation. The stepwise regression analysis of family time together, presented in Table 8, may be interpreted as highlighting the importance of both family strengths and spouse's appraisal of the situation. Thirty-three percent of the variance in family time together was explained by the military member's expectation of family time together (15%), the spouse's sense of family-Army fit (12%), and the spouse's commitment to the Army lifestyle (6%).

Table 8
Stepwise Regression Analysis of Critical Stressors,
Strengths, and Supports in Explaining Variability
in Family Time Together

Critical Variables	Beta	R^2	F	$p =$
Military member's expectation of family time together	.29	.15	17.16	.0001
Spouse sense of family-Army "fit"	.15	.27	14.31	.0002
Spouse commitment to Army lifestyle	.20	.33	11.75	.0001
Multiple correlation		.33	21.04	.0001

Discussion

This investigation attempted to identify those pressures (stressors and strains) and family resiliency factors (strengths, supports, and appraisals) that could explain the variability in African-American enlisted family adaptation to reassignment in Western Europe. This study attempted to advance the understanding the resiliencies of both African-American and enlisted military families for they represent the most understudied groups in the armed forces.

The findings of this investigation point to the importance of an ecologically oriented theoretical perspective to the study of African-American families (Staples, 1976). The Resiliency Model of African-American Family Adaptation (McCubbin, McCubbin, Thompson, & Thompson, 1995) described in this investigation appears to have some relevance and merit to guide future research and our understanding of why some families are more capable of recovering from crises than others. The critical variables of the pile-up of stressors and strains, and particularly family strengths, supports, and coherence, appear to be of central importance in explaining African-American enlisted family adaptation. This general observation appears to be congruent with the ecologically oriented African-American family research, which emphasizes the functional value of the community, the survival strategies for coping, and the importance of internal family strengths in African-American families (see McAdoo, 1981, 1983; Peters, 1976; Scanzoni, 1971).

It should not be surprising to note the importance of coherence (family-Army fit) in explaining African-American enlisted family adaptation. As Peters and Massey (1983) noted, there are

African-American families whose total lives unfold within a uniquely oppressive environment. Because of their cultural identity, these families have a negative status in their host society, thus deterring their capability to provide for their basic needs. In this respect, African-American families are encumbered by the constant threat and actual periodic occurrences of intimidation, discrimination, or denial because of race. They experience MEES—Mundane Extreme Environmental Stress, or a set of conditions that are sometimes subtle, sometimes overt, are pervasive and continuous and may be debilitating (Pierce, 1975). Therefore, to what degree African-American families "fit" into the Army lifestyle is influenced by the manner in which they are treated, by the intensity of the military situation, and by the pervasiveness of their sense of discrimination.

Even while faced with the possibility or even incidents of the mundane stress of discrimination and racism in the Army, African-American families appeared to be resilient and adaptive to the unique demands of Army life. They demonstrated resilient adaptation even in a foreign country, where another form of discrimination, the rejection of African-American soldiers and their families by the European community, may emerge. African-American soldiers are professionals and they revealed a deep commitment to the special mission of the military. They appeared to be willing to invest in a military career and attempted to cope with the hardships of that lifestyle (McCubbin, Patterson, & Lavee, 1983). African-American families indicated that their sense of coherence, of "fit" in the Army, is also dependent upon the support they receive from the community. The predictability of work and family life, and the degree to which the spouse feels accepted and supported in the Army, are other factors that determine the level of family coherence. Furthermore, the African-American families' sense of influence and control over future assignments, their active recreation orientation, and their confidence in the Army's ability to care for them in the case of armed conflict in Europe all facilitate the family's development of a sense of fit. African-American families appear to have a stronger sense of coherence, or fit, if they feel they belong, have some say about their future, have some degree of predictability in their lives, and feel their families will be cared for should a crisis emerge.

Given the special demands of the military profession, especially in foreign countries, spouse self-reliance (i.e., ability to manage the children and finances, to make decisions, and to handle difficulties should they emerge) gains added importance. This is a major factor in African-American family adaptation. This confidence in the spouse's self-reliance appears to be enhanced if the military member has a greater repertoire of coping skills, such as knowing the language, being able to drive, etc. It is reasonable to assume that African-American soldiers' coping skills are then communicated and shared with other family members, particularly with their spouses. Furthermore, the spouse's self-reliance and the soldier's confidence in the spouse's self-reliance were enhanced by both the soldier's and the spouse's commitment to the Army lifestyle. By accepting the hardships of military duties, which is part of a commitment to the Army lifestyle, spouses are more likely to take charge of the family situation. The African-American soldier's primary responsibility is to the military and its mission and thus the family is encouraged to be self-sufficient.

At first glance, it was surprising to note the importance of military member agreement on traditional family roles. It was found to be a positive factor in the soldiers' confidence in their spouses' self-reliance. However, given the realistic demands of Army life in Western Europe (e.g., soldiers' heavy involvement in mission-related activities), it is not surprising that spouses are called upon to "take charge of" family matters and family responsibilities. This is a "traditional-homemaker responsibility" for spouses, even though spouses were also likely to be employed on a full-time basis. If families agreed to function along these traditional lines, there was a greater sense of confidence in spouse's self-reliance.

This emphasis on traditional family roles, with the husband as decision-maker and the spouse as the homemaker, appeared to run contrary to the finding that spouse employment is critical to family adaptation. On the other hand, it is reasonable to infer that spouse employment is also an economic matter for these African-American military families. Even though spouses are called upon to take charge of family matters as one of their major homemaker responsibilities, they are also called upon to contribute to the family's economic well-being. Predictably, a spouse's employment was also positively related to her active involvement in the community, the length of time she had been in Western Europe (to find a job), and to the number of times she had been to Western Europe.

Military life in an overseas assignment is demanding. For the most part, soldiers are called upon to develop their military-related skills and abilities to the highest possible level. This high level of readiness is vital to the defense of the United States and its allies. Consequently, the soldier's time is at a premium. The Army's demand for more and more of the soldier's time leaves little time for the soldier to attend to personal and family responsibilities. Family time, the opportunity to invest in and develop marital and parent-child relationships, is likely to be curtailed by these ever-present competing demands. However, African-American enlisted family adaptation is positively related to both the military member's and the spouse's investment in family time for togetherness. In stressful situations, it is important for families to structure, organize, plan for, and seize those precious moments of family time together. In the case of African-American enlisted families, this investment appears to pay off in promoting the well-being of family members and minimizing stress.

It was surprising to observe the relative absence of stressors and strains in the final set of explanatory variables. The accumulation of stressors and strains before, immediately following, and during the initial period of adjustment to the stressor of relocation, while initially important, appeared to lose their predictive value when considered along with the family's internal strengths, the personal resources of individual members, and the buffering influence of the family members' appraisal of the situation, their sense of coherence or "fit" in the Army community.

The simultaneous consideration of stressors, strains, strengths, supports, and coherence, the elements of resiliency, is important in the systematic study of families under stress. While the resiliency framework has served as a useful guide in the selection and analysis of these important variables, researchers have yet to gain a full appreciation for the processes by which African-American military families adapt to change. This investigation attempted to shed light upon the strengths of African-American families in the military, and in this respect it has confirmed the importance of coherence, spouse self-reliance, spouse employment, and family time together as critical attributes of African-American enlisted families. As the Army and other branches of the Armed Services move forward with their family life programs and prevention-oriented family centers, they should consider which policies and programs can be strengthened or introduced to enhance significant strengths in African-American enlisted military families.

As noted in previous research (Hansen & Hill, 1964; Hill, 1958; McCubbin, 1979), the family's adaptation to stressful situations may be influenced by the community's "blueprint" for coping. In other words, the community's offerings of both opportunities and guidelines for managing stress are likely to shape the course as well as the outcome of family adaptation. In this investigation, spouse employment and the family's sense of "fitting in" or coherence are paramount and they point to the importance of the Army's policies and community efforts in support of African-American families. It seems reasonable to take the position that African-American enlisted families would benefit from the Army's commitment to and investment in policies that lead to job opportunities for spouses, increasing the spouse's self-confidence and self-reliance, and promoting support and a sense of community. Additionally, Army policies that give priority to spouses' learning the language and culture and acquiring skills for negotiating and enjoying their experience in the country would benefit the enlisted soldier through increased morale, sense of coherence, and self-confidence.

It is no small matter that the soldier's and family's sense of coherence is linked to their trust and confidence in the Army's plan to care for families in case of armed conflict or war. A well-developed and refined family program must be clearly communicated to and understood by the soldiers and their families. Clearly, these African-American enlisted families feel that they are an integral part of the Army's defense posture. They sense that their presence in a foreign country is not only to support the soldiers, but to serve as a symbol of United States involvement in and commitment to its allies. The presence of Army families may be viewed as a deterrent to military foreign invasion. Soldiers are expected to fight harder when their families are nearby. By the same token, to be effective the soldier must also feel confident that the Army will "take care of its own" families. Some families wondered whether they were really the deterrent force. Some believed that American families were there because if they were harmed or threatened, the United States would react swiftly and decisively as a matter of national security and foreign policy. The Army's investment in families and the preparation for their safety, in case of danger, appears to play a meaningful role in ensuring the readiness of our soldiers on foreign soil.

Notes

1. The author returned to active duty to design and conduct this investigation. This project was funded by the Agricultural Experiment Station, University of Wisconsin–Madison and University of Minnesota, the Center for Excellence in Family Studies and the Institute for the Study of Resiliency in Families.

2. The author acknowledges that the motivation for this special project on African Americans resulted from extensive dialogue with Dr. Marie F. Peters, colleague and friend, whose conceptualization of mundane stress served as an important guide in the conduct of this study. Additionally, the author thanks the invaluable contributions of Dr. Joan Patterson and Dr. Yoav Lavee to this project and to earlier versions of this chapter.

References

Antonovsky, A. (1979). *Health, stress, and coping.* San Francisco: Jossey-Bass.

Brown, R. J. (1993). Broader social issues: Policies, programs and services geared to military families. In F. W. Kaslow (Ed.), *The military family in peace and war* (pp. 163-172). New York: Springer.

Hansen, D., & Hill, R. (1964). Families under stress. In H. Christensen (Ed.), *Handbook of marriage and the family* (pp. 782-819). Chicago: Rand McNally.

Hill, R. (1958). Generic features of families under stress. *Social Casework, 39*, 139–150.

Hunter, E. (1982). *Families under the flag: A review of military family literature.* New York: Praeger.

Hunter, E.J., & Nice, D. S. (1978). *Military families: Adaptation to change.* New York: Praeger.

Kaslow, F.W. (1993). *The military family in peace and war.* New York: Springer.

Kupchella, D. L. (1993). Social policy and planning and legislative considerations. In F. W. Kaslow (Ed.), *The military family in peace and war* (pp. 241-250). New York: Springer.

Lavee, Y., McCubbin, H.I., & Patterson, J.M. (1985). The double ABCX model of family stress and adaptation: An empirical test by analysis of structural equations with latent variables. *Journal of Marriage and the Family, 47*, 811-825.

McAdoo, H. (1981). *Black families.* Beverly Hills, CA: Sage.

McAdoo, H. (1983). Societal stress: The black family. In H. McCubbin & C. Figley (Eds.), *Stress and the family: Vol. 1, Coping with normative transitions* (pp. 178-187). New York: Brunner/Mazel.

McCubbin, H.I. (1979). Integrating coping behavior in family stress theory. *Journal of Marriage and the Family, 41*, 237–244.

McCubbin, H.I., & Dahl, B. (1976). Prolonged family separation: A longitudinal study. In H. McCubbin, B. Dahl, & E. Hunter (Eds.), *Families in the military system* (pp. 112-144). Beverly Hills, CA: Sage.

McCubbin, H.I., Dahl, B., & Hunter, E. (1976). *Families in the military system.* Beverly Hills, CA: Sage.

McCubbin, H. I. & McCubbin, M.A. (1993). Coping with health crises: Resiliency model of family stress, adjustment and adaptation. In C. Danielson, B. Hamel-Bissell, & P. Winstead-Frye (Eds.), *Families, health and illness* (pp. 21-63). New York: Mosby.

McCubbin, H.I., McCubbin, M.A., Thompson, A.I., & Thompson, E.A. (1995). Resiliency in ethnic minority families: A conceptual model for predicting family adjustment and adaptation. In H.I. McCubbin, E.A. Thompson, A.I. Thompson, & J.E. Fromer (Eds.), *Resiliency in ethnic minority families: Native and immigrant American families, Volume 1* (pp. 3-48). Madison, WI: University of Wisconsin System.

McCubbin, H.I., Olson, D., & Zimmerman, S. (1986). Strengthening families through action research. In R. Rapoport (Ed.), *Children, youth and families: The action research relationship* (pp. 126-165). New York: Cambridge.

McCubbin, H.I., Patterson, J., & Lavee, Y. (1983). *One thousand Army families: Strengths, coping, and supports.* St. Paul: University of Minnesota.

McCubbin, H.I., Sussman, M., & Patterson, J. (1983). *Social stress and the family: Advances and developments in family stress theory and research.* New York: Haworth.

McCubbin, H.I. & Thompson, A.I. (1992). Resiliency in families: An East-West perspective. In J. Fischer (Ed.), *East-West directives in social work practice: Tradition and change.* (pp. 103-130). Honolulu: University of Hawaii.

McCubbin, H.I., Thompson, A.I., Thompson, E.A., Elver, K.M., & McCubbin, M.A. (1994). Ethnicity, schema, and coherence: Appraisal processes for families in crisis. In H.I. McCubbin, E.A. Thompson, A.I. Thompson, & J.E. Fromer (Eds.), *Sense of coherence and resiliency: Stress, coping, and health* (pp. 41-67). Madison, WI: University of Wisconsin System.

Military Family Research Institute. (1995). *Military adolescents: Their strengths and vulnerabilities.* Scranton, PA: Marywood College.

Nice, D. S. (1993). The military family in the health care system. In F.W. Kaslow (Ed.), *The military family in peace and war* (pp. 191-213). New York: Springer.

Orthner, D. (1980). *Families in blue: A study of married and single parents of families in the U.S. Air Force.* Greensboro, NC: Family Research and Analysis.

Peters, M. (1976). *Nine black families: A study of household management and childbearing in black families with working mothers.* Ann Arbor, MI: University Microfilms.

Peters, M., & Massey, G. (1983). Mundane extreme environmental stress in family stress theories: The case of black families in White America. In H. McCubbin, M. Sussman, & J. Patterson (Eds.), *Social stress and the family: Advances and developments in family stress theory and research* (pp. 193-218). New York: Haworth.

Pierce, C. (1975). The mundane extreme environment and its effect on learning. In S.G. Brainard (Ed.), *Learning disabilities: Issues and recommendations for research* (pp. 111-119). Washington, DC: National Institute of Education.

Rakoff, S., & Doherty, J. (1989). *Army family composition and retention* (Report No. 6054). Alexandria, VA: U.S. Army Research Institute for the Behavioral and Social Sciences.

Scanzoni, J. (1971). *The black family in modern society.* Boston, MA: Allyn & Bacon.

Staples, R. (1976). *Introduction to black sociology.* New York: McGraw Hill.

Thompson, E.A., McCubbin, H.I., Thompson, A.I., & Elver, K.M. (1995). Vulnerability and resiliency in Native Hawaiian families under stress. In H.I. McCubbin, E.A. Thompson, A.I. Thompson, & J.E. Fromer (Eds.), *Resiliency in ethnic minority families: Native and immigrant American families, Volume 1.* (pp. 115-131). Madison, WI: University of Wisconsin System.

Chapter 6

Housing and Neighborhood Satisfaction of Single-Parent Mothers and Grandmothers[1]

Marilyn L. Cantwell and Dorothy I. Jenkins

An increasing number of poor, minority women are heading households with children. Because a proportion of these women are "at-risk" single-parent mothers and single-parent grandmothers, it is becoming very important to understand the problems and conditions of their housing and neighborhood environments. Such an understanding can serve as a basis for developing personal and neighborhood resources to help these families cope with the conditions of their daily life.

Research Objectives

For the purposes of this study, three research objectives were identified. This study would: explore a model of neighborhood satisfaction by looking at local facility use, neighborhood condition, and social and demographic components; identify a model for dwelling satisfaction by looking at specific housing conditions and social and demographic components; and compare models for single-parent mothers and single-parent grandmothers.

This chapter will report the perceptions of these African-American single-parent mothers and grandmothers and discuss the conditions of their individual housing units and neighborhoods. Finally, suggestions will be made for improving the situation for these at-risk groups.

Review of Literature

The Single Parent and the
Single Grandparent

Single women who head households increasingly constitute a large proportion of the U.S. population. According to recent reports, families maintained by women with no husband present doubled between 1970 to 1990, rising from 5.5 to 10.9 million (U.S. Department of Commerce, 1990). Female-headed families rose from 11% of family households in 1970 to 15% in 1980 and 17% in 1990. Single women maintained 44% of black families. Nearly half of all children will at some time live in a single-parent, usually female-headed, household; these children will often experience a sharp decline in their standard of living.

On all indicators of objective housing quality, women who head households appear to be experiencing shelter deficits (Winter & Morris, 1982; Birch, 1985; Franck & Ahrentzen, 1989). They are more than likely to live in housing defined as inadequate by the U.S. Census. Women heads of households are twice as likely as men to live in inadequate housing and, since women earn 33% to 50% of their male counterparts, they are not as likely to be able to afford better alternatives (U.S. Department of Commerce, 1990). Additional research in this area is needed to better evaluate existing housing and neighborhoods and to design more appropriate environments and strategies for future single parents and their children.

The U.S. Department of Commerce (1993) estimates that 33.2 million children under the age of 18 live with their grandparents or other relatives. In about a third of these cases, neither parent is present and the grandmother or great-grandmother is playing a critical role as surrogate parent (Minkler & Roe, 1993). While multigenerational households have long been commonplace in working-class communities and in African-American and Hispanic households of all income levels, the current trend cuts across all class and racial lines. These arrangements are most prevalent in inner cities throughout our country, where drugs and other social ills have taken their toll. These grandparents face numerous problems.

The salience of the grandmother role and the symbolic meaning of grandchildren are mediated by two constructs: personal circumstances, and situational contexts (Timberlake & Chipungu, 1992). Housing and neighborhood conditions are major components of these constructs. Therefore, it is important to direct research toward better understanding these components.

Housing and Neighborhood Satisfaction

The importance of neighborhood and housing varies greatly among people living in a city. An understanding of how certain factors account for differences in the importance of neighborhood and housing can help strengthen urban community development, neighborhood revitalization, the loyalty and attachment of residents to a neighborhood as well as the quality of life for individual households.

Despite the relatively high numbers of single-parent women heading households, very little attention has been paid to housing and neighborhood perceptions of this group. With few exceptions, the relationship between female households and physical characteristics of their housing and neighborhood environments has received little attention (Galster & Hesser, 1981; Herting & Guest, 1985).

The standards or criteria used to assess housing and neighborhoods are thought to be the product of past experience, adaption processes, aspiration levels, and individual personality characteristics (Rodgers, 1982). Earlier studies in which the relationship between race and residential satisfaction was examined suggested that different races use similar criteria to evaluate housing and neighborhoods and that Blacks' dissatisfaction with the environment was principally a function of inferior housing condition (Cook, 1988; Crull, Bode, & Morris, 1991; Fried, 1982). Other studies have started from the premise that housing and neighborhood satisfaction is shaped by objective characteristics of the environment, characteristics of the respondents, and respondents' subjective beliefs, perceptions, and aspirations (Galster & Hesser, 1981; Weidemann, Anderson, Butterfield, & O'Donnell, 1982).

Over the years, housing researchers focused on various aspects of an individual's housing environment and neighborhood condition. Included in their assessments are: physical structure (size and number of rooms, condition of plumbing, and structural repair needs); housing site (size of yard and quality of landscaping); immediate neighborhood (proximity of and relation to neighbors); and local community (proximity to schools, churches, and shopping and access to public services) (Gruber, Shelton, & Godwin, 1985; Ha & Weber, 1991). Many of the same variable groupings are used in the current study.

Methodology

Sample

The sample of single-parent grandmothers and single-parent mothers was drawn from a data set of a larger study consisting of 1,200 interviews from a haphazard multi-stage sample of residents from a 1,000 block area of a predetermined geographic area of Baton Rouge, Louisiana. Fourteen of the respondents of the original sample were single-parent grandmothers, all of whom were African-American. Seventy-four of the respondents were single-parent mothers, of whom 51 were African-American. Sixty-eight percent of the single-parent mothers were African-American, and 32% of this group were White. For the purposes of this study, "single-parent grandmothers" are defined as grandmothers who are the only adult present in their household without a parent present, or with a parent who is under 21 years old. Single-parent mothers must be the only adult present, with all children under 21 years of age.

Data Collection

Data were collected in house-to-house personal interviews over a period of 18 months. Structured questionnaires were administered by a specially trained member of the local community. The study included questions about the physical adequacy of the housing unit, community services, satisfaction, sense of community, local facility use, social and neighborhood support services, public services, and demographic and socioeconomic data.

Data Analysis

Model specification was determined by previous research and features of the data set. Two dependent variable categories were identified: Neighborhood Satisfaction and Dwelling Satisfaction. Forward stepwise regression analysis was then used to study the relationships between variables.

Previous research has identified several variables that are hypothesized to be important to neighborhood and dwelling satisfaction. Ideally one would like to use all these variables to predict a model for each concept. However, due to the variability of the sample size for the two groups (single-parent mothers and single-parent grandmothers) not all of the variables could be used in an equation predicting neighborhood satisfaction and dwelling satisfaction. Therefore, in order to select important independent vari-

Table 1
**Factors Predicting Neighborhood Satisfaction
of Single-Parent Mothers**

Variable Number	Variable Name	Factor Loading
	Local Facility Use	
10	Availability of grocery stores	.978
12	Availability of stores and businesses	.984
14	Availability of churches and synagogues	−.425
17	Availability of recreational activities	−.552
11	Use of grocery stores	.657
13	Use of stores and businesses	.822
15	Use of churches and synagogues	.539
18	Use of neighborhood services	.600
	Neighborhood Condition	
21	Vacant/decaying buildings	.389
22	Cost of housing	.325
23	Vandalism	.708
24	Burglaries	.750
26	Rats	.316
28	Litter and garbage	.673
29	Stray animals	.672
31	Drugs	.458
32	Lighting	.408
	Social/Demographic	
69	Employment	.781
90	Housing tenure	.466
103	Age	−.388
106	Race	.310
108	Income range	−.627
104	Vehicle ownership	.696
35	Change in neighborhood condition	.325
41	Helped or helping neighbors	.311

ables, a two-step process was used. Principal component analysis was first used to group and weigh the variables into smaller conceptual groups, or factors. Next, those variables most heavily weighted within each of the factors were selected to use in a forward stepwise regression to determine an equation predicting neighborhood satisfaction and dwelling satisfaction for each subsample. The variables were added one by one to the model and were checked to determine their importance to the model as specified. This analysis meets the criterion that fewer variables than the number of subjects be included in the final equation (see Tables 1, 2, 3, and 4).

After the proposed models were developed, specific models for each category were formulated by forward stepwise regression. The specific models identified variables in each of the two areas, neighborhood and dwelling satisfaction, by order of importance. The specified models differed for the single-parent mothers and grandmothers. For the single-parent mothers, neighborhood condition and local facility use had greater effects than social/demographic variables on neighborhood satisfaction. Social/demographic variables and the use of local facilities had a greater effect for neighborhood satisfaction for single-parent grandmothers. Dwell-

Table 2
Factors Predicting Neighborhood Satisfaction
of Single-Parent Grandmothers

Variable Number	Variable Name	Factor Loading
	Local Facility Use	
10	Availability of grocery stores	.907
12	Availability of stores and businesses	.903
14	Availability of churches and synagogues	− .244
16	Availability of health and medical services	.310
17	Availability of recreational activities	− .222
11	Use of grocery stores	.415
13	Use of stores and businesses	.419
15	Use of churches and synagogues	.376
18	Use of neighborhood services	.235
	Neighborhood Condition	
21	Vacant/decaying buildings	.567
22	Cost of housing	.286
23	Vandalism	.427
24	Burglaries	.750
25	Muggings	.566
26	Rats	.288
28	Litter and garbage	.743
29	Stray animals	.436
30	Street maintenance	.763
31	Drugs	.329
32	Lighting	.545
	Social/Demographic	
69	Employment	.781
90	Housing tenure	.466
103	Age	− .285
106	Race	.310
108	Income range	.696
104	Vehicle ownership	− .310
35	Change in neighborhood condition	.425
41	Helped or helping neighbors	.301

Table 3
Factors Predicting Dwelling Satisfaction
of Single-Parent Mothers

Variable Number	Variable Name	Factor Loading
	Housing Condition	
93	Plumbing	.650
94	Heating system	.436
95	Water supply	.405
97	Roof	.285
98	Walls	.417
100	Windows	.555
101	Exterior condition	.468
	Public Services	
49	Street mainenance	.452
52	Street lighting	.535
60	Recreational facilities/parks	.676
	Social/Demographic	
88	Type of structure	.230
90	Housing tenure	−.320
69	Employment status	.781
103	Age	.459
106	Race	.354
108	Income range	−.689

ing satisfaction for both parent groups was related to specific housing condition and social/demographic variables.

Results

Characteristics of Sample

The average age of the single-parent mothers in the sample is 30 years old. They have lived in their neighborhoods an average of 9.6 years and in their current homes an average of 4 years. Only 29% own their homes. The average value of their homes is $14,511. Fifty-four percent of the single-parent mothers reported their incomes to be below $10,000. Twenty-one percent earn between $3,001 and $7,000, nearly 14% indicated that their incomes were $3,000 or less, and another 14% reported incomes between $7,000 and $10,000 (Table 5). The average age of the single-parent grandmothers in this study is 53.8 years old. They have lived in their neighborhoods an average of 15.7 years and in their current homes an average of 13.6 years. Only 36% own their homes. The average

Table 4
Factors Predicting Dwelling Satisfaction
of Single-Parent Grandmothers

Variable Number	Variable Name	Factor Loading
	Housing Condition	
93	Plumbing	.657
94	Heating system	.424
95	Water supply	.403
97	Roof	.453
98	Walls	.568
100	Windows	.779
101	Exterior condition	.470
	Social/Demographic	
88	Type of structure	.368
90	Housing tenure	.466
91	Want to own dwelling	.986
69	Employment status	.781
103	Age	– .288
104	Vehicle ownership	– .310
106	Race	.418
108	Income range	– .677

value of their homes is $18,658. Sixty-nine percent of the single-parent grandmothers indicated an income range of below $10,000 and 21% have an annual income of between $3,001 and $7,000. Fourteen percent reported incomes of $3,000 or less and another 14% have incomes between $7,001 and $10,000 (Table 5).

Perceptions of Neighborhood and Housing

Seventy-nine percent of the single-parent grandmothers rate their neighborhoods as an excellent or good place to live, and most are very strongly (36%) or strongly (43%) attached. Thirty-six percent feel that neighborhood conditions have improved in the last year or two; 43% feel it has remained the same, and 21% feel that it has declined. Fifty-seven percent of this group own a vehicle.

The single-parent mothers do not rate their neighborhoods as favorably as the single-parent grandmothers. Only 6% rate it as excellent and 32% as good, while 44% rate it as fair and 18% as poor. Only 15% feel that neighborhood conditions have improved in the last year or two; 34% feel it has remained the same, while 33% feel that is has declined. Thirty percent of the single-parent mothers own a vehicle.

Table 5
Characteristics of Sample[a]

Variable	Single-Parent Mothers (*n* = 74)	Single-Parent Grandmothers (*n* = 14)
Average age	30	54
Income range		
Below $10,000	54%	49%
Below $3,000	18%	14%
$3,001 – $7,000	22%	21%
$7,001 – $10,000	14%	14%
$10,001 – $25,000	24%	23%
Over $25,000	7%	7%
No response	15%	21%
Average housing value	$14,511	$18,658
Tenure		
Own	29%	36%
Rent	68%	64%
Other	3%	0%
Race		
African-American	68%	100%
White	32%	0
3 No Response		
1 Mixed		

[a] Secondary analysis from a haphazard multi-stage sample.

Specified Models

Single-Parent Mothers' Neighborhood Satisfaction. For single-parent mothers, 18 variables in the specified model accounted for .46 of the variance. This model is shown in Table 6. The contributing variables include several representing the original proposed categories of neighborhood conditions, local facility use, and social/demographic characteristics. For this model, single-parent mothers' neighborhood satisfaction depended upon their perception that their neighborhood was free of stray animals, vacant and decaying buildings, vandalism, burglaries, and rats. It also depended upon adequate lighting and street maintenance, reasonable cost of housing, satisfaction with their dwelling, and their reported age. The order of the variables as presented in Tables 6, 7, 8, and 9 represents the order of variable contribution to the model as directed by the stepwise regression procedure. A maximum improvement tech-

Table 6
Summary of Stepwise Regression Analysis for
Neighborhood Satisfaction of Single-Parent Mothers

Variable	R	R^2	F	p
Model F-ratio = 17.67				
Stray animals	.062	.062	3.78	.056
Vacant/decaying buildings	.057	.119	3.67	.060
Available health & medical facilities	.039	.159	1.58	.115
Vandalism	.039	.198	2.65	.109
Use of stores and business in area	.033	.231	2.27	.137
Age	.025	.256	1.76	.189
Change in neighborhood condition	.020	.277	1.45	.233
Burglaries	.016	.294	1.18	.281
Street maintenance	.031	.325	2.24	.140
Use of churches & synagogues	.021	.346	1.60	.211
Use of services in area	.021	.368	1.57	.215
Satisfaction with dwelling	.020	.388	1.52	.223
Cost of housing	.016	.404	1.24	.271
Helped or being helped	.012	.417	0.93	.340
Available churches & synagogues	.014	.431	1.10	.298
Available recreation facilities	.015	.447	1.16	.285
Rats	.008	.455	0.601	.442
Lighting	.006	.461	0.469	.497

nique was employed to find the "best" variables for the models of dwelling and neighborhood satisfaction for the two subject groups.

Single-Parent Mothers' Dwelling Satisfaction. The model specified for dwelling satisfaction included ten variables, accounting for .54 of the variance (Table 7). These variables fall into the two original categories of housing condition and social/demographic characteristics. Housing conditions that helped to predict dwelling satisfaction include the degree to which plumbing, windows, the water system, exterior condition, and walls do not need improvement. The predictor social/demographic characteristics include vehicle ownership, being employed, having a higher income range, and being African American.

Single-Parent Grandmothers' Neighborhood Satisfaction. For single-parent grandmothers, the specified model accounted for .96 of the variance in neighborhood satisfaction (Table 8). Although only nine variables are included in the model, they account for a very high percentage of the variance. The variables represent the original neighborhood satisfaction categories, including local facil-

Table 7
Summary of Stepwise Regression Analysis for
Dwelling Satisfaction of Single-Parent Mothers

Variable	R	R^2	F	p
Model F-ratio = 47.97				
Plumbing	.251	.251	18.45	.000
Windows	.096	.347	7.99	.006
Heating system	.054	.402	4.81	.032
Vehicle ownership	.041	.444	3.92	.053
Water supply	.026	.470	2.54	.117
Exterior condition	.019	.490	1.93	.170
Employment status	.020	.511	2.09	.154
Income range	.005	.516	0.494	.485
Race	.010	.526	0.988	.325
Walls	.010	.536	1.04	.311

ity use and social/demographic characteristics. Specifically, to the extent that single-parent grandmothers perceive their neighborhoods to be free of rats and vacant/decaying buildings, they tend to be more satisfied. Their neighborhood satisfaction also depends upon the extent to which they perceive health and medical facilities and grocery stores to be available and whether they use these services and stores. Being employed, owning a vehicle, and being African American were the important social/demographic variables.

Table 8
Summary of Stepwise Regression Analysis for
Neighborhood Satisfaction of Single-Parent Grandmothers

Variable	R	R^2	F	p
Model F-ratio = 248.17				
Employment status	.430	.430	6.81	.028
Use of area services	.400	.831	19.05	.002
Rats	.132	.964	26.28	.001
Vacant/decaying buildings	.014	.979	4.16	.087
Use of grocery stores in area	.008	.987	3.17	.134
Vehicle ownership	.001	.909	15.07	.017
Race	.009	1.00	5.61	.098
Available health & medical facilities	.000	1.00	228.21	.004

Single-Parent Grandmothers' Dwelling Satisfaction. The model specified to predict dwelling satisfaction for the single-parent grandmothers accounted for .99 of the variance (Table 9). This model contained variables related to housing condition and social/demographic characteristics. Residents who perceived their walls, heating systems, plumbing, water supply, and roofs as not needing improvement were more satisfied. Those who wanted to own their home, had higher incomes, had lived in their homes longer, lived in single-family detached homes, owned a vehicle, and were African American tended to be more satisfied with their dwellings.

Table 9
Summary of Stepwise Regression Analysis for
Dwelling Satisfaction of Single-Parent Grandmothers

Variable	R	R^2	F	p
Model F-ratio = 162.52				
Walls	.547	.547	13.29	.003
Heating system	.263	.810	13.92	.003
Plumbing	.059	.870	4.13	.072
Water supply	.019	.890	1.45	.262
Want to own dwelling	.015	.905	1.13	.321
Housing tenure	.029	.935	2.77	.146
Income range	.024	.960	3.14	.136
Race	.010	.970	1.39	.302
Type of structure	.006	.977	0.82	.430
Roof	.019	.995	9.32	.092
Vehicle ownership	.003	.999	6.27	.241

Conclusions and Recommendations

Conclusions

It is difficult to define and measure neighborhood and housing quality and satisfaction. This concept may include the physical features of the dwelling, the presence or absence of neighborhood services, and the fit between specific neighborhood or unit characteristics and the occupant. Residents' attitudes and behaviors are also important in defining and measuring housing and neighborhood satisfaction. Research that contributes to an understanding of dwelling and neighborhood satisfaction can affect the social, political, and economic fabric of a community.

Several findings stand out in this investigation. Based on the objectives of the study, to explore models of neighborhood satisfaction and dwelling satisfaction for each population group and then compare these models, the data point to several differences between the two population groups. For single-parent mothers and single-parent grandmothers the proposed model of neighborhood satisfaction included eight variables identifying both availability and use of local facilities, nine specific neighborhood condition variables and eight social/demographic variables (Tables 1 and 2). The specified model identified the important neighborhood satisfaction variables for single-parent mothers (Table 6). Those local facility variables that were identified in the specified model for neighborhood satisfaction of single-parent mothers were: the availability of health and medical facilities, churches and synagogues, and recreational facilities; the use of stores and businesses, churches, and synagogues; and services in the area. The specific neighborhood condition variables identified were stray animals, vacant/decaying buildings, vandalism, burglaries, and rats. The social/demographic variables that were identified in the specified model for single-parent mothers were age and change in neighborhood condition (Table 6).

For single-parent grandmothers the specified model indicated different variables in each of the three categories as important predictors of neighborhood satisfaction (Table 8). Only three local facility variables were identified for single-parent grandmothers: use of area services, grocery stores in the area, and available health and medical facilities. Rats and vacant/decaying buildings were the neighborhood condition variables that were specified for neighborhood satisfaction for this population group. Employment status and race were the important specified social/demographic variables for neighborhood satisfaction of single-parent grandmothers (Table 8).

The specified model predicted neighborhood satisfaction better for single-parent grandmothers than for single-parent mothers. The model for single-parent mothers included a greater number of variables, each contributing less to the overall effect of the equation, with neighborhood condition variables having the greatest impact. For neighborhood satisfaction, the variance explained by the equation was .46 for single-parent mothers and .96 for single-parent grandmothers.

There were differences in the predicted and specified models for dwelling satisfaction between single-parent mothers and single-parent grandmothers (Tables 3, 4, 7, and 9). In this research three areas of dwelling satisfaction were identified for each population group as predictors of dwelling satisfaction: housing condition, public services, and social/demographic variable (Tables 3 and 4). For the single-parent mothers the specified model indicated the physical features of the dwelling; plumbing, windows, heating systems, water supply, exterior condition and walls were the variables of importance. There were no public service variables indicated and only three social/demographic variables were indicated as important to the model: vehicle ownership, income range, and race (Tables 3 and 7). The specified model for single-parent grandmothers in the study indicated a greater number of social/demographic variables important in dwelling satisfaction (Table 9). Wanting to own their own dwellings, current tenure, income range, race, type of structure, and vehicle ownership were important indicator variables for this population group (Table 9). The important physical features variables of dwelling satisfaction for single-parent grandmothers were the housing condition variables of walls, heating systems, plumbing, water supply, and condition of the roof (Table 9).

Specific physical conditions of housing, walls, plumbing, water supply, heating/cooling systems, and exterior condition appeared to contribute to the explanation of the different residential experiences of single-parent mothers and grandmothers. The social/demographic characteristics of vehicle ownership, housing tenure, race, income, and employment status are included in the model and contribute to the full range of what is important to respondents.

It was expected that both differences and similarities would exist in the criteria used among single-parent mothers and single-parent grandmothers. According to the data, single-parent mothers and single-parent grandmothers were not equally satisfied with their housing or neighborhoods. Single-parent grandmothers rated their neighborhoods and dwellings higher than single-parent mothers. Based on the regression analysis, not many of the social/demographic variables contributed to neighborhood satisfaction of single-parent mothers.

It is interesting to note that one of the predictors of dwelling satisfaction for single-parent mothers is race. Traditionally, the expectations for obtaining high-quality housing have been lower for African Americans than for Caucasians. This expectation is likely to be based upon a realistic evaluation of the ability to obtain high-quality, affordable housing. Presumably, biases still exist that discriminate against African-American single-parent households.

Continued study of the factors that increase satisfaction across groups and the distinct elements that increase satisfaction among subgroups will serve to define appropriate strategies and opportunities for those whose housing and neighborhoods are inadequate. Once housing strategies and opportunities are defined, community network development can be initiated through public/private partnerships addressing these issues specifically.[2]

An issue that needs to be further explored is the relative condition and economic history of the two groups studied here. Although the single-parent grandmothers report lower current incomes than the single-parent mothers, they are living in houses that have a higher economic value and perceive their neighborhoods to be better places to live. Although the grandmothers are single now, perhaps they were part of a multi-wage-earner household earlier and were able to accumulate additional economic resources. This may account for their slightly better housing and neighborhood conditions.

Recommendations

There are several recommendations for this study. Innovative information-gathering techniques that could expand the data collection from specified populations should be investigated. One such technique is Visitor Employed Photography (VEP). VEP involves the participants and/or investigator taking pictures of an area of the living environment that is either a help or a hindrance to living independently. As the picture subject is identified, and the picture taken, the participant is asked to elaborate on the reason for the picture. In addition, the surroundings are recorded so that the subject's context is also part of the interview record. Collecting visual information, such as photographs, would improve the ability of researchers to define and measure various elements of housing and neighborhood quality and satisfaction. This data-collection method would provide images of specific elements of the housing and neighborhood conditions that affect satisfaction. These pictures also serve as an extension to the statistical data so often relied upon in housing and neighborhood studies.

Specific strategies and opportunities should be developed to assist those whose dwellings and neighborhoods are inadequate. Some of these strategies and opportunities might include: analyzing physical design aspects and suggesting improvements; providing service delivery to the residents; educating residents about available programs and the qualifications for home acquisition and improvement; and developing resident "mentoring" and "self-help" workshops. Neighborhood work/service cooperatives could be organized, and resident networking programs such as neighborhood watch programs could be developed. Support networks and educational programs for local neighborhood businesses could be investigated, and the services of local labor union retirees could be focused on job skill development and retooling.

It is important to recognize the fact that one of the strongest determinants of housing satisfaction among single-parent mother or single-parent grandmother households was being able to live well independently. The strategies suggested above could help provide increased levels of independence for these populations.

Notes

1. This research was supported by Mid-City Redevelopment Alliance and General Health, Inc., Baton Rouge, Louisiana.

2. The sample of single-parent grandmothers is too small to permit other comparisons that might be extended from this model: a) never-married single-parent households, and b) white single-parent grandmothers heading second-generation families.

References

Birch, E. (1985). *The unsheltered woman: Women and housing in the 80's.* New Brunswick, NJ: Center for Urban Policy Research, Rutgers University.

Cook, C. C. (1988). Components of neighborhood satisfaction. *Environment & Behavior, 20,* 115–149.

Crull, S., Bode, M. E., & Morris, E. W. (1991). Two tests of housing and neighborhood satisfaction. *Housing and Society, 18,* 53–64.

Franck, K., & Ahrentzen, S. (1989). *New households, new housing.* New York, NY: Van Nostrand Reinhold.

Fried, M. (1982). Residential attachment: Sources of residential and community attachment. *Journal of Social Issues, 38,* 107–119.

Galster, G. C., & Hesser, G. W. (1981). Residential satisfaction—Compositional and contextual correlates. *Environment & Behavior, 13,* 735–758.

Gruber, K. J., Shelton, G. G., & Godwin, D. D. (1985). Housing satisfaction and type residence. *Housing and Society, 12,* 97–106.

Herting, J. R., & Guest, A. M. (1985). Components of satisfaction with local areas in the metropolis. *The Sociological Quarterly, 26,* 99–115.

Ha, M., & Weber, M. (1991). The determinant of residential environmental qualities and satisfaction: Effects of financing housing programs and housing regulations. *Housing and Society, 18,* 65–76.

Minkler, M., & Roe, K. M. (1993). Grandmothers as caregivers, raising children of the crack cocaine epidemic (Vol. 2). In D. E. Biegel & R. Schulz (Eds.), *The family caregiver applications series.* Newbury Park, CA: Sage.

Rodgers, W. L. (1982). Density, crowding, and satisfaction with the residential environment. *Social Indicators Research, 10,* 75–102.

Timberlake, E. M., & Chipungu, S. S. (1992). Grandmotherhood: Contemporary meaning among African-American middle-class grandmothers. *Social Work, 37,* 216–222.

U.S. Bureau of the Census. (1983). *1980 census of population: General population characteristics.* Washington, DC: U.S. Government Printing Office.

U.S. Department of Commerce. (1990). How we're changing. *Current Population Reports,* Special Studies Series, P-23, No. 170.

U.S. Department of Commerce. (1993, April). Bureau of Census, P20-467, Household and family characteristics, March 1992. *Current population reports.* Washington, DC: U.S. Government Printing Office.

Winter, M., & Morris, E. W. (1982). Housing conditions, satisfaction, and conventionality: An analysis of the housing of female-headed households. *Housing and Society, 9,* 70–86.

Weidemann, S., Anderson, J. R., Butterfield, D. I., & O'Donnell, P. M. (1982). Residents' perceptions of satisfaction and safety—A basis for change in multifamily housing. *Environment & Behavior, 14,* 695–724.

Chapter 7

Healing Forces in African-American Families

Cherie A. Bagley and Juanitaelizabeth Carroll

African Americans have always had to contend with pressures due to the burdens of racism and oppression. Race significantly impacts their lives and they continue to contend with socioeconomic difficulties in the nineties. Because of this impact, those working with African Americans in the mental health professions must consider and understand their social context (Hines & Boyd-Franklin, 1982).

African-American Families
and Mental Health

Historically, African Americans have instituted their own indigenous support systems (Poole, 1990). The core family has been a strong support system along with the church; black organizations such as the National Association for the Advancement of Colored People and Urban League; and black-owned businesses, such as hairdressers and funeral homes (Figure 1). Role models and mentors are frequently obtained through these kinds of organizations and black-owned media sources such as *Ebony, Jet, Essence*, and *Black Enterprise*. The church, the first fully owned and controlled African American institution, has been an especially powerful support (Nelsen, Yokley, & Nelsen, 1971). The black church housed an organizational structure well suited as an organ of socialization, inspiration, communication, training, and healing.

Because most agencies of the white community resisted serving African Americans, the black church exercised a social welfare function providing banks, housing, institutions of learning, health care, job service, and legal advice (Wimberley, 1989). The church not only provided services denied by the larger community but tangibly affirmed the worth and dignity of African Americans in

Figure 1
Indigenous Support Systems
in African American Families

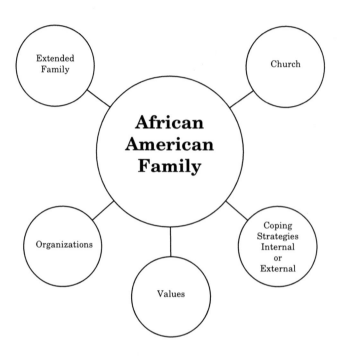

their charge. The black church's greatest mission may be ably reflected in a cry popularized by the Reverend Jesse Jackson, it kept hope alive.

In this chapter we will discuss (1) stressors occurring in African-American families, (2) resources that are used to combat the debilitating effects of these stressors, giving emphasis to the role of the black church and healing forces found within the indigenous support systems, (3) church and community as elements of resiliency, (4) the importance of these identified resources in counseling African American families at risk, and (5) offer guidelines for counseling with these families.

At various times in life, African Americans may be at risk for mental health problems (Ramseur, 1991). African Americans may be at risk to suffer emotional turmoil because of frequent rejection and ostracism, societal exclusion, and negativity. The emotional consequences of these factors may be gender-related as some psychological research links females to depression (McGrath, Keita, Strickland, & Russo, 1990) and males to anger (Jones, Gray, & Jospitre, 1982). Members of both sexes are often described as having bad attitudes when they are not in agreement with mainstream society. This presents a paradox because often African Americans differ in perspective from the values or opinions of white society (Sue & Sue, 1990).

Recognition of one's racial identity provides a forum for the various attitudes an individual presents when confronted with racism, such as denial, shock, cultural immersion, or biculturality (Helms, 1990; Parham, 1989). Racial identity attitudes are not regarded as stable until adolescence or adulthood (Whaley, 1993). Across the life cycle, with each crisis or setback a person may develop a different attitude. Depending on how severe the oppressive attack, one might: (1) suffer and recover; (2) continue suffering and maintain a life of bitterness and failure, or demonstrate maladaptive behavior; (3) maintain an attitude of indifference toward society and perceive and accept the glass ceiling effect (societal limitations); or (4) develop an attitude of acceptance or challenge toward living in two worlds, one African-American and one white (Dodson, 1988; Lacayo, 1989).

For a better understanding of how these stressors affect African-American families, more studies are needed that document black family structure and the variety of lifestyle patterns within black family life. For example, egalitarianism between the sexes is often the case in two-parent black families, but some traditional attitudes may coexist (Barbarin, 1983; Thomas & Dansby, 1985; Willie, 1988).

The extended family retains a primary role in the black family and functions as a cooperative network. The extended family can be extensive: parents, grandparents, cousins, nieces, nephews. Black family reunions are often a facilitator of kinship bonds despite geographical distance. Numerous researchers view the composite strengths of black families (collective cooperation, strong extended family bonds, religious exposure, strong work ethic, and egalitarianism between the sexes) as qualities that promote recovery from adversity (Nobles, 1988; Peters & Massey, 1983; Thomas & Dansby, 1985; White & Parham, 1990).

Dodson (1988) discusses three approaches to studying the black family: (1) cultural ethnocentrism, (2) cultural relativism, and (3) the social class approach. Cultural ethnocentrism examines the black family as it assimilates to American society. Frequently the black family is viewed as not measuring up, and they are described as structurally disorganized and unstable. Nearly all literature discussing the African-American family refers to the Moynihan report of the 1960s as the perpetrator of many negative stereotypes regarding the black family (Billingsley, 1968, 1974; Dodson, 1988; Spaights, 1990; White & Parham, 1990). Cultural relativism incorporates the background and experiences of the family to understand a particular group's dynamics and holds that everyone possesses a culture. Black culture is distinguished from white culture and many connect black family patterns with African heritage (Dodson, 1988; Myers, 1988; Nobles et al., 1987; Nobles, 1988). This view focuses more on the strengths inherent in the black family. The social class perspective advocates the control of socioeconomic factors when conducting research on black families, and as a result, differences between Blacks and Whites will disappear. This approach states that many times social class categorizations of income and education are not uniform in comparing Blacks with Whites and may provide misleading information. Blacks in the same occupation and income level as Whites may not have access to the same resources (Dodson, 1988).

Black families confront a variety of mental health challenges, such as homicide, violence, incarceration, teen pregnancy, substance abuse, relationship issues (communication, money, sex), depression, stress, barriers to achievement, lack of reinforcement, parenting, single parenting, self-esteem, unemployment, and discrimination (Baker, 1987; Jackson & Sears, 1992; Spaights, 1990; White & Parham, 1990). How African-American families cope with these psychosocial issues varies. While this chapter focuses on those who seek help, there are many who never enter traditional mental health centers. For this reason, it is vital that alternative community resources be made available.

Obtaining mental health services has often been a negative experience for Blacks and their behaviors and attitudes have been mislabeled or misunderstood (Nobles et al., 1987; Nobles, 1988). One has only to review the literature to find the many comparisons made between Whites and Blacks, with Blacks appearing deficient. White and Parham (1990) discuss the fallacy of viewing Blacks with models that were normed on Whites. Caution should be exercised in interpreting racially comparative data.

The Church as an Indigenous and
Healing Institution

Many African Americans at the turn of the century bore witness to a prevailing spirit of creativity and optimism. This spirit emanated from the African American Church with vigor. Surviving the bewilderment of emancipation from slavery, reconstruction of the south, and the pathos of the depression, a majority of African Americans suffered the paralyzing effects of a post-oppressive reaction syndrome (PORS), an original term defined as the psychological effects remaining in response to the aforementioned social ills (Anderson, 1988; Hines & Boyd-Franklin, 1982; Billingsley, 1968).

The odious intent of centuries of racial oppression worked its evil:

> "When you determine what a man shall think, you do not have to concern yourself about what he will do. If you make a man feel inferior, you do not have to compel him to accept an inferior status, for he will seek it himself. If you make a man think that he is justly an outcast, you do not have to order him to the back door; he will go without being told; and if there is no back door his very nature will demand one" (Woodson, in Kimbro & Hill, 1991, p. 56).

African Americans experienced horrific violence from lashings to tarring and feathering. African Americans lived within a societal standard that rejected their very being and erected roadblocks to thwart their advancement. In response, many succumbed to the manifestations of PORS. These manifestations were rage, self-debilitating behaviors, somatic pathology, antisocial acting out, Black-on-Black crime, depression, isolationism, and weakened social interactions (Hines & Boyd-Franklin, 1982; Billingsley, 1968). The slave system had a negative impact on the family system. Captors disregarded the family by severing kinship ties and displaying inhumane treatment. Males were denied roles as husbands and fathers. There existed a general lack of support or protection for the family unit (Hines & Boyd-Franklin, 1982; Billingsley, 1968). Succeeding generations experience these effects indirectly in the forms of family disruption, inadequate health care, unemployment, underemployment, and social degradation. Social forces have oppressed the African-American worker and a majority of blacks are at lower level positions. Although jobs may be attainable, those jobs available may lack economic, social, and psychological gratification and may be regarded as menial. Many may accept this status though capable of more, not wanting to confront tremendous frustration and opposition (Billingsley, 1968). The majority self-mobilized into a swelling under-class, which is still evident today. Aspirations were strangled and self-destructive behaviors flourished. With so many obstacles, most strove only for menial employment despite their intellectual gifts. Contempt, disrespect, and exploitation within the race grew more commonplace. Alcoholism, addiction, and other means of anesthetizing themselves from the pain of their environment were commonly practiced, and the health of the middle-aged adult often deteriorated beneath the burdens of overwork and poverty.

African Americans hurtled beyond the paralyzing effects of PORS at the turn of the century. A major tool and healing element was found in religious institutions (Poole, 1990). Galvanized by a growing tide of individual acts defying racism, denominations of the black church dropped their denominational separation. The result was a veritable tower of strength, courage, and progress. The tower included Black Methodist, Baptist, Holiness, Presbyterian, Pentecostal, Nationalist, Muslim, and many other congregations briefly uniting as the "black church." The race clung to this tower throughout the era of advocacy for civil rights.

This "black church" was often the center in a hub of activity and proactive attitudes prevailed. Preaching inspired and influenced African Americans to believe they were special, persons of historic merit, descended from a great people because of race and color. This presented a self-concept in sharp contrast to centuries of being despised, rejected, and too often grievously persecuted for these same attributes.

Steeped in the religion of their ancestry, Africans who were enslaved and brought captive to America continued the practices of their African Traditional, Islamic, or Christian religions until the cruel opposition of slave holders forced such practices to cease or go underground (Barrett, 1974). Remnants of this tradition are evident in retentions such as folk tales (e.g., Bre'r Rabbit), folk medicines and remedies, dance, arts, crafts, and childhood rhymes. It was to the slave holders' advantage to intermingle African tribes in order to maintain their disparity (Lincoln, 1974, 1989). The enslaved might otherwise think to unite and overthrow their oppressors. Immediately upon arrival in America the African transplants were usually placed with African people of a different family, culture, and language than their own (Washington, 1989). This impeded the sharing of religious observances. Although scholars contend that the black church was the first organization of the African-American slave transplants (Nelsen, Yokley, & Nelsen, 1971).

Prior to becoming institutionalized, religion was retained and practiced individually by men and women disparagingly referred to as "witchdoctors and medicine men." These authorities were consulted clandestinely by slaves. The earliest religious organizations consisted of the Brush or Bush Arbor Churches. A few daring souls would literally gather in the brush or bushes for worship out of view of their enslavers. With subsequent generations the heritage of African-American religious traditions grew weaker. Once the movement towards westernized Christian evangelization of the slaves began, a majority of the slaves adopted the religious practices of their enslavers.

The enslaved attended religious worship for more than spiritual reasons, as it was often an opportunity for socialization or escape from obligatory duties. Toward the end of the 1700s, the thumb of oppression became more firmly imposed, even in worship. Rather than finding relief or relaxation in church, many slaves chafed to hear humility, tolerance, and fellowship preached while from the same lips they were ordered to segregate themselves to the farthest parts of the church building and not allowed to speak, teach, or satisfactorily participate in the life or organization of the church. Sentiment grew among the slaves for holding meetings independently and thereby increase their benefit to one another.

Up to emancipation, the black church had served important educational functions by providing a sanctioned meeting place and an outlet for oratory, the physical, and cultural arts: industry, carpentry, decoration, sewing, music, singing, and prose, as well as providing organization, administration, and leadership opportunities to spirits hampered from free expression. Lovers of education managed to press through the sieve of resistance and obtain instruction about the alphabet, arithmetic, reading, writing, and sometimes recitation of the great classics. After emancipation, those starving for education learned more in church school reading from the bible than from inadequate textbooks in segregated schools for former slaves. These schools were established by the freedmen's bureau and northern missionary societies (Anderson, 1988).

The church prior to emancipation was unparalleled as a leadership training forum. Denied voice in the white churches and institutions, procedures observed over the years in their master's organizations were engrafted by older members into the day-to-day workings of the early black churches. Without textbooks, many aspired to the only tolerated expression of leadership, the ministry (Woodson, 1972).

Through industrialization, the African-American church remained the paramount institution of the African-American community. Those African Americans entering the entrepreneurial and professional ranks have found that the best way to reach African Americans has been through the church (Woodson, 1972; Poole, 1990).

Churches became the spawning grounds for job-matching services, housing corporations, banks, business ventures, schools, universities, and many creative agencies of self-help. Mt. Olivet Baptist Church of New York City spearheaded the establishment of the YMCA and houses for young women, providing affordable housing for those coming to the cities to obtain work (Woodson, 1972). This was the era of a new contingent and it was necessary because most institutions of the white community resisted serving African Americans (Wilmore, 1990). When the white banks refused to lend money to entrepreneurs or prospective homeowners, the church rallied and started its own credit union (Wimberly, 1989, 1991). When people were refused housing, the church rallied to create housing. When people were refused education, the church rallied to create its own institutions of learning. When they were refused hospital care, churches such as St. Stephen's African Methodist Episcopal of Chicago laid the groundwork for hospitals like Provident Hospital.

Many voices today contend that the black churches have outlived their usefulness. Most persons are alienated from the types of activities that were practiced and encouraged by church members of the previous half century. Churches that attract African Americans today provide different types of services. These churches pronounce false the alarm that the African American Church is a relic. Church-sponsored programs can act as healing forces to families. A New York congregation sponsors city-wide oratorical and essay contests for children to promote education. A Chicago church sponsors health screenings for hypertension, diabetes, and so on, along with health education and exercise programs for senior citizens.

Other churches focus on health care and operate Holistic Centers that combine spiritual and physical health care and provide staff physicians and health personnel. Family ministries are operated; one church provides a committee of professional personnel (e.g., teacher, social worker, police officer, businessman, psychologists, etc.) to plan activities and improve services to families.

These programs focus on topics relevant to African Americans such as violence, sexuality, divorce, depression, and AIDS.

Churches may more effectively break destructive cycles by bringing social services to the people. These programs can work to affirm competencies and strengths families already possess (Pointsett & Russell, 1988; Littlejohn-Blake & Darling, 1993).

Most African Americans have some experience with organized religion. For example, a couple first consulted their minister for counseling and were subsequently referred to family therapy. The minister was relieved at this decision because his counseling of the couple was too time-consuming and there was concern about over involvement because the husband was a member of the church deacon board. The wife was more comfortable counseling with a therapist. This referral process can work both ways between therapist and clergy.

Counseling in the church should have its place and its limitations. The church has historically been a resource for African Americans and a better working relationship could be forged between clergy and therapists. Churches have historically been embraced by African-American families whereas psychotherapy continues to be stigmatized in the African-American community (Richardson, 1991; Solomon, 1990).

Stressful Conditions Experienced

Family life in the 1990s is increasingly fast paced. Technological and societal change often create pressure for the individual and when the individual suffers, the family also suffers. Within this stressful environment, the African-American family is in crisis, undergoing a process of dismantling and decay (Skinner-Hughes, 1992). Family members often feel distress at the inability to achieve a goal or maintain a certain level of functioning. Distress occurs when an individual experiences a sense of frustration or dissonance and feels unable to effectively resolve or master his or her goal (Peters & Massey, 1983). There is a combination of emotional and tangible problems. Stress can be derived from either external or internal sources. External stress can be described as pressure placed upon the individual by an outside force: possibly an institution, another person, or an object. An example of external stress would be an administrative decision to change a job classification when the change is unwanted by the employee.

Internal stress derives from the individual, through their own mental states or behaviors that produce negative outcomes or the lack of a coping response. Internal mediators of stress are described as personality factors that influence the individual's response to stress. In African-American families stress is often a combination of external and internal forces. People differ in their psychological defenses, coping resources, and personal predispositions. Three identified internal mediators are: 1) *Locus of Control*: the perception that life is controlled by the individual or by the external environment; 2) *Learned Helplessness*: the length of time one remains at a task if it is perceived nothing can be accomplished; and 3) *Self Concept*: how positive self-evaluation differs in possibility thinking from negative self-evaluation (Smith, 1985).

Although all people experience problems and may seek counseling, people of color experience a twofold impact of conflict, at an individual level and at a societal level. Smith (1985) encourages the identification of these levels (society vs. individual) in working with people of color and suggests the Stress-Resistant-Delivery Model as a guide in counseling. The model seeks to identify the stressors, outline and implement stress resistant forces, and deliver services to the client. Smith's model incorporates the social system and life experience in working with minorities. This is crucial because African Americans have frequently been misunderstood when viewed as separate from their social context (Dilworth-Anderson & McAdoo, 1988; Nobles, 1988).

Counseling as a Healing Force

Healing forces are defined as factors contributing to the physical, mental, or spiritual health of the individual or family. When African Americans have a problem they generally first look within their indigenous support systems; the family, church, black organizations and businesses. If there is a health problem African Americans may use the physician, but if they are without a regular doctor or insurance they may rely more on emergency rooms or walk-in treatment at a clinic (Cheatham, Shelton, & Ray, 1987).

Counseling can teach families and individuals to contend with situational events, strengthen self-esteem, and adopt coping strategies to rebuild strength after a predicament. Counseling with African Americans is facilitated by awareness of the following factors (Copeland, 1983; Barbarin, 1983):

a) An understanding of racism

b) Knowledge of forces that combat stressors and maintain personal strength

    c)   Utilization and knowledge of coping techniques to assist in healing from emotional pain

    d)   Cultural understanding

One of the observations made of the counseling process is that Blacks who enter a mental health setting when geographically surrounded by Whites will invariably discuss racial experiences in that environment. The authors cannot recall any African-American client contact without discussion of their perceptions of the impact of racism. In clinical experience in a predominantly white community and mental health setting serving few African-American clients, racial issues and problems are voluntarily discussed with an ethnic therapist. An advantage of providing an ethnic therapist from a visibly recognizable ethnic group (VREG) is the automatic promotion of the topic of racism. This may occur because the client recognizes skin color that promotes a set of behaviors from society, and feels safe in exploring the issue of race in the therapy environment. A therapist of the same race or ethnicity validates the client's perceptions of the environment because the therapist, although promoting and guiding the healing process, has experienced similar dynamics. Self-disclosure by the therapist of racial situations and experiences can be helpful to the client.

    Critics often say this can lead to "over identification" with the client, but sharing selected racial experiences can have the effect of reducing client distress and offering validation during periods of incongruence when their ideas are invalidated elsewhere. It may help the clients view their own experience in a larger context outside of self and feel more secure. This may promote analytical problem solving or the development of coping strategies to contend with inexpedient and unwanted events. None of the African-American adults in this observation have crossed the therapy door without an acknowledgment of racism. Being able to release the mask a client wears in society has healing effects.

    The schemata depicted in Figure 2 indicates the flow of events during a counseling interaction with African-American persons when race is a factor in addition to the problem stressor. Coping strategies and racial combativeness aid in empowering the individual or family. Racial combativeness is defined as an attitude of challenge to myths or stereotypes that negate the African-American person's self-image or self-esteem. It can be manifested as an internal resolve or a verbal reeducation. Internal resolve involves objective analysis and decision making regarding a problem situation that allows for resolution of the problem. This resolution produces emotional or internal satisfaction. Verbal reeducation can be described as a form of cognitive restructuring. An individual actively articulates and changes his or her perception of the problem through discussion or receipt of new information.

Figure 2
Counseling Process

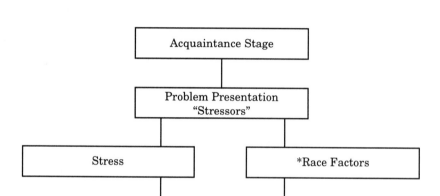

*(Ethnic person differs in counseling interaction due to these components)

The mental health system is often gender based: Societal sex roles teach women to be open, supportive, and receptive and males to be more independent (Gilligan, 1982). Counseling involves embracing someone else's opinion and a degree of dependency. This is contrary behavior for males and particularly African-American males, who may still embrace traditional masculine concepts that reinforce the attitude that others are not to be trusted or embraced for help. In the first author's clinical experience, women are more frequently receptive to counseling. Men come in more frequently at the urging of the spouse or due to divorce or relationship difficulty.

Clients rarely fully embrace all the information imparted by a therapist. Many times much counsel is rejected, but the therapist can continue to repeat a potential solution if thought to be valuable or ask the client to envision ideas that would remedy the situation. Client attitudes influence the therapeutic process and a range of attitudes has been observed in counseling African Americans. Attitudes that impede counseling include:

Limited Help: Clients may have difficulty when they do not wish to engage in self-examination or share feelings. This client may terminate prematurely.

Quick Fix: Clients decide they have found the solution and the therapist believes they are just beginning.

Semi-Voluntary: Clients who are coming at the insistence of someone else and see no point in coming (e.g., marital counseling, to repay a debt).

Dependent: Expects the therapist to do everything, constantly calling for advice and advocacy.

Attitudes that facilitate counseling include:

Resilience Maximized: Client acknowledges problem and takes some responsibility for it. Able to articulate errors they may have made and to entertain new behaviors or cognitions.

Willing to Trust: Client has some *trust* in a few people and is willing to interact and receive feedback regarding his or her own behavior. Willing to acknowledge racial issues but refrains from viewing the situation as global.

Trust is critical to the process of therapy. This has always been an issue for African Americans in mainstream society and suspiciousness in the beginning may be natural. If not adequately addressed, this may negatively influence the counseling process.

Persons who do not recover from maladaptive behavior often exhibit these traits: 1) selfishness and focusing solely on their own perceptions and opinions; 2) an unwillingness to change; 3) lack of a strong sense of direction; 4) lack of understanding of the sociopolitical structure or how oppression occurs—the ethnic person may believe the stereotype "you're so different from the masses of blacks"; 5) procrastinating, waiting for someone else to deliver or define them; and 6) lack of coping strategies or resources.

In clinical practice one who has a receptive attitude to suggestions as opposed to a defensive posture may more readily see improvement in maladaptive symptoms. For example, a client who questions and debates everything the therapist says exhibits distrustful behavior even when matched for race. It is acknowledged that this behavior may be adaptive in cross-cultural interactions. Having a commitment to the process of maintaining appointments and participation in health care are helpful elements. Rarely does a client improve solely because of the therapist's actions; there must be an interactive process that occurs between the therapist and client where the client is challenged to work on his or her issues (Gary, 1985).

To facilitate the healing process a therapist should work to provide these components: trust, camaraderie, knowledge, racial and cultural understanding, advocacy, and self-disclosure (both therapist and client).

Many times, the African-American therapist is trained in practicums to work with white families and no cross-cultural training is given. Rarely is an African-American client available to the therapist in training. Training has often taken the color blind approach, where race is disregarded and universality is emphasized (Hines & Boyd-Franklin, 1982). Many black therapists and psychologists advocate an Afrocentric approach. This approach includes the idea that Blacks are an African people and their behaviors and perceptions must be viewed with this in mind (Jackson & Sears, 1992; Myers, 1988; Nobles, 1987).

It is proposed that therapists wishing to become licensed to work with ethnic persons first indicate substantial knowledge of or experience with the ethnic group. Psychological healing is aided by compassion, support, and an intelligent understanding of the environment. Frequently for minorities, their perspective may be submerged or invalidated by others and reinforcement for ideas is inconsistent in the daily environment. This excludes the all-black environment, which may have different dynamics.

Programs that target oppression and educate the African-American community in prevention principles are called for so that people will not become dysfunctional because they lack the knowledge and use of principles that promote mental health. Prevention principles are defined as strategies or techniques that a person uses in anticipation of a crisis situation. For example, (1) utilizing a method of decision making, (2) developing a list of available resources to diminish stress prior to becoming distressed, or (3) attending an educational group to increase knowledge (e.g., substance abuse). If a person becomes a client, they deserve freedom from the labels and victimization of traditional therapy. Perhaps the *Diagnostic and Statistical Manual* (*DSM-IV*) needs a category of "societal oppression" so that one will not be diagnosed as a patient when one has been a victim. Those who are receptive to the principles of prevention are receptive to healing and even though they may experience a setback they learn from the trauma and advance to perform greater tasks.

The following are clinical case examples of clients who presented for therapy and some suggested healing forces that promote resiliency in African-American families.

Clinical Case Examples

Case 1: African-American female, late 20's, single, professional student.

This client, a medical student, was referred by her physician for stress and difficulty with digestion. A periodic flare up of ulcers occurs with severe pain but the client masks pain because in her words "sickness is weakness." In therapy, she is distressed at her mother's illness and the anxiety that creates.

Church membership in her town is a source of strength and she speaks of frequent attendance. She wishes to connect with a church in the new area. Frequently she states "I don't know how to relax" and that being in control is important. Discussions in treatment center on stressors of racial discrimination and family concerns. Treatment involved relaxation as a primary goal.

Healing forces: Church membership and involvement; Learn relaxation techniques and use on a regular basis; Delegate family responsibilities to other members and relinquish powerbroker position; Commitment to achieve goals; Progression of time in medical school–acknowledge medical school as a stressful process; Support network with other medical students; Counseling (articulate problem, develop a strategy, provide support); Problem Solving Racial Dilemmas/Racial awareness (involves devising traditional and innovative methods to contend with racial barriers which encourage success and/or survival in the environment).

Diagnosis: Adjustment Disorder with Physical Complaints

Sessions: 7 individual

Case 2: Couple, remarried; African-American male, mid 30's; African-American female, late 20's, professional couple.

Both clients have previously been married and are three months into this marriage. Conflict exists over celebration of holidays, money, and ambition. The wife enjoys holidays for family, closeness, relationships, and gifts while the husband ignores holidays and often works. He is self employed, very money oriented and ambitious. She is professional, makes little money, which is okay, but enjoys her career. She feels half of what he owns is hers but he disagrees and says not so, this is his business. He stated that "money is number one and if the relationship detracts from my career, I must let the marriage go." The wife disagrees with much of what her spouse says but never verbalizes disagreement. These issues were not discussed prior to marriage. He suggests divorce, obtaining a prenuptial agreement, and then remarrying. He is disappointed that his wife is not maintaining her attractive appearance as prior to marriage. He insists on her being dressed well to shop at the grocery store. She has not met his family nor has her name been placed on any accounts. She states "I want to share something with you like a joint bank account." They are not sharing anything. It is "his" and "mine" rather than "ours." Both speak of enjoying church membership in the community and met through mutual church attendance. They enjoy the dramatic choir and find it inspirational and energizing. Throughout the ordeal, the wife placed value on regular church attendance and valued church friends' support and the worship service as empowering.

Healing forces: Church participation; Confront conflictual issues; Acceptance of fundamental differences; Acknowledge insufficient information regarding each other and extended family; Rebuild wife's self-esteem; Extended family support (visits, discussion); Adjustment process of divorce; Validation and support in decision making; More focus placed on career (provided stability); Discussion of relationship issues–values (diversion from developing negative thoughts); Reading assignments "Men Who Hate Women and the Women Who Love Them"; Lack of role model for marriage and developing a realistic model; Receptive attitude.

Diagnosis: Adjustment Disorder Unspecified

Sessions: 1 couple, 16 individual. Husband attended only the first session.

Case 3: African-American family. Father, late 40's; mother, early 40's. Five children, ages 16, 15, 10, 9, and 8.

This family sought counseling due to poor communication and excess tension and fighting in the home. In particular, intense discussion occurred between the parents and between the mother and eldest daughter. Resolution was sought to the family conflict. All members attended the first session but the eldest daughter had to attend work and left. The eldest also found some place to go the second session and was offered individual counseling regarding past sexual abuse by an uncle. The marriage was seen as the major issue and marital counseling began. Religion was a strong factor in this family and guided their life stringently. Issues that surfaced: decision-making, feeling supported and cared for, quality time spent together, communication, and forgetting the past. The husband verbalized "I am the head of the family and should make the decisions." The wife agrees but neither feels this is what occurs. The husband did not feel supported in decision making and the wife felt all decisions regarding the children were made by her. The family was given homework assignments to work on their relationship and terminated after 7 sessions.

The eldest daughter attended 14 individual sessions with the goal of establishing her independence from the family and focusing on issues of former child abuse. She states "All I need to do is become independent of my parents and get out of the house and everything will be fine." Extreme behaviors of fighting with the parents verbally and physically were reduced through counseling and moving after high school graduation. The daughter is rebellious toward the family religion which distresses the family.

Healing forces, parents: Clarification of roles and expectations; Acceptance of limitations in marital relationship; Parental flexibility (not forcing but allowing choices); Strong religious involvement, frequent attendance throughout the week and on Sunday. The family lived by their religious doctrine and were disciplined and highly achievement oriented.

Healing forces, daughter: Reduction of extreme behavior; Gained more independence and reduced extremism; Counseling provided a forum to focus on self exploration and goal setting; gaining emotional control; Encourage responsibility—make appointments and keep them; Family acceptance of her rejecting the family religion, desire to discuss in counseling the role of religion in her life.

Diagnosis: Parent-Child Problem

Sessions: 7 family, 14 individual teen

Case 4: African-American male, early 30's; African-American female, late 20's, professional couple.

This couple planned marriage but barriers were always erected by the man. The woman feels the man discusses marriage but never gets specific and feels he is afraid of marriage. He keeps changing the dates. He has previously been married and the woman has never married. They appear to be opposites in many ways, such as she prefers the city, he the spaciousness of the country. They are of the same religion and mention it as a strong family value in both of their extended families. The couple needs assistance in processing their conflict and a decision regarding their future relationship. He is the traditional man and states "My mother stayed home and took care of the children and a wife should stay home and have a career after the children are grown." The woman is a feminist and adamant about having a career. Both are children of physicians, and the woman was impacted by parental divorce; her mother was left penniless and always submerged her needs to the spouse who departed. She feels a career is insurance against this dilemma and verbalizes "I'm scared marriage means losing my independence."

Healing forces: Communication and racial awareness; Called and requested an ethnic therapist for counseling assuming a commonality of belief. Recognition of conflicting racial identity stages between them impacting the relation; Articulate real feelings regarding expectations of relationship and marriage, confronting whether and when to marry; Discussion of compromising—realized they couldn't or were not willing to give up traditional or feminist views; Develop support network: involved move to another geographical area; focus on achievements, careers, and socialization for both individuals.

Diagnosis: Adjustment Disorder Unspecified

Sessions: 5 couple, 14 individual

Case 5: African male, mid 40's, married 15 years, two sons (ages 15 and 8); recent graduate.

This was a crisis intervention case. African man devastated that his wife left and may divorce him and unable to receive gratification from his recent graduation since the spouse left. Coming to counseling was a major decision because he states "therapy is something for weak people." Despite this view, he came because he feared his potential behavior. Experiences symptoms of not sleeping well, slow responses, distraught, angry, and hurt. He became animated if asked about the disagreement between he and his spouse. He states "I will not tolerate another man raising my children and I will take action." Currently taking some medication to help with sleep.

Healing forces: Communication and racial awareness; sought out an ethnic friend to refer him to an ethnic therapist assuming a commonality of belief. Initiating phone contact and counseling session; Need for reassurance and support; Discuss and articulate his emotions to reduce level of anger.

Diagnosis: Marital Problem

Sessions: 1

Case 6: Middle and lower income urban community of Rochester, New York comprised of 50% African Americans, 60% working mothers and 40% working mothers with preschool children.

Female physician who is a member of an historic African American Church in the community encounters repeated crises attempting to find reliable child care. More and more members of the church and community had the same problem. There was inadequate child care for middle and lower income working parents. The church leadership was approached until they agreed to support establishment of a weekday nursery.

Healing forces: Church leadership and community support. The church supported the physician's work to establish a nursery. Church members as well as members of neighboring church and community agencies were drawn into the problem of inadequate child care. Eventually, the weekday nursery becomes the first Head Start eligible child care center in the city. In a few years the nursery grew into a child care center. Low and middle income working parents of the community finally had access to quality childcare for their preschool children, and to after-school care for school age children. Previously, except for private homes, no such service existed.

Case 7: African-American community members of the church and community discuss a growing problem where 2nd, 3rd and 4th grade children exhibit "Third Grade Syndrome" when children's academic performance takes a precipitous drop in Southside Chicago.

> The church assumed leadership of five area neighborhoods to address problems of Third Grade Syndrome and other issues such as: disintegration of public education, violence and negative gang activity exhibited by adolescent and young adult males.
>
> *Healing forces*: The church initiated several programs to address these concerns. The Student Triumvirate Education, Empowerment and Intervention Program (STEEP) is an after-school program combining academic and social services including academic enrichment and mandatory social work interviews. Another program, Building African American Christian Men (BAACM) aims to defuse violent tendencies of Black-on-Black crime and provide a source of nurture and security to offset the lure of gang fellowship and drug addiction.

Mediating Stress in the African-American Community

From these case studies one can see the value placed upon the church and selection of an ethnic therapist in counseling. Assumptions are made that a common belief system exists. Under stressful circumstances, having someone to talk with or provide support can mediate a crisis situation. Mental health outreach in the community should be better linked to indigenous resources. Youth and family centers, churches, and housing developments are likely to be drawing cards for participation in mental health services (Thomas & Dansby, 1985). Church has been an all encompassing institution for Blacks and provides many resources such as leadership and psychosocial support (Gary, 1985; Nobles, 1988; Poole, 1990). Historically, African Americans were grounded in religion and spirituality and these beliefs contribute to the survival skills of Blacks (Pointsett & Russell, 1988; Richardson, 1991). Some select counselors based on religious affiliation (Richardson, 1991). A religious or spiritually connected person is viewed positively as "one who will help." Collaborative relations between clergy and counselors could promote dissemination of health information and reduce the mental health stigma. Simultaneously, counselors may reach larger numbers of people, gain acceptance, and increase their understanding of African-American health issues through church and community linkages. The church is central to healing in the African-American community due to aggregate endorsement and support (Pointsett & Russell, 1988; Richardson, 1991; Solomon, 1990; Thomas & Dansby, 1985). Certain factors aid an individual in healing:

1. Religion (Belief in power of prayer/higher being); Churches are useful for counseling as a familiar and supportive environment and for exploring the context of religion to the individual. A referral system is needed between clergy and therapists. The use of group work and advocacy could be promoted in churches to link health resources to the community. Recognition of the central role of the black church by professionals represents empowerment of the African-American family and could enhance service delivery. The church promotes self-esteem, identity, and strengthens individual and family bonds.

2. Someone to tell their story to who understands what they're experiencing. This would include an understanding of the sociopolitical power structure. Oral tradition (sharing stories generationally) has flourished in African-American families.

3. Access to a support network whether individual, spouse, family, or kin to rely on.

4. Financial resources can buffer the situation (e.g., purchasing power/ownership, fixing one's home, travel/leave nonsupportive environment for more supportive environment).

5. Counseling—obtain information and help with decision making. Process of time and integration of situation with objective information provided from a knowledgeable source.

6. Process emotion: Expression of affect, appropriate interpretation, labeling, and expression of feelings.

7. Attitude of challenge: Requires rejection of societal values that exclude minorities or are in contradiction to the ethnic person's self-esteem.

8. Self-esteem: Strong, positive, internal sense of self is established.

9. Boldness: Take initiative and maintain assertive behavior.

10. Support groups

11. Communication

12. Compromise

Healing can be promoted by collective groups who have oppression in common. Forums or support groups where people can
share their experiences and not feel stigmatized are important.
More group forums on oppression should be organized because group
involvement is often well accepted by minorities. Frequently, intellectual discussion groups flourish, but what they lack is the
additional component of healing from the emotional effects of hurt,
bitterness, depression, or anger. Gary (1985) discusses depression
and black men, citing sociocultural factors as important predictors
of depression. Sociocultural factors such as a support network
(relationships), religious involvement, and community participation may mediate stress.

Financial resources buffer stress because many clients report shopping for purchases such as furniture or jogging clothes
makes them feel better. Stress appears to minimize autonomy and
"having something" and the means (money) to obtain material goods
gives the person a sense of control or empowerment. This may be
why one sees differences in the depression level between unemployed and employed black men, where levels of depression were
lower in employed males (Gary, 1985).

Self-esteem is defined as feelings of self-worth, ranging from
high to low and acts as a buffer—when destructive circumstances
occur the person is able to assess and know what his or her strengths
are to combat the negativity or criticism experienced.

Racial awareness is necessary for ethnic people to prevent
internalization of the flourish of negativism encountered. Rather
than becoming a person who doesn't listen to anyone, it is a fine
balancing act to determine whose guidance the African-American
individual or family can listen to versus avoid.

In addition, when a person is in the minority, there is
strength in possessing a sense of boldness, courage, or assertiveness
to challenge systems that are unjust. Proactive behavior is helpful
because this allows the person to distance his or her reactive behavior (emotion) in order to understand that change is necessary
and action is needed. After processing the emotion (reactionary
behavior) and allowing it to be a temporary state, logical analysis
and proactive behavior may become more useful (Gary, 1985).

In summary, the healing forces in African-American families are as follows:

Healing Forces

Support Networks (Family, Extended Family, Positive Relationships)	Self-Esteem
	Oral Tradition
	Racial Awareness
Religious Involvement	Boldness/Attitude of Challenge
Community Participation	Proactive Behavior
Receptive Attitude	Positive Communication
Financial Resources	Counseling
Achievement/Accomplishment	Compromise

Promoting Healing in the African-American Community

Those who counsel with African-American families should have an awareness of the forces that promote healing. There should be recognition that an African-American individual's heritage differs from a person of Eurocentric background. Recognition would involve a therapist's knowledge of the culture, an awareness of African retentions such as the concept of oral tradition, and knowledge of the impact of values, religion, and oppression in the client's life.

There is great value in matching African-American clients with a therapist of the same race. Many times in this pairing the therapist can divulge to the client what others cannot say and promote the process of trust, which enhances self-disclosure. This is not to disfavor cross-cultural counseling matches, which also have their value. Same-race matches are not always possible due to a lack of ethnic therapists. The supply of ethnic therapists should be increased along with training for mainstream counselors in cultural awareness and sensitivity.

Churches are already an indigenous resource and could be better utilized to promote mental and physical health, and the referral system between clergy and therapists could be improved. Training alternative providers in the church and community could help extend support systems for African-American families because they do not frequently use traditional mental health centers. Ethnic professionals who are called upon to provide services to the church should receive payment for services rendered to acknowledge the value of those services. Some have stated they are expected to volunteer professional service without renumeration and have felt demeaned in the process.

We advocate an increase in knowledge, especially among mental health professionals, of the healing forces used as resources in African-American families. Cultural competence is important and does not occur happenstance. Training programs in counseling may wish to consider licensing or certifying persons for cultural competence in order to promote and ensure the process of healing for African-American families or other ethnic groups.

Where African Americans receive healing is not as important as the experience of strengthening and empowerment. The identification of these resources promotes awareness and healing within the individual, family, and culture.

References

Anderson, J.D. (1988). *The education of Blacks in the South, 1860–1935.* Chapel Hill: University of North Carolina Press.

Baker, F. M. (1987). The Afro-American life cycle: Success, failure, and mental health. *Journal of the National Medical Association, 79,* 625–633.

Barbarin, O. (1983). Coping with ecological transitions by black families: A psychosocial model. *Journal of Community Psychology, 11,* 308–322.

Barrett, L. (1974). African religions in the Americas. In C.E. Lincoln (Ed.), *The black experience in religion* (pp. 311–340). Garden City, NJ: Anchor Press/Doubleday.

Billingsley, A. (1968). *Black families in White America.* New York: Simon & Schuster.

Billingsley, A. (1974). *Black families and the struggle for survival.* New York: Friendship Press.

Cheatham, H.E., Shelton, T.O., & Ray, W.J. (1987). Race, sex, causal attribution and help-seeking behavior. *Journal of College Student Personnel, 27,* 559–568.

Copeland, E.J. (1983). Cross-cultural counseling and psychotherapy: A historical perspective, implications for research and training. *Personnel and Guidance Journal, 62,* 10–15.

Dilworth-Anderson, P., & McAdoo, H.P. (1988). The study of ethnic minority families: Implications for practitioners and policy makers. *Family Relations, 37,* 265–267.

Dodson, J. (1988). Conceptualizations of black families. In H. P. McAdoo (Ed.), *Black families* (2nd ed., pp. 77–90). Newbury Park, CA: Sage.

Gary, L. (1985). Depressive symptoms and black men. *Social Work Research and Abstracts, 21*, 21–29.

Gilligan, C. (1982). *In a different voice.* Cambridge: Harvard University Press.

Helms, J.E. (Ed.). (1990). *Black and white racial identity: Theory, research, and practice.* Westport, CT: Greenwood Press.

Hines, P.M., & Boyd-Franklin, N. (1982). Black families. In M. McGoldrick, J. K. Pearce, & J. Giordano (Eds.), *Ethnicity and family therapy.* New York: The Guilford Press.

Jackson, A.P., & Sears, S.J. (1992). Implications of an Africentric worldview in reducing stress for African American women. *Journal of Counseling and Development, 71*, 184–190.

Jones, B.E., Gray, B.A., & Jospitre, J. (1982). Survey of psychotherapy with black men. *The American Journal of Psychiatry, 139*, 1174–1177.

Kimbro, D., & Hill, N. (1991). *Think and grow rich: A black choice.* New York: Fawcett Columbine.

Lacayo, R. (1989, March). Between two worlds. *Time, 133*, 58–68.

Lincoln, C.E. (Ed.). (1974). *The black experience in religion.* Garden City, NJ: Anchor/Doubleday.

Lincoln, C.E. (1989). The development of black religion in America. In G. Wilmore (Ed.), *African American religious studies* (pp. 5–21). Durham: Duke University Press.

Littlejohn-Blake, S.M., & Darling, C.A. (1993). Understanding the strengths of African American families. *Journal of Black Studies, 23*, 460–471.

McGrath, E., Keita, G.P, Strickland, B.R., & Russo, N.F. (1990). *Women and depression.* Washington, DC: American Psychological Association.

Myers, L.J. (1988). *Understanding an Afrocentric worldview: Introduction to an optimal psychology.* Dubuque, IA: Kendall/Hunt.

Nelsen, H.M., Yokley, R.L., & Nelsen, A.K. (1971). *The black church in America.* New York: Basic Books.

Nobles, W.W. (1988). African-American family life: An instrument of culture. In H. P. McAdoo (Ed.), *Black families* (pp. 44–53). Newbury Park, CA: Sage

Nobles, W.W., Goddard, L.L., Cavil, W.E., & George, P.Y. (1987). *African-American families: Issues, insights, and directions.* Oakland: Black Family Institute.

Parham, T. A. (1989). Cycles of psychological nigrescence. *The Counseling Psychologist, 17*, 187–226.

Peters, M.F., & Massey, G. (1983). Mundane extreme environmental stress in family stress theories: The case of black families in white America. In H. I. McCubbin (Ed.), *Social stress in the family: Advances and developments in family stress therapy research* (pp. 193–218). New York: Haworth.

Pointsett, A., & Russell, A. (1988). Black churches: Can they strengthen the black family? *American Visions, 3*, 9–11.

Poole, T.G. (1990). Black families and the black church: A sociohistorical perspective. In H.E. Cheatham & J.B. Stewart (Eds.), *Black families* (pp. 33–48). New Brunswick, NJ: Transaction.

Ramseur, H.P. (1991). Psychologically healthy black adults. In R.L. Jones (Ed.), *Black psychology* (pp. 353–378). Berkeley: Cobb & Henry.

Richardson. B.L. (1991). Utilizing the resources of the African American church: Strategies for counseling professionals. In C.C. Lee & B. L. Richardson (Eds.), *Multicultural issues in counseling: New approaches to diversity,* Alexandria, VA: American Association for Counseling and Development.

Skinner-Hughes, L. (1992). Managing conflict within the African American family. *The Journal of Christian Education, 49,* 26–27. Nashville: African Methodist Episcopal Church.

Smith, E. J. (1985). Life stress, social support, and mental health issues. *The Counseling Psychologist, 13,* 537–579.

Solomon, B.B. (1990). Counseling black families at inner-city church sites. In H.E. Cheatham & J.B. Stewart (Eds.), *Black families* (pp. 353–372). New Brunswick, NJ: Transaction.

Spaights, E. (1990). The therapeutic implications of working with the black family. *Journal of Instructional Psychology, 17,* 183–189.

Sue, D.W., & Sue, D. (1990). *Counseling the culturally different* (2nd ed.). New York: John Wiley.

Thomas, M.B., & Dansby, P.G. (1985). Black clients: Family structures, therapeutic issues and strengths. *Psychotherapy, 22,* 398–407.

Washington, J.R. Jr. (1989). Folk religion and Negro congregations. In G. Wilmore (Ed.), *African American religious studies* (pp. 53–59). Durham: Duke University Press.

Whaley, A.L. (1993). Self-esteem, cultural identity, and psychosocial adjustment in African American children. *The Journal of Black Psychology, 19,* 406–422.

White, J.L., & Parham, T.A. (1990). *The psychology of Blacks* (2nd ed.). Englewood Cliffs, NJ: Prentice Hall.

Willie, C.V. (1988). *A new look at black families* (3rd ed.). New York: General Hall.

Wilmore, G.S. (1990). *Black religion and black radicalism.* Maryknoll: Orbis Books.

Wimberly, E.P. (1989). Pastoral counseling and the black perspective. In G.S. Wilmore (Ed.), *African American religious studies* (pp. 420–428). Durham: Duke University Press.

Wimberly, E.P. (1991). *African American pastoral care.* Nashville: Abingdon.

Woodson, C.G. (1972). *The history of the Negro church.* Washington, DC: The Associated Publishers.

Chapter 8

The Lack of Prenatal Care in Poor Urban African-American Postpartal Women

A Phenomenological Study

Carol Sue Holtz

Within the United States, the state of Georgia, with 12.4 deaths per 1,000 live births, and the District of Columbia, with 20.7 deaths per 1,000 live births, rank highest in infant mortality rates ("Study Finds," 1993). African-American infant mortality rates in Georgia are 2.3 times higher than the rates for European Americans ("Infant Mortality," 1992). Georgia and other southeastern states lead the nation in infant mortality rates, mainly due to differences in the population distribution. Georgia's overall infant mortality rate reflects a higher proportion of African Americans (27%) than the United States as a whole (12%) (Georgia Department of Human Resources, 1990). In addition, Georgia has a substandard health care delivery system in rural areas and lacks adequate outpatient services and preventive care departments (Hill, 1992).

Inadequate prenatal care is a major problem in Georgia. During the 1980s the use of prenatal care decreased. Only 60% of African-American women and 80% of European-American women received prenatal care in the first trimester of pregnancy.

All states must provide Medicaid coverage for pregnant women and children through age five whose family incomes reach up to 133% of the poverty level (Georgia Department of Human Resources, 1990). Georgia recently increased its rate to 150% of poverty level ("Profiling the Poor," 1992). Georgia also has a new pilot program, Healthy Mothers: Babies Best Start (Maternal and Child Institute, Inc., 1993), a prenatal health care incentive program sponsored by Grady Memorial Hospital, the Atlanta business community, and the Maternal & Child Health Institute, Inc. This free program provides women in Fulton and DeKalb Counties (located within metropolitan Atlanta) with educational information and discounts for goods and services. This program encourages women to start prenatal care early and to continue throughout pregnancy.

Infant mortality data within the metropolitan Atlanta counties of Cobb, DeKalb, and Fulton indicate that African-American women are twice as likely to experience an infant death compared to European-American women. This is primarily due to the increased incidence of low birthweight babies (less than 2,500 grams or 5.5 lbs.) among African-American mothers (Georgia Department of Human Resources, 1990). The purpose of this study was to describe the lived experiences of 15 poor, urban African-American women who received no prenatal care.

Literature Review

All studies reviewed are from data collected from different regions of the United States. Prenatal care utilization is highly associated with the reduction of infant mortality rates (Binkin, Rust, Kam, & Williams, 1988; Hale, 1990; Hill, 1990; Reed, 1986). Ideally, pregnant women should have 13 prenatal visits for a full-term pregnancy, with more visits if health problems occur. The minimum standard is nine visits. Twice the number of African-American mothers, as compared to white mothers, receive late prenatal care or no care at all (David & Collins, 1991; Hale, 1990; Murray & Bernfield, 1988; Zambrana, Dunkel-Schetter, & Scrimshaw, 1991).

Women covered by Medicaid do not obtain prenatal care as early in pregnancy or make as many visits as women with private insurance. The Medicaid process is so time consuming that many women are well into pregnancy before eligibility is established. Furthermore, Medicaid clinics are often overburdened and unable to schedule appointments promptly (Brown, 1988). According to Brown, "There continues to be a lack of parity in access to health care, and the differences in economic levels clearly contribute to the lack of access to health care" (p. 71).

Ropers (1991) and others have reported that some African Americans above the poverty line also have less access to medical care than European Americans (Blendon, Aiken, Freeman, & Corey,

1989; Kleinman & Kessel, 1987; Reed, 1986). Brown (1988) stated that each dollar spent on prenatal care saves $3.38 for long-term care for a surviving, but sickly, low birthweight baby during his/ her first year of life. It is recognized that prenatal care is valuable and cost effective, and yet usage remains low, especially among poor African Americans. African-American women are twice as likely as European-American women to have babies who die within the first year of life (Blendon, Aiken, Freeman, & Corey, 1989; Brown, 1988; David & Collins, 1991; Kempe et al., 1992; Kleinman & Kessel, 1987). Many researchers believe that the ultimate success of efforts to improve pregnancy outcomes depends on ensuring that prenatal care begins in the first trimester and continues regularly throughout pregnancy (Hulsey, Patrick, Alexander, & Ebeling, 1991; Kempe et al., 1992; Moore, Origel, Key, & Resnik, 1986; Murray & Bernfield, 1988; Petitti, Coleman, Binsacca, & Allen, 1990; Zambrana et al., 1991).

Some studies addressing the racial disparity in low birthweight infants found higher rates of maternal high-risk conditions in African-American women, including hypertensive disorders, chorioamnionitis (infection in uterine membranes), chronic urinary tract infections, and sexually transmitted diseases (Kempe et al., 1992; Kleinman & Kessel, 1987). The negative impact of stress resulting from racism, sexism, and social classism greatly contributes to African-Americans' health problems throughout the U.S. (Berg, 1993).

The Georgia Department of Human Resources (1990) reported that preterm births account for two-thirds of African-American infant mortality. The role of prenatal care in the prevention of low birthweight, especially among urban, poor African Americans, is well documented. Low birthweight babies are 40 times more likely than normal weight babies to die in the first four weeks of life. During the 1980s, more than 80,000 infants born in Georgia were low birthweight, weighing between 3 lbs. 5 oz. and 5 lbs. 6 oz. In addition, 15,000 babies born in Georgia were very low birthweight, weighing under 3 lbs. 5 oz. and were at 200 times greater risk than normal weight babies. Many factors associated with low birthweight are often preventable or manageable. These include the lack of adequate and timely prenatal care, malnutrition of the mother, substance abuse by the mother during pregnancy, and other problems such as diabetes, hypertension, and unplanned pregnancy (Georgia Department of Human Resources, 1990).

According to the Healthy People 2000 report by the U.S. Department of Health and Human Services (1992), an expectant mother with no prenatal care is three times more likely to have a low birthweight baby. Despite the importance of early prenatal care in protecting against low birthweight and infant deaths, nearly one of every four pregnant women in the United States receives no care in the first trimester of pregnancy. A disproportionate number of these mothers have low incomes, received less than a high school education, or are very young. Healthy People 2000 (1992, p. 70) reported that in order to substantially improve maternal and infant health by the year 2000:

(1) Infant mortality rates must be reduced to no more than 7 deaths per 1,000 births (a 31% decrease)

(2) Low birthweight must be reduced to no more than 5% of live births (a 28% decrease)

(3) First trimester prenatal care must be increased to at least 90% of live births (an 18% increase)

Research Design

In this exploratory and descriptive study, phenomenological methodology was used. Phenomenology, a theoretical perspective as well as a research methodology, is based on the qualitative research paradigm. Phenomenological research methodology is concerned with the understanding of human beings and the nature of their transactions with themselves and their surroundings. Data are organized non-numerically and interpreted to discover patterns and themes through techniques such as observing, documenting, analyzing, and interpreting attitudes, patterns, and characteristics. Data are recorded in field notes, diaries, and handwritten or taped interviews, often in response to open-ended questions (Burch, 1989; Lincoln & Guba, 1985; Omery, 1983).

This study concerning poor, urban, postpartal women was based on face-to-face audio-taped interviews with 15 participants, using open-ended questions as a guide. Participants were interviewed once in the postpartum hospital setting and again two to four weeks later, in their home environments. Each interview lasted 45 minutes to one hour. The 15 participants met the selection criteria by being African-American, poor urban women who had received no formal prenatal care and had delivered an infant within one to four days prior to entering the study. Subjects were between the ages of 18 and 45 and demonstrated the ability and willingness to communicate openly. The researcher contacted the nursing staff of the various postpartal units of the large metropolitan Atlanta hospital and explained the study. Staff were extremely helpful in supplying names and room numbers of patients who met the study's selection criteria. On some occasions they reviewed the nursing Kardex to obtain names and room numbers of potential participants. After gathering a list of potential participants the researcher went to each potential participant's room, explained the study and invited her to participate. The selection of each participant, who met eligibility criteria, was based on whether the potential participant verbalized an interest in the study and her willingness and ability to be reflective of her feelings and thoughts. The researcher did not reject any of the potential participants for the study, but two women declined participation in the study because they stated they did not want to reveal details of their drug use. After the women were selected and agreed to participate, they were asked to sign an informed consent form. Their home addresses and phone numbers (if available) were obtained and the first interview appointments were made. All participants requested the first interview to begin immediately after signing the consent form.

All mothers in this study were single and received Aid to Families with Dependent Children (AFDC). Most lived in public housing and were unemployed. Some mothers used drugs, alcohol, and tobacco during pregnancy, and many were actively receiving rehabilitation after delivery. Outcomes of the 15 babies born of mothers in this study included: one death, two with intrauterine growth retardation (IUGR) who were low birthweight, one with respiratory distress, one with a fractured mandible acquired from a difficult delivery, two with sepsis (a generalized infection in the blood stream), and eight in good condition.

All audiotapes were transcribed. An ethnographic software package (Ethnograph) was used to convert the transcripts into a format that allowed for the written transcripts to be placed in the left-hand margin of the page and allowed space on the right-hand margin of the page for the coding of the transcripts, line by line. Transcripts were coded first into general categories and again into smaller subcategories.

Findings

Four major reasons for avoiding prenatal care, identified by the author of this study and supported by her doctoral dissertation committee, were identified: (1) Keeping to Myself—My Choice; (2) Keeping to Myself—Not My Choice; (3) Wanting/Needing; and (4)

Making It. Keeping to Myself—My Choice described the numerous reasons why mothers voluntarily remained isolated from doctors and clinics. Keeping to Myself—Not My Choice described mothers who involuntarily kept away from doctors and clinics because of environmental and social forces. Wanting/Needing described many basic unfulfilled needs of high priority in mothers' lives. Making It addressed the positive and often quite creative ways mothers improved their lives, using self-care behaviors and survival techniques.

Theme I. Keeping to Myself—My Choice

Participants stayed away from prenatal clinics by their own choice for five main reasons: (1) It's nobody's business; (2) Hassles with prenatal care; (3) It hurts; (4) It's not worth the trouble; and (5) Worrying about drugs, alcohol, and tobacco.

Nobody's business. Some mothers stated that they wanted no one to know their personal life story. They felt that if they went to a prenatal clinic, others would expect them to reveal facts concerning their personal lives. Many stated, "It's nobody's business," expressing their need to maintain their pride and dignity and revealing that they did not trust the confidentiality of health care providers at the local clinic (sometimes located within only a few blocks of their residence). They believed that others would know their personal situation and gossip about them. Some mothers stated that they already had numerous other small children very close in age, and they would be embarrassed for others to know that they were unable to prevent another pregnancy.

Hassles with the prenatal care. Some mothers perceived that the health care system requires numerous documents, long waits for appointments, and long waits in the health department clinics. Limited availability of prenatal care services in needed locations and an increased number of private practice physicians who will not take Medicaid made access difficult.

It hurts. Some mothers believed that the examination and lab work related to prenatal care include painful procedures that they wished to avoid. One mother had the following remarks concerning her fear of painful procedures:

> I didn't go to the clinic because for one thing, I don't like needles. They keep shooting and shooting those things in your arms to get your blood.

Not worth the trouble. Not all women believe that prenatal care is important and worth the effort; some believe that it is needed only if the woman is ill. Some mothers were unfamiliar with the concept of prenatal care. Others feared the medical procedures. When asked if she believed if prenatal care was beneficial, one mother made the following comment: "Yeah, they check you and things. I honestly, really don't know what they do." Another mother made the following statement:

> I didn't like it at all . . . because they really don't do anything for you. I don't see much sense in going. They don't do nothing for you but weigh you and measure your stomach.

Worrying about drugs, alcohol, and tobacco. Some mothers worried about the legal problems of drug use in pregnancy and the consequences of getting caught, being sent to jail, and losing custody of their children. This theme also included the mothers' concerns about drug, alcohol, and tobacco use in pregnancy and the effects on their babies' health. One woman reported:

> No one in this neighborhood ever goes to the prenatal clinic. But my sister, who lives in another place, went a few times. The clinic is right nearby. Nobody goes 'cause they on drugs and they're afraid to be checked. They don't care about themselves or the baby, but they still be afraid the baby will be taken away.

Theme II. Keeping to Myself—Not My Choice

Some participants avoided prenatal care for reasons that were not within their control. Mothers often felt all alone, perceived danger inside their homes, perceived danger outside their homes, did not have transportation, or did not have anyone to watch their children while they were away.

All alone. Participants who felt all alone reflected a variety of thoughts and feelings. Some mothers had few childhood memories or adult experiences of close family or friendship ties. Others were lonely for adult companionship. Many women stated that they would make it on their own and did not need, want, or expect help from others. Significant others, family, friends, or neighbors did not always provide a sufficient and/or reliable network system. Many mothers had previous disappointing experiences when depending on others, or they recounted tales of other women who had been let down. Some participants agreed that it is better not to expect anything from others than to be let down by unfulfilled expectations. Because of their social isolation, mothers found it very difficult to trust others (such as health care providers) and did not have support or encouragement from friends or family to seek prenatal care.

Some participants had close relationships with family members who did not reside within a convenient commuting distance. Some family or significant others were presently incarcerated, and others had died of various causes, including drug-related violence. Some family and significant others resided near by, but inadequate transportation or previous unsatisfactory relationships prevented a continuation of close ties. Other participants had legal fears related to substance abuse during pregnancy and wished to remain anonymous and hidden from family, friends, and/or legal authorities in order to prevent attention being directed toward themselves. Therefore, they did not get prenatal care. One mother described the following negative experience of being let down by family or friends:

> I hangs by myself. I don't like a lot of crowd. I like to be by myself. It causes a lot of problem when you're with a lot of people. You just can't trust some people. Some people you can trust, some you can't. I don't want to take no chance. I see a lot of people get hurt like that, so I just like to be by myself. I have a friend, she used to stay with me; I got sick and went to the hospital and she took my food stamps and my AFDC check and that's the reason I don't trust nobody and I ain't going to no prenatal clinic.

Danger inside my home. Some mothers were presently living in fear of violent activities inside their home, perpetrated by male significant others (none were married), which caused them to focus on protecting themselves and their children. Obtaining prenatal care for a present pregnancy was given low priority.

Danger outside my home. Other participants were concerned about external neighborhood violence and did not leave their homes often. Many mothers had barred their windows and doors and forbidden their children to play anywhere but within their apartments. One mother described her immediate external environment:

It's a drug area. Lots of people get high all the time. There are shootouts and fights and all that. Every time you look around, you can't even sit out on your front porch. Your child can't play out on the playground because someone's out there smoking crack. You've got to keep to yourself, and keep your kids locked up inside all the time.

No one to watch the kids. Some mothers' lack of child care prevented them from leaving their homes for any length of time. The logistics of making a bus journey to a health clinic, bringing an older infant and other small toddlers, with food, diapers, bottles, and extra clean clothing, was too overwhelming. Some participants lived in areas that were not on a bus line, and the walking distance was too difficult for a pregnant mother with small children. If these women left their homes for a long period of time, the older children coming home from school (some as early as 2:30 PM) would not have anyone to escort them from the school bus or to let them into their homes. The women believed that their neighborhoods were too dangerous for their children to be permitted a house key and after-school independence.

No transportation. Mothers often expressed that their lack of transportation prevented them from traveling to a health clinic to obtain prenatal care. Some did not live near public transportation and/or could not afford the fares.

Theme III. Wanting/Needing

Mothers expressed many unmet basic "wants or needs." They sometimes perceived their unfulfilled wants or needs to be of a higher priority than obtaining prenatal care for their recent pregnancy. Mothers frequently stated that they, at different periods in time, "wanted or needed" one or more of the following: better housing, baby supplies, birth control/sterilization, abortion, treatment for illnesses, good food, a decent job, and drug and alcohol treatment. Mothers living in extreme poverty supported by AFDC, food stamps, public housing, and WIC often did not have enough of the minimum basic needs required for themselves and their children. One mother described her overwhelming problems with public housing,

Twelve people are living here in this apartment, four adults and eight children. My sister and me, we each had our last baby just one week apart. I'm wanting to get into Section 8 housing, but it takes a whole year. I made an application for it. This place is so nasty. They never fix it up. They don't want to do noth'n here. It takes so long to get things fixed. We've lived here for four years and we still don't have heat in the upstairs bedrooms.

Another mother stated the following concerning her need for Pampers. "Well, I don't have no Pampers and no money for them. The only thing I have is just stuff for the baby from the first baby. I didn't know I was going to have her, so soon."

Another mother addressed her unsuccessful and frustrating experience with condom use, and "wanting or needing" a more reliable birth control method.

I used condoms. They was just too old, I think. That's another thing. Somebody needs to tell people if you use old condoms, they could break and then you get pregnant. I used them and I still got pregnant.

One mother had the following remarks about abortion.

I really thought I wouldn't need prenatal care, 'cause back then, I was thinking about getting an abortion. Then I changed my mind, but I never did think about taking up prenatal care. My Momma didn't kill me, so I decided to keep the baby. You never know what might happen to my child, he might come out being a good football player or someth'n.

Another mother made the following comment about abortion.

He wasn't planned. I couldn't take the pills 'cause of my blood pressure, so I didn't have no kind of nothing. So I ain't thinking I could get pregnant right away. All of the sudden I started miss'n my period and I said, 'Gads, I got pregnant!' I was scared to tell the dude that I'm pregnant. I was think'n about having an abortion, but I waited, I waited and waited and waited. I waited too long. I guess I was scared.

Another mother expressed her feelings concerning her lack of employment, which also related to her need for child care.

The government, they always holler'n they want people off welfare. All you got to do is . . . it ain't but one simple answer, provide adequate child care, after school care for the kids who's go'n to school. Include middle school stu-

dents, not necessarily the high school students. Child care
for little kids and for babies; hey, they will have so many
people go'n to work, man there ain't gonna be no jobs left.
I mean, 'cause like I'm used to working, okay, I got a mind,
a serious mind.

Theme IV. Making It

Some mothers in this study used a variety of strategies for "making it." This term refers to all self-care behaviors and survival
techniques in their daily attempts to cope with the oppressions of
racism, classism, and sexism. These women were strong, flexible,
and adaptable, and quite creative in working with or around the
majority culture's social and health care systems. They believed
they were in the process of obtaining their dreams and goals or, as
they said in their own words, "making it." They were coping with
limited resources, such as inadequate housing, small budgets,
external neighborhood violence, internal family violence, and
unplanned pregnancies. They were actively involved in making a
better life for themselves and their children, hoping to attain more
adequate housing in safer neighborhoods, job skills, more education that might lead to higher paying jobs, adequate food and
clothing, and/or a drug- and alcohol-free body. Some women actively participated in job training or education and enrolled in
drug and alcohol treatment centers. Others were improving their
relationships with their children or making their environment safer
by acquiring better housing or fortifying their present location.
Some mothers were involved in daily exercising, making nutritious
meals with low food budgets, and trading child care services with
neighbors.

Summary

The purpose of this study was to describe the lived experiences of
15 poor, urban African-American women who received no prenatal
care. From the data collected, major themes and subcategories
were developed that described the lived experiences of these
mothers.

Most mothers seemed concerned about violence inside and
outside their homes and were struggling daily with inadequate
housing, transportation and babysitting problems, a lack of baby
supplies, and incomplete nutritional knowledge. Many had thought
about obtaining an abortion early in pregnancy and all mothers in

the study wanted either a tubal ligation or Norplant to prevent future pregnancies.

Recommendations

Based on the interview data, the following recommendations can be made.

The positive benefits of prenatal care should be stressed. Public and private radio and TV could be used to make announcements that clearly state specific benefits of prenatal care for both mothers and their babies.

Mothers attending prenatal clinics should be encouraged to give verbal or written evaluations of the facilities as well as the care and attitudes of health care providers, and health care providers should respond to the critiques by making needed changes.

Access to prenatal health care clinics should be improved. All pregnant women needing public transportation funds should be given a free van ride or bus tokens to get to prenatal clinics. Adequate child care services should be provided at all prenatal clinic locations, requiring no reservations.

The milieu of the prenatal care clinic setting should be improved. A special area should be set aside for walk-in prenatal visits. No one should ever be turned away from prenatal care clinics. In-service cultural and class sensitivity programs, which include instructions for addressing the drug and alcohol using pregnant client, should be provided to encourage a more caring, non-threatening, nonpunitive atmosphere. This information should also be incorporated into the program curricula of medical, nursing, and social work schools. Convenient, nutritious, and reasonably priced box lunches might be provided for all mothers and children waiting for prenatal care appointments.

Multiple services at one convenient setting (one-stop shopping) should be provided. Convenient multiple services at prenatal clinics might include the following: (a) nutritional counseling; (b) contraceptive counseling; (c) case workers and social workers available for processing paperwork for Medicaid, WIC, food stamps, and applications for subsidized housing; (d) general psychological counseling and/or drug and alcohol treatment; (e) general prenatal classes, including exercise instruction; (f) used clothing (maternity and all size children's), used toys, baby furniture, and baby care appliances resale shop; and (g) parenting classes teaching infant child care and home safety.

A variety of incentives to encourage mothers to regularly attend all prenatal clinic visits could be initiated. Some examples might include a raffle of baby care items for all mothers attending a prenatal clinic, a daily drawing for free box lunches, and a free infant layette for mothers attending all prenatal care clinic visits.

All of the previously mentioned suggestions need community and corporate financial support to provide the additional costs, but, if one takes into consideration the cost of neonatal intensive care for low birthweight babies, these projects may be real "bargains" in both savings and improving infants' lives. Money spent proactively to increase attendance in prenatal care and decrease use of high-cost infant care would be an excellent investment.

References

Berg, C. (1993, January 28). *Sociodemographic and behavioral characteristics of black and white mothers of very low and normal weight infants in Georgia, 1986–1988.* Paper presented at the meeting of the Community Forum on Children and Families, Atlanta, GA.

Binkin, N., Rust, A., Kam, R., & Williams, R. (1988). Racial differences in neonatal mortality. *American Journal of Diseases of Children, 142,* 434–440.

Blendon, R., Aiken, L., Freeman, H., & Corey, C. (1989). Access to medical care for black and white Americans. *Journal of the American Medical Association, 261,* 278–281.

Brown, S. (1988). *Prenatal care: Reaching mothers, reaching infants.* Washington, DC: National Academy Press.

Burch, R. (1989). On phenomenology and its practices. *Phenomenology and Pedagogy, 7,* 188–217.

David, R., & Collins, J. (1991). Bad outcomes in black babies: Race or racism? *Ethnicity and Disease, 1,* 236–244.

Georgia Department of Human Resources. (1990). *Infant health in Georgia: Progress during the 1980's.* Atlanta, GA: Author.

Hale, C. (1990, January/February). Infant mortality: An American tragedy. *The Black Scholar,* 17–26.

Hill, C. (1992). Reproduction and transformation of health praxis and knowledge among Southern Blacks. In H. Baer & Y. Jones (Eds.), *African Americans in the South* (pp. 34–59). Athens: The University of Georgia Press.

Hill, I. (1990). Improving state medicaid programs for pregnant women and children. *Health Care Financing Review 1990 Annual Supplement,* 75–87.

Hulsey, T., Patrick, C., Alexander, G., & Ebeling, M. (1991). Prenatal care and prematurity: Is there an association in uncomplicated pregnancies? *Birth, 18,* 146–152.

Infant mortality rate is still high in Georgia. (1992, October 22). *Atlanta Journal and Constitution,* p. D4.

Kempe, A., Wise, P., Barkan, S., Sappenfield, W., Sachs, B., Gortamaker, S., Sobol, A., First, L., Pursley, D., Rinehart, H., Kotelchuck, M., Cole, S., Gunter, N., & Stockbauer, J. (1992). Clinical determinants of the racial disparity in very low birth weight. *New England Journal of Medicine, 327,* 969–973.

Kleinman, J., & Kessel, S. (1987). Racial differences in low birth weight. *New England Journal of Medicine, 317,* 749–753.

Lincoln, Y., & Guba, E. (1985). *Naturalistic inquiry.* Beverly Hills, CA: Sage.

Maternal and Child Institute, Inc. (1993). *Healthy mothers: Babies best start.* Atlanta, GA: State of Georgia, Human Resources Department.

Moore, T., Origel, W., Key, T., & Resnik, R. (1986). The perinatal and economic impact of prenatal care in a low-socioeconomic population. *American Journal of Obstetrics and Gynecology, 154,* 29–33.

Murray, J., & Bernfield, M. (1988). The differential effect of prenatal care on the incidence of low birthweight among blacks and whites in a prepaid health care plan. *New England Journal of Medicine, 319,* 1385–1391.

Omery, A. (1983). Phenomenology: A method for nursing research. *Advances in Nursing Science,* 49–63.

Petitti, D., Coleman, C., Binsacca, D., & Allen, B. (1990). Early prenatal care in urban black and white women. *Birth, 17,* 1–5.

Profiling the poor: A litany of social ills. (1992, April 19). *Atlanta Journal and Constitution,* D7.

Reed, W. (1986). Suffer the children: Some effects of racism on the health of black infants. In P. Conrad & R. Kern (Eds.), *The sociology of health and illness: Clinical perspectives* (pp. 272–280). New York: St. Martin's Press.

Ropers, R. (1991). *Persistent poverty.* New York: Plenum.

Study finds Georgia and D.C. lead nation in infant deaths. (1993, January 8). *Atlanta Journal and Constitution,* p. 1.

U.S. Department of Health and Human Services. (1992). *Healthy people 2000.* Boston: Jones & Bartlett Publishers.

Zambrana, R., Dunkel-Schetter, C., & Scrimshaw, S. (1991). Factors which influence the use of prenatal care in low income racial-ethnic women in Los Angeles County. *Journal of Community Health, 16,* 283–295.

II. Family Relationships

Chapter 9

Level of Satisfaction in African-American Marriages
A Preliminary Investigation

Michael E. Connor

Consistent with the pathological, negative orientation approach prevalent in social science research, the literature on marital relationships emphasizes problems in marriage—divorce, working through conflict, separation, mediated settlement, monetary issues, discipline problems, abuse, child custody, etc. One is hard-pressed to find much in the "professional" literature that relates to successful marriages. The studies regarding marital relationships that do exist tend to reflect a "negative orientation," focusing on the timing of divorce, women's perceptions of equity in marriage, differing and divergent directions people take within marriage, and learning to share custody of children after divorce (Ahrons & Rodgers, 1987; Heaton, 1985; Heaton & Albrecht, 1991; Little, 1982; Traupman & Hatfield, 1983). Researchers have even discussed satisfaction in remarriage (Vemer, Coleman, Granong, & Cooper, 1989), yet little has been published on satisfaction in marriage.

Glenn (1991) wrote, "There is no good evidence on the trend in marital success in the United States in recent years. There is of course ample evidence on trends in divorce . . ." (p. 261). He indicated that "the probability of attaining marital success, in a first marriage or at all, has declined in recent years" (p. 268). Glenn felt that Americans have given up on the ideal of marital permanence and thus are less than committed to marriage. Heaton and Albrecht (1991) suggested that many individuals remain in unhappy marriages because they are unaware or fearful of the alternatives.

It is not surprising, therefore, that the tools that social scientists use to assess marriage also have a negative, pathological orientation. There seems to be little need or desire to assess that which makes marriages work. The assumption seems to be that "healthy" families take care of themselves and/or that by studying dysfunctional families, the needs of both functional and dysfunctional families can be determined. Filsinger (1983) discussed several tools researchers use to assess couples. The Spouse Observation Checklist (Weiss & Perry, 1983) is a cognitive-behavioral checklist oriented to clinical work; the Marital Interaction Coding System–III (Weiss & Summers, 1983) uses a complex, rated system in which trained coders observe problem-solving attempts; the Marital Satisfaction Inventory (Snyder, 1983) tries to assess attitudes and beliefs regarding the marital relationship; the Marital Communication Inventory (Schumm, Anderson, & Griffin, 1983) helps counselors assess communication patterns in the marriage; the Dyadic Adjustment Scale (Spanier & Filsinger, 1983) attempts to measure marital adjustment; the Inventory of Marital Conflict (Hudgens, Portner, & Kearney, 1983) attempts to describe and type marital relationships using vignettes depicting common problem areas; the Marital Agendas Protocol (Notarius & Vanzetti, 1983) helps therapists assess a couple's presenting problem; the Family Environment Scale (Moos, 1974) measures the family social environment; the Family Inventory of Life Events and Changes (McCubbin & Patterson, 1983) looks at the impact of life stress on the family; and the Family Adaptability and Cohesion Evaluation Scales (Olson & Portner, 1983) can be used to help diagnose families in difficulty. This is not an exhaustive list, but a representative sample of the tools available.

None of these tools seem to include input from couples who have experienced conflict and "worked through" it. Additionally, none of them seem pertinent to the assessment of marital or relationship strengths. Each seems to imply that by somehow determining the areas of stress, conflict, and problems, marital issues can be resolved. Given the clinical orientation of the assessment devices, this approach is not surprising. One wonders, however, if the approach is somewhat lacking. That is, there may be more value in assessing couples who remain together after many years of marriage, who are reasonably satisfied with their marital relationship, and who acknowledge problematic areas—both past and present. Data suggest that most divorces occur early in marriage

(Bozett & Hanson, 1991) and that second marriages tend to break up during the first four years of the marriage (Visher & Visher, 1983). Thus, researching couples whose marriages have lasted seven years or longer might shed some light on those relationships perceived to be "successful." It is possible that these couples hold the key to understanding the dynamics of working through marital conflict and moving towards marital satisfaction.

Because little or no information was found in the scientific literature regarding marital satisfaction, popular literature was also reviewed. Interestingly, numerous articles were readily available, many with "catchy" titles (e.g., "Mates For Life," "Staying Married," "Happily Ever After," "Keeping Love Alive," "Marriages Made to Last," "The Friendship Factor In Marriage," "How To Stay Married," and "Ties That Bind"). Lauer and Lauer (1985) found that in long-term successful marriages, spouses viewed one another as friends—often best friends. These respondents tended to like one another as people, enjoyed time together, viewed their mate as interesting, saw marriage as a long-term commitment, and desired to work through conflict (learning to communicate was important). Humor was reported as an important personality trait, most subjects reported satisfactory (not perfect) sex lives, and the couples recognized that it was more important to give rather than receive. In short, these couples appeared to be motivated and willing to work toward mutual satisfaction in their relationships. These authors found similar and related results in a later study (Lauer, Lauer, & Kerr, 1990), which surveyed 100 couples who were married at least 45 years. This sample showed high agreement on a variety of issues, including family finances, recreation, religion, affection, sexual relations, goals, household chores, career decisions, major decision making, philosophy of life, friends, and time together. Additionally, the couples reported they were in an intimate relationship with someone they liked and enjoyed being with, they were committed to the relationship and to their partners, and they recognized and appreciated the role of humor.

Yager (1988) emphasizes friendship in marriage—especially after the birth of a child, when stress can be especially high. The couple must set aside time for one another, do things together, share with one another and work as a team. Kantrowitz, Wingert, Gordon, and Michael (1987) emphasize that couples must put forth energy toward building a fulfilling life together. They believe that Americans are currently taking marriage more seriously (other researchers question this, see Glenn, 1991) and they note a drop in the divorce rate in 1986 (4.8 per 1000). According to U.S. News &

World Report, divorce in the United States reached a peak in 1981 when it was 5.3 per 1000. These researchers note that divorce most often occurs four years into the marriage, is highest for childless couples or those with one child and couples who are between 25 and 29 years of age. It is also noted that, contrary to popular belief, the divorce rate does not rise for men in their 40s or 50s (the so-called "mid-life crisis" years). In fact, numerous authors write about the positives of marriages during the mid-life years. For example, Wakin (1985) suggests that marriages during these mid-years are more fulfilling—that the couple can become closer when children leave. He views this time as more peaceful, less demanding with more satisfaction—if the marriage was solid early on.

Curran (1983), writing about middle-class dominant culture families, lists and discusses several "traits of healthy" families. Among these traits are: family members communicate and listen to each other; they affirm and support one another; they respect and trust one another; they maintain a sense of humor and value play; they share leisure time together; they share responsibilities; they have a sense of family, which includes tradition, values, religion, and rituals; and they respect the privacy of each member. Klagsbrun (1985) believes that lasting marital relationships endure and are mutually satisfactory. She asserts that marriages that survive are characterized by: the ability to change and to tolerate change; the ability to live with the unchangeable; the assumption of permanence; trust; a balance of power among the members; enjoyment of one another; a shared history that is valued; and luck. Respondents in Gaylin's study (1991) offered a wide variety of views and opinions regarding what they felt made a marriage work. Learning to compromise, learning to tolerate one's spouse, being compatible, valuing companionship and humor, and working to keep romance alive were mentioned. DeAngelis, Scarf, and Viscott (1992) offered seven "secrets" of successful marriages:

> Understanding the emotional baggage one brings to the marriage;
>
> Recognizing that being in love fades and you must work at love;
>
> Learning to be yourself rather than trying to remake yourself to fit your spouse;
>
> Being aware that men and women communicate differently;

Being aware that when couples fight, they often are not fighting about the real issues;

Recognizing that sex indicates the state of the entire relationship; and

Avoid letting ups and downs of life divide you.

Few of these writers/researchers have included input from minority families/couples in their articles. In fact, as with many areas of social science research, people of color are simply ignored, treated as pathological entities or perceived as dark-skinned white people. Regarding African-American families, the usual focus of social science investigation continues to be on single-parent homes, father absenteeism, delinquency, family violence, low self-esteem, teen pregnancy, school drop-out issues, deprivation, etc. Crohan and Veroff (1989) did look at "dimensions" of marital well-being among white and black newlyweds. They concluded that "happiness" is the major factor as relates to couple satisfaction. They also reported that income is positively related to feelings of competence for Blacks (negatively related for Whites) and that premarital cohabitation is negatively associated with happiness for Blacks but not for Whites. They point out that Whites are more career-minded due to greater opportunity for them and that living together prior to marriage has different meaning for Blacks and Whites. The perception seems to be that what is known about and works for Whites will simply generalize to other populations and that nothing positive can be gleaned from studying black intact families. Obviously this negative approach lacks appeal and relevance for individuals of these populations and for individuals who wish to work with these populations. Specifically as relates to successful African-American marriages, little is found in the scientific literature. Hill (1971) and Smith, Burlew, Mosley, and Whitney (1978) attempt to deal with this issue by looking at black family strengths. They find strong work, achievement, and religious orientation in black families, plus strong kinship bonds and role flexibility.

Magazines that focus on the black community (especially *Essence Magazine*) do occasionally deal with black couples staying together, often with suggestions to overcome or avoid problems. Marshall (1985), for example, acknowledges the impact of racism and economics on black couples and suggested that a couple must commit to each another, work together, and move toward sexual equity. Ray (1988) focuses on financial constraints affecting black couples and realizes that love is not enough, that the couple must learn to work out financial problems, that they need to respect one another and develop skills to negotiate conflict. Pressley (1987) looked at successful two-career black couples and underscores the need for shared roles, the development of decision-making skills, and learning to work together. Hayes (1988) reports that black couples must learn to talk about racism, bigotry, and social pressures they face on and off the job. She also emphasizes learning to listen, discussing important issues (in a loving manner), enjoying sex and intimacy, learning to deal with frustration, and becoming friends.

Pinkney (1993) wrote that the many problems confronted by African-American couples are reflections of life in a racist society and that few vestiges of the original African family system remain. Staples and Johnson (1993) also discuss African marriages and how they were eradicated by Whites during slavery. These authors discuss intergroup tension between women and men, which they see as the legacy of racism. Staples and Johnson note "Black Americans' acceptance of Western forms of marriage is inconsistent with the customs of their African heritage" (p.139). Pinkney (1993) further notes that while problems abound among low socioeconomic status (SES) Blacks, there is a growing middle class that is characterized by "stable family relations" (p. 85). Additionally, he notes "in the vast majority of black families . . . dominance is shared between the mother and the father . . . " (p. 89). Aldridge (1991) reviews selected research on black men and women in relationships and summarizes the qualities that the population feels are important. These include understanding, honesty, warmth, dress, open communication, sharing, respectability, independence, listening skills, proper manners, support, and maturity. She believes that strategies for building and maintaining healthy relationships are crucial for the survival of African Americans. Unfortunately, Staples and Johnson (1993) note that due to the institutional decimation of black males (including the high mortality rate, lack of education and employment opportunities, high incarceration levels—all of which are directly related to the impact of racism and ghetto living), the majority of black women will never marry—thus there will always be a large percentage of incomplete and unstable African-American homes.

The purpose of this preliminary descriptive research is to sample black adults who have been married six years or longer to determine how they perceive their relationship, what they perceive to be the major factors in making their relationships last, and what they believe it takes to make marriages survive. The primary goal is to learn if there are issues this population is successfully confronting that might be shared with other black persons/couples in an attempt to enhance their own marital relationships—present or future.

Subjects

The subjects for this research are African-American men and women who perceive their marriages as stable, who have been married for at least six years, and who are between the ages of 25 and 75. An attempt was made to attract a cross-section of persons who primarily reside in the Greater Los Angeles area.

Questionnaires were given to black colleagues to make available to their associates, to black adults at a large shopping mall, and to black adults at an outdoor concert. Additionally, the media (radio, television, and newspapers) was contacted to help inform listeners, readers, and viewers of the request for married volunteers to participate in this research.

Methodology

After reviewing the tools listed above (page 160) it was determined that none of them was wholly satisfactory in attempting to elicit the type of information desired in this survey. Therefore, a Marriage Questionnaire (MQ) was developed (see Appendix A). This questionnaire elicited some background information, asked the most influential factor in making their marriage work, asked what "element" is most significant in making any marriage work, and requested each respondent to answer twenty-two (22) True-False questions regarding their perception of their marriage.

Additionally, the Marital Satisfaction Inventory (MSI) was given to a number of participants to determine how they would respond to it. Fifty (50) sets of questionnaires (MSI and MQ) were handed or mailed to subjects known to be married six years or longer. Additional packets (46–MQ only) were handed out at an outdoor music festival to black adults who identified themselves as being married six years or more. Some respondents were given more than one packet to give to friends who they thought would participate. Stamped, addressed return envelopes were provided to all participants, along with a cover letter explaining the project, provision for a $5.00 token of appreciation, and a stamped envelope (to be addressed) to receive a copy of the results (see Appendix B).

Additionally, eighteen (18) Marriage Questionnaires were completed at a large shopping mall in the area. An attempt was made to elicit responses from both couples and individuals (when one member of the couple was not present). When these participants felt their spouse would participate, they were provided with a coded questionnaire to take home (along with a stamped addressed envelope in which to return the questionnaire). Relevant questionnaires were numbered in a manner in which a couple (not the specific person) could be identified as being a couple: 1001, 2001; 1002, 2002; 1003, 2003; etc., with numbers beginning with 1 being female and 2 being male. However, it was not necessary that both members of the couple complete the forms in order to participate. Names were not to appear on any forms. Thus, care was taken to mask the identity of all respondents.

In total, one hundred (100) MSI forms and one hundred fourteen (114) MQ forms were dispensed. Half of the forms were given to men and half to women.

Finally, eleven (11) black couples who had been married between 8 and 14 years were interviewed separately in an effort to get some further notion as to what they felt kept their marriages together. The couples were asked four specific questions:

1. What makes for success in marriage?

2. What have you done to keep your marriage together?

3. What are/were some of the problems you confronted and overcame in your marriage?

4. Do black couples face unique issues and challenges in making marriage work?

Both husbands' and wives' responses were recorded. The couples were interviewed separately so as to limit interaction and potential bias of their responses. The couple's interview averaged forty eight (48) minutes.

Results

Of the 50 MSI forms given to women, 29 were returned, and of the 50 MSIs given to men, 26 were returned. Thirty six of 57 women and 32 of 57 men completed the MQ. The completion-return rate was higher for those who were handed the forms than for those who received forms in the mail (or from friends).

Men sampled are older (44.35 versus 40.42), more educated (15.55 years versus 14.96 years), have more children (2.36 versus

2.19), are married slightly longer (16.55 years versus 16.23 years) and report higher combined family income ($62,700 versus $58,500) than women sampled. Interestingly, women tend to rate both self and mate more satisfied in marriage than men rate themselves and their spouse (88% of women rate selves as good or excellent and 84% spouse perception as good or excellent). Black men and women tend to agree on the most influential factors in making

Table 1
Qualities For Success In Own Marriage

Women	Men
1. Communication/Understanding	1. Friendship/Love/Trust
2. Friendship/Love/Trust	2. Communication/Understanding
3. Commitment	3. Commitment
4. Religion	4. Religion
5. Children	5. Children
6. See below*	6. (Sex)

*There was no 6th item for women.

Table 2
Qualities For Success In Marriage In General

Women	Men
1. Friendship/Love/Trust	1. Friendship/Love/Trust
2. Communication/Understanding	2. Communication/Understanding
3. Commitment	3. Commitment
4. Sex	4. Sex
5. Religion	5. Religion
6. See below*	6. (Money)

*There was no 6th item general trend for women.

their own marriages last and on the significant elements that make for lasting marriages in general.

Regarding their own marriages, women rated communication/understanding first and friendship, love, and trust second while men reversed this order. Women and men agreed that commitment to the relationship, religion, and having children were next in order. Men listed sex as sixth (see Table 1).

As relates to significant elements in marriages in general, black men and women also agreed on the elements and the order: friendship, love, and trust; communication/understanding; commitment to the relationship; sex; and religion. Men also listed money (see Table 2).

Additionally, couples' responses were summarized on the twenty-two True-False MQ statements. Answers were grouped into high agreement (90%), moderate agreement (80%), and low agreement (70% and below) categories. Statements with which the couples demonstrated high agreement include:

1. I look forward to getting old with my spouse.
6. We have equal say in how we spend money.
7. We share responsibilities in rearing our children.
9. Our friends believe we have a strong marriage.
21. We enjoy our time together.

Moderate agreement statements include:

3. My mate is easy to talk with.
8. It is easy to make decisions with my spouse.
10. We have a mutually satisfactory sex life.
11. We are financially stable.
13. My mate likes the way I treat him/her.
15. I like the way I treat my mate.
17. We enjoy leisure time together.
22. I prefer to be with my friends (This had a moderate high false rating).

Low agreement statements include:

2. I often say "I love you" to my spouse.
4. My mate thinks I am easy to talk with.
5. We share household responsibilities.

12. We argue about money.

14. I am more responsible than my spouse with the children.

16. We take regular vacations.

18. We take separate vacations.

19. We enjoy an active social life.

20. We have hobbies together.

The MSI indicates couples with low levels of dissatisfaction (that is, they are satisfied). An interesting pattern emerges where the trends for each couple are essentially the same. These couples tend to see themselves as happily married with low levels of global distress. They are moderately satisfied with the amount of understanding and affection expressed by their spouse; they believe they are able to problem solve their differences; they are satisfied with the quality and quantity of leisure time together; they don't disagree about the management of family resources; they are generally satisfied with their mutual sexual lives; they are satisfied with parent-child relationships at home; and there is minimal conflict between the spouses as relates to child rearing. However, a percentage do report histories of unhappy childhoods and/or disharmony in *their* parents' marriages. Also, the role orientation scale is higher for males than females, suggesting shared household responsibilities and decisions—not surprising in black families.

Responses to the interview questions generally concur with the MQ results. The eleven couples believe that marital success is related to learning to live together, to compromise, to adjust, to enjoy one another, and they value friendship, commitment, and love. They indicate that much time, energy, and work (especially in the earlier years) went into the relationship. They continue to do things as a unit and they share household chores (note all the couples were dual-earner households). Primary problems centered around issues of learning to accept one another, issues in living together, money disagreements, and the impact of children. And, these couples were very clear that racism was a problem they had to confront on a daily basis—three of the eleven couples were aware of the resultant stress that problems of racism added to their personal lives—for example, taking the stress out on one another before learning more adaptive ways of dealing with it.

Discussion

The sample selected to participate in this project can be classified as educated, middle-income, and middle-aged with relatively small families (two or more children). In many ways, their perceptions of traits in marital happiness overlap with those presented by Curran (1983), Klagsbrun (1985), Lauer and Lauer (1985; Lauer et al., 1990) in that communication, commitment, love, and trust are valued. However, as with other studies about black couples, there are some important differences. Both of the partners work outside the home, they share in financial decision making, and they share with child-rearing. In this sample, women perceive themselves and their mates as slightly more satisfied with the relationship than men perceive themselves and their mates. Perhaps this slight difference is due to black women being more comfortable with the realities of the relationship (racism, finances, children, self, etc.) or with the men having a greater need/desire to pursue more than what they currently possess. These respondents report looking forward to growing old with their spouse, which can be considered indicative of acceptance and perhaps comfort in the relationship. Interestingly, these people tend to believe they "express" love and affection towards one another (AFC-MSI Scale), but the MQ responses indicate they don't say "I love you" often. I would like to explore this more fully in a follow-up study, which might inquire more directly about how affection is expressed. Perhaps related to this is the MQ response that difficulties exist relative to talking/problem solving together—or perhaps expressed affection means different things to different people.

A few respondents expressed concern about the "intimate" nature of certain questions, primarily dealing with sexuality (an older population) and income (apparently across the age spectrum). A total of seven persons declined to complete the questionnaire citing these issues. This reluctance was anticipated.

These respondents indicate (MQ) they do not have either active social lives or share hobbies in common. This is likely due to the fact that they were very busy with their work, childrearing, and household tasks and they have not prioritized to the extent that these are highly perceived ideas or needs.

The eleven interviewed couples offer additional insight regarding situations confronted in African-American marriages in the United States. These couples all tended to feel communication, commitment, sharing of responsibilities, and friendship are required for marital success. All were very adamant that black couples had to endure far more than white couples to survive (racism, discrimination, dual-worker homes, childrearing in a hostile environment, inappropriate school curriculum for their children, perceived insensitivity on the job from coworkers, ongoing financial constraint, and locating adequate housing with reasonable neighbors were all mentioned, plus the unique problems confronting black men in the U.S.). These couples also talked about the impact of their own families of origin, of religion, and of a belief in marriage and family. The importance of the extended family was very significant in emotionally supporting these couples. Problems confronted and dealt with primarily centered around finances—getting overly extended, credit card management, lack of sound financial planning and displacement of anger—taking frustrations out on one another, which often had to do with problems at the workplace (e.g., failure to get promoted, racial jokes/insensitiveness, perceived powerlessness on the job, etc.). For example, three woman spoke to some extent about younger Whites whom they had trained getting promoted above them.

It is of interest that somehow these subjects figured out what was going on or at least adjusted in a manner such that they seemed to turn to one another for support, strength, and help. It is also of interest that each couple seems to have a social support network (similar to themselves) with whom they interact, socialize, and problem solve. There seems to be a "catharsis" about these social interactions. This social support can be viewed as a logical expansion of the black extended family. Both men and women discussed a small group of close friends with whom they'd had a relationship for many years—often prior to getting married. Apparently, this small group of close friends (sometimes including family members) had matured and developed into important primary relationships that seem to be cherished and valued by both spouses.

Clearly, these "pilot study" couples do not have perfect or problem-free households, but they appear to be motivated and committed to their marital/familial relationships.

In summary, this preliminary descriptive investigation regarding black married men and women yields some interesting results and certain trends, and it suggests direction for future research.

First, contrary to popular literature, these respondents are willing to share information regarding their relationships; they do value, love, and respect one another. They work on communication and are committed to one another and to their marriages. In general, they appear to be well adjusted and satisfied with their mate and marriage, and look forward to growing old together. Families are small, both people work (have careers), they are committed to the relationship, they value communication, and racism has had an impact on their lives.

This population seems to be mature, educated, financially stable, and successful. It is likely that financial stability is a very important variable as relates to marital stability. Clark-Nicolas and Gray-Little (1991) remark that "the connection between economic resources and marital success may be more intricate in black families" (p. 646). They note the lack of resources as a stressor, but when resources are adequate this may facilitate family life. Aldridge (1991) and Staples and Johnson (1993) also make this point. For example, Aldridge writes: "Some social scientists maintain that at the core of the problems in black . . . marital relationship is the perennial difficulty obtaining jobs and adequate incomes necessary for satisfying relationships" (p. 41). And, as Pinkney (1993) notes, these economic difficulties are the result of a racist, bigoted society. One can assume that certain interrelated prerequisites to successful marriage exist: Education—this allows a "stake" in the future, some assurance of a decent job, financial security, and some control over one's destiny; Maturity (age)—suggests the ability to work towards common goals, be comfortable with one's faults and weaknesses (acceptance); Financial stability—the avoidance of the stress of poverty provides a sense of fulfillment, comfortable existence, and time and energy to grow together; and Commitment to the relationship—the desire to stay together, develop patience and understanding and to value the other person.

Finally, these results suggest certain direction for future research that focuses on married black adults.

First, there is an obvious need to increase the sample size, to draw from a larger potential pool, and to subject the results to more rigorous statistical analysis. As relates to California, while it is likely the population will again self-select, it is important that the population be drawn from a wider geographical area throughout the state.

Second, the MSI would be eliminated as it did not offer anything beyond what was obtained with the MQ. Since the MSI is a clinical tool dealing with potential problem areas, it is not surprising it was of limited value with this population. The MQ would be expanded to include more information about how decisions are made, how love/affection is expressed, what are shared duties and responsibilities, and what are future goals. Additionally, a selected group, say, 20% of the respondents, would be interviewed to gain a greater sense of their perceptions and philosophies and issues about married life. The twenty-two (22) True-False questions would be expanded to a Likert-type scale.

Third, the respondents would be asked directly what advice/ insight they would or could offer other black couples as relates to acquiring satisfaction in marriage—especially as relates to financial difficulties, childrearing, the impact of poverty and racism, and household responsibilities.

As relates to dealing with the stress of racism, more information is needed in understanding how these couples are coping. Specifically, an attempt should be made to determine just how these successful black couples deal with issues of racism at home and at work. That is, what are their perceptions of the issues and how are they dealing with them? Additionally, it is of interest to determine what these couples are doing to help their children survive in an often hostile environment. If the "pilot study" couples are similar, it is likely these people acknowledge, confront, and support one another in dealing with racial issues directly, especially those who have been together ten years or longer.

Finally, I do believe the negative orientation to problem solving so pervasive in our society is a problem itself. It is unclear what can be learned to help people solve problems by simply looking at problems. Rather, it seems to make sense to try and look at solutions. As relates to marriages, Pines (1991) encourages couples to focus on the positives rather than the negatives. This doesn't suggest you ignore problems, but rather that you build the relationship on its strengths and use these strengths to solve problems. This certainly seems reasonable!

Appendix A
Marriage Questionnaire

Male____ Female____ Age____ Years Married____
Number of children____ Age of Oldest____ Age of Youngest_____
Religion_____
City of Residence_____ No. of yrs.____ Buying__ Renting__
Occupation_____ No. of yrs. in this line of work_____
Education (yrs.)_____ Combined Family Income_____

Overall, how do you rate your marriage? Excellent__ Good__ Fair__ Poor__
Overall, how do you feel your spouse would rate your marriage?
                              Excellent__ Good__ Fair__ Poor__

What has been the most influential factor in making your marriage last over the years?_____

What element is the most significant in making a marriage survive?_____

_____

circle one

T	F	1. I look forward to getting old with my spouse.
T	F	2. I often say "I love you" to my spouse.
T	F	3. My mate is easy to talk with.
T	F	4. My mate thinks that I am easy to talk with.
T	F	5. We share household responsibilities.
T	F	6. We have equal say in how we spend money.
T	F	7. We share responsibilities in rearing our children.
T	F	8. It is easy to make decisions with my spouse.
T	F	9. Our friends believe we have a strong marriage.
T	F	10. We have a mutually satisfactory sex life.
T	F	11. We are financial stable.
T	F	12. We argue about money.
T	F	13. My mate likes the way I treat him/her.
T	F	14. I am more responsible than my spouse with the children.
T	F	15. I like the way I treat my mate.
T	F	16. We take regular vacations.
T	F	17. We enjoy leisure time together.
T	F	18. We take separate vacations.
T	F	19. We enjoy an active social life.
T	F	20. We have hobbies together.
T	F	21. We enjoy our time together.
T	F	22. I prefer to be with my friends.

Appendix B
Cover Letter

You are probably aware that the divorce rate for Black couples (and others) is very high. In attempting to understand this, research usually looks at negatives—what's wrong with Black men/Black women, etc. I tend to believe this approach is erroneous—that if we want to try and keep marriages together we must study/understand those who have been together for many years. Thus, this research.

Each of you (the couple) is being asked to complete 2 questionnaires—It will take 30–45 minutes of your time. Please *do not* discuss your answers with each other as that will invalidate the procedures.

Each form is identified by a red form number code 10_(female) or 20_(male). This is the *only* identification on the forms—do not write your name anywhere. Please use a black PENCIL to complete the questions.

When both of you have completed the tests, please clip everything together, put inside the enclosed large addressed envelope and put in the mail. I am able to offer you a small token ($5.00/couple) of my appreciation for your time and effort. To receive the money put your name and address on the enclosed envelope and return separately to me. Also, please indicate if you'd like a summary of this study.

I sincerely appreciate and thank you for your help.

Respectfully,

Michael E. Connor, Ph.D.

References

Ahrons, C. R., & Rodgers, R. H. (1987). *Divorced families.* New York: Norton.

Aldridge, D. P. (1991). *Focusing: Black male-female relationships.* Chicago: Third World Press.

Bozett, F.W., & Hanson, S.W. (1991). Cultural change and the future of fatherhood and families. In F.W. Bozett & S.M. Hanson (Eds.), *Fatherhood and families in culture context.* New York: Springer.

Clark-Nicolas, P., & Gray-Little, B. (1991). Effects of economic resources on marital quality for black couples. *Journal of Marriage and the Family, 53*, 645-656.

Crafton, B. (1989). Happily ever after. *Family Circle.* p.168.

Crohan, S. E., & Veroff, J. (1989). Marital well-being among white and black newlyweds. *Journal of Marriage and the Family, 51*, 373–383.

Curran, D. (1983). *Traits of a healthy family.* Minneapolis, MN: Wiston Press.

DeAngelis, B., Scarf, M., & Viscott, D. (1992). 7 secrets of successful marriages. *Relationships, 1*, 3–14.

Filsinger, E. E. (1983). *Marriage and family assessment.* Beverly Hills, CA: Sage.

Gaylin, J. (1991, August). Secrets of marriage. *Parents*, 75–78.

Glenn, N. (1991). The recent trend in marital success in the United States. *Journal of Marriage and the Family 53*, 261–270.

Hayes, J. (1988). Staying married strategies. *Essence Magazine*, p.89.

Heaton, T. B. (1985). The timing of divorce. *Journal of Marriage and the Family, 47*, 631–639.

Heaton, T., & Albrecht, S. (1991). Stable unhappy marriages. *Journal of Marriage and the Family, 53*, 747–758.

Hill, R. B. (1971). *The strengths of black families.* New York: Independent Publisher's Group.

Hudgens, A., Portner, J., & Kearney, M. (1983). Capturing marital dynamics: Clinical use of the inventory of marital conflict. In E.E. Filsinger (Ed.), *Marriage and family assessment.* Beverly Hills, CA: Sage

Kantrowitz, B., Wingert, P., Gordon, J., & Michael, R. (1987, August 24). How to stay married. *Newsweek.*

Klagsbrun, F. (1985). *Married people—Staying together in the age of divorce.* New York: Bantam Books.

Lauer, J., & Lauer, R. (1985, June). Marriages made to last. *Psychology Today.*

Lauer, R. H., Lauer, J. C., & Kerr, S. T. (1990). The long-term marriage: Perceptions of stability and satisfaction. *International Journal of Aging and Human Development, 31*, 189–195.

Little, M. (1982). *Family breakup.* San Francisco: Jossey-Bass.

Marshall, P. (1985, February). Ties that bind. *Essence Magazine.*

McAuliffe, K. (1987). Trends in divorce. *U.S. News and World Report* 102:68.

McCubbin, H.I., & Patterson, J.M. (1983). Stress: The family inventory of life events and changes. In E.E. Filsinger (Ed.), *Marriage and family assessment.* Beverly Hills, CA: Sage.

Moos, R. (1974). *The family environment scale.* Palo Alto, CA: Consulting Psychologists Press.

Notarius, C.I., & Vanzetti, N.A. (1983). Family adaptability and cohesion evaluation scales. In E.E. Filsinger (Ed.), *Marriage and family assessment.* Beverly Hills, CA: Sage.

Olson, D.H., & Portner, J. (1983). Family adaptability and cohesion evaluation scales. In E.E. Filsinger (Ed.), *Marriage and family assessment.* Beverly Hills, CA: Sage.

Pines, A. M. (1991, October/November). When the heat fades: Why do some marriages glow while others flicker out? *Modern Maturity*, 30–34.

Pinkney, A. (1993). *Black Americans* (4th ed.) Englewood Cliffs, NJ: Prentice Hall.

Pressley, P. V. (1987, March). Families that work. *Essence Magazine.*

Ray, E. C. (1988, February). Love is not enough. *Essence Magazine.*

Schumm, W.R., Anderson, S.A., & Griffin, C.L. (1983). The marital communication inventory. In E.E. Filsinger (Ed.), *Marriage and family assessment.* Beverly Hills, CA: Sage.

Smith, W.D., Burlew, A.K., Mosley, M.H., & Whitney, W.M. (1978). *Minority issues in mental health.* Reading, MA: Addison-Wesley.

Snyder, D.K. (1983). Clinical and research applications of the marital satisfaction inventory. In E.E. Filsinger (Ed.), *Marriage and family assessment.* Beverly Hills, CA: Sage.

Spanier, G.B., & Filsinger, E.E. (1983). The dyadic adjustment scale. In E.E. Filsinger (Ed.), *Marriage and family assessment.* Beverly Hills, CA: Sage.

Staples, R., & Johnson, L. B. (1993). *Black families at the crossroads: Challenges and prospects.* San Francisco: Jossey-Bass.

Traupman, J., & Hatfield, E. (1983). How important is marital fairness over the lifespan. *International Journal of Aging and Human Development, 17,* 89–101.

Vemer, E., Coleman, M., Granong, L.H., & Cooper, H. (1989). Marital satisfaction in remarriage: A meta-analysis. *Journal of Marriage and the Family, 51,* 713–725.

Visher, E.B., & Visher, J.S. (1983). *Stepfamily workshop manual.* Towson, MD: Stepfamily Association of America.

Wakin, E. (1985, June). Keeping love alive. *50 Plus.*

Weiss, R.L., & Perry, B.A. (1983). The spouse observation checklist: Development and clinical applications. In E.E. Filsinger (Ed.), *Marriage and family assessment.* Beverly Hills, CA: Sage.

Weiss, R.L., & Summers, K.J. (1983). Marital interaction coding system III. In E.E. Filsinger (Ed.), *Marriage and family assessment.* Beverly Hills, CA: Sage.

Yager, J. (1988, March). The friendship factor in marriage. *American Baby,* 65.

Chapter 10

Variation in Adolescent Pregnancy Status

A National Tri-Ethnic Study

Velma McBride Murry

Adolescent sexual activity has been the topic of great discussion over the past 15 years. What has become apparent is that, in most instances, adolescents' decisions to initiate and continue sexual intercourse, to use contraception, if sexually active, and their method of resolving a pregnancy result from a series of choices. Whether these choices are implicit or explicit, active or passive (Moore & Burt, 1982), approximately 45% of females and 65% of males have engaged in sexual intercourse by age 18. One million become pregnant each year; 300,000 decide to abort. Of those who decide not to have an abortion, 90% decide to keep and raise their babies. Further, distribution of adolescent birth rates by race indicates that, in 1989, births to females ages 15 to 19 represented 190,000 Whites, 140,000 Blacks, and 10,500 to individuals of other racial backgrounds (National Center for Health Statistics, 1989).

In light of these data, continued concern has been expressed about the disproportionate representation of black youth in rates of sexual activity, pregnancy, and childbirth. Available studies indicate that black adolescent females become sexually active younger (Bauman & Udry, 1981; Newcomer & Udry, 1985; Zelnik, Kantner, & Ford, 1981), with average age at sexual onset about 14.4 years (Zabin, Smith, Hirsch, & Hardy, 1986; Zelnik & Shah, 1983). In addition, compared to white adolescents, black girls are more likely to experience pregnancy during adolescence (Henshaw & Van Vort, 1989; National Center for Health Statistics, 1989), are 2.5 times as likely to carry the pregnancy to term, and are 5.5

times as likely to be single mothers (Bumpass & McLanahan, 1987; U.S. Bureau of the Census, 1987). The majority of these studies, however, compare adolescents of color to Whites and are based on the use of unbalanced research designs, with regard to family structure, geographic residence, and socioeconomic status.

In addition, research studies of sexual activity among Hispanic youths were almost nonexistent until the mid-1980s. Recent reports indicate that approximately half of never-married Hispanics age 15–19 have experienced sexual intercourse. Further, Hispanics tend to be older than Blacks, yet younger than Whites, at sexual onset. Although the fertility rates among Hispanic and black adolescents are quite similar, over half of Hispanics are married at the time of first birth (Aneshensel, Fielder, & Becerra, 1989; Brindis, 1992; Darabi, Dryfoos, & Schwartz, 1986).

Recognizing that Hispanics are not a homogeneous group, some within-group investigations have been conducted. Results from a national study (Durant et al., 1990) of Hispanic adolescents living in the United States revealed that a greater proportion of Cubans had experienced sexual intercourse (69%), followed by those of Central/South American (56%), Puerto Rican (40%), and Mexican-American (39%) origins. Average age at sexual onset, across each Hispanic group, was 15.3 years. In terms of adolescent fertility rates, Puerto Ricans had the highest rate of births (62.4 per 1000), followed by Mexican Americans (42 per 1,000), and Cubans (7 per 1,000).

Children having children is problematic for many reasons. First, adolescent childbearing disrupts the sequence of events traditionally associated with adulthood status, such as completing school, having some work experience, marriage, and then childbearing (Hogan & Kitagawa, 1985). Those bearing children "off-time" are confronted with inadequate economic and social resources, limited education, and low-paying jobs, which increases the possibility of relying on public assistance for financial and medical support. Further, having children during adolescence presents numerous complications for their offspring, such as low birthweight and its associated problems (Hayes, 1987).

There are no conclusive solutions to reduce the rate of childbirth to unmarried adolescents, but there is a general consensus that something has to be done. In response to the "adolescent pregnancy epidemic," the National Research Council established a panel to study this phenomenon. After a thorough examination of existing research and programs, this panel recognized the significance of moral, religious, and political questions that surrounded decisions about adolescent pregnancy. Emphasized in their report was the interrelatedness of "youth employment, poverty, poor education, single-parent families and adolescent pregnancy" (Hayes, 1987).

In the quest to encourage adolescents to delay the onset of first sexual intercourse and reduce the number of births to adolescents, little is known about those who are sexually active, but have avoided pregnancy and subsequently childbearing. Such investigations may provide insights into the mechanisms and processes that these females utilize to protect themselves from risk of unplanned pregnancy.

In this chapter, a within-group tri-ethnic study was conducted on a nationally representative sample of black, Hispanic, and white adolescent females who are at high risk for early childbearing because of their sexual histories and life circumstances, but who have nevertheless avoided this life transition. A study of this nature seems important because while many adolescents are engaging in sexual activity and becoming parents at a young age (Hogan & Kitagawa, 1985; Rhodes & Jason, 1990), there are also many who choose not to become mothers at this developmental stage.

This chapter is divided into three sections. A conceptual framework for the present study is discussed in the first section. Supportive empirical findings regarding selected components of that framework are also included in this section. Next, using data obtained from a national probability sample, the conceptual model is empirically tested. The last section includes a brief summary of major findings of the study and suggestions are offered for how our society can be instrumental in preparing adolescents to make responsible sexual decisions. As readers explore the areas discussed in this chapter, they should be reminded that the majority of research on adolescent sexuality is based on nonrepresentative data obtained from low-income Blacks and middle-income Whites, with few investigations on Hispanics, other adolescents of color, or middle-income Blacks.

Theoretical Explanations

Attempting to understanding the sexual decision-making processes of adolescents is a complex phenomenon. According to Franklin (1988), issues related to adolescent sexuality can be best understood by considering the interactions between the individual's characteristics, her environment, and specific aspects of her experiences.

Franklin used a modified version of Bronfenbrenner's (1979) ecological model of human development to explain adolescent sexuality because: (a) it offers a systematic framework for examining this
issue and (b) it stresses the importance of interactions between
characteristics of people and their environments and contends that
the "main effects are in the interactions" (Bronfenbrenner, 1979,
p. 22). This model contains four components operating on the
following levels: *individual*, *family*, *sociocultural*, and *social structural*. The individual level focuses on personal characteristics and
includes historical and background information (Belsky, 1980). The
family level includes an analysis of family characteristics, structure, and dynamics that shape adolescents' decisions about sexual
activity. Sociocultural level of analysis focuses on values and
belief systems that influence individual and family characteristics,
whereas social structural emphasizes the role of major social institutions in shaping adolescents' decisions about sexual behavior
(Franklin, 1988).

Individual

Biological Factors

One common perspective of adolescent sexual activity is that age
at sexual onset is a result of instinctual, biologically driven, sexual
impulses that occur during puberty.

Thus, declining age at first coitus and increased incidence of
pregnancy and childbearing among adolescents can be attributed
to the occurrence of early sexual maturation among today's females. This finding, however, seems to be more germane to white
adolescents (Magnusson, Stattin, & Allen, 1986; Udry, 1979). Similar studies conducted on black youth are inconclusive. For
example, some researchers have suggested that, although Blacks
reach sexual maturity slightly earlier than their white counterparts, biological maturation has little influence on timing of sexual
intercourse (Moore, Simms, & Betsey, 1986). Others report no
significant relationship between age at menarche and early sexual
onset among Blacks (Westney, Jenkins, Butts, & Williams, 1984).
In contrast, based on an examination of black adolescents included
in a nationally representative sample, Leigh and associates (1988),
as well as Murry (1992), found that early sexual maturation was
significantly related to sexual onset among black females. The
significance of pubertal development and sexual activity primarily
among Hispanics has been ignored.

Contraceptive Behavior. Several social and demographic characteristics are related to contraceptive use among adolescents.
These include race, socioeconomic status, family stability, and religiosity. Researchers frequently report that adolescents of color,
Hispanics and Blacks, are less effective contraceptive users compared to their white counterparts (Darabi, Dryfoos, & Schwartz,
1986; Zelnik, Kantner, & Ford, 1981). This difference, however,
seems to disappear when such factors as socioeconomic status and
family stability are taken into account (Hofferth, 1987; Zelnik &
Kantner, 1977). Greater evidence of contraceptive use occurs among
black and white girls with higher socioeconomic status, greater
family stability, and higher levels of religiosity (Zelnik, Kantner, &
Ford, 1981). In fact, results from a within-group comparison of
black adolescents in Chicago revealed that as socioeconomic status
increased the likelihood of these girls having used contraception at
first coitus also increased (Hogan & Kitagawa, 1985). Further,
studies have also shown that when black girls do use contraception, they are more likely to select a prescribed method at first
sexual intercourse. In contrast, their counterparts from other racial backgrounds tend to select less reliable over-the-counter methods (Zelnik, Kantner, & Ford, 1981).

Sexual Knowledge. Going beyond models of factors influencing sexual behavior, a great deal of research has focused on the
role of sexual knowledge about contraception and reproduction on
the sexual activity of adolescents. It has been well documented
that most adolescents have limited and often incorrect information
about contraception and reproduction (Freeman, Rickels, Mudd, &
Huggins, 1982; Zelnik & Kantner, 1977). Inadequate sexual knowledge puts adolescents at risk of pregnancy and sexually transmitted diseases because, more often than not, they believe that they
know what they are doing. On the contrary, results from a national study revealed that less than half of white (43%), black
(17%), and Hispanic (24%) adolescent girls knew the "least" fertile
period in a woman's cycle (Palmer & Murry, 1994). Similar findings were reported by Zelnik and associates over a decade ago
(1981).

Studies evaluating the influence of sexual knowledge on adolescent sexual behavior have been less consistent. Some researchers report that adolescents who are adequately informed about
sexual matters are more likely to delay sexual onset. Further,
those with accurate contraception and reproductive knowledge are
more likely to be effective contraceptive users and tend to be less
vulnerable to unintended pregnancies (Fox, 1980; Murry, 1992;

Scott-Jones & Turner, 1988). Another view is that providing factual knowledge increases curiosity, thereby encouraging sexual experimentation (Rossa, 1983), and there are those who suggest that sexual knowledge neither fosters nor inhibits sexual experimentation among adolescents (Newcomer & Udry, 1985).

Family

Several aspects of the family have been identified as important antecedents of adolescent sexual behavior, including family income, family structure, parental control, and family sexuality socialization (Miller & Jorgensen, 1988; Murry, 1994b).

Family Income. Having middle to high incomes and educated parents appear to place adolescents at less risk of early sexual onset, pregnancy, and motherhood (Forste & Heaton, 1988; Hogan & Kitagawa, 1985; Zelnik, Kantner, & Ford, 1981). One explanation for this finding is that these families tend to place higher value on achievement, thus encouraging their adolescents to delay sexual activities in order to accomplish future goals (Miller & Sneesby, 1988). A second reason is that these adolescents may also see a more direct connection between achievement and employement than other adolescents who do not have educated or employed parents.

Family Structure. Most studies have found single-mother households to be a significant factor in adolescent sexual behavior patterns (Evans, 1987; Grief, 1985; Hogan & Kitagawa, 1985; Moore & Burt, 1982; Zelnik, Kantner, & Ford, 1981). Compared to those in two-parent households, daughters of single mothers appear to be at greater risk of early sexual onset, pregnancy, and childbearing for several reasons. First, their mother's dating practice may enhance the acceptability of sex outside of marriage (Fox, 1980; Moore, Peterson, & Furstenberg, 1986; Newcomer & Udry, 1985). Second, daughters of female-headed families may be given messages that husbands are not essential to raise a family. Father-absent families may also give sons distorted views about raising a family. For instance, sons may receive the message that one does not have to be committed to marriage or childrearing in order to father children (Gibbs, 1992). There are, however, no empirical data to substantiate these explanations.

However, Thornton (1980) and others (Ladner, 1971; McLanahan & Booth, 1991) have suggested that norms are not directly transmitted from parental status. The decreased parental supervision, availability, and guidance, often associated with single-mother households, may explain variations in the sexual behavior of their daughters as compared to those in two-parent households (Hogan & Kitagawa, 1985).

Parental Control. The extent to which the presence and absence of constraint or control affects the sexual behavior of adolescents is unclear. One position maintains that premarital sexual activity occurs when parents have inadequate control over adolescents. It is through parental control that adolescents learn to conform to societal expectations regarding appropriate and inappropriate behavior. Results from several studies have indicated that when parents, specifically Blacks, define limits, supervise their daughters' dating habits, and have open talks about sexual issues, their daughters are more likely to delay sexual onset, pregnancy, and childbearing (Abrahamse, Morrison, & Waite, 1988; Hogan & Kitagawa, 1985; Murry, 1994b; Scott-Jones & Turner, 1988). However, Wilson (1982) and others (Bolton, 1980; Hogan & Kitagawa, 1985; Zelnik et al., 1981) have pointed out that protecting adolescents, particularly urban adolescents, from the negative influences of their environment may be difficult for parents. The task becomes even more difficult for adolescents living in poverty, where more traditional pathways to adulthood status (i.e., employment, independent living arrangements, and marriage) are not readily available.

Using one aspect of parental control, Miller and associates (1986), in their study of white adolescents, found a curvilinear relationship between degree of parental strictness and adolescent sexual activity. That is, parents who are very lenient in imposing rules and restrictions or those using high degree of control tend to have daughters who engage in sexual activity at an earlier age. The lowest level of sexual activity was found among daughters of parents who exercised moderate control.

Family Sexuality Socialization. Because parents and adolescents often do not agree on the level of communication that has taken place, disagreement continues to exist regarding the relationship between family communication about sexual issues and adolescent sexual activity (Newcomer & Udry, 1987; Warren, 1992). Results from one retrospective study revealed that adolescent daughters' perceptions of their parents' attitudes toward sexual involvement and childbearing significantly discriminated between those who were childbearers, sexually active, and virgins (Evans, 1987). Similar findings were reported by Freeman and Rickles (1993) in their attempt to differentiate between urban African-American adolescent females who were never-pregnant, aborters, and mothers.

The family environment, though a major influence on adolescent development, does not act in isolation. One's sociocultural experiences, for example, play an important role in determining sexual attitudes, beliefs, and behaviors.

Sociocultural

Religiosity

Religious institutions transmit numerous messages about sexuality. It has been suggested that religious teachings influence conformity by providing meaning to and defining norms for sexual conduct, thus constraining sexual behavior through fear of institutional sanctions (DeLamater, 1981), particularly among Whites. Empirically, the relationship between church attendance and sexual behavior patterns among adolescents of color has not been well substantiated. Available studies provide some evidence suggesting that black and Hispanic adolescents who attend church frequently are less likely to engage in premarital sexual activities (Durant, Pendergrast, & Seymore, 1990; Murry, 1994a; Zelnik et al., 1981). Moreover, according to Hayes (1987), those who frequently participate in religious services may have stronger social supports to enforce more conservative behavior norms.

However, some researchers have pointed out that highly religious adolescents may actually be more vulnerable to pregnancy and parenting than their nonreligious counterparts. Religious adolescents tend to be more ambivalent about their sexuality and may, therefore, be less inclined to select effective contraceptive methods that require advance planning or a doctor's appointment (Abrahamse, Morrison, & Waite, 1988; Studer & Thornton, 1987; Zelnik, Kantner, & Ford, 1981).

Social Structural

According to Davis (1989), adolescent sexual behavior is socially shaped and is, therefore, an outcome of changes in our modern society. For example, increased divorce rate, greater incidence of children being raised in single-parent households, separation of work and home, urbanization and mobility, increased access to cars, as well as technological advances, have greatly affected the degree to which adolescents' activities are outside direct parental/adult supervision (Beeghley & Sellers, 1986). Decreased parental supervision allows adolescents to plan their social lives, including opportunities to have sex, with greater autonomy.

Employment Opportunities. Labor force participation is often associated with greater independence among adolescents. Some researchers have suggested that adolescents who work more than 15 hours per week are more distant from their parents, tend to have less ambition for college, and are more likely to engage in high-risk behaviors (Mortimer & Finch, 1986; Steinberg, Greenberger, Garduque, & McAuliffe, 1982).

The benefits of employment may outweigh the costs. Having the opportunity to work seems especially important for minority and urban youths. According to Alter (1987), having jobs after school appears to decrease urban adolescents' vulnerability to the pressures of their neighborhood. Moreover, Moore and Werthheimer (1984) have pointed out that a major predictor of fertility rates among minority youth is their perception of decline in future opportunities as a result of early childbearing. According to these researchers, lowest fertility rates occur among adolescents who have the best alternatives to motherhood (e.g., education, employment, and economic independence). Results from a recent investigation also provide support for this finding. Specifically, employed black adolescent females were more likely to delay sexual onset than were those who were unemployed or had never worked (Murry, 1994a). One explanation offered for this finding is that employed adolescents may have more limits placed on their independence and greater regulation of their free time, resulting in fewer opportunities to engage in sexual activities.

Access to Health Care Services. The extent to which various human services and resources are available seems to greatly affect adolescents' decisions regarding reproduction. For example, structural barriers to clinic access are directly associated with adolescents' use of reproductive health care services. Barriers may include transportation problems, inconvenient hours, requirement of parental consent, perception that such services are not confidential or are not geared toward their age group, costs of service, and poor clinic location (Chilman, 1988). In fact, these barriers may explain why many adolescents do not use more effective contraception, do not seek abortions until after the first trimester, or why those who carry pregnancies to full-term wait until 16 to 19 weeks into gestation before seeking prenatal care (Cates, 1980; Hardy & Zabin 1991; Hayes, 1987).

Regardless of the adolescent's decision, being sexually active but successfully avoiding pregnancy seems to suggest that some have the abilities to negotiate the transition to adulthood through pathways others than "off-time" motherhood.

Based on this literature review the following questions were posed and empirically tested:

1. To what extent do individual, family, sociocultural, and social structural factors explain variation in the pregnancy status of black, Hispanic, and white sexually active adolescent females?

2. Within this context, what specific variable(s) accurately predict whether these individuals will be classified as never-pregnant, aborters, or adolescent mothers?

Method

Sample

The data set utilized to test these questions is the 1988 National Survey of Family Growth Cycle VI (NSFG). These data were collected by the National Center for Health Statistics, with a nationally representative sample of females of childbearing age (15–44) living in the United States. Completed interviews were obtained from 8,450 women. NSFG includes an array of highly structured questions about the contraception and pregnancy histories, reproductive knowledge and sex education, sexual activity patterns, and a wide range of social, economic, and family characteristics of women living in the United States.

A total of 3,839 females, 875 Blacks, 363 Hispanics, and 2601 Whites, were selected for this study. The adolescent girls were ages 15–21, unmarried, and did not have children. This age range was selected because the extant data set does not include women younger than age 15. Second, within American society, 21 is the most consistently recognized age at which individuals have adult privileges and responsibilities. Third, the need for advanced education in order to obtain employment delays the time at which individuals *usually* marry or become parents, both symbols of adulthood status in America.

For analytical purposes, subjects were stratified according to pregnancy status. Of the 875 Blacks included in the study, 477 (55%) were never-pregnant, 116 (13%) aborted, and 282 (32%) were mothers. Among Hispanics (n = 363), 259 (71%) were never-pregnant, 63 (17%) aborted, and 41 (12%) were mothers. For Whites

(n = 2621), 2301 (87%) were never-pregnant, 269 (10%) aborted, and 51 (2%) were mothers.

Measures

Pregnancy status was measured in terms of whether respondents had never experienced a pregnancy, were pregnant but aborted, were pregnant and carried first pregnancy to full-term.

Individual factors measured included: (a) educational attainment; (b) current age; (c) age at sexual onset; (d) contraceptive and reproductive knowledge; (e) contraceptive behavior; and (f) self-perception of the adequacy of sex education received

Family factors measured included: (a) family structure; (b) family income; (c) family sexuality socialization; (d) parental control; and (e) mother's educational attainment.

Sociocultural factors measured included: (a) religious affiliation and (b) church attendance.

Social structural factors measured included: (a) access to reproductive health care services and (b) employment status.

Results

In order to examine within-group differences, separate analyses were conducted for each ethnic group. Frequencies, means comparisons, and hierarchical discriminant function analyses were utilized in this investigation. Discriminant function analyses were used to unravel the individual, family, sociocultural, and social structural factors that distinguished adolescents by pregnancy status. Such information will enable us to better focus intervention and educational programs toward identifying factors associated with less sexual risk taking within each ethnic group.

Test for Within-Group Differences

Chi-square and one-way ANOVAs were prepared on the data to test for within-group differences among the selected variables.

Blacks

Results revealed significant differences among the pregnancy status groups in regard to education, family structure, poverty status, mother and daughter's employment status, religious affiliation, church attendance, and parental control. Overall, never-pregnant and aborters completed more years of schooling, were less likely to drop out of school, were more likely to be raised in biologically intact families, were more likely to describe their parents as moderate disciplinarians, had higher reported family income, were more likely to be employed, more likely to have working mothers, less likely to report no religious affiliation, received more education from their parents on the following topics: anatomical and physiological issues, how pregnancy occurs, and sexually transmitted diseases. Although the majority of respondents were of Baptist persuasion, never-pregnant and aborters attended church more frequently than adolescent mothers.

Data on sexual history and experiences of each tri-ethnic group by pregnancy status are included in Table 1. Findings for Blacks indicate that aborters and adolescent mothers reached puberty earlier than never-pregnant. In addition, adolescent mothers initiated sexual intercourse earlier than both never-pregnant and aborters, and aborters were older than adolescent mothers at first pregnancy.

Hispanics

Significant within-group differences were observed on the following variables: age, educational attainment, family income, mother's educational attainment, and mother and adolescent's employment status. Specifically, never-pregnant and aborters tended to be younger, completed more years of schooling, were more likely to live with both biological parents, reported higher family incomes and higher educational attainment for their mothers, and were more likely to report that they, as well as their mothers, worked either part-time or full-time. Other differences noted were that, in contrast to aborters and adolescent mothers, never-pregnant were more likely to describe their parents as moderate disciplinarians. A greater proportion of adolescent mothers and never-pregnants reported having communicated with their parents about sexual issues.

Results of the Hispanic females' sexual history and reproductive behavior are displayed in Table 1. Findings indicate that adolescent mothers reached puberty earlier than the never-pregnant and aborters. Yet, aborters became sexually active earlier than both adolescent mothers and the never-pregnant. Further, aborters were slightly younger than adolescent mothers at first pregnancy.

Table 1
Sexual History and Reproductive Behavior
of Tri-Ethnic Groups by Pregnancy Status

Black	Pregnancy Status		
Variable	Never Pregnant (n=477)	Abortion (n=116)	Mothers (n=282)
[c]Puberty onset (yrs.)	12.7	12.1	12.3
[a]Sexual onset (yrs.)	15.9	15.8	14.7
[a]Age at 1st pregnancy (yrs.)	–	17.0	15.6

Hispanic	Pregnancy Status		
Variable	Never Pregnant (n=259)	Abortion (n=63)	Mothers (n=41)
[c]Puberty onset (yrs.)	12.5	12.2	11.9
[a]Sexual onset (yrs.)	16.5	14.6	15.7
[c]Age at 1st pregnancy (yrs.)	–	16.2	16.9

White	Pregnancy Status		
Variable	Never Pregnant (n=2301)	Abortion (n=269)	Mothers (n=51)
[c]Puberty onset (yrs.)	12.6	12.6	12.6
[a]Sexual onset (yrs.)	16.5	15.4	16.1
[c]Age at 1st pregnancy	–	17.4	17.1

Significant differences between groups (Chi–square and one–way ANOVA tests):
[a]$p<.001$
[b]$p<.01$
[c]$p<.05$

Whites

Within-group comparison of never-pregnant, aborters, and mothers revealed statistically significant differences in education, family structure, poverty status, mother and adolescent employment status, parental control, religious affiliation, and church attendance. More specifically, in contrast to their adolescent mother counterparts, Whites who were never-pregnant and aborters tended to drop out of school less often and consequently completed more years of education. In addition, the never-pregnant and those who aborted were more likely to be raised in biologically intact families, reported higher family incomes, were more likely to report full-time employment for their mothers, less likely to indicate that they had never worked, and attended church more frequently than adolescent mothers. The never-pregnant and adolescent mothers were more likely to describe their parents as moderate disciplinarians.

As noted in Table 1, regardless of pregnancy status, Whites reached puberty, on average, about the same age (12.6 years). Aborters became sexually active earlier than both adolescent mothers and never-pregnants and were older at first pregnancy than adolescent mothers.

Discriminant Function Analysis

A separate discriminant function analysis was conducted on each race/ethnic group to determine the extent to which the study variables accurately distinguish respondents by pregnancy status. The discriminant procedure results in a forecasting function, which is comparable to the F test and the R in a typical multiple regression analysis. The analysis maximized the separation of the designated groups. It is most easily interpreted by an examination of the structure coefficients, which are the correlations between the discriminant function and each study variable. A total of 19 study variables were entered into each model and subjected to a stepwise regression analysis. A stepwise procedure was selected for several reasons. It allows one to identify variables that are superior predictors, thus eliminating weak predictors. In addition, this procedure simplifies the identification properties of common properties among the predictor variables without sacrificing too much classification. Prior probabilities of outcome groups were set at the sample proportion of cases actually falling within each group. The results from this test will be discussed separately for each ethnic group (see Table 2).

Blacks

As shown in Table 2, these variables correctly classified 80% of the cases overall for Blacks, accurately distinguishing 90% of the cases as never-pregnant, 80% of the cases as adolescent mothers, and 38% of the cases as aborters. Within this group, aborters were more difficult to classify than either of the other two groups. Ten variables remained in the final model. The most important predictor of pregnancy status for Blacks was current age. Perception of the adequacy of sex education received was the second strongest predictor, followed by age at sexual onset, dropout rate, pregnancy

Table 2
Stepwise Selection Summary of Discriminant Function Analysis of Pregnancy Status for Tri-Ethnic Groups

Variable[a]	Standardized Discriminant Coefficients[b]
Black Adolescents	
Age	−0.76
Adequacy of sex information	0.46
Age at sexual onset	0.44
Dropout rate	−0.41
Pregnancy education	0.32
Family income	0.31
STDs education	−0.29
Contraception education	−0.26
Access to reproductive health care	−0.24
Contraceptive knowledge	0.21
Significance of model	
Wilks' lambda = .35, p <.001, Eigenvalue = 1.27	
Classification accuracy	
Never pregnant 90.0%, Aborters: 38.0%, Mothers: 80.4%	
Total cases correctly classified: 80.0%	
Hispanic Females	
Education	−1.68
Age at conception	−1.60
Adequacy of sex information	1.60
Age	1.18
Age at sexual onset	0.83
Contraception education	0.75
Employment status	−0.65
Parental control	−0.62
Pregnancy education	0.53
Mother's education	−0.45
Family structure	−0.40
Significance of model	
Wilks' lambda = .001, p<.001, Eigenvalue = 195.55	
Classification accuracy	
Never–pregnant: 100%, Aborters: 81.7%, Mothers: 82.1%	
Total cases correctly classified: 94.8%	

Table 2 (continued)
Stepwise Selection Summary of Discriminant Function
Analysis of Pregnancy Status for Tri–Ethnic Groups

Variable[a]	Standardized Discriminant Coefficients[b]
White Females	
Age at conception	1.21
Age	−0.50
Education	0.47
Dropout rate	0.37
Contraception use at last coitus	0.22
Employment status	−0.20
Age at sexual onset	−.16
Pregnancy education	.15
Significance of model	
Wilks' lambda = 0.005, p<.0001, Eigenvalue = 136.56	
Classification accuracy	
Never–pregnant: 100%, Aborters: 100%, Mothers: 84.0%	
Total cases correctly classified: 99.7%	

[a]Variables are ordered as selected in stepwise procedure.
[b]Variables included reached significance at p ≤.05.

education from parents, poverty status, STD and contraception education from parents and access to reproductive health care. Contraceptive knowledge, though significant, provided the least amount of power to the discriminating function.

Hispanics

The final model correctly classified 95% of the cases overall for Hispanics. In terms of specific classification, the selected variables correctly distinguishing 100% of those who were never-pregnant, 82% of aborters, and 82% of adolescent mothers. Eleven variables remained in the final model. Education was the most important factor distinguishing the three groups, followed by age at conception, self-perception of the adequacy of sex information received, current age, age at sexual onset, contraception education from parents, employment opportunities, parental control, pregnancy education from parents, and mother's education. Family structure was the last variable entered into the model, suggesting little contribution in classifying the three groups (see Table 2).

Whites

Whites correctly classified 100% of the cases overall for the eight variables remaining in the final model. Classification by specific pregnancy status revealed that 100% of the never-pregnant and aborters were correctly classified and 84% of adolescent mothers. The main contributor to the discriminant function was age at conception, followed by current age, education, school dropout rate, contraception use at last coitus, employment opportunities, age at sexual onset, and pregnancy education from parents.

Discussion

This study attempted to enhance our understanding of factors that decrease sexually active adolescents' vulnerability to early pregnancy and childbearing. In addition, emphasis was devoted to differentiating between those who have successfully avoided pregnancy from those who have become pregnant and aborted, and those who became pregnant and decided to keep and raise their child. Several patterns emerged from this investigation. Although it is commonly assumed that the majority of sexually active adolescent girls have become pregnant, results from the present study revealed that regardless of ethnicity, more than half of a nationally representative sample of black, Hispanic, and white adolescent girls had successfully avoided pregnancy. A second pattern observed was the limited proportion of girls in each ethnic group that had obtained an abortion. Although national statistics show that approximately 45% of pregnant adolescents decide to abort, results from the present study reflect the following rates: Hispanics (17%), followed by Blacks (13%), and Whites (10%). Inconsistent findings may be attributed to several factors. First, separate statistics are often not reported by race/ethnicity. Second, few studies have specifically examined pregnancy resolution among Hispanics. Third, most studies compare non-whites to Whites, without distinguishing non-Whites according to race/ethnicity (Murry, 1994a). Finally, when race and ethnicity are considered, comparative studies on Blacks and Whites have shown no statistical differences in the proportion of pregnancies ended by abortion (Children's Defense Fund, 1988; Hayes, 1987; Henshaw & Van Vort, 1989; Voydanoff & Donnelly, 1990).

An examination of within-group differences shows that the proportion of females who had become adolescent mothers was greater among Blacks than Hispanics and Whites. The ratio imbalance of adolescent mothers among Blacks may be a function of family income status. Specifically, a major proportion of Blacks in general, and black adolescent mothers specifically, reported incomes at or below poverty. The relationship between poverty and adolescent pregnancy and childbearing has been well documented. Living in poverty places adolescents at greater risk of early pregnancy and childbearing because poor families are more likely to be single-parent headed, creating conditions for reduced parental supervision of adolescents' dating activities. "This autonomy provides more opportunities for sexual initiation and activity" (Voydanoff & Donnelly, 1990, p. 29). In addition, being poor also increases the likelihood that adolescents will have fewer opportunities to move into adulthood status through more socially acceptable pathways, such as advanced education, employment, marriage, and then having children (Abrahamse et al., 1988). This finding suggests the need to improve the financial well-being of poor families as efforts are undertaken to combat unplanned pregnancy and childbirths to adolescents.

A fourth general pattern that emerged in this study was related to the final discriminant function models. The models appear to be a "better" fit for classifying the pregnancy status of Whites and Hispanics than for Blacks. In fact, using the selected study variables resulted in correctly classifying from 95% to 100% of the Hispanics and Whites, compared to approximately 80% of the cases for Blacks. Overall, the analyses were somewhat less accurate at predicting the group status of aborters who were Black. This may have occurred because abortion is a much rarer event than never being pregnant or adolescent motherhood among Blacks (Zelnik, Kantner, & Ford, 1981). At the same time, these findings may imply greater similarity between Blacks who successfully avoid pregnancy and those who abort. In fact, results from the classification procedure show that 52% of those who aborted were misclassified as never-pregnant. The inability to differentiate between these two groups also may have occurred because when a pregnant adolescent aborts, she appears to be quite similar to her counterpart who has never been pregnant (Freeman & Rickels, 1993; Zabin, Hirsch, & Emerson, 1989). The similarity between black aborters and never-pregnants warrants further investigation.

Finally, it seems important to highlight that, although successfully avoiding motherhood, the majority of these tri-ethnic girls, were *not* taking precautions to protect themselves from sexually transmitted diseases. This behavior can have deadly consequences. The spread of HIV cases among adolescents is probably more common than is recognized. Parents, educators, the media, and medical practitioners can no longer ignore dealing with issues of feelings and relationships in counseling, teaching, and advising adolescents about sexuality. Rather than taking the position that adolescents should be encouraged to "just say no," more initiatives need to be taken to educate adolescents to effectively protect themselves from STDs. Further, encouraging our youth to "wait until you are married to have sex" is not working. The latest survey figures indicate that the majority of adolescents have already engaged in sexual intercourse by the time they complete high school (Centers for Disease Control, 1992; Forrest & Singh, 1990).

Predicting whether sexually active Blacks will successfully avoid pregnancy, abort, if pregnancy occurs, or become adolescent mothers appears to be related to a combination of individual, family, and social structural factors. Knowing the adolescent's current age was the most important discriminating factor. Determining just *why* age emerged as such a powerful predictor goes beyond the scope of these data. One plausible explanation is that age may indirectly reflect a number of factors. For example, never-pregnant and aborters, though younger than adolescent mothers, were older at sexual onset. Further, being older at the time of sexual onset may also have given these girls more time to mature emotionally and cognitively. Thus they may have had greater ability to anticipate consequences and weigh the future costs and outcome of their behavior. In fact, most research suggests that sometime during adolescence young people reach a level of cognitive development needed to fully comprehend the risks they are taking (Rodman, Lewis, & Griffith, 1984). In addition, age at sexual onset plays an integral role in adolescents' decisions regarding contraceptive use. Older sexually active teens are more likely to be effective contraceptive users and are more likely to use low-risk methods (i.e., birth control pills) (Jones & Philliber, 1983; Murry, 1994a). In fact, when data from the present study are examined for contraceptive use patterns, sexually active, never-pregnant girls were more likely to report using a method at first and last coitus.

The ability to make informed and rational decisions regarding one's sexuality has also been associated with exposure to sexuality information. Although the role of parental sexuality socialization in adolescent sexual behavior is inconclusive, results from the present study provide support for those suggesting that parental discussion about topics related to sexually transmitted diseases and how pregnancy occurs appear to have encouraged black adolescents to avoid pregnancy and childbirth (Fox, 1980; Scott-Jones & Turner, 1990). Findings from the present study also point to the significance of reproductive health care services in discriminating Blacks by pregnancy status. For example, in contrast to aborters, never-pregnants and adolescent mothers were less likely to have obtained a medical (reproductive) check up within the past year. According to Brazzell and Acock (1988), as well as Henshaw and Silverman (1988), adolescents who abort tend to have greater access to medically safe clinics. In fact, aborters in the present study tended to select a wider range of medical services than the other two groups.

Based on variables included in the final discriminant model, individual, family, and social structural factors emerged as important predictors of Hispanic females' vulnerability to pregnancy and adolescent motherhood. The data reflect clear distinction between never-pregnants, aborters, and adolescent mothers. Educational aspirations and employment opportunities played a major role in their decision to prevent an unplanned pregnancy. The relationship between academic career and employment aspirations and sexual risk taking has been reported in previous studies on non-Hispanic youth (Hayes, 1987; Miller & Sneesby, 1988; Hogan & Kitagawa, 1985). Results from one study revealed that sexually active adolescents who indicated that having a baby would impede or interfere with their desire to obtain a college education or training beyond high school were more proactive in either preventing a pregnancy or having an abortion if a pregnancy occurred (Freeman & Rickels, 1993).

Having a job after school also seems to encourage delayed adolescent motherhood among Hispanics. Employed youth may be less at risk because there is less "free" time to socialize, thus allowing less time to engage in sexual activity (Alter, 1987). Or educational and occupational aspirations may reflect adolescents' perception of the opportunity structure. Thus being employed may symbolize the channels for future career opportunity, particularly for low-income youth, in lieu of childbearing.

Family-based sexuality socialization was also an important discriminant among Hispanics. It was interesting to note that Hispanic adolescent mothers and never-pregnants were just as likely to have communicated with their parents about how pregnancy occurred. At the same time, having such information had greater influence on the sexual decisions of the never-pregnant. It seems important to mention, however, that the present data do not allow one to determine the timing or purpose of these discussions. It is possible, for example, that parents did not begin these conversations until they discovered that their daughters were sexually active or already pregnant (Thornburg, 1985).

Findings also provide support for the importance of parental control in reducing adolescents' vulnerability to unplanned pregnancy. Available data on white youths show that adolescents are at less risk if their parents exercise moderate control (Miller, McCoy, Olson, & Wallace, 1986). Contrary to this finding, being subjected to a high degree of parental control appears to have reduced their daughters' risk of pregnancy and childbearing. For example, of the three groups, Hispanic never-pregnants were more likely to describe their parents as "very strict." The extent to which parental control affects the sexual behavior of adolescents is unclear. This finding, however, suggests the need to consider the significance of ethnicity/race in unraveling the relationship between parental control and sexual risk taking among adolescent females.

Another noteworthy finding was the high dropout rate among Hispanic aborters. The causal direction of this relationship is unclear. At the same time, this finding may indirectly imply that these girls had lower educational aspirations or were having problems with school. Further, "some adolescents may lower their aspirations and leave school after becoming pregnant" (Voydanoff & Donnelly, 1990, p. 58). Several studies have shown greater likelihood of pregnancy occurring among adolescent females under these circumstances (Dawson, 1986; Hogan & Kitagawa, 1985; Moore, Sims, & Betsey, 1986). This finding further suggested the interrelatedness of academic performance and adolescent pregnancy.

Finally, having relatively well-educated mothers seemed to protect sexually active Hispanic females from becoming pregnant. This finding is consistent with several other studies (Furstenberg, Brooks-Gunn, & Morgan, 1987; Miller & Sneesby, 1988). Although most studies have shown that mother's education is a powerful inhibitor of early sexual onset, Zabin and Hayward (1993) also found that higher parental educational attainment reduces the chances of unplanned pregnancy among their sexually active daughters. Parent's education symbolizes not only academic training, but also may reflect parent's income level and neighborhood quality, as well as perceptions and expectations for the future. Taken together, the differences noted here seem to reflect resource availability. Those with the greatest amount of resources are fundamentally different from those without, in terms of confronting problems, future goals, and opportunities, all of which have been associated with adolescent females' sexual experiences, regardless of race/ethnicity.

Although few studies have considered within-group differences among Whites, results identify specific factors that "best" discriminate between never-pregnants, aborters, and adolescent mothers. The variables are, primarily, individually based, with pregnancy education from parents being the only family-based factor that emerged in the final model. Similar to their black counterparts, current age was the most important factor predicting the likelihood that sexually active Whites will successfully avoid pregnancy and subsequently adolescent motherhood. As stated earlier, the association between age and pregnancy status is unclear. One plausible explanation for this link is that the never-pregnant, though about the same age at interview as the other two groups, may have been older at sexual onset. The significance of age at sexual onset and pregnancy risk has been well documented. Delaying the onset until late adolescence and beyond increases the probability of safer sexual practices among adolescents, in terms of effective and consistent use of contraception (Hogan & Kitagawa, 1985; Moore, Sims, & Betsey, 1988; Murry, 1994a).

A similar pattern for dropout rates, employment status, and adolescent pregnancy status observed among Blacks and Hispanics also occurred among Whites. Never-pregnant Whites were less likely to drop out of school and more likely to be employed full-time. This finding may be a reflection of the never-pregnants' future educational goals and viewing an unplanned pregnancy and possible birth as a "serious impediment to their life goals" (Voydanoff & Donnelly, 1990, p. 58). In addition, the link may be a function of their own mothers' educational attainment and employment status. Mothers of never-pregnants were more likely to work full-time and had completed more years of schooling than the mothers of either of the other two groups. Further examination of the relationship between education and employment goals and sexual behavior of white adolescents is warranted, given the economic climate of the United States and predictions for job opportunities during the 21st century.

Conclusions

Given that the majority of adolescents are sexually active by the time they graduate high school (Hayes, 1987), rather than continuing to determine *why* adolescents are having sex, attention should be devoted to assisting them in making responsible decisions that place them at less risk of pregnancy and "off-time" motherhood. Such information may be garnered by conducting more in-depth investigations on those who are sexually active but have successfully avoided pregnancy. To date, limited attention has been given to this subgroup of adolescents. The present study was an attempt to increase the knowledge base about these individuals. One of the important conclusions from this study is that sexually active adolescents are more likely to avoid pregnancy when they have access to resources that provide opportunities for youth to obtain adulthood status through more traditional pathways, as well as avenues to prevent unplanned pregnancies and "off-time" motherhood.

References

Abrahamse, A. F., Morrison, P. A., & Waite, C. J. (1988). Teenagers' willingness to consider single parenthood: Who is at greater risk? *Family Planning Perspectives, 20,* 13–18.

Alter, C. F. (1987). Preventing family dependency. *Society, 24,* 12–16.

Aneshensel, C. S., Fielder, E. V., & Becerra, R. M. (1989). Fertility and fertility-related behavior among Mexican-American and non-Hispanic white females. *Journal of Health and Social Behavior, 30,* 56–76.

Bauman, K., & Udry, J. R. (1981). Subjective expected utility and adolescent sexual behavior. *Adolescence, 14,* 527–538.

Beeghley, L., & Sellers, C. (1986). Adolescents and sex: A structural theory of premarital sex in the United States. *Deviant Behavior, 7,* 313–336.

Belsky, J. (1980). Child maltreatment: An ecological analysis. *American Psychologist, 5,* 320–335.

Bolton, F. G., Jr. (1980). *The pregnant adolescent: Problems of premature parenthood.* Beverly Hills, CA: Sage.

Brazzell, J. F., & Acock, A. C. (1988). Influences of attitudes, significant others, and aspirations on how adolescents intend to resolve a premarital pregnancy. *Journal of Marriage and the Family, 50,* 413–425.

Brindis, C. (1992). Adolescent pregnancy prevention for Hispanic youth: The role of schools, families, and communities. *Journal of School Health, 62,* 345–351.

Bronfenbrenner, U. (1979). *The ecology of human development.* Cambridge, MA: Harvard University Press.

Bumpass, L. L., & McLanahan, S. (1987). Social background, not race, conditions for black premarital childbearing. *Family Planning Perspectives, 19*, 219–220.

Cates, W., Jr. (1980). Adolescent abortions in the United States. *Journal of Adolescent Health Care, 1*, 18–25.

Children's Defense Fund. (1988). *Teenage pregnancy: An advocate's guide to the numbers.* Washington, DC: Author.

Chilman, C. S. (1988). Never-married, single, adolescent parents. In C. S. Chilman, E. W. Nunnally, & F. M. Cox (Eds.), *Variant family form* (pp. 17–37). Newbury Park, CA: Sage.

Centers for Disease Control. (1992). Sexual behavior among high school students. *Morbidity and Mortality Weekly Report, 40*, 882–885.

Darabi, K. F., Dryfoos, J., & Schwartz, D. (1986). Hispanic adolescent fertility. *Hispanic Journal of Behavioral Sciences, 8*, 157–171.

Davis, R. (1989). Teenage pregnancy: A theoretical analysis of a social problem. *Adolescence, 93*, 19–28.

Dawson, D.A. (1986). Effects of sex education on adolescents' behavior. *Family Planning Perspectives, 18*, 162-170.

DeLamater, J. (1981). The social control of sexuality. *Annual Review of Sociology, 7*, 263–290.

Durant, R. H., Pendergrast, R., & Seymore, C. (1990). Sexual behavior among Hispanic female adolescents in the United States. *Pediatrics, 85*, 1051–1058.

Evans, R. C. (1987). Adolescent sexual activity, pregnancy, and childbearing: Attitudes of significant others as risk factors. *Child and Youth Services, 9*, 75–93.

Forrest, J.D., & Singh, S. (1990). The sexual and reproductive behavior of American women: 1982–1988. *Family Planning Perspective, 22*, 206–214.

Forste, R. T., & Heaton, T. B. (1988). Initiation of sexual activity among female adolescents. *Youth and Society, 19*, 250–268.

Fox, G. L. (1980). The mother-adolescent daughter relationship as a sexual socialization structure: A research review. *Family Relations, 29*, 21–28.

Franklin, D. L. (1988). Race, class, and adolescent pregnancy: An ecological analysis. *American Journal of Orthopsychiatry, 58*, 339–354.

Freeman, E. W., & Rickels, K. (1993). *Early childbearing: Perspectives of black adolescents on pregnancy, abortion, and childbearing.* Newbury Park, CA: Sage.

Freeman, E. W., Rickels, K., Mudd, E. B., & Huggins, G. R. (1982). Never-pregnant adolescents and family planning programs: Contraception continuation and pregnancy risk. *American Journal of Public Health, 72*, 815–822.

Furstenberg, F.F. Jr., Brooks-Gunn, J., & Morgan, S.P. (1987). Adolescent mothers and their children in later life. *Family Planning Perspectives, 19, 142-151.*

Gibbs, J. T. (1992). The social context of teenage pregnancy and parenting in the black community: Implications for public policy. In M. K. Rosenheim & M. F. Testa (Eds.), *Early parenthood and coming of age in the 1990's.* New Brunswick, NJ: Rutgers University Press.

Grief, G. (1985). Children and housework in the single father family. *Family Relations, 34*, 353–357.

Hardy, J. B., & Zabin, L. S. (1991). *Adolescent pregnancy in an urban environment: Issues, programs, and evaluation.* Washington, DC: The Urban Institute Press.

Hayes, C. (1987). *Risking the future: Adolescent sexuality, pregnancy, and childbearing* (Vol. 1). Washington, DC: National Academy Press.

Henshaw, S. K., & Silverman, J. (1988). The characteristics and prior contraceptive use of U.S. abortion patients. *Family Planning Perspectives, 20,* 158-168.

Henshaw, S. K., & Van Vort, J. (1989). Teenage abortion, birth, and pregnancy statistics: An update. *Family Planning Perspectives, 21,* 84–88.

Hofferth, S. L. (1987). Factors affecting initiation of sexual intercourse. In S. L. Hofferth & C. D. Hayes (Eds.), *Risking the future: Adolescent sexuality, pregnancy and childbearing* (Vol. 2, pp. 7–35). Washington, DC: National Academy Press.

Hogan, D. P., & Kitagawa, E. M. (1985). The impact of social status, family structure, and neighborhood on the fertility of black adolescents. *American Journal of Sociology, 19,* 825–855.

Jones, J., & Philliber, S. (1983). Sexually active but not pregnant: A comparison of teens who risk and teens who plan. *Journal of Youth and Adolescence, 12,* 235–251.

Ladner, J. A. (1971). *Tomorrow's tomorrow: The black woman.* Garden City, NJ: Doubleday.

Leigh, G. K., Weddle, K., & Loewen, I. R. (1988). Analysis of timing of transition to sexual intercourse for black adolescent females. *Journal of Adolescent Research, 3,* 333–345.

Magnusson, D., Stattin, H., & Allen, V. L. (1986). Differential maturation among girls and its relation to social adjustment in a longitudinal perspective. In D. L. Featherman & R. M. Lerner (Eds.), *Lifespan development* (Vol. 7). New York: Academic Press.

McLanahan, S., & Booth, K. (1991). Mother-only families: Problems, prospects, and politics. In A. Booth (Ed.), *Contemporary families: Looking forward, looking back.* Minneapolis: National Council on Family Relations.

Miller, B. C., & Jorgensen, S. R. (1988). Adolescent fertility-related behavior and its family linkages. In D. Klein & J. Aldous (Eds.), *Social stress and family development.* New York: Guilford Press.

Miller, B. C., McCoy, J. K., Olson, T. D., & Wallace, C. M. (1986). Parental discipline and control attempts in relation to adolescent sexual attitudes and behavior. *Journal of Marriage and the Family, 48,* 503–512.

Miller, B. C., & Sneesby, K. R. (1988). Educational correlates of adolescents' sexual attitudes and behavior. *Journal of Youth and Adolescence, 17,* 521–530.

Moore, K., Simms, M. C., & Betsey, C. L. (1986). *Choice and circumstance.* New Brunswick, NJ: Transaction Books.

Moore, K. A., & Burt, M. R. (1982). *Private crisis, public cost.* Washington, DC: Urban Institute Press.

Moore, K. A., Peterson, J. L., & Furstenberg, F. F. (1986). Parental attitudes and the occurrence of early sexual activity. *Journal of Marriage and the Family, 48,* 777– 782.

Moore, K. A., & Werthheimer, R. F. (1984). Teenage childbearing and welfare: Prevention and ameliorative strategies. *Family Planning Perspectives, 16,* 285–291.

Mortimer, J., & Finch, M. (1986). The effects of part-time work on adolescent self-concept and achievement. In P. Borman & J. Reisman (Eds.), *Becoming a worker.* Norwood, NJ: Ablex.

Murry, V. M. (1992). Sexual career paths of black adolescent females: A study of socioeconomic status and other life experiences. *Journal of Adolescent Research, 7,* 4–27.

Murry, V. M. (1994a). Black adolescent females: A comparison of early versus late coital initiators. *Family Relations, 43,* 342–348.

Murry, V. M. (1994b). Socio-historical study of African American adolescent females sexuality: Timing of first coitus 1950 through 1980. In R. Staples (Ed.), *The black family: Essays and studies* (pp. 52–65). Belmont, CA: Wadsworth.

National Center for Health Statistics. (1989). *Trends in teenage childbearing: United States 1970–81.* Series 21, No. 41, Hyattsville, MD: United States Department of Health and Human Services.

Newcomer, S. F., & Udry, J. R. (1985). Parent-child communication and adolescent sexual behavior. *Family Planning Perspectives, 17:* 169–174.

Palmer, J. T., & Murry, V. M. (1994). *Sexual knowledge and sexual behavior: Tri-ethnic comparison of black, Hispanic, and white adolescents.* Unpublished manuscript.

Rhodes, J. E., & Jason, L. A. (1990). A social-stress model of substance abuse. *Journal of Consulting and Clinical Psychology, 58,* 395–401.

Rodman, H., Lewis, S. H., & Griffith, S B. (1984). *The sexual rights of adolescents: Competence, vulnerability, and parental control.* New York: Columbia University Press.

Rossa, M. W. (1983). A comparative study of pregnant teenagers, parenting attitudes, and knowledge about sexual and child development. *Journal of Youth and Adolescence, 12,* 213–223.

Scott-Jones, D., & Turner, S. L. (1988). Sex education, contraceptives and reproductive knowledge, and contraceptive use among black adolescent females. *Journal of Adolescent Research, 3,* 171–187.

Steinburg, L., Greenberger, E., Garduque, L., & McAuliffe, S. (1982). Adolescents in the labor force: Some costs and benefits to schooling and learning. *Education and Policy Analysis, 4,* 363–372.

Studer, M., & Thornton, A. (1987). Adolescent religiosity and contraceptive usage. *Journal of Marriage and the Family, 49,* 117–128.

Thornburg, H.D. (1985). Adolescents' sources of information about sex. *Journal of School Health, 51,* 274-277.

Thornton, A. (1980). The difference between first generation fertility and economic status of second generation fertility. *Population and Environment, 3,* 51–72.

Udry, R. (1979). Age at menarche, at first intercourse, and at first pregnancy. *Journal of Biosocial Science, 11,* 433–441.

U.S. Bureau of the Census. (1987). *Statistical abstract of the United States: 1986* (107th ed., No. 84). Washington, DC: U. S. Government Printing Office.

Voydanoff, P., & Donnelly, B. W. (1990). *Adolescent sexuality and pregnancy.* Newbury Park, CA: Sage.

Warren, C. (1992). Perspectives on international sex practices and American family sex communication relevant to teenage sexual behavior in the United States. *Health Communication, 4,* 121-136.

Westney, O. E, Jenkins, R. R., Butts, J. D., & Williams, I. (1984). Sexual development and behavior in black adolescents. *Adolescence, 9,* 557–568.

Wilson, W.J. (1982). Inner-city dislocations. *Society, 21,* 80-86.

Zabin, L.S., & Hayward, S.C. (1993). *Adolescent sexual behavior and childbearing.* Newbury Park, CA: Sage.

Zabin, L. S., Hirsch, M. B., & Emerson, M. R. (1989). When urban adolescents choose abortion: Effects on education, psychological and subsequent pregnancy. *Family Planning Perspectives, 21,* 248–255.

Zabin, L. S., Smith, E. A., Hirsch, M. B., & Hardy, J. B. (1986). Ages of physical maturation and first intercourse in black teenage males and females. *Demography, 23,* 595–605.

Zelnik, M., Kantner, J. F. (1977). Sexual and contraceptive experiences of young unmarried women in the United States, 1971 and 1976. *Family Planning Perspectives, 9,* 55–71.

Zelnik, M., Kantner, J. F., & Ford, K. (1981). *Sex and pregnancy in adolescence.* Beverly Hills, CA: Sage.

Zelnik, M., & Shah, F. K. (1983). First intercourse among young Americans. *Family Planning Perspectives, 2,* 64–70.

Chapter 11

"Being There"

The Perception of Fatherhood Among a Group of African-American Adolescent Fathers

William D. Allen and William J. Doherty

The life experiences of adolescent mothers and the outcomes for their children are important social concerns that continue to be well researched (Furstenberg, Brooks-Gunn, & Morgan, 1987; Hofferth & Hayes, 1987). Most of the remedial educational and employment programs addressing adolescent parenting focus on the needs of the adolescent mother and her child (Dunston, Hall, & Thorne-Henderson, 1987). However, compared to adolescent motherhood, relatively little is known about adolescent fatherhood despite increased scholarship during the past decade (Connor, 1988; Elster & Lamb, 1986; Freeman, 1989; Hendricks, 1983; Robinson, 1988b; Sullivan, 1986).

Much of this recent work presents demographic and statistical information about young fathers and their behavior (Battle, 1988; Parke & Neville, 1987). There has been less research into the more subjective aspects of adolescent fatherhood. In order to understand adolescent fatherhood in its proper context, the quantitative and qualitative aspects of these young men's experiences must be integrated. Empirical (Robinson, 1988a) and anecdotal (Dash, 1989) evidence suggests that many adolescent fathers value fatherhood as a significant component of their self-identity. These adolescents cite fatherhood as a salient role that provides a unique sense of purpose to their lives. The authors of this chapter pursued a number of questions regarding adolescent fatherhood: What do adolescent fathers mean when they use the term "fatherhood"? Does it refer solely to the biological role in parenthood, or does it reflect some of the broader social and cultural expectations of fathers in contemporary American society? How do adolescent fathers develop their perceptions of fatherhood? Are these perceptions reflected in their actual paternal behavior?

To begin to answer these questions, the researchers interviewed a group of ten African-American adolescent fathers. To gain a clearer understanding of what being a father meant to these adolescents, the researchers asked them to discuss their perceptions of fatherhood and their opinions on how these perceptions arose. The potential influence that the perception of fatherhood had on their conduct as fathers was explored. Finally, the possibility was considered that building on these adolescents' strengths might provide a useful approach for improving their life experiences as well as those of their natal partners and children.

Conceptual Frameworks

The current study is grounded in the theory known as symbolic interactionism. This conceptual framework focuses on the connection between symbols and the interactions that define and maintain these symbols. Symbolic interactionism encompasses a broad range of theoretical principles and empirical approaches (LaRossa & Reitzes, 1993). This study was guided by the three fundamental principles of symbolic interaction suggested by Blumer (1969):

(1) People act on the basis of the meanings that things have for them.

(2) Meanings emerge through social interactions.

(3) Meanings are managed through an interpretive process.

Symbolic interaction provides a powerful tool for discerning the meaning of fatherhood among adolescent fathers. The principles outlined above help to clarify the experiences and behaviors of these young men. In a study of prospective adolescent fathers, Westney, Cole, and Munford (1986) cited the work of Carl Rogers and his emphasis on the link between self-perception and behavior. They suggested that given this link, "It could be assumed that the degree to which the prospective father perceives himself as a father would influence his behavior [in that role]." The concepts of identity and role (LaRossa & Reitzes, 1993) are also important to our discussion of the term "fatherhood." How adolescent fathers think of themselves and how they see themselves reflected in society are important influences on the roles they take with their natal partners and children. These roles were believed to be based upon:

(1) Modeling the behavior of their own fathers and other significant men in their lives.

(2) Their subjective sense of being "fathered" or of not being "fathered," in the sense of being parented by a significant male in their lives.

(3) The current depiction of fathers in society and their perceived role(s) in the family.

(4) Their perception and evaluation of the performance of African-Americans as fathers.

This study also uses two concepts from human ecology theory (Bubolz & Sontag, 1993). One of these concepts, the interdependence of people and their environments, suggests that both human and environmental factors interact to determine the course and quality of these young fathers' lives (Westney, Brabble, & Edwards, 1988). A second concept, the ability (or inability) of people to exert control over their environments, is related to the first. It suggests that the transition to parenthood for young fathers is heavily influenced by the environment in which the pregnancy, birth, and neonatal experiences occur. Social service, governmental, and legal institutions often combine to minimize adolescent fathers' ability to play supportive roles in the lives of their families.

The belief in the importance of context in understanding the experience of adolescent fathers led to the consideration of the social contexts of the subjects' perceptions (McAdoo, 1993). It is impossible to understand either the antecedents or the consequences of adolescent fatherhood without incorporating the social, ethnic, and historic context in which these young men live. The analysis sought to avoid minimizing possible socioeconomic influences on the young men in the sample, as well as cultural factors that mediate the impact of those influences on them and their families (Allen, 1982). One of the concerns was the ability to make meaningful distinctions between subjects primarily on the basis of ethnicity. This was a major consideration in the decision to focus the present study on African-American adolescent fathers.

The major findings of this exploratory study emerged from the empirical process rather than from a priori hypotheses. Thus, the process was not begun with a set of experimental statements to be proved or disproved. However, Blumer's three principles coupled with a review of the literature on adolescent fathers suggested what might be found. It was suspected that the subjects' perceptions of fatherhood would affect their paternal behavior. It was also expected that these perceptions would emerge from social interactions with other family members and peers. Finally, it was thought that the interplay of the young men's perceptions and their paternal behavior would demonstrate a continual process of redefinition and mutual influence.

Background

Adolescent fathers are said to be responsible for 116,000 live births annually (Barth, Claycomb, & Loomis, 1988), though this figure may be conservative as 65% of birth certificates for adolescent mothers under age twenty fail to indicate a father (Smollar & Ooms, 1987). Although many of the fathers and mothers are similar in age, not all fathers of babies born to adolescent mothers are themselves adolescents. Precise estimates of the number of adolescent fathers are difficult to ascertain because of the relatively low avowal rate of paternity by adolescent males (Wattenberg, 1990) and the social stigma attached to early childbearing.

In the introduction to their descriptive study of adolescent fathers, Barret and Robinson (1982) stated that "adolescent fathers are both under-researched and clinically under-served." The limited understanding of adolescent fathers and their needs reflects a lack of coverage by many disciplines, including the family social sciences. A recent issue of *Family Relations* (October, 1991) focusing on "Adolescent Pregnancy and Parenting" did not include any articles on adolescent fatherhood.

Several explanations have been presented for the gap in the literature. Traditionally, childbearing and childrearing issues have been associated with women. For this reason, adolescent parenthood has been conceptualized as a female issue, hence the relative wealth of research on adolescent mothers. Historically, the tendency has been to portray adolescent fathers as villains, worthless victimizers who were primarily interested in sexual self-gratification (Young, 1954; Vincent, 1956). These portrayals were more reflective of social values about teen pregnancy and parenting than the actual experience of adolescent fathers. The legacy of such portrayals and the stigma associated with them is one of the reasons adolescent fathers have remained such a mystery in the literature (Battle, 1988).

Many researchers have found adolescent fathers elusive and difficult to reach (Barret & Robinson, 1982; Christmon, 1990a; Robinson, 1988b). Young fathers often deny paternity or are purposefully not named by the mothers (Hardy, Duggan, Masnyk, & Pearson, 1989). At least one study has also documented lower levels of trust in some fathers versus non-fathers (McCoy & Tyler, 1985). Given the negative portrayal of adolescent parents in the media, it should not be surprising that most adolescents are reluctant to be associated with such images.

Several methodological problems have added to the current lack of understanding of adolescent fatherhood (Robinson, 1988b). The use of inferential rather than direct methods of study leaves researchers vulnerable to accepting the perspective of adolescent mothers, who often have relationship problems with the adolescent fathers in question. Similarly, asking adults who were adolescent fathers to recollect their experiences may rely too much on perspectives that have subsequently been affected by unrelated influences. Even the term "adolescent father" has not always been well defined, with some researchers applying it to men in their twenties who happen to be natal partners with women in their teens.

Of major concern are studies that combine subjects from different ethnic groups with little or no analysis of ethnicity's contribution to observed differences in the behavior and attitudes of subjects. The literature reflects little analysis of the influence that ethnicity has on which young men become involved with their children and the degree of that involvement. This is surprising, since there is good evidence that ethnic differences have an impact on adolescent fathers' preferences regarding pregnancy resolution (Marsiglio, 1989; Redmond, 1985). Ethnicity is an important factor in differing rates of pregnancy termination among ethnic groups (Zelnik, Kantner, & Ford, 1981). Since African-American adolescents are much more likely than European Americans to encourage their partners to continue pregnancies and take them to term, they are disproportionately more likely to become adolescent fathers as a result of those pregnancies. However, this fact has tended to be lost when ethnicity is reduced to being a "risk factor" associated with becoming an adolescent father (Marsiglio, 1987; Robbins, Kaplan, & Martin, 1985.)

In one study, young African-American men were found to be more likely to have been responsible for a non-marital birth than European Americans, but much less likely to be living with the child. Although this researcher does not state categorically that this reflects ethnically based attitudes about out-of-wedlock births or living arrangements, one might conclude from the discussion of these findings that in general, young African-American men do not value fatherhood or family as highly as their counterparts in other ethnic groups. The authors of this chapter believe a more probable alternative hypothesis is that the conflict between strong convictions about responsibility to family and weak ability to fulfill those responsibilities drove these young fathers out of relationships and away from their children (Connor, 1988; Wilson, 1987).

Ethnicity, removed from its sociopolitical context, may be a poor predictor for risk of becoming an adolescent father (Howell & Frese, 1982; Taborn, 1988). Other factors such as peer attitudes towards sexuality, family structure and history regarding early childrearing, and ethnocultural socialization may interact to promote adolescent fatherhood as a salient option for some African-American adolescents (Christmon, 1990b; Hogan & Kitagawa, 1985). Such interactions may also help researchers understand ethnic differences in paternal involvement among adolescent fathers (Parke & Neville, 1987; Sullivan, 1986). Indeed, studies on adolescent mothers have shown that African-American adolescent mothers report higher levels of father participation than European Americans (Danziger & Radin, 1990; Farber, 1990).

One of the strongest influences on an adolescent father's involvement with his family is his access to and success in the world of employment (Redmond, 1985). Adolescent fathers who have jobs have been found to be more involved in their children's lives than those without steady employment or who are chronically unemployed (Danziger & Radin, 1990). This supports the work of Wilson (1987) and others, who pointed to the lack of jobs and employment opportunity as fostering a sense of frustration in fathers. Since providing for the economic and material needs of their families is a significant part of a father's role (Comer, 1989; Taylor, Leashore, & Toliver, 1988), one might expect that the historical lack of employment for teenagers (particularly African-American males) is potentially devastating to their attempts at fulfilling paternal responsibilities. Not only is lack of employment a major source of concern (Elster & Panzarine, 1983), but adolescent fathers are frustrated that the lack of employment often prevents them from meeting their paternal aspirations (Marsiglio, 1989).

Adolescent fathers have both direct and indirect effects on their children (Furstenberg, 1976; Lamb & Elster, 1985; Rivara, Sweeney, & Henderson, 1986; Vaz, Smolen, & Miller, 1983). Examples of direct effects might include providing food, clothing, and disposable diapers for the children. Examples of indirect effects are the adolescent father's emotional and economic support to the mother. Paternal support often enables her to better cope with the demands of childrearing, which benefits the child indirectly. There is increasing evidence that adolescent fathers want to be (and in fact are) involved with their "procreated" families (Klinman, Sanders, Rosen, & Longo, 1986; Robinson & Barret, 1986).

The fact that many adolescent fathers do not live with either their natal partners or their children does not preclude the possibility of their having a positive effect on both (Kahn & Bolton, 1986; Furstenberg, 1976). Most adolescent fathers typically maintain some level of involvement with their children (Rivara, Sweeney, & Henderson, 1986), although there is evidence that the level of such involvement appears to decrease over time, particularly among fathers who do not marry their children's mothers (Furstenberg, Brooks-Gunn, & Morgan, 1987). Perhaps this is because although many adolescent fathers show a keen interest in participating in the upbringing of their children, these young men are caught in a developmental dilemma. As one theorist indicated, "The cognitive and emotional capacities most essential to empathic, mature parenting are likely to be those least available to adolescent boys still engaged in struggles around separation from their own parents" (Applegate, 1988).

The adolescent father's perception of fatherhood may be a primary influence on his performance in that role (Westney, Cole, & Munford, 1986). Remarkably little attention has been focused on this subjective aspect of adolescent fatherhood. Several researchers have approached the issue by posing such questions as "How do you feel about becoming a father out-of-wedlock?" or "Do you think that this pregnancy will affect your life?" (e.g., Hendricks & Montgomery, 1983). There have also been attempts to determine the possible relationship between the adolescent father's self-image and his willingness to be involved with the mother and child (Hendricks & Montgomery, 1983; Robinson & Barret, 1987). Looking specifically at parental responsibility, Christmon (1990a) found that the assumption of parental responsibility was more influenced by the adolescent father's own self-image and role expectations than by those of his partner or his parents. Also, adolescents who had good self-images (defined as a well-developed sense of himself and his potential in his environment) seemed better prepared to negotiate complex developmental tasks more typical of young adulthood (such as fatherhood).

Christmon's work on paternal perceptions is similar to the present study in that both explored the adolescent father's perception of himself as a father, and both interviewed small, nonrepresentative samples of African Americans. Caparulo and London (1981) also conducted face-to-face interviews, although they interviewed adolescent couples (as opposed to just the fathers). They explored the impact that adolescent fathers had on their partners and the father-mother-infant relationship. They found that the adolescent fathers in their study had a "dramatic" influence on their natal partners, and that these young men took their paternal responsibility very seriously.

Methods

Ten African-American adolescent males from a metropolitan area (Minneapolis-Saint Paul, MN) participated in this study. Given the social stigma attached to early parenthood, many of the participants in the study might never have openly discussed their experiences as fathers. It was also suspected that most of these young men's abilities to express themselves through conversation might be better than either their reading or writing skills. Standardized questionnaires or surveys seemed less efficient methods for exploring the meaning of fatherhood than a more flexible, personal approach, such as in-depth interviews. It was felt that such interviews could retrieve more of the rich nuances of their lives. They might also facilitate the inclusion of unexpected material that emerged during the course of each interview.

As noted earlier, one of the reasons for limiting the sample to African-American adolescent fathers was that meaningful comparisons between ethnic groups (particularly when based on such a small sample) would be inadvisable. The investigators also agreed with others who have found that much of the research including African-American adolescents as subjects reflects ethnocentric biases in both research design and interpretation of results (McKenry, Everett, Ramseur, & Carter, 1989; Wilkinson, 1987). As the principal investigator was African American, the authors hoped to limit the effects of such bias, although it was realized that ethnicity alone would not guarantee his ability to accurately record, interpret, or present the experiences of the adolescent fathers. In a broader sense, exploring this particular issue provided the potential for mutual benefit as a result of the research process (Boss, 1987). While the researchers increased their understanding of the experience of adolescent fatherhood, the participants increased their understanding of their paternal aspirations by discussing these ideals explicitly (Dilworth-Anderson & McAdoo, 1988).

The Participants

For the purposes of this study, an "adolescent father" was defined as a male, biological parent between the ages of 15 and 19. The terms "father," "mother," and "child" refer to the participant, his natal partner, and their child, respectively, unless otherwise noted. In an attempt to obtain a sample group whose experiences of fatherhood would be roughly comparable, the investigators tried to find participants whose children had been born within two years of the interview. Fathers who had more than one child were asked to choose one "focal child." Questions exploring paternal involvement and responsibility referred to this child.

Participants for the study were solicited from community- and school-based programs for adolescent fathers, although programs for adolescent mothers were also contacted. Participating organizations were asked for their critique of the project and advice on how to improve the chances of retrieving the maximum amount of information during the interviews. Agency administrators were also asked for their help in finding suitable candidates for the study. For some organizations, such as the school system, this took the form of permission to display a poster describing the project on their premises. In some cases, staff members suggested adolescent fathers in their client base who they believed might be willing to participate in the study. A decision was then made either to provide these fathers with the investigator's name and telephone number or to ask them for consent to have the investigator contact them.

The Questionnaire

A primary task during the preliminary stages of the project was the development of an instrument to guide each interview. The central research question focused on the meaning of fatherhood, and that theme was enlarged upon by exploring the participant's experiences with his own father and details of the participant's current relationship with his child. The resulting questionnaire was composed of three sections. The first section gathered demographic data on the young fathers, their natal partners, and their children. The second section explored each participant's relationship with his child. The young fathers were asked to discuss their feelings towards their children and to describe specific behaviors they engaged in while with their children. The third section focused on the discussion of each adolescent's perception of what fatherhood meant to him, building on the demographic and experiential information from the prior two sections as a foundation.

This last section of the questionnaire and the corresponding portion of each interview were especially important. It was here that participants defined fatherhood in their own words, discussed their views on the importance of fathers to families (if any), and described their opinions of what made someone a "good" father. The young fathers were encouraged to discuss their experiences with their own fathers and whether these experiences matched their previously expressed ideals about fatherhood. They were also asked to evaluate themselves as they imagined others might perceive their performance as fathers (e.g., "Based on what you're doing now, when your child gets to be your age, how might he (she) rate you as a dad?"). The interviewer concluded by giving participants an opportunity to identify any remaining aspects of their experience as fathers that had not been discussed.

The Interview

Each potential subject was presented with a description of the study and the general format of the interview. If the young father agreed to participate, a mutually acceptable time and location for the interview were chosen. The locations were selected to provide for the security and convenience of the participants. Special efforts were made to select interview sites in easily accessible, public places. Food concession areas of shopping malls at off-peak hours and quiet rooms in libraries turned out to be good sites. The interviews were one-on-one dialogues; neither representatives of social service organizations nor other members of the participant's family or social network participated.

After introductions, the interviewer and participant searched together for a space in which a frank discussion could be conducted in a relatively undisturbed manner. This search for a quiet corner served as a cooperative task that provided an opportunity to establish some rapport before the formal interview began. Another such opportunity occurred during the first 10–15 minutes of each interview, during which the interviewer reviewed the basic reasons for doing the study. At this time, various logistic details such as explaining the need for audiotaping and obtaining written consent were resolved. With the preliminaries accomplished, the interviewer progressed through the questionnaire with each participant. The sessions typically took two to three hours, although one interview lasted over five hours.[1] Finally, each participant received a small, cash honorarium of $10, expressing appreciation for his willingness to participate in the study. It was hoped that this gesture would also enable these young men to realize their contribution to the solution of problems faced by young parents like themselves.

Analysis

Each interview was audiotaped to ensure an accurate record of the participants' responses. During the interviews, the investigator also noted various verbal responses and nonverbal cues (such as body language and facial expressions). These notations were added to a set of summary notes compiled after each interview and designed to facilitate interpretation of the audiotapes. The summary notes included subjective impressions and reactions recorded immediately following the interview. These summary notes along with the audiotapes were used to develop a descriptive log for each interview.

A predominant theme or set of themes was identified for each interview log. This process also produced a wealth of quotations that characterized the sentiments of each young father and form the basis of the results reported below. The quotations are word-for-word transcriptions from the audiotapes. The quotations in this chapter are used to convey some of the wonder, pride, frustration, and bewilderment that the participants expressed during the interviews.

After interview logs were prepared for each participant, they were compared to discover common themes. The investigators were also interested in understanding possible explanations for differences between the participants' perceptions of fatherhood and paternal performance. Tables were developed to summarize the various demographic, evaluative, and subjective information from the group that helped to identify common trends among the young fathers and provided a basis for discussion of the differences among them. Although many topics were discussed in the course of the interviews, the tables focus on those most directly relevant to the research questions and the participants' responses to them.

Results

Before the major findings relating to this group's perceptions of fatherhood are presented, objective and self-evaluative data in their responses will be summarized. Table 1 shows demographic data on the participants, their partners, and their children. The young fathers in this study ranged in age from 15 to 19, with a group mean of 16.5. The ages of the mothers were typically similar to the participants' ages at the time of the child's birth, though in a few cases the father was two to three years older. The children ranged in age from six weeks to just under three years. Most of the fathers in this group had a single child. In the case of the three participants who had more than one child, the focal child tended to be the oldest. All but one of the adolescents were pursuing either a high school diploma or G.E.D. (if still in school), or entering the job market at entry level positions in blue-collar trades or the service industries. They reported jobs paying from $200 to over $800 per month. Only one father reported receiving public assistance. In general, this group did not appear to be economically stressed and did not indicate that lack of money was a primary concern.

Table 1
Summary Demographics

Subject	Subject's Age	Partner's Age	Number of Children	Focal Child's Age
MM	17	17	1	14 mos.
ET	17	17	1*	2 mos.
GK	18	19	1	12 mos.
TE	18	17	1	16 mos.
DC	19	17	1	30 mos.
BM	19	16–18	3	24 mos.
RJ	19	19	2	36 mos.
FQ	19	18	1	5 mos.
DJ	16	14–17	4	12 mos.
JJ	15	18	1	2 mos.

*ET claimed that there was a child in another state that he thought of as his own, even though it was not his biological offspring.

Table 2 summarizes the participants' appraisal of two key relationships: (1) their relationship with their natal partner, and (2) their relationship with the focal child. Each young father was asked to use a Likert scale (1 = Not very close, 2 = Close, and 3 = Very close) to characterize the quality of the two relationships. All participants indicated that they had been dating the mothers for at least one year prior to the pregnancy, and some had known the mothers for three or more years. It is interesting to note that half of the participants rated the relationship with their child higher (or closer) than the relationship with the mother. Most participants initially described themselves as being on "good terms" with the mothers, but later elaborated more complex and often problematic relationships. None of the adolescent fathers in the study were married, and only three indicated that they believed marriage was a possibility for themselves and the mother in the future.

Table 2 also summarizes the participants' living arrangements and a measure of paternal involvement. Two fathers lived together with the mothers and children (one in his parents' household, the other independently). The remainder lived with their

Table 2
Involvement with Partners and Children

Subject	Relationship with Partner*	Living with Partner	Relationship with Child*	Time Spent with Child
MM	2	No	3	Ev-Oth-Day
ET	1	No	2	Ev-Oth-Day
GK	1	No	3	Ev-Oth-Day
TE	1	No	2	Once/week
DC	3	No	2	Ev-Oth-Day
BM	2	No	3	Every Day
RJ	3	Yes	2	Every Day
FQ	1	No	2	Once/week
DJ	3	No	2	Ev-Oth-Day
JJ	3	Yes	3	Every Day

*Rating system: 1 = "Not very close."
                 2 = "Close."
                 3 = "Very Close."

own mothers or other members of their extended families. In order to summarize the participants' responses on involvement, three categories were created for Time Spent With Child: Every day, Every other day, and Once a week. Three fathers indicated that they spent an hour or more with their children "every day." Five fathers said they saw their child "every other day" on average. The remaining two saw their children less frequently, typically on a weekly basis. It is important to note that for many participants, there were occasional periods during which they did not see their child for more than a week or more. These lapses appeared to coincide with relationship difficulties between the participant and the mother. It is also significant that only one non-residential adolescent father saw his child every day.

The participants used the time spent with their children in a variety of ways. The activities they reported included playing indoors and outdoors, watching TV, going to the park or for walks, reading to the children, eating together, fishing, and swimming. In addition to such recreational activities, some of the participants spoke of routine child-care tasks such as feeding, bathing, and putting their children to sleep. When asked if they were specifically responsible for child-care duties, the fathers' responses ranged from "no" to "I do everything that she (the mother) does." Some of the young men expressed confidence in their ability to care for their children on their own for extended periods. Others seemed to suggest that their child-care responsibilities were contingent on what the mothers let them do. In other words, they would be willing to do anything that the mothers did, but were presently not providing much in the way of comprehensive child care beyond occasional baby-sitting. Several fathers indicated that they gave portions of their salaries to the mothers to provide for the material needs of their children. However, it was in the role of emotional support that they saw themselves as most effective.

Table 3 provides a summary of the four ratings of fatherhood that each father was asked to do. In this set of ratings, participants were asked to use a ten-point Likert scale ranging from "0" for "Terrible" to "10" for "Excellent." If the participant felt unable or unwilling to do a rating, a "—" was recorded. Participants were first asked to rate their own fathers and then to rate themselves in the role of father. The first of these helped the interviewer to begin exploring the nature of each participant's experience with his own father. The next three were designed to allow the adolescents to speculate on themselves as fathers, and on how others might view their paternal performance. These ratings taken together formed a subject-defined measure of their performance as fathers. They also provided a basis for the discussion of congruencies or incongruencies in the participants' paternal aspirations and their actual paternal behavior.

Developing a Perception of Fatherhood

In our attempt to identify common themes in the participants' responses, we found it helpful to compare their answers to the two key questions in the questionnaire. Table 4 contains brief paraphrases of the participants' responses to the question: "What does being a father mean to you?" This question typically came at the midpoint during the interviews, after we had discussed the young

Table 3
Ratings of Fatherhood*

Subject	Rate Your Father	Rate Yourself	Partner's Rating of You	Child's Rating of You
MM	—	5	—	10
ET	8	7	6	7
GK	5	10	8	10
TE	10	7	7	—
DC	0	9	8	9
BM	10	10	8	8
RJ	2	9	9	9
FQ	0	7	7	9
DJ	—	—	10	10
JJ	5	7	5	7

*Rating system: 0 = "Terrible."
              10 = "Excellent."
              — = "Can't or don't want to rate."

men's lives, their relationships with their partners, and their feelings toward and interaction with their children. It was the adolescent's first formal opportunity to subjectively express his perception of fatherhood. Among the most common themes that emerged from the responses were those of responsibility, love, caring for others, and being a provider.

Table 5 shows the responses to a restatement of the research question: "What makes someone a good father?" This phrasing allowed participants to take a more objective approach in answer-

Table 4
"What does being a father mean to you?"

Father	Response
MM	A boost in self-esteem, makes me feel proud.
ET	Makes me happy. It's a blessing from God.
GK	Responsibility, love.
TE	Being there for your kid.
DC	Responsibility and being there.
BM	Taking care of responsibilities.
RJ	Responsibility, taking care of my kids.
FQ	Being a provider. Loving and understanding.
DJ	Knowing yourself. Being connected with your child.
JJ	Taking care of somebody, responsibilities.

ing the question. In most cases, the participants used this second opportunity to amplify their responses to the earlier question, "What does being a father mean to you?" Although responsibility and involvement with children were among the two most cited attributes, the phrase that seemed to best embody this group's perceptions about what made someone a good father was *"being there."*

Table 5
"What makes someone a good father?"

Father	Response
MM	Maturity and family focus (vs. individual).
ET	Being there, responsibility.
GK	Being there, caring, responsibility.
TE	Shouldering your responsibility.
DC	Being there with your kid.
BM	Spending time with your children.
RJ	Being with your family, being there for your kids.
FQ	Being there for everything.
DJ	Understanding, knowledge of yourself.
JJ	Be around and show them that you love them.

Major Themes

"Being There"

To this group of adolescent fathers, the phrase "being there" seemed to crystallize the perception of fatherhood. They typically used this phrase in one of two related contexts. The first of these was in the sense of being physically and emotionally present in the lives of their children. In response to the question of what made someone a good father, GK responded:

> Being there, caring, responsibilities again. There's a lot of things you can say about how to be a good father. The most important thing? . . . being there, I would say. Being there as a father figure.

In a similar vein, FQ said:

I think the most important thing is to be there for my daughter. I need to give her love and understanding. A father is the one who make[s] you smile. Being a father means being there for everything.

The stories the young men provided to demonstrate the ways they were "there" for their children were convincing and often touching. When asked to describe what his son typically did when he saw his father, MM said:

When he sees me, he'll do his little thing. Like he'll smile or act like he don't see me. But if I say "OK, I'm leavin' now . . . " then he'll look back and open his arms and start runnin' to me. And when he was little, he'd always, like you know, his eyes would light up, his whole face would light up. He doesn't even do that when his mom picks him up.

Similarly, the youngest father, JJ, recalled seeing his child for the first time:

I didn't want to be there; I don't like blood . . . . I went to the hospital from a basketball game. My cousin and his girlfriend came over and said "Your son has been born!" I said, "Oh, God!" . . . [but then] I held him, and I could tell right then I was gonna like him.

Later, JJ discussed his aspirations for the future and how having a child would affect them:

I want to be in professional sports (a basketball player) or a lawyer. If I could do it over, I would not be a father right now, but he's here and I'm glad he's here. Even though he's just a little baby, when he hears my voice he'll look around, and he grabs my finger.

[What if you had to chose between him and a career?]

Oh . . . [Thinks for a second] I think I'd choose him. Right now, I'd choose him over anything.

One of the reasons the phrase "being there" might have been so significant to these young fathers is that they did not perceive that they could consistently provide for the material needs of their children in more conventional ways. Eight of the ten young men interviewed were working and had money enough to contribute to their partners and the children. However, the amount and predictability of these financial resources were typically low. Since most participants did not live with their children, their opportunities to interact with the children were usually limited. Therefore, the time they spent with their children took on great symbolic significance.

The second context in which these young fathers used the phrase "being there" referred to having been present at the birth of their children. Some of them spoke of their participation in the delivery process. The fathers who witnessed the births echoed FQ:

> I just think that a father should be in there, to go through the experience, you know, to see what the mother goes through. And really, when you're in the operating room or the birthing room, that really starts it all. It's like you see your son or daughter come out and you're there, and that's where everything starts.

And according to DC:

> I just about faded when I saw that. That was a weird experience! It's hard to tell what you feel when you're inside that room. It was like movies at school, but being there is something else.
>
> [Do you think it made a difference, your being with the mother?]
>
> Yeah, I'm sure it did. Instead of her going through it by herself, holding nobody's hand, you know, she had me there.

After more than a year, MM spoke of the impact the birth of his son made on him as if it had just happened:

> I came to the hospital with a close friend, actually, he's the godfather. Things were a little tough between me and the mother, but I told [the partner] I would at least stay until she was done. When he popped out, I was like [looks surprised]! And I woke up a half-hour later. (laughs) Luckily, my buddy was in there with me and he caught me. I was out and when I woke up I was lookin' at the television, I was lookin' around and I said "What happened? Where'd they go?" And they brought me in the room and I looked at him again. It was like, man! It was hard to believe. I was, shocked, you know, flabbergasted!
>
> [Were you glad you were there?]
>
> YEP! It made me feel a lot better. Then that way, you know for myself and when he gets older, [and says] "Were you there?", I'll say, "Yep!, I seen your little butt fall on the table." (laughs) Yeah, it made me feel really good.

Responsibility

In addition to "being there," another theme that repeatedly came up during the interviews was responsibility. Several of the young fathers in the study cited responsibility as the most significant aspect of their perception of being fathers, as in this quote from RJ:

> Responsibility. There's a lot of responsibility with two kids. I remember going to temporary agencies, just tryin' to get diapers for [child]. My neighbors ask me if we want to go out to the bar, but they know we can't afford to go most of the time.

In a similar vein, GK spoke about how the multitude of responsibilities was often his biggest concern:

> All the responsibilities, I would say. I didn't think there was this much responsibilities. I mean, there's *hundreds* of 'em! Some weeks I plan for me and [child] to do somethin' the whole week and it's like, and I didn't know in-between he was going to wet his clothes, and now I gotta change him, and I gotta do this, and I gotta take him to the doctor . . . .

Many of the fathers were very specific about the behaviors and level of involvement that established that they were fulfilling their paternal responsibility. Their responses to questions such as how much time they spent with the children, or what specific activities they engaged in, demonstrated they had more than a casual observer's knowledge of their children. Only one or two of the participants were vague or evasive about what they actually did to live up to their definitions of good fathers. In response to an inquiry about the kind and frequency of his child-care responsibilities, one father who was still in school began:

> I want to be there whenever she need somethin'; if she drop a toy or somethin', I make sure I'll pick it up and give it back to her.
>
> [How much time do you spend with your daughter?]
>
> As much as my schedule permits, [but] when I bring her to my house, it's always overnight.
>
> [How often is that?]

> Well . . . very rarely . . . her grandmother knows I'm okay but she also knows the type of people I hang out with. So when I ask to take the baby, they want to know, "Where you takin' her?" So, I stay away as much as I can. I don't want to intrude on their comfort.
>
> [When last were you able to take her overnight?]
>
> (Silence.)

The apparent contradiction between this participant's intentions and his actual paternal behavior is not unique to adolescent fathers (see the discussion of the asynchrony between the culture and conduct of fatherhood in LaRossa, 1988). Part of the problem in this particular instance could have been the lack of clarity in the term "child care." For the purposes of this study, the term child care meant attending to the physical needs of the children as a primary caregiver. Several of the fathers initially equated the term with financial support, as in "child support." Even with these occasional misunderstandings, it is accurate to say that most of these adolescents perceived themselves as significantly involved in the lives of their children. Many of the adolescent fathers in this study were pushing the mothers for even more time with their children. Typical of the strong sense of responsibility expressed by these young fathers was this statement by MM:

> My mom and my grandmother raised me. My dad? All I know is that his name was ——, and when I was about [child]'s age he left my mom. So, my mindset is that I want to be everything that he wasn't to me. Meanin' I want to be *something* to my son. I want to be a [cherished] memory, I don't want to be like just a name. My mom was talkin' about finding my dad, and I was like "Well, go ahead . . . I don't care." I don't want to be like that with [child]. I want to be part of his life. I want him to say, "My dad is right there." I want to take him to ball games, I want to keep him strong, I want to *be* his life.

This response was typical of the adolescent fathers in this group and many of them were quite knowledgeable about their children. They proudly quoted birth statistics and could be very specific about their children's current developmental progress in areas such as walking or toilet-training. All but one of the participants predicted being involved to some extent in the lives of their children in the future. Some even thought they would continue to be involved in relationships with the mothers, although as previously noted, most did not see these relationships evolving into marriage. Their primary sense of responsibility was to their children as opposed to the children's mothers.

The Influence of the Participants' Own Fathers

The adolescent fathers in this study felt very strongly that fathers were important to families. Most were convinced that their involvement with their children today would provide the basis for mutually enhancing relationships with their children in the future. When asked why fathers were important, many of the fathers' responses were similar to RJ's:

> Yes I think fathers are important. Like, my mom was a single parent, and I saw what she went through. She taught me a lot of responsibility, but she could really have used some help. I think they [fathers] can help the mom and the family.

Several of the participants felt that it was particularly important that male children have their father's involvement. As GK explained:

> I think fathers are important, especially for boys. Every child needs a role model; boys need fathers as a role model.

As important a role as they assign to the father, the participants were not expressing negative evaluations of their mothers in making these statements. Each participant went to some length to make it clear that they felt their own mothers had made heroic efforts to raise them. The role they felt fathers played was one of augmenting, rather than competing with or replacing, mothers. This group also had strong feelings about the influence that their own fathers had on their lives. For some of them, this was a positive influence that had helped them to shape their own positive views on fatherhood. But for others, recalling memories of their fathers was painful because they were struggling with feelings of not being "fathered" in a consistent and caring manner. Some of the participants' fathers had left their families of origin when the participants were two to three years of age (about the same ages as their own children). Their sense of abandonment comes across clearly in MM's recollection of his family's receiving a Christmas card after no contact in several years:

> I don't want to be negative, but I have to be negative. My father? 'Course I think if he was any kind of a man he would have least acknowledged me. I mean, that's what hurts me more than anything else, that he never even, you know . . . I mean a card? Paper's nothin' . . . .

Adding to their sense of ambivalence, some of the participants now perceived themselves to be in problematic family relationships that were similar to those in which their fathers had been (and left). Eight of the participants indicated that like themselves, their fathers had become parents while still in their teens. Three of the participants reported experiencing relationship problems with their natal partners. These problems were serious enough for them to characterize the relationships as "not very close." Almost all of the participants also spoke of problems in dealing with the mother's extended family. All of these aspects of their own situation seemed to reflect the earlier experience of each participant's own father. A consequence of this dilemma was that several participants had difficulty rating their fathers. For instance, the three participants who rated their fathers the highest (10), initially appeared almost apologetic about having to discuss their fathers. They went on to say that they really did not know their fathers personally, and were rating them based on hearsay from their mothers and other relatives. Only later as the interviews progressed did deeper feelings such as this response from DC emerge:

> [Tell me about your dad.]
>
> I don't even know who he is. He left when I was two. I guess after my second birthday he decided he didn't want to be around no more and just left.
>
> [Would you like to meet him someday?]
>
> If I could, yeah. If I could see him, just to see him; just to know what he looks like . . . . And what's messed up is that my mom ain't got no pictures of him. So I couldn't even look at a picture of him and see what he looked like. She said she never got around to takin' any pictures. I was like, "You ain't got no pictures of him?" She said, "I didn't get no pictures of him. We weren't into picture-takin' back then." (Then in a puzzled voice, he wondered out loud) Back in the '70s . . . ?
>
> [If you could see him, what would you say to him?]
>
> I'd probably tell him about himself! I don't know, I think I'd be in a state of shock. I don't know . . . I wouldn't say

nothin' to him . . . but . . . I'd probably cuss him out! (laughs) . . . . But, really I don't know . . . (and then, after a pause, sadly) . . . I don't know what I'd do.

Obstacles to Being Fathers

Relationships With Partners

There were three categories of problems that this group of adolescent fathers felt hindered their attempts at involvement with their children. Foremost among these obstacles was the relationship between the participant and his partner. Even though most of the fathers described themselves as being on "good terms" with their partners, during the course of all the interviews it became clear that they were having problems working through their dual roles as partners and as fathers. For some of the fathers, there was a sense of confusion and conflict between adolescent perspectives on dating and adult perspectives on committed relationships and parenting. The problem could be summarized in the question, "Am I my girlfriend's 'man' or my baby's father?" According to DJ:

It's one thing to be a boyfriend, another to be a father. Well, let me put it like this. Being a father takes you away from being a boyfriend. You have to deal with the baby and the mom. Being a boyfriend, it's just the mom.

[Could you give me an example of why that's a problem?]

Being a father, mom has a male friend over, he picks up the baby, I want him to put my baby down. Then [the mother] want to fight over who controls the baby.

Many of the relationship problems the participants spoke about were rooted in the divergent socialization of females and males. This divergence seemed to foster two very different and often irreconcilable perspectives on basic issues such as intimacy, trust, and approaches to childrearing. Lacking the skills to reconcile these perspectives, the participants were in what must have seemed an "unwinable" position. If they stayed in the relationships, they faced problems with their partners and limited access to their children; if they left, they were condemned for taking advantage of their partners and abandoning their children. However, it would be inaccurate to describe the relationship problems of the participants and their partners as solely the result of conflict in gender socialization. The root problem seemed to be the stability and maturity of the relationships themselves. Though many of the fathers had been involved in long-term relationships with the mothers at the time of the births, the pregnancies tended to complicate the dynamics in these relationships. They added one more potential source of disagreement and conflict for the couple. Often, these conflicts appeared as struggles for control of the children. DJ, the father quoted above, continued:

> Just say she gets mad at me and says, "You can't see your child." I say "I don't even want to see you no more" and then if I don't see her, I don't see my baby. And then so I say it's best that we stay away from being obligated to each other.

In another example, DC discussed how these difficulties directly affected his desire to be involved with his son:

> Well, like when me and [partner] weren't fond of each other, it kept me and my son apart. She would always [say] "I don't want to see you today," or I would want to see my son, and me and her were fightin'. I would say "Well, I'm comin' over . . . " and she say "No, you don't," and leave. And I would come over there and she'd be gone.
>
> So she was makin' me madder and madder, 'til I really got sick of it and I never came around for a long time. And then she was like, "Dang! . . . ," I mean, she knew that [child] needed a dad, so she wised up and she started lettin' me get closer to him.

This particular young man, when asked how he learned about being a father, reported how he deliberately sought and found jobs in the school nursery and later at a home daycare center in order to learn how to be "good at taking care of babies." It was hard to believe that he would have gone to that much effort simply to fight with the mother. His desire to be involved with his son was seen as a primary motivation for taking these steps. He and other participants came to see their natal partners as obstacles to such involvement, particularly when the relationship between them was strained. This situation was often compounded by the participant's lack of relationship management skills. As adolescents, many of them did not fully understand what concepts such as trust, communication, and mutual respect meant, but they had to try to negotiate these concepts with their natal partners in the context of intimate relationships.

Problems With the Natal
Partner's Family

The mother's extended family could also present a formidable obstacle to the participants' performing their roles as fathers. Often, the participant was perceived positively by the partner's family until the announcement of pregnancy. From that point on, the relationship between the participant and the partner's family seemed to become increasingly strained, hitting a low point at the time of delivery. More than one young father described the experience of standing on one side of the delivery table and attempting to support his partner, while the partner's mother stood on the opposite side and cursed at him. GK provided one of the most dramatic examples of this type of conflict. When asked how he got along with his partner's family, he hesitated before replying:

> Umm . . . I would say . . . I don't know . . . because, well . . . when she was pregnant, everything was going along fine until about the sixth month. Then they didn't want to have anything to do with me. It was like . . . on Easter me and a friend went over to her house and her brothers actually shot at us! And that stopped me from going over for about two months. Went back again and that time her dad threatened to kill me if I didn't get out of his yard, and all this . . . It's been . . . It's been like hell . . . .

The problem often extended to friends and acquaintances of the mother, as well as to the participant's own family and friends. Mutual friends who seemed supportive of the relationship often conspired to destroy one partner's sense of trust and commitment in the other. RJ discussed how this affected the period during his partner's pregnancy and how they decided to handle the problem:

> Oh, we were havin' problems even before I found out she was pregnant. In fact, I was the one to convince her not to have an abortion. Trust is still a big issue for us. She don't have friends and I don't have friends 'cause we don't trust each other. I can trust her, but I don't trust her around her friends. She don't trust none of my friends, either. So, we have an agreement just to hang together.

Problems With Social
Institutions

For some of the participants, the hospital or clinic where their baby was born was their first experience with the social institutions they would increasingly need to negotiate as fathers. It was heartening to hear that some of the fathers were welcomed by the hospital staff; two spoke with pride of participating in the deliveries by cutting the umbilical cords of their children. Other institutions were not always so open. Some fathers felt that society in general (and social service institutions such as public assistance and child protection in particular) often operated in a way that prevented them from being good fathers. Though a few of them also saw the courts as their last resort for solving problems that kept them from seeing more of their children, when the courts exhibited what they perceived to be a bias toward the mothers, it struck them as yet another example of how "the system is stacked against the father." Yet in spite of such real and perceived obstacles, some participants were willing to take extraordinary measures to care for their children, as this incident from GK's early parenting experience shows:

> My son was seven months old and he had a bite mark on his face. I asked [partner] who did it, she said she didn't know. I asked her did she take him [to the emergency room], 'cause at the time she was staying at a place where cats and dogs was, and I figured, Well, if a dog or somethin' bit him, he should go in for shots.

> So I take him to the hospital. They look at him and they document it and they tell me, "Well, maybe you oughta take him to St. Joe's [foster home agency] and let them do some documents." Well, I made it to St. Joe's, they told me give 'em [child] and I can go. And I'm thinkin', I'm bringin' my son here, I want to know what's goin' on. They tell me, "We can't."

> When I call up there or when I went back there, they tell me I can't even see my son. They took him and told me, "Even though you're the father we can't tell you nothing. We have to notify the mother, let her know her son is here, let her know who brought him." Even though I'm the one who brought him.

> Later, when I asked the county about the report concerning the bite marks, they told me, "We can't tell you anything; that information is confidential." (After a pause, with a perplexed look on his face) . . . I'm the one who made the report . . . .

Myths and Realities

Earlier, this chapter cited the social stigma that adolescent fathers face as a possible explanation for why they are such a difficult group to reach and to serve. The young men in this group also spoke of negative stereotypes and images that hindered their development of positive self-identities as fathers. GK was clear about what he wanted for his child.

> I don't want my son growin' up like I did. There's a lot of kids who don't have fathers, or if they do have fathers they're in jail or on drugs or not working or don't care about anything else . . . so what [if] they're a father.

> If you look at it, there's probably more dads out there that's not doin' what they should be doin' for their children, than there is dads doin' everything they can.

At one point in the discussion, GK stated his resolve that his son "see that his dad was not what he sees in society." This was a sentiment that most of these participants shared. In stereotypical images, African-American men appear as athletes, entertainers, and criminals but seldom as bankers, doctors, and lawyers. Even less seldom do African-American adolescents see themselves or adults depicted in family settings. The result is a social reproduction of both these negative images and the biases behind the images. In the face of these negative stereotypes, it not surprising that images of African-American men functioning in healthy ways, or in "traditional" family contexts, are often met with the protest, "But that isn't realistic . . . " by both African Americans and non-African Americans alike. These images represented another example of institutional barriers to the participants' attempts to be good fathers.

GK also speculated on the possible reasons many young men chose not to stay with and support their natal partners and children. When asked what happens to the dads out there who were "not doing what they should be doing," he replied:

> They go out and they do the same thing again. They go out and they have another baby thinking its gonna be joy and "Well, you know, I'm going to have a son, and he's gonna be just like me, grow up to look just like me . . . ." And that girl or that woman does the same thing his previ-

ous relationship did, so that throws him to do the same thing he did before. You know, "Well, I'm tired of going through it; just [dump her]," and go out and do the same thing. Then you got three babies, four babies, five babies, six babies, and its on. Until maybe one day, he finally find someone who'll settle down, get married, have children, live a life.

The account of this scenario was a sobering illustration of the potential consequences of the relationship problems outlined earlier. It also made the researchers wonder whether any of the participants with more than one child had experienced this chain of events. This hypothetical scenario was recalled during the interview of a father who appeared to validate GK's theory. According to DJ, when he became sexually intimate with the young women he was dating, he articulated certain "ground rules":

I establish that with basically any females that I have a child with. I tell 'em we can't be together. They say, "Well why not? How're we gonna be a family?" I tell them we can be a family, "I can be a father to my child, regardless, and a friend to you but that's no more, no less." Then they say, "But why?" and I say, "Because, the logistics . . . I mean, where the . . . the practicality . . . the formality of our relationship is us bein' a couple."

We argue, we fight. Then they say, "I hate you, I don't want to see you no more." I say "I don't want to see you no more either." And then we still have this little baby, right here that needs both of us . . . .

The last paragraph of this quote is a part of the interview with DJ that immediately preceded the discussion of conflict in his relationship with his partner, and control of his child as discussed earlier. DJ was one of two participants who had more than one child with different natal partners. The reason why some young men impregnate more than one mother is a subject that demands more research and is beyond the scope of this chapter. However, the similarity between GK's hypothesis about young men who father more than one baby and DJ's actual experiences seems compelling.

The participants in this study, like other adolescents, may have engaged in sexual intercourse as one part of a larger strategy to find love, nurturing, and acceptance in their relationships. Unlike some of their peers who used contraceptive measures or perhaps were just more fortunate, these young men impregnated their partners. At first, many of them were slow to realize the profound consequences of early pregnancy for themselves, their partners, and for the children. Usually, these consequences begin to dawn on them following the exhilaration surrounding the birth of their children. However, it would appear that some fathers (like DJ) do not fully comprehend the consequences of early pregnancy and parenting until several children have been born, if then. This lag time between discovery of the impregnation and full comprehension of paternal responsibility seemed to be shorter in fathers with only one child. Almost immediately, these participants saw their lives as fundamentally changed.

Discussion

Some of the decisions made during the design and execution of this study limit the generalizability of the results of this study to other groups of adolescent fathers. The small sample size and the exclusive focus on African-American adolescent fathers are two of the most obvious examples of these limiting factors. It is suspected that much of what the participants in this study reported about their lives would probably apply to adolescent fathers from different ethnic, socioeconomic, and geographic backgrounds. Nonetheless, it cannot be assumed that the specific experiences detailed in this study will necessarily be true for other young fathers.

There have been few longitudinal studies of adolescent fathers, which limits researchers' understanding of this group. The fact that the participants were only interviewed once leaves the study vulnerable to the charge that a longitudinal project may have produced quite a different picture of these adolescent fathers' actual involvement over time. More research is needed in order to better understand what happens to adolescent fathers and their families as they struggle to overcome both the mundane problems in any close relationship and the unique challenges of early parenthood. This study is also limited because the perspective of others in the young men's ecology was missing. It would have been interesting to hear from the mothers about their perceptions of the relationship and to learn their evaluation of the participants as fathers. The study may also have benefited from watching the young fathers interacting with their children in order to better validate their claims of paternal involvement.

Finally, the investigators realize that the adolescent fathers who chose to participate in this study defined themselves as fathers in part by being involved with their children. Therefore, the finding that they are committed to their offspring might appear tautological. Unless a way can be found to explore the perceptions of uninvolved fathers, only adolescent fathers who choose to be involved can be spoken of with certainty. Researchers need to understand the experience and motivation of fathers who do not choose to be involved with their children. This does not invalidate the significance of the findings of the present study or diminish the experiences of the young fathers who agreed to participate in this study. Rather, the incomplete nature of this study and the current literature should create a sense of urgency for more exploration and analysis of this issue.

The influence of the participants' family of origin on their belief systems should not be underestimated. As others have shown (Christmon, 1990b), this may have played a pivotal role in both their decision-making regarding the prospect of fatherhood and in their current thinking about the paternal role. When asked how their families felt about their early transitions to fatherhood, most participants indicated that parents and siblings were accepting, though reluctant (because of the timing). It has already been noted that many of the participants' fathers were themselves adolescent fathers. What these young men saw modeled in the way of close heterosexual relationships in their families of origin (or more specifically, the problems associated with such relationships) may also have been influential in their current relationships with their natal partners. It is certainly not the case that all or most African-American youth grow up in households without their fathers as was the case for so many of the participants in this study. However, there is little doubt that this absence was a primary influence on the participants' perceptions of fatherhood. Their strong desire to be involved with their children was in large part a reaction to their conviction that they would have benefited from the involvement of their own fathers.

Another primary influence on the perception of fatherhood was ethnocultural socialization regarding the role of men in families. Cazenave (1981) wrote about the significance of responsibility to the African-American men he surveyed about family life and fatherhood. His respondents stated that "responsibility was the key to manhood." This is consistent with the work of other prominent family scholars writing about the role of fatherhood in the African-American community (McAdoo, 1993; Taylor, Leashore, & Toliver, 1988). This finding seemed to hold true for the adolescent fathers in this study as well, even though many did not have fathers in the households they grew up in. That suggests that there were other sources of ethnic socialization within their ecology that communicated the significance of responsibility. According to the young men in the present sample, these included older siblings, grandfathers, uncles, and significant women in their lives (e.g., their mothers). A more subtle example of ethnocultural socialization was the group's consensus on how they were doing as fathers in comparison to other fathers they knew. Connor (1983) surveyed the perceptions of fatherhood among African-American adult males. One of his findings was that these adult fathers perceived themselves to be "more involved" with their own children than they perceived other African-American fathers were with their offspring. This also seemed to hold true for the adolescent fathers in the present study. Of the ten participants, eight were convinced that they were doing a better job at being fathers than were the other adolescent fathers whom they knew. None of the fathers perceived himself to be a less effective or less involved parent than other fathers.

The participants in this study reflected the themes of being responsible for the welfare of one's family and providing for their material and emotional needs when they spoke of "being there." To some readers this phrase (and the value it implicitly epitomizes) would appear in contradiction with research such as the finding that African-American adolescent fathers are much less likely to live with their partners (and the children) than other ethnic groups (e.g., Marsiglio, 1988). However, this may be like comparing apples to oranges. What this type of discrepancy actually highlights is the difference between an ethnic group's values about fatherhood and the conduct of a specific group of individuals within that ethnic group. Recall the phrase used by GK regarding paternal responsibility: " . . . there's probably more dads out there that's not doin' what they should be doin' for their children." GK believed that fathers should be responsible for their children, but he felt he was not able to live with his own child due to relationship problems with his natal partner and her family. However, he clearly stated that his preference would have been to be living with the mother and child. Thus, the fact that he was not living with them did not preclude him from embracing the value that he should be living with his "procreated" family.[2]

Many of the young fathers in this study seemed to be searching for meaningful connections with other African-American men, especially older men who they might use as role models. This manifested itself in their recollections of their grandfathers, older brothers, and uncles, and in their respectful treatment of the interviewer. Most of the young men appeared to truly appreciate the chance to open up and express their experiences of being adolescent fathers with another African-American man. It is important to find ways to harness this dynamic in attempts at supporting these young fathers. Mental health professionals acknowledge that African-American adolescent males are a particularly difficult population to reach and serve (Hendricks, 1983; Smith, 1988). This is even more true for adolescent fathers (Hendricks & Solomon, 1987). Therefore, programs staffed primarily with European-Americans (particularly women) functioning as social workers or guidance counselors will probably not be as effective as programs that are staffed by workers with whom the young fathers can more readily identify as role models and possible mentors. Services to African-American adolescent fathers must solicit and include the participation of adult African-American men in order to be effective (Battle, 1988). In addition to motivating adolescents, participation in mentoring programs can benefit the adult men as well. Such relationships represent concrete opportunities to build communities and improve the prospects for all African Americans.

Clearly, African-American men have to be in a position to become and remain positive role models for younger men and boys. This cannot happen if they are denied the very opportunities that society expects them to motivate younger men to seize. These opportunities include access to adequate education and to gainful employment. Similarly, it may be difficult (though not impossible) for older men who have not been in stable and supportive relationships or had positive family experiences to provide support to younger men such as the adolescent fathers in the present study. These young men are often grappling with serious relationship and family life issues of their own. If society is to be successful in serving the needs of these adolescent fathers, the larger needs of the communities from which they emerge must be kept in mind.

Conclusion

In many ways, the ten young fathers in this study were traveling a similar road, a road filled with childhood dreams hastily recast, and challenges faced before their time. When the participants spoke of the obstacles to "being there," their frustration and their sense of determination could be heard. Sometimes their lives as they perceived them could be seen: filled with a seemingly endless chain of obstacles to maintaining stable relationships with either their natal partners or their children. Many of these young men lacked the relationship skills necessary for negotiating their roles as partners and as co-parents. This directly affected their roles as fathers in their own eyes and in the eyes of the various other layers of their ecology: family, friends, schools or employers, social service agencies, legal and government institutions, and society.

And yet, despite these problems, their response to the question "What does being a father mean to you?" still seemed to fill these young men with a sense of expectation about the future rather than with regrets about the past. Most described the experience as having changed them in some inexplicable, yet fundamental way. When asked how being a father made him feel, MM said:

> It kinda gives you, it's a . . . it's an unexplainable feeling. Like when I was in the delivery room and he came, and he was there, you know, and he looked at me . . . it was like, you're in awe. That's the best way I can say it, you're in awe! You're like, wow! He looks at you and, and your body like tingles . . . it's almost like catching the Holy Ghost or something!

The majority of the adolescent fathers in this study appeared truly dedicated to being involved with their children and performing their roles as fathers, as they understood that role. Regardless of the empirical evidence suggesting less involvement by adolescent fathers over time, it is important not to lose sight of this group of fathers' sense of commitment. Therein might lie the key to ensuring a continuing commitment to their children over time, and perhaps even to their natal partners.

It would be a shame if the positive outcomes that some researchers have reported for adolescent mothers were primarily the result of these individuals being fortunate exceptions to a more typical negative life course. Similarly, it is important to have greater expectations for these adolescent fathers and their families. It is crucial that they not have the "odds" unnecessarily stacked against them because the institutions responsible for supporting them do not understand their experience or their needs. It is also crucial that better ways can be found to reach adolescent fathers earlier during their partners' pregnancies and to recruit them into roles as responsible, involved fathers. If it is true, as Blumer (1969) suggests, that "people . . . do not act toward culture, social structure, or the like; they act toward situations," there is reason for optimism regarding the prospects for adolescent fathers. Many of these young men prioritize their roles as fathers highly, even though they see themselves as coming to the role prematurely. With the appropriate support they should be able to overcome the developmental and structural obstacles to their becoming good fathers, and be truly successful at "being there."

Society has a moral obligation as well as a practical interest in preventing adolescent pregnancies. To be successful at this, however, more may have to be done than simply urging young people to abstain from sexual intimacy. The profound connections between early pregnancy and other social issues must be faced, such as the continuing effects of the lack of educational and employment opportunity in many neighborhoods, poor access to and utilization of family planning services, and the continuing legacies of ethnic and gender discrimination. This will require a rethinking of many preconceived ideas about adolescent sexuality, adolescent pregnancy, and in particular adolescent fathers. These interviews created the conviction that the will and desire to be good fathers is a rich resource in these young men that has yet to be fully tapped.

Notes

1. Two pilot interviews were conducted to provide a better sense of potential problem areas in the interview process. These pilots were very useful in uncovering wording that some of the young fathers found confusing. Although the responses from the young fathers who took part in the pilot interviews are not reflected in the summary data, their experiences were generally consistent with those of the other young fathers in the study.

2. A similar confusion can be seen regarding ethnic values about out-of-wedlock births among African-Americans. There is a perception in some academic and political circles that African-Americans favor having children out of wedlock. Specific behavior patterns in the African-American community, such as avoiding pregnancy termination and multigenerational acceptance of and support for children born out of wedlock, have been misinterpreted as a preference among African-Americans for adolescent pregnancy and parenting. When statistics on out-of-wedlock births to certain age groups of African-American women are relied upon as proxies for the underlying values about children and family, researchers risk misinterpreting observable ethnocultural trends, and perpetuating ethnocentric stereotypes. The young fathers in this study all stated that they would have preferred to become fathers later in life. Moreover, none of them expressed a desire (or value) to have their own children become parents at the relatively early ages they themselves did. These statements represent their values about the inappropriateness of early parenting.

References

Allen, W. (1982). Black family research in the U.S.: A review, assessment, and extension. *Journal of Comparative Family Studies, 9,* 167–189.

Applegate, J. (1988). Adolescent fatherhood: Development perils and potentials. *Child and Adolescent Social Work Journal, 5,* 205–217.

Barret, R., & Robinson, B. (1982). A descriptive study of teenage expectant fathers. *Family Relations, 31,* 349–352.

Barth, R.P., Claycomb, M., & Loomis, A. (1988). Service to adolescent fathers. *Health and Social Work, 13,* 277–287.

Battle, S. (1988). The black adolescent father. *Urban League Review, 12,* 70–83.

Blumer, H. (1969). *Symbolic interactionism: Perspective and method.* Englewood Cliffs, NJ: Prentice-Hall.

Boss, P. (1987). The role of intuition in family research: Three issues of ethics. *Contemporary Family Therapy, 9,* 147–159.

Bubolz, M., & Sontag, S. (1993). Human ecology theory. In P. Boss, W. J. Doherty, R. LaRossa, W. Schumm, & S. Steinmetz (Eds.), *Sourcebook of family theories and methods: A contextual approach* (pp. 419–448). New York: Plenum.

Caparulo, F., & London, K. (1981). Adolescent fathers: Adolescents first, fathers second. *Issues in Health Care of Women, 3,* 23–33.

Cazenave, N. (1981). Black men in America: The quest for manhood. In H. McAdoo (Ed.), *Black families.* Beverly Hills, CA: Sage.

Christmon, K. (1990a). Parental responsibility of African-American unwed adolescent fathers. *Adolescence, 25,* 645–653.

Christmon, K. (1990b). The unwed father's perceptions of his family and of himself as a father. *Child and Adolescent Social Work Journal, 7,* 275–283.

Comer, J. (1989). Black fathers. In S. Cath, A. Gurwitt, & L. Gunsberg (Eds.), *Fathers and their families* (pp. 365–84). Hillsdale, NJ: The Analytic Press.

Connor, M. (1983). *Black male attitudes towards fathering: A follow-up report.* Presented at the Western Psychological Assoc. Annual Conference, San Francisco.

Connor, M. (1988). Teenage fatherhood: Issues confronting young, black males. In J. Gibbs (Ed.), *Young, black, and male in America* (pp. 188–218). Westport: Auburn House.

Danziger, S., & Radin, N. (1990). Absent does not equal uninvolved: Predictors of fathering in teen mother families. *Journal of Marriage and the Family, 52,* 636–642.

Dash, L. (1989). *When children want children.* New York: William Morrow & Co.

Dilworth-Anderson, P., & McAdoo, H. (1988). The study of ethnic minority families: Implications for practitioners and policymakers. *Family Relations, 37,* 265–267.

Dunston, P., Hall, G., & Thorne-Henderson, C. (1987). Black adolescent mothers and their families: Extending services. *Child & Youth Services, 9,* 95–110.

Elster, A., & Lamb, M. (1986). *Adolescent fatherhood*. Hillsdale, NJ: Erlbaum.

Elster, A., & Panzarine, S. (1983). Adolescent fathers: Stresses during the gestation and early parenthood. *Clinical Pediatrics, 22*, 700–703.

Farber, N. (1990). The significance of race and class in marital decisions among unmarried adolescent mothers. *Social Problems, 37*, 51–63.

Freeman, E. (1989). Adolescent fathers in urban communities: Exploring their needs and role in preventing pregnancy. *Journal of Social Work and Human Sexuality, 8*, 113–131.

Furstenberg, F. (1976). *Unplanned parenthood: The social consequences of teenage childbearing*. New York: Free Press.

Furstenberg, F., Brooks-Gunn, J., & Morgan, S. (1987). *Adolescent mothers in later life*. Cambridge: Cambridge University Press.

Hardy, J., Duggan, A., Masnyk, K., & Pearson, C. (1989). Fathers of children born to young urban mothers. *Family Planning Perspectives, 21*, 195–163.

Hendricks, L. (1983). Suggestions for reaching unmarried, black adolescent fathers. *Child Welfare, 62*, 141–146.

Hendricks, L., & Montgomery, T. (1983). A limited population of unmarried adolescent father. *Adolescence, 18*, 201–210.

Hendricks, L., & Solomon, A. (1987). Reaching black male adolescent parents through nontraditional techniques. *Child & Youth Services, 9*, 111–124.

Hofferth, S., & Hayes, C. (1987). *Risking the future* (Vol. 2). Washington, DC: National Academy Press.

Hogan, D., & Kitagawa, E. (1985). The impact of social status, family structure, and neighborhood on the fertility of black adolescents. *American Journal of Sociology, 70*, 825–855.

Howell, F., & Frese, W. (1982). Early transition into adult roles: Some antecedents and outcomes. *American Education Research Journal, 19*, 51–73

Kahn, J., & Bolton, F. (1986). Clinical issues in adolescent fatherhood. In A. B. Elster & M. E. Lamb (Eds.), *Adolescent fatherhood* (pp. 141–154). Hillsdale, NJ: Erlbaum.

Klinman, D., Sanders, J., Rosen, J., & Longo, K. (1986). The teen father collaboration: A demonstration and research model. In A. Elster & M. Lamb (Eds.), *Adolescent fatherhood* (pp. 155–170). Hillsdale, NJ: Erlbaum.

Lamb, M., & Elster, A. (1985). Adolescent mother-infant-father relationships. *Developmental Psychology, 21*, 768–773.

LaRossa, R. (1988). Fatherhood and social change. *Family Relations, 37*, 451–457.

LaRossa, R., & Reitzes, D. (1993). Symbolic interactionism and family studies. In P. Boss, W. J. Doherty, R. LaRossa, W. Schumm, & S. Steinmetz (Eds.), *Sourcebook of family theories and methods: A contextual approach* (pp. 135–163). New York: Plenum.

McAdoo, J. (1993, January). The roles of African-American fathers: An ecological perspective. *Families in Society*, 28–35.

McCoy, J., & Tyler, F. (1985). Selected psychosocial characteristics of black unwed adolescent fathers. *Journal of Adolescent Health Care, 6*, 12–16.

McKenry, P., Everett, J., Ramseur, H., & Carter, C. (1989). Research on black adolescents: A legacy of cultural bias. *Journal of Adolescent Research, 4,* 254–264.

Marsiglio, W. (1987). Adolescent fathers in the United States: Their initial living arrangements, marital experience and educational outcomes. *Family Planning Perspectives, 19,* 240–251.

Marsiglio, W. (1988). Commitment to social fatherhood: Predicting adolescent males' intentions to live with their child and partner. *Journal of Marriage and the Family, 50,* 427–441.

Marsiglio, W. (1989). Adolescent males' pregnancy resolution preferences and family formation intentions. *Journal of Adolescent Research, 4,* 214–237.

Parke, R., & Neville, B. (1987). Teenage fatherhood. In S.L. Hofferth & C.D. Hayes (Eds.), *Risking the future: Adolescent sexuality, pregnancy and childbearing* (Vol. 2, pp. 145–173). Washington, DC: National Academy Press.

Redmond, M. (1985). Attitudes of adolescent males toward adolescent pregnancy and fatherhood. *Family Relations, 34,* 337–342.

Rivara, F., Sweeney, P., & Henderson, B. (1986). Black teenage fathers: What happens when the child is born? *Pediatrics, 78,* 151–158.

Robbins, C., Kaplan, H., & Martin, S. (1985). Antecedents of pregnancy among unmarried adolescents. *Journal of Marriage and the Family, 47,* 567–583.

Robinson, B. (1988a). Teenage pregnancy from the father's perspective. *American Journal of Orthopsychiatry, 58,* 46–51.

Robinson, B. (1988b). *Teenage fathers.* Lexington, MA: D. C. Heath.

Robinson, B., & Barret, R. (1986). *The developing father.* New York: Guilford.

Robinson, B., & Barret, R. (1987). Self-concept and anxiety of adolescent and adult fathers. *Adolescence, 22,* 611–616.

Smollar, J., & Ooms, T. (1987). *Young unwed fathers: Research review, policy dilemmas, and options.* Washington, DC: Catholic University of America.

Smith, L. (1988). Black adolescent fathers: Issues for service provision. *Social Work, 33,* 269–271.

Sullivan, M. (1986). *Teen fathers in the inner city: An exploratory ethnographic study.* New York: Vera Institute of Justice.

Taborn, J. (1988). Adolescent pregnancy: A medical concern. *Urban League Review, 12,* 91–99.

Taylor, R., Leashore, B., & Toliver, S. (1988). An assessment of the provider role as perceived by black males. *Family Relations, 37,* 426–431.

Vaz, R., Smolen, P., & Miller, C. (1983). Adolescent pregnancy: Involvement of the male partner. *Journal of Adolescent Health Care, 4,* 246–250.

Vincent, C. E. (1956). *Unwed mothers.* New York: The Free Press.

Wattenberg, E. (1990, March-April). Unmarried fathers: Perplexing questions. *Children Today,* 25–30.

Westney, O., Brabble, E., & Edwards, C. (1988). Human ecology: Concepts and perspectives. In R. Borden & J. Jacobs (Eds.), *Human ecology—Research and applications* (pp. 129–137). College Park, MD: Society for Human Ecology.

Westney, O., Cole, O., & Munford, T. (1986). Adolescent unwed prospective fathers: Readiness for fatherhood and behaviors toward the mother and expected infant. *Adolescence, 21,* 901–911.

Wilkinson, D. (1987). Ethnicity. In M. Sussman & M. Steinmetz (Eds.), *Handbook of marriage and the family* (pp. 183–210). New York: Plenum.

Wilson, W. (1987). *The truly disadvantaged: The inner city, the underclass, and public policy.* Chicago, IL: The University of Chicago Press.

Young, L. (1954). *Out of wedlock.* New York: McGraw-Hill.

Zelnik, M., Kantner, J., & Ford, K. (1981). *Sex and pregnancy in adolescence.* Beverly Hills, CA: Sage.

Chapter 12

African-American Couples' Lived Experience of Infertility[1]

Su An Arnn Phipps

Approximately 15 to 20% of couples in the United States, or over 10 million people, experience difficulty in conception during their childbearing years (Link & Darling, 1986). This unanticipated circumstance carries psychosocial and spiritual consequences of varying intensity for both individuals and couples. Kalmuss (1987) describes the risk of infertility as 1.5 times higher for black women than for white women. According to the United States Public Health Service (1985) and Hirsch and Mosher (1987), the distinct epidemiologic profile of infertile persons in the U.S. is of older couples, who are more likely to be Black, with less than a high school education and with no previous children. Yet, no research or literature was found that describes black couples' infertility experience, or discusses the cultural or socioeconomic influence on couples' involuntary childlessness. The meaning of their infertility experience is unknown.

Methods

The study described in this chapter is part of a larger project investigating couples' infertility taking the factors of race and socioeconomic status into consideration. The study method was phenomenology, an inductive research method that has as its goal the description of "the total systematic structure of lived experience, including the meanings that these experiences have for the individuals who participated in them" (Omery, 1983, p. 50). The researcher investigates informants' perceptions of how they live and experience their world on an everyday basis. The researcher must set aside or "bracket" his or her knowledge, values, and views about the experience being studied (Oiler, 1982) in order to identify, rather than verify pre-existing notions of reality (Reimen, 1986). Informants' experiences are assumed to provide essential truths about reality (Spiegelburg, 1976) that are difficult, if not impossible, to uncover through more objective methodology. Three essential steps of the phenomenological method are to: 1) investigate particular phenomena; 2) investigate general essences; and 3) apprehend essential relationships among essences (Spiegelburg, 1976). Essences are defined as "unities of meaning intended by different individuals in the same acts or by the same individuals by different acts" (Natanson, 1973, p. 14). The purpose of this study was to investigate the meaning of infertility to African-American couples of lower socioeconomic status, to describe the general essences through induction of themes and categories, and to investigate relationships among these essences. The study question was "What is the lived experience of infertility for black couples of low socioeconomic status?"

Research Design

Informants

A purposive sample of eight African-American, lower socioeconomic status couples was used to identify the common infertility experience of this group. Couple socioeconomic status was determined using Hollingshead's Four Factor Index of Social Status (1975), which categorizes status based on one's level of education and type of occupation. The study method was an unstructured interview conducted in couples' homes or at a university office.

The eight husbands ranged in age from 27 to 40 years, with a median age of 34 years, and a mean age of 32.5 years. All had completed high school. Five had completed at least one year of college or had special training following high school graduation. None had a college degree. Examples of husbands' occupations include a carpenter, nursing assistant, janitor, and barber.

The eight wives ranged in age from 23 to 37 years, with a mean age of 31.2 years, and a median age of 34 years. The wives were generally more highly educated than their spouses. Three had attended some college or trade school. Four had associate degrees and one had a baccalaureate degree. One of the wives was working as a secretary/receptionist, and another was a beautician student. Two wives were registered nurses, although one was not

Couple Informants

Husbands		Wives	
Age	Education:	Age	Education:
x = 32.5	High School = 3	x = 31.2	High School = 0
median = 34	Partial College or Trade School = 5	median = 34	Partial College or Trade School = 3
range = 27–40	Associate Degree = 0	range = 23–37	Associate Degree = 4
	Baccalaureate = 0		Baccalaureate = 1

employed. One wife was a laboratory technician, and another worked for an answering service. The other two wives were seeking employment. The median combined family income ranged from $20,000 to $25,000. All of the couples identified themselves as Protestant, or more specifically as Christian or Pentecostal.

Couples included in the study were those who had never conceived, or having already had children, were unable to become pregnant while currently attempting. Couples who had experienced more than one early miscarriage were not included. For couples who already had children, these children could be in the home through birth, adoption or foster care. Two couples had adopted children, and two couples had one biological child. The origin of couples' infertility was undetermined in 3 couples, involved a known female factor in four couples, and an identified male factor in one couple.

Some of the couples had not sought medical diagnosis or treatment and were uncertain why they were unable to conceive. Two of the couples were in the diagnostic phase of treatment at the time of the interview. The length of time couples had been attempting pregnancy varied. The longest period of time was 13 years. Couples participating in infertility support groups, such as

Infertility Origin	Length of Time Attempting Pregnancy
Undetermined = 3	7 - 12 months = 1
Male Factor = 1	13 - 18 months = 2
Female Factor = 4	31 - 36 months = 2
	37 - 48 months = 1
	over 5 years = 2

RESOLVE, or who were participating in in vitro fertilization were excluded from the study.

Data Collection

Informants were recruited from notices placed in newspapers, at junior colleges and physician offices, or by referral from individuals known by the researcher. Once the study procedure was explained and couples indicated their willingness to participate, a convenient interview time was established. Spouses were interviewed separately, in private, and asked to describe what it is like as a man or a woman not to be able to have a baby when they wanted to. Spouses were then brought back together for the couple interview. Consistent with phenomenological method, the only interview question asked was "What is it like for you as a couple not to be able to have a baby when you want to?" Other questions were only asked for purposes of amplification or clarification. After audiotapes were transcribed verbatim onto a computer, a software package was used to process the data.

Data Analysis

Transcriptions were analyzed using Colaizzi's (1978) method of phenomenological analysis. The procedural steps consist of: 1) listening to and reading informants' descriptions to acquire a feeling for their content; 2) extracting significant statements; 3) formulating meanings for the statements; 4) organizing clusters of themes from aggregate formulated meanings; 5) comparing theme clusters to original descriptions to validate clusters and examine discrepancies; 6) developing an exhaustive description of the phenomenon; and 7) having informants review the exhaustive description for validation of the original experience. The number of couple interviews was determined with the saturation of data. Data saturation refers to the repetition and confirmation of data gained as one conducts a qualitative study (Streubert & Carpenter, 1995). The results presented here are preliminary data, as feedback has not been received from all of the African-American consultants and the exhaustive description is currently in the couple validation process.

Findings

Nine couple categories were induced from the data. These include: 1) evaluation of the meaning of childlessness; 2) emotions experienced with infertility; 3) coping; 4) marital functioning; 5) relation-ships; 6) health care; 7) time; 8) expenditures; and 9) self-perception.

Evaluation of the Meaning of Childlessness

Three theme clusters were induced in the category, Evaluation of the Meaning of Childlessness. These were *perceptions of infertility, desire,* and *envisioned future.* These couples perceived involuntary childlessness as a major stressor, but only one of many life issues. They viewed infertility as a couple problem, rather than an indi-vidual problem. Their infertility was a blocking of a life goal resulting in sorrow, confusion, and frustration for both partners and a feeling of being "passed by."

Infertility sometimes led to putting the couple's future on hold, a perceived inability to plan for the future. The desire for a child, frequently a son , was shared by the couple. Both felt a void, an incompleteness in their lives, and a feeling of being different from other couples.

> Wife: "Now they're getting pregnant. You know, it was kinda, it hurt you know, and you kind of feel like you're the oddball. As a couple, we felt like we stuck out like a sore thumb. You know, here we are, the only ones who can't seem to have children."

Although couples had anticipated having children prior to mar-riage, their desire grew after marriage and after being around children. The yearning for a child is continuous. Couples had envisioned themselves experiencing joy at conception and birth; parenting a child, loving, nurturing and guiding him. Often couples had an ideal number of children in mind, as well as the spacing of the children. Although having biological children was preferred, adoption was discussed as an acceptable answer to their childless-ness.

Emotions Experienced With Infertility

Couples' emotions experienced with infertility included *frustration* from internal and external pressure to conceive and subsequent failure, and uncertainty about the present or future possibility of conception. Infertility only added to the frustration couples experi-enced with other life stressors.

Sorrow was intense for both spouses, sometimes leading to despondency or depression. It occurred monthly with menses, with awareness of others' pregnancies and seeing others' children at holidays and family gatherings. At times sorrow overshadowed spouses' attempts to comfort each other. *Anger* accompanied the perceived unfairness of their circumstances; at not conceiving when their desire is so strong; at others' ease of conception; at the mistreatment and abuse of children. One wife stated, regarding the couple's relatives (fictitious names):

> Wife: "Some things I can't handle. And again, I can't handle Julie and Harold having one baby that's 10 months old and another one due any day, and neither one are working and they don't own a crib. So I'd like to go and take the baby, 'cause we could do better for the baby. We could give the baby a better home. It wouldn't want for anything. And so it's hard . . . I don't think it's fair of these women to go to abortion clinics to get rid of babies when my husband and I want a baby. I don't think it's fair that these women on welfare can have all these kids, and you got two people who are working."
>
> Husband: "Um hmm."
>
> Wife: " . . . and we want a baby" (crying). Husband takes hand.

In spite of these emotions, couples maintained *hope* over time and found it was important to their outlook. Couples spoke of their faith in God and God's provision. Their hope was increased by others' "miracle" pregnancies. Couples also saw hope in pregnancy with time, with treatment or technology.

Coping

Couples coped with their intense emotions through *avoidance* and other *cognitive processes*. These couples often chose not to think about or discuss their childlessness with one another. After a time, they tended to ignore it, to keep *going on*, to keep trying but not focusing on it or making it a priority in their lives.

Couples attempted to refocus their energies by pursuing mutual interests or distracting themselves through work.

> Husband: " . . . Sometimes we laugh about it, because we wonder when we would fit a child in, knowing that we'd just work our schedules around that because our week is busy now . . . And I guess it's good 'cause that keeps us

> from thinking about those types of things. I don't, we're
> not going to dwell on it as much as we used to, at least not
> to the point where we did. . . . Our week now is pretty
> busy, so it's, it keeps your mind off those types of things."

They entertained only the positive thoughts, looking toward the
future rather than at the past, including their unsuccessful attempts or a disappointing medical diagnosis. Their *faith in God*
meant believing in God's provision and seeking God through prayer.
Although they did not understand God's reasons for their infertility, their belief that God was in control, and their faith in God's
goodness brought an assurance and hope for the future. With that
assurance, couples were willing to keep trying or to accept their
childlessness and go on with living. *Couple togetherness* was also
described as an important coping factor. Couple's love for one
another was described as a major strength. Facing infertility together eased the stress. Spending time together, becoming closer,
and demonstrating their love through caring behaviors were helpful. Spending time interacting with or *being around children* temporarily lessened the pain of childlessness, and these times were
selectively chosen. *Spouses' coping styles* served to support one
another, but were not necessarily similar or at times even compatible. While some differences were attributed to gender, asynchro-
nous styles contributed to anger, distancing, and conflict between
the spouses. Spouses' attempts at humor were sometimes successful, but at other times were seen as not taking things seriously
enough.

Marital Functioning

Some couples described their marriages as stronger and more *united*,
because of their experience. Although some spouses had considered divorce at one time, they decided to stay together. Couples
viewed marriage as a covenant relationship, not to be destroyed by
infertility. Infertility required an evaluation of their marriage,
and a determination of their priorities, determining to remain with
their spouse and the possibility of not having children.

> Wife: "Well, like I said earlier, it affected a lot, I think, at
> the beginning when we first found out that there was a
> problem. But we actually probably wanted to break up
> and just forget it because maybe it was me, maybe it was
> him, and we didn't want to ruin each other's life, and like I
> said, it was just love that kept us together and we had to

just overcome that and say which do we want, to be alone and unhappy or together and happy? . . . So . . . we decided to stay together and take whatever comes. We're hoping for a child."

Spousal support through verbal encouragement and reinforcement, listening, and other caring behaviors added to couples' feelings of unity. There was absolution between the dyad, even though blame was expected by some spouses. Support was sometimes difficult when one was struggling or overwhelmed with his or her own emotions (e.g., a husband not knowing how to make things better for a crying wife).

Men tended not to express their feelings in an effort to protect their wives or to decrease their wives' pain. However, support using a logical approach didn't seem supportive to wives when emotions were intense.

Communication was central to marital unity. *Open communication* with sharing of thoughts and feelings was essential for a healthy marriage, but difficult as one risked being vulnerable. Sharing one's individual experience brought understanding and was essential when working on the couple experience. On the other hand, avoiding the topic of infertility, or *closed communication,* affected coping and resolution of other life matters, frequently leading to misunderstanding and distancing.

> Husband: "I'm sure there's some thing she would do to try to expose herself to me and vice-versa. And through that, I guess we began to see each other. We sat down at one point and just explained. We never lost sight of the fact that we loved each other."

A wife described changes in their relationship over time when they weren't sharing thoughts and feelings:

> Wife: " . . . that would help. Just spending time with each other. And then after a while it just got to the point where it was more arguing. I don't know if it's ah, him blaming me and me blaming him, or if it's just that we don't know where to turn anymore. And our frustrations just build up to where it becomes an argument. I don't know if a lot of relationships wound up that way but I hate that ours did or has. I wish it would change. It seems as though because we don't have children that we are in fact becoming child-like. It's weird. It's weird."

Relationships

Relationships with *family* and *others* were affected by the infertility experience. While couples recognized supportive efforts, the end result was that they felt pressured by others, particularly parents, and they felt pain when family and others knowing and unknowingly made hurtful comments. Spouses decided not to discuss infertility outside the marriage and to maintain their privacy. This added to feelings of isolation and not fitting in, but was seen as an important protective mechanism. In this group of informants, husbands' families provided less support than their wives' families, and sometimes erected barriers, which resulted in emotional distancing of the couple.

Both the husbands and the wives described their relationships with *God* as positive and supportive. God was important in the couples' daily lives. They sought God and God's direction more during this experience. God could be trusted. Couples had faith in God's timing, fairness, and omnipotence and that God would bless them with children if that was God's will for their lives:

> Wife: "Or when someone's been waiting for it for a long time like us."
>
> Husband: "Yeah."
>
> Wife: "I think that gives us more hope, though. 'Cause we feel like, well, God could do it for them."
>
> Husband: "Yeah, then He could do it for us."
>
> Wife: "He's not partial."
>
> Husband: "No."

Another couple illustrates this theme:

> Husband: "As I know is, what I said is, that God never wastes any time. His timing is right."
>
> Wife: "Something like—It's gotten so I tell Him to hurry. I did. He knows everything. He understands I don't want to wait either. I told Him, 'We got the house now. Let's get busy' (laughing). I know you're not supposed to be disrespectful, but He understands me."

A third couple commented:

> Husband: "But if He says, 'Go see medical help,' yes I will."

Wife: "Yeah we're just prayin' . . . and if that's the direction we go, fine. He can do it any way He wants. He's God. Who are we to tell Him what to do, and how to do it (laughing). Right?"

Health Care

Health care, particularly infertility *treatment*, was not a financial possibility for most of the couples in this group. Seeking medical assistance for infertility was a major decision, filled with uncertainty and avoided by some. It meant admitting a fertility problem and failure. The threat of *diagnosis* of a fertility problem jeopardized one's self-concept as fertile and implied a problem with one's sexuality.

When treatment was sought, it was only after couples' efforts failed, after a minimum of two years. For the majority it was unavailable or limited by finances or insurance plans:

Wife: "I need medical help desperately right now and I have called a couple of clinics. I don't know what will happen with it. Everybody has a budget or a sliding scale, payment scale. It is kind of bad when you can't even pay the least amount you have to pay. So, I just say, 'Can I just bring in whatever I can bring in and when I get a little bit more I'll bring it?' Some say, 'Okay that's fine.' But then others say, 'No, I can't help you.' I desperately need medical help right now and if I don't get my condition taken care of then there won't be any children."

Time

The category of time was induced from the data with the themes of *aging* and *waiting*. Couples felt the pressure of time, primarily because they wanted to be young parents or because they wanted to conceive before older family members died.

The *waiting* for pregnancy was discouraging, painful, and difficult for most. Faith in God lessened the pain, with the belief that they will conceive at the right time.

Expenditures

Couples expended energy or *effort* in pursuing pregnancy. For these couples that meant adopting healthy habits, investigating appropriate, and at times, free health care.

Couples focused their efforts on their marriages and spousal support, in being positive and hopeful. As previously mentioned, *finances* limited diagnosis or treatment, as well as some demonstrations of spousal support.

Self-Perception

Couples perceived themselves as different from others, but spouses had individual issues to resolve. For husbands, having a child, particularly a son, was a demonstration of *manliness*. Their security as fertile men was shaken by wives' requests for diagnostic testing. Men also believed that their role was to shield their wives from pain and sorrow when possible. This meant suppressing or concealing their own emotions in order to be strong for their wives. For men, crying in front of spouses was described as a sign of weakness.

Wives expressed guilt at not fulfilling their perceived *roles as wives and as women*, of not bearing a child for their spouse. Women tended to feel responsible for the couple's infertility, even when a formal diagnosis wasn't present.

Both spouses discussed confidence in being good *parents*. They related experiences with children that validated they would do well. Being able to provide a home and necessities was important to them and demonstrated their readiness and willingness to be responsible parents.

Discussion

The experience of involuntary childlessness is painful and frustrating to couples of all cultures, but may be intensified for black couples, as African-American families are traditionally centered around children, and being a mother or father is a salient role (Crosbie-Burnett & Lewis, 1993). This group of informants demonstrated numerous strengths while experiencing both a situational and a developmental crisis. In order to survive and cope with the crises, spouses evaluated their past and present to determine their future. Rather than divorcing or conceiving outside of marriage, dyads chose to retain their marriage and identity as a couple. This is in sharp contrast to the cavalier attitude of black males depicted by the media. This choice meant couples had to develop new coping strategies or enhance those currently existing, to work through conflict and develop mutual understanding. Informants experienced sorrow, anger, and frustration at the uncertainty and perceived unfairness of their childlessness, yet were working at

managing the stresses associated with their experience by supporting one another, focusing on other aspects of living, adopting a
positive approach and having faith in God, God's timing and provision. This was not readily accomplished in light of the unavailabil-
ity or lack of access to available social and economic resources,
particularly those related to health care. Rather than expending
energies in external activities, interests, and supports, the couples
tended to invest in building a strong marital relationship by improving couple communication, affirming one another and engaging in caring behaviors. Their shared concept of God and level of
couple spirituality helped to strengthen their relationship.

Infertility required a reassessment of who the couple was in
relation to their family and community. Couples in this study
tended to isolate themselves from others to protect themselves from
discomfort, feelings of differentness, and others' perceived insensitivity. Their response to extended families was somewhat surprising, as one might expect kin to be a major support. However, even
though some familial support was present, couples often emotionally distanced themselves as a result of pressure or conflict related
to family values, or desires, and the dyads' need for privacy. Couples
seemed unwilling to rely on informal support networks, because
others had not lived through their experience, and spouses believed they would not find meaningful support there.

Implications

The study of couple infertility provides a rich opportunity to explore family resiliency in light of both situational and developmental crises. Books and television programs on infertility describe
the experiences of middle and upper income families, primarily
white, going through expensive and time-consuming treatment. The
media also tend to focus on birth control and fertility rates of
African Americans, on problems of female-headed families with
numerous children, and the image of paternal neglect of children.
These presentations serve to emphasize infertile couples'
differentness by their failure to conceive. In addition, there is
little public support of their intense desire to have children in light
of their economic circumstances. It is as if their problem or experience does not exist or has no relevance to society. Unfortunately,
they receive little or no support and their strengths go unrecog-
nized.

The need for infertility services is projected to increase for
all racial and socioeconomic groups in the coming years (Aral &

Cates, 1983; Hogue & Mollencamp, 1984), related to the rise in sexually transmitted diseases, medical advancements and delayed childbearing (Sherris & Fox, 1983; Moore & Spadoni, 1984; Goldsmith, 1989). In the event of health care reform, more couples will have access to health care and infertility services. The provision of holistic care will be impossible without an understanding of racial and socioeconomic contexts of couple infertility.

Note

1. This research was funded by a grant from the National Institute of Health.

References

Aral, S. O., & Cates, W.J. (1983). The increasing concern with infertility. Why now? *Journal of the American Medical Association, 250,* 2327–2331.

Colaizzi, P.F. (1978). Psychological research as the phenomenologist views it. In R. Vails & M. King (Eds.), *Existential phenomenological alternative for psychology* (pp. 48–71). New York: Oxford University Press.

Crosbie-Burnett, M., & Lewis, E.A. (1993). Use of African-American family structures and functioning to address the challenges of European-American post divorce families. *Family Relations, 42,* 243–248.

Goldsmith, M.F. (1989). Silent epidemic of 'social disease' makes STD experts raise their voices. *Journal of the American Medical Association, 261,* 3509–3510.

Hirsch, M.D., & Mosher, W.D. (1987). Characteristics of infertile women in the United States and their use of infertility services. *Fertility and Sterility, 47,* 618–625.

Hogue, C. J., & Mollencamp, M. (1984). The increasing concern with infertility. (Letter). *Journal of the American Medical Association, 252,* 208.

Hollingshead, A.B. (1975). *Four Factor Index of Social Status.* Unpublished working paper, Yale University, Department of Sociology.

Kalmuss, D.S. (1987). The use of infertility services among fertility-impaired couples. *Demography, 24,* 575–585.

Link, P.W., & Darling, C.A. (1986). Couples undergoing treatment for infertility: Dimensions of life satisfaction. *Journal of Sex and Marital Therapy, 12,* 46–59.

Moore, D.E., & Spadoni, L.R. (1984). Infertility in women. In K. Holmes, P. Mardly, P.F. Sparling, & P. J. Wiesner (Eds.), *Sexually transmitted diseases* (pp. 763–773). New York: McGraw-Hill.

Natanson, M. (1973). *Edmund Husserl: Philosopher of infinite tasks.* Evanston, IL: Northwestern University Press.

Oiler, C. (1982). The phenomenological approach in nursing research. *Nursing Research, 31,* 178–181.

Omery, A. (1983). Phenomenology: A method for nursing research. *Advances in Nursing Science, 5,* 49–63.

Reimen, D.J. (1986). The essential structure of a caring interaction. In P. Manhall & C. Oiler (Eds.), *Nursing research: A qualitative perspective* (pp. 69–84). Norwalk, CT: Appleton-Century-Crofts.

Sherris, J.D., & Fox, G. (1983). Infertility and STD: A public health challenge. *Population Reports, L,* 114–151.

Spiegelburg, H. (1976). *The phenomenological movement.* The Hague: Martinus Nijhoff.

Streubert, H., & Carpenter, D. (1995). *Qualitative research in nursing: Advancing the humanistic imperative.* Philadelphia: Lippincott.

U.S. Department of Health and Human Services, Public Health Service. (1985). Infertility—United States, 1982. *Morbidity and Mortality Weekly Report, 34*(14), 197–199. Washington DC: U.S. Government Printing Office.

Chapter 13

Observing Mother-Daughter Interaction in African-American and Asian-American Families

Nancy A. Gonzales, Yumi Hiraga, and Ana Mari Cauce[1]

There has been a surge of interest in ethnic diversity within the social sciences in recent years. Prompted by broad social, political, and historical trends within the United States, strong incentives now exist for the inclusion of persons of color in social and psychological research in this country. The "decade of ethnicity," a phrase coined by Shweder and Sullivan (1993) to describe the emergence of ethnic diversity as a viable research agenda in the 1990s, is being received with a multitude of mixed reactions. Those who value ethnic research are optimistic about the opportunity to generate a more nearly *universal* psychology that will be valid for a wider range of cultures. In designing efforts to operationalize this objective, however, investigators are faced with countless methodological questions and challenges. What constitutes an "ethnic" group, and how does ethnicity relate to other concepts such as culture, nationality, race? Will diverse groups consent to participate in research? How should they be recruited? Are standard research measures, theories, and methodologies appropriate for use with culturally distinct populations?

Studying Multiple Ethnic Groups: Is It a Bad Idea?

One fundamental question that must be addressed by researchers who wish to study diverse populations is whether to focus exclusively on a single ethnic group in an effort to understand a "culturally specific" phenomenon, or whether to include more than one group in a single study. Opposing positions on this issue have been backed over the years by strong theoretical as well as political appeals. On one side of the debate are those who argue that ethnic populations should not be studied in relation to each other, because of the inevitable tendency to view one group (typically the non-"mainstream" group) as deficient by comparison. Indeed this is the argument we have advanced in our own work, and it is a position that is fueled by the fact that social science research has been used historically to support damaging ethnic stereotypes and deleterious social policies. Much of the "ethnic" research conducted in this country within the last decade has focused specifically on single ethnic populations in response to these concerns, and typically has not sought to generalize findings across groups.

Persuasive arguments have also been advanced for research that applies constructs and theories across diverse groups in order to directly examine ethnic differences. This position assumes that all groups share at least some "universal" features by virtue of their shared humanity, and to the extent that theories are not equivalent across ethnic groups, theoretical perspectives may be broadened at the same time that the unique role of culture is revealed (Berry, Poortinga, Segall, & Dasen, 1992; Betancourt & Lopez, 1993). An argument for multigroup studies can also be advanced on a practical level. In this country, at this time, representative samples in most cities are by definition *multi*-ethnic, often including groups which can be divided into several categories of national origin, language, and immigration/acculturation status. It is this very aspect of American culture that challenges educators and mental health professionals charged with the responsibility of providing services that are "sensitive to differences" that may exist. Research designed to identify ethnic differences and similarities across groups, especially that which has implications for public health and public policy, is thus becoming increasingly important.

As more investigators respond to the call for multiethnic research, they will be challenged to bridge substantive theoretical interests with cross-cultural strategies. In the pages to follow, we will outline several challenges that we encountered in a study designed to examine the psychosocial development and psychological adjustment of African-American and Asian-American adolescents living in the Pacific Northwest. Rather than review results from the project that have been presented elsewhere (Mason, Cauce, Gonzales, Hiraga, & Grove, 1994b; Mason, Cauce, Gonzales, &

Hiraga, 1994a; Gonzales, Cauce, & Mason, 1995a), this chapter will discuss several methodological questions that were raised in planning and implementing the project.

The Research Plan: Confronting Ethnocentric Biases

The study was part of a larger project designed to prospectively test an ecological model of socioemotional development within two groups of ethnic families, Asian-American and African-American. The family was viewed as a direct source of socializing influence, and as both a mediator and moderator of influences external to the family. External factors included aspects of the neighborhood environment, adolescent peer groups, parents' work environments, and extra-familial social ties. The study plan called for interviews with parents and adolescents, using standard questionnaire measures assessing each domain of influence, every year for three years, as adolescents moved from junior high school into high school.

Given the fact that the study utilized an ecological perspective, which interprets behavior in context, it was not subject to some of the interpretive biases associated with a decontextualized approach to the study of ethnic families (Liddle, 1987; Szapocznik & Kurtines, 1993). Furthermore, Anglo-American families were not included as a reference group, and the study would assume no evaluative stance with respect to differences that might be revealed between Asian-American and African-American families. Nevertheless, we remained concerned with the degree of ethnocentric bias that might be introduced by our approach to studying these families.

Because we planned to examine similar processes within both groups of families, our methodology required that we choose *one* set of measures that could be applied to *both* groups. Consequently we were operating on the assumption that "universal" dimensions could be used to characterize family functioning within two distinct cultural groups. Much of the available socialization literature, however, had focused almost exclusively on white, middle-class families. Research on Asian-American and African-American families was notably lacking at the time the study was developed. Our selection of measures accordingly remained rooted in mainstream psychology. The following study developed out of our concern that the chosen self-report measures had demonstrated no evidence of cross-ethnic equivalence (see Hui & Triandis, 1985, for a discussion of this issue), and thus might lead to erroneous conclusions regarding family influences. A second study was thus planned with a subsample of families who were videotaped while engaging in a structured family interaction task. This study was designed to provide objective ratings of actual family behavior that would serve as criterion against which to validate the self-report measures.

Description of the Study

Because a large percentage of African-American youths live in single, mother-headed households, we decided to focus on mother-child interactions, and not include father-child dyads or larger family units. Given the fact that interactions between mothers and their adolescent children are known to vary with the sex of the child, and after discovering during initial recruitment efforts that adolescent females were more willing to participate than males, we also decided to restrict the investigation to mother-daughter interactions. Finally, the study was limited to the examination of three aspects of the mother-daughter relationship. Maternal warmth/ support and maternal control were chosen as dimensions of parenting that have been repeatedly identified in the literature as critical (Maccoby & Martin, 1983), and as potentially "pancultural" (Minturn & Lambert, 1964). In addition, parent-adolescent conflict was included due to its prominent role within the family during early adolescence (Steinberg, 1990). The plan was thus to obtain observational ratings of maternal warmth/support, maternal restrictive control, and parent-adolescent conflict for 60 families within each ethnic group.

Procedure

The videotaped family interaction task was modeled after procedures commonly used in observational research to generate family discussions on topics that are personally relevant to each participating family (Robin & Weiss, 1980). Prior to the videotaped discussion, mothers and daughters were asked to independently complete a battery of questionnaires which included the Issues Checklist (IC; Prinz & Kent, in Foster & Robin, 1988). The IC is a measure of parent-adolescent conflict that asks respondents to identify and rate sources of conflict that they have had in the past months from a list of 44 potential topics of disagreement. After independently completing this questionnaire, mothers and daughters were comfortably seated in a small discussion room equipped for videotaping. They were given 5 minutes to jointly review their lists and to select the single most problematic source of conflict, immediately followed by 10 minutes in which to discuss and reach an agreement regarding the chosen topic.

Observational Coding. Behavioral ratings of parental support, parental restrictive control, and parent-adolescent conflict were based on a modified version of a global coding system developed by Sarason, Pierce and Sarason (1990). The original coding system consisted of 37 items, which are rated by independent coders on a 6-point scale ranging from 1 (not at all) to 6 (extremely), yielding 4 primary factors: parental warmth/support toward child, child warmth/support toward parent, parental restrictiveness, and degree of dyadic conflict (Sarason, Pierce, & Sarason, 1990). Items that were most representative of the constructs specifically targeted by the survey measures were chosen to index parental warmth, parental control, and conflict. This was done in order to maximize the conceptual and operational fit between the content of the self-report items and the coded behaviors.

Self-Report Family Measures. The Child-Rearing Practices Report (CRPR; Block, 1965) was originally developed as a self-descriptive instrument, but has been revised to be used as a child-report measure of parental socialization practices. Parents and adolescents completed their respective versions which required them to indicate, on a 5-point Likert scale (1 = definitely false to 5 = definitely true), the accuracy of a number of statements as they apply to the behavior of the mother. Previous studies have revealed that a 40-item, two-factor solution best describes response patterns obtained from parents and college-age students (Rickel & Biasatti, 1982). The two-factor solution was utilized in the present study, yielding scale scores for the following dimensions: parental warmth/support (support), and parental restrictiveness/control (control).

The Issues Checklist (IC; Prinz & Kent, in Robin & Foster, 1984) as described above was used as a measure of parent-adolescent conflict. Respondents indicate first whether each of the 44 issues has been broached during the past 4 weeks, how often each issue was discussed, and then rate the average anger intensity of those discussions. These reports yield three scores: the total number of issues, the average anger intensity, and a weighted frequency by anger intensity score. The average anger intensity score has been shown to discriminate between distressed and non-distressed families, and was used as a measure of parent-adolescent conflict in the present study (Robin & Foster, 1984; Prinz, Rosenblum, & O'Leary, 1978).

Criterion Measures. Three indicators of development outcome were included as criterion upon which to assess the concurrent validity of the family measures. All three outcomes—academic achievement, behavior problems, and symptoms of depression—have been linked to family influences within the developmental and clinical literature. Academic achievement was based on self-reported grades, which have been recommended as appropriate and reliable indicators of current school performance (Dornbusch et al., 1987). The Child Behavior Checklist (CBCL; Achenbach & Edelbrock, 1983) is a widely utilized instrument for assessing parents' perception of their children's behavioral (externalizing) and emotional (internalizing) problems. The externalizing subscale from the CBCL was used to index adolescent behavioral problems. The Child Depression Inventory (CDI; Kovacs, 1981, 1986) is the most commonly cited and thoroughly researched self-report measure of childhood depression and was used to index depressive symptomatology (Finch & Conway, 1985).

Observing Ethnic Families:
Methodological Issues and Findings

The primary aim of the study was to examine the validity of survey measures of parenting behavior and parent-adolescent conflict. In designing and implementing the study, however, several additional methodological questions related to observational research with ethnic minority families were raised. Thus a strategy that was selected to address one set of methodological questions, in fact introduced a new set of concerns. These will be discussed in the sections to follow.

Recruitment: Where Oh
Where Are You?

Before we began the project, we had some doubts about whether we could recruit a sample of 60 African-American and 60 Asian-American families to participate in a laboratory-based research project, especially a project that asked them to reveal family dynamics to a group of researchers and a video camera. We were located in a psychology department that routinely recruited families for videotaping, but noted the conspicuous lack of families of color among the ranks of those filing in and out of various labs in the department. We had no reason to think that ethnic families were purposefully being excluded by investigators who typically advertised on a community-wide level, but suspected that there might be ethnic differences in willingness to volunteer for such studies.

As we had suspected, we found tremendous differences in our ability to recruit the families in which we were interested. Potential adolescents and parents were contacted through a variety of formal and informal networks within various community organizations and schools. This strategy proved to be quite effective as a method of reaching the African-American community, which tends to be racially segregated in the Seattle area. Many families live in predominantly African-American neighborhoods and attend schools in which African-American students are in the majority. In addition, after-school activities, including local teen hangouts, tend to be racially homogeneous. Thus we were able to locate large groups of potential participants with relative ease. Furthermore, many of the African-American adolescents expressed immediate interest in participating in the study. We were likely aided by the fact that we were offering $50 for participation in the project, and our research staff itself was multiethnic. Two of the current authors are Latina, one is Japanese American, and our research staff included an ethnically diverse group of research assistants, including African-American students. In general, African-American mothers were also interested in participating in the study.

While initially encouraged by the positive response we had received in our recruitment efforts, we soon discovered many of the obstacles that prevent otherwise interested families from being included in laboratory-based research. The African-American families as a group experienced a number of difficulties that served as barriers to participation. The university was located some distance from many of the families who had to deal with transportation limitations, along with generally busy schedules and limited resources. Fifty percent of the sample included single mothers, and 86% of the mothers in the sample held full-time jobs. Some held more than one job, worked weekends, or attended classes themselves, and the majority had more than one child at home. In addition, for many families, the interview was to be their first time on the campus of a large university, which likely heightened their perceptions of the task as intimidating. Despite the fact that we had more than enough families who had agreed to participate within just a few months of our start date, and we began to make transportation and in-lab babysitting available, it took the better part of a year to complete interviews with 60 families.

The final sample of African-American adolescents in the study had a mean age of 13 years, 3 months.[2] Approximately one third of these adolescents were living with both biological parents, while another third were living in single-parent households (all of them lived with their mothers), and the remaining third were living in a variety of extended and blended family structures. Income level varied considerably among the families. Approximately 32% of the families reported a household income at or below $15,000, 36% reported income levels between $15,000 and $30,000, and 32% had incomes greater than $30,000.

In recruiting the Asian-American sample, we encountered a different set of problems that ultimately proved more difficult to circumvent. Although it has often been the case that Asian Americans have been grouped into one category, there are many differences between the various Asian-American groups. These differences include language, value systems, communication patterns, and immigration patterns, all of which become relevant when doing research with these populations.[3] In the initial stages of the study, we originally planned to examine only Japanese-American families so as to avoid grouping individuals who have very different cultural backgrounds. However, due to several problems that will be described, we were unable to recruit a large enough sample of Japanese-American families. Consequently we altered our plans midstream and decided to include Chinese-American families. Japanese- and Chinese-American families share many cultural patterns and are more similar to each other in terms of acculturation and immigration patterns in the Pacific Northwest than other Asian groups. Yet even this combination of Asian groups was not ideal.

Furthermore, even after deciding to sample both Japanese- and Chinese-American families, we ran into difficulties finding these populations. Although Seattle is a mecca for Asian Americans, most of the Japanese and Chinese Americans are spread out across the greater Seattle area. Seattle no longer has a "Chinatown," but rather, an "International District" consisting of many Asian groups. Unlike the African-American community, or even other newer Asian communities, Japanese and Chinese Americans do not, for the most part, congregate in one place. This is related to generational status, particularly for Japanese Americans. Japanese Americans tend to be third and fourth generation, thus more integrated into mainstream society. Few are recent immigrants. Since these families were spread across the city, obtaining our sample was very difficult. None of the schools had a predominant Japanese- or Chinese-American population. Youth clubs catering to Asian youth were nonexistent. We needed to search far and wide for our sample.

In addition, many of the adolescents who responded to our flyers and posters turned out to be biracial, in that one parent was Japanese or Chinese American while the other parent was of a different race. Yet these children considered themselves "Japanese American" or "Chinese American" (Cauce et al., 1992). Again, we attributed this to the degree of acculturation of these groups and to high outmarriage rates. We had to exclude these families from the study. Whereas some of the adolescents who responded to our advertisements for African-American teenagers were also biracial, a far greater number and a greater proportion of these youths were not. In contrast, biracial Asian-American adolescents were more likely to respond to our recruitment efforts than monoracial Asian-American adolescents.

By far, however, the greatest difficulty we faced in finding an Asian-American sample was simply a low response rate to all of our efforts at recruitment. It has been noted that Japanese- and Chinese-American families value privacy, particularly with respect to the family, and they are less willing to reveal information about themselves, much less anything that might be construed as negative. "Saving face"—that one be well perceived by others— is important in Japanese and Chinese cultures. It is related to shame, which is another important concept within both cultures. Feelings of "saving face" and shame both guide and motivate behavior in terms of conforming to society or family expectations; an individual avoids losing face or bringing shame to one's family at all costs (see Huang & Ying, 1989). Discussion of personal or family problems in front of others, rather than keeping it within the family or close friends relates to a "loss of face." The Asian-American families that we approached were clearly reticent about engaging in such an activity. Many families who agreed to participate in the larger study balked at the idea of being videotaped. Unlike the African-American sample, in which many of the teenagers knew each other and to some extent supported each other to enter the study, few of the Asian-American teenagers knew each other. The net result of our efforts over a 9-month period resulted in a total of 33 families, only 55% of the targeted sample. The adolescents in the Asian-American sample had a mean age of 12 years, 11 months. The majority (88%) of these adolescents lived with both biological parents in homes that were primarily middle-class.

Reactions to Direct
Observation: "Where's the
Camera?"

In addition to our concerns about ethnic differences in participation rates, we also noted differential responses to the study procedures. Once in the laboratory setting, the African-American families demonstrated no apparent distress or inhibition about the nature of the task or the research setting. We believe that their comfort may have been facilitated by the fact that an African-American researcher was present during all sessions, and that our research staff took other steps to create a warm and inviting environment. By and large, the African-American families appeared to take the task seriously, but seemed to relax and enjoy the procedure. When given instructions to resolve a chosen conflict, for example, many mothers approached the task as an opportunity to "really work something out" with their daughters. Some even wanted to continue with their discussions beyond the allotted 10 minutes in order to "finish what they had started."

Rather than being inhibited by the presence of a camera, many of the families seemed to enjoy being videotaped. Indeed, many of the adolescents, and a few of the mothers, couldn't resist the temptation to "ham it up" for the camera. Several families asked to watch themselves on videotape at the end of the study, and found it humorous and informative. This is not meant to imply, however, that the interactions were uniformly pleasant. Several of the mother-daughter interactions were obviously conflictual and upsetting. Even in these cases, however, the mothers and daughters both seemed willing to acknowledge their difficulties during open-ended interviews that occurred at the end of the session. Furthermore, immediately following the videotaped interaction, mothers and daughters completed questionnaires that asked them to rate their own interactions on several dimensions. In response to the item "to what extent was the discussion you just had about this topic similar to other discussions you have had with your daughter/mother on this topic," 86% of the adolescents and 79% of the mothers responded "quite a bit" or "very, very much."

The Asian-American families as a group had a markedly different response to the study. Even though families were informed about the study procedures before they came to the laboratory, many of the families appeared uncomfortable during the task. In some of the interactions, the conversations appeared stilted, as though the mothers and daughters wanted to look "good" for the camera. This aspect was also accentuated by the dressed up appearance of many of these mothers. Unlike the African-American families, these families appeared more acutely aware of the video camera. Again, this may have to do with the importance of "putting on a good face." Rather than openly expressing disagreement or disclosing potentially revealing information, the Asian-American mothers and daughters often preferred to shield themselves from the view of the camera and to whisper. It seemed as though these families avoided "hot" topics and felt uncomfortable discussing conflict, as evidenced by uncomfortable giggles, silences, inability to find a topic of conflict, and discussions that did not directly focus on the conflict. These families were either tremendously inhibited by the experimental procedure, or they simply do not engage in conflict in the same manner as families typically studied in observational research. For instance, one mother and daughter pair spent most of the interaction laughing uncontrollably, rather than coming up with solutions to their conflict. Hsu, Tseng, Ashton, McDermott, and Char (1985) hypothesized that this pattern may be due to the cultural emphasis on harmony in social relations, which downplays disagreement with one another.

Coding Family Interactions: "That's not how I see it!"

One of the most intriguing aspects of doing observational research with ethnic families is that there are such obvious differences in communication patterns and styles of expression that are both fascinating and enjoyable to behold. We were entertained by the spontaneity, wit, and humor of several of the African-American families, and impressed by the candor with which they discussed sensitive issues. We were equally impressed by the subtle way in which Asian-American families seemed to communicate so much by saying so little. We were touched by the many, varied displays of tenderness of the mothers in both groups who helped their daughters reason through personal dilemmas, giggled with their daughters, and fussed with their clothes and hair. Unfortunately, the available coding systems that have been developed to rate family interactions do not account for these rich and subtle communications, nor the striking differences that we observed. Indeed, in an effort to maximize interrater reliability, many coding systems attempt to disallow for the possibility that the same construct might be operationalized by different behaviors, or that the same behavior might have a different meaning within different families.

For this reason, the choice of an appropriate observational coding system proved even more challenging than the selection of paper-and-pencil measures for the original study had been. Despite the fact that observational techniques had proliferated as a method for studying families within developmental psychology, clinical psychology, and family studies, few studies at the time had yet to include ethnically diverse families. Since coding systems had not been developed for either Asian-American or African-American families, we were left with the choice of using an existing system with codes that might not accurately capture the patterns of interaction in these families, or developing entirely new coding schemes. Given the fact that we had hoped to use the same coding system for both groups, yet the primary purpose of the study was to obtain behavioral ratings that would serve as culturally anchored validity criterion within each group, we opted for a combined "etic-emic" strategy.

Cross-culturalists make a distinction between culture-specific and culture-general (or universal) aspects of behavior. The former are referred to as emic, the latter as etic aspects. Using what has been called an "iterative" approach (Berry et al., 1992), we chose an available coding system (imposed etic), and then scrutinized the system for cultural appropriateness and modified it in an emic phase. A combined etic-emic approach has been recommended by Triandis (1978), and it is claimed that with such an instrument, an emically defined etic construct is obtained that can be used for comparisons.

To assist us in this process, we sought consultation from two expert panels, one from the African-American community and one from the Asian-American community, each of which consisted of parents, psychology graduate students, and mental health professionals (social workers and psychologists). These panels were asked to review the coding system and to provide information about the appropriateness of the codes for defining the constructs. In addition, consultants viewed and coded tapes and helped to develop culturally appropriate criterion upon which to base behavioral ratings. Our experiences in working with the community consultants was informative, both in terms of providing information about the validity of the coding scheme and as a source of information about culturally important family dynamics that we were missing with our chosen measures.

African-American Families. The panel of African-American consultants included 5 mental health professionals (1 psychologist and 4 social workers) working in a community mental health agency, and 3 mothers who were asked to attend a series of 3 meetings to discuss the coding system and to review videotapes. The first question we asked of the group was whether the 3 family constructs were meaningful from a cultural standpoint, and whether the chosen codes accurately captured these dimensions.

For the most part, the panel of experts agreed that parental warmth/support, parental restrictive control, and conflict were salient features of mother-daughter relationships. Furthermore, when asked to place individual items on the coding system into one of these categories, the proportion of correctly identified items was consistently high. Correct identification was indicated when an informant accurately identified an item as belonging to the conceptual category (i.e., one of the three subscales) to which it belonged in the coding system. Out of the 17 core items used to index the three dimensions of interest, 14 items were correctly labeled by all 8 consultants. Three items that yielded less than perfect agreement were items on the maternal control factor, which were each misidentified by only one consultant as indices of parent-adolescent conflict.

In addition to agreeing that the dimensions and codes were appropriate, our expert panel also advised that we were omitting other features of parenting, such as socialization regarding racial issues, that they believed were important for maturing adolescents. This particular issue we found difficult to address with our coding strategy, but agreed that it is worthy of further attention. The community consultants also suggested that we had overlooked the crux of good parenting by failing to assess the "positive" control strategies that African-American mothers used to set clear and firm rules, and to establish themselves as influential authority figures in the eyes of their children. As one social worker expressed it, "the strength of the African-American mother is in her power . . . she's compassionate, yet uncompromising and tough when she has to be." Given the unanimous feelings of the group that this was important, new items were added to the coding system in an effort to capture this aspect of control.

In fact, this dimension of parental control is not new to the developmental or family literature. "Firm" control (versus "lax" control) was first identified by Schaefer (1965) and is conceptually related to the "demandingness" component of Baumrind's authoritative parenting style (1971). Of interest here is that not only was firmness also being identified by our consultants, but it was viewed as perhaps the most important feature of socialization in the African-American family. Furthermore, "firm" control was described by the panel as being "uncompromising" and "tough," qualities which are most frequently used to describe the "authoritarian" style (Baumrind, 1971).

We did not attempt to directly test Baumrind's (1971) tripartite model of parenting style (i.e., authoritative, authoritarian, permissive). However, the feedback that we obtained in our work with community consultants has led us to question the cross-cultural validity of the authoritarian and authoritative distinction with African-American families. Others have entertained similar questions, including Baumrind herself, who reported that authoritarian parental control may not lead to the same negative outcomes for African-American children that are observed within white, middle-class populations (Baumrind, 1972; Steinberg, Mounts, Lamborn, & Dornbusch, 1991). Similarly, our quantitative analyses indicate that higher levels of restrictive parental control may be associated with better outcomes for African-American adolescents living in high-risk neighborhoods (Gonzales et al., 1995b; Mason et al., 1994a). Though it is not our intention to present analyses from the larger study in the present discussion, this point illustrates the importance of examining research theories and measures for cross-ethnic equivalence.

Asian-American Families. Whereas African-American and Anglo families often communicate disagreement and power in a verbal manner, such as by arguing and giving orders, Lebra (1976) reported that in Asian cultures, people communicate conflict nonverbally, such as by facial expression, and by empathic means. Communication in general tends to be nonverbal, indirect, and implicit. We found this to be true when working with the Asian-American sample. During the family interactions, the Asian-American families were indeed less direct with each other and less revealing of their thoughts and feelings. This was true to such an extent that we, and some of our trained coders, still remain uncertain about how to interpret many of these interactions. Consequently, we experienced greater difficulty applying the chosen coding system with the Asian-American sample. Even our panel of experts had a difficult time reaching agreement when interpreting the videotaped interactions. Our struggles were likely compounded by the fact that the group was made up of a combination of Chinese-American and Japanese-American students and professionals who also varied widely in generation status.

Despite these difficulties, identical items were used to index the three subscales (maternal support, maternal restrictive control, parent-adolescent conflict) for the Asian-American and African-American families. For each of these items, however, our consultants recommended different operational criteria, which allowed us to capture "emic" aspects of the constructs. Additionally, a number of new items were added to the coding scheme solely for the Asian-American families in an attempt to assess dimensions that seemed of unique relevance to this group. For instance, two items were added to the coding scheme based on the previous work by Bell, Bell, and Munakata (1989). One item, "daughter is dependent upon the mother to provide ideas, solutions, and thoughts," was used to measure *amae*. *Amae* is a Japanese term used to describe a cultural pattern of getting what you want by depending on another. In their work coding the interactions of Japanese families, Bell et al. (1989) report that Japanese coders often have difficulty understanding the American concept of "power" in interpersonal relations. Conversely, U.S. coders find the concept of *amae*, which is related to interpersonal power, difficult to grasp. Another item was added to capture the contrast between *tatemae* and *honne*, Japanese terms that reflect the extent to which an individual is revealing true feelings versus what is expected of her (allowing the social standard to dictate one's behavior).

Although the concepts of *tatemae*, and *honne* and *amae* are directly taken from the Japanese culture, similar ideas exist in the Chinese culture. Similar to Japanese Americans, Chinese Americans are expected to suppress their emotions, especially in public situations, which may again be related to saving face. In addition, interdependence or dependence is highly encouraged in the Chinese family (Huang & Ying, 1989). Because of the similar values and ideas in the two cultures, we applied these concepts to both groups: Chinese- and Japanese-American families.

Ethnic Biases Among Coders

Our experiences in refining the coding system and viewing tapes, particularly those within the Asian-American sample, told us that we might well get different ratings depending on whom we chose to code the videotapes. We felt quite strongly about having coders who were of the same ethnic background as the families they would rate because of the potential for biases stemming from the subjective, and perhaps ethnocentric, judgments of independent coders. Since ethnic families had rarely been included in observational family research, however, the issue of ethnic biases among data coders had not been previously addressed. Thus, we also decided to include Anglo-American coders for each group in order to examine differences in ratings between coders of similar (ingroup) and dissimilar (outgroup) ethnicity.

A total of 6 female coders were trained to code the African-American tapes, 3 African-American and 3 non-African-American coders. Not surprisingly, we found much less agreement among this group of coders than we had among the expert panel. The training process involved 72 hours of reviewing items, viewing and coding tapes, reviewing and discussing ratings and discrepancies, and attempting to reach a consensus. Though it is not possible to review all of the interesting observations we made during this training process, one issue was repeated time and again throughout the process. Many times when coders in the project disagreed about items during training, their impressions hinged on the degree to which they perceived the African-American mothers as being "harsh" in their responses. Behavior viewed as potentially rejecting and/or critical by non-African-American coders, was often seen as appropriately "firm" behavior by the African-American coders. An example that we have used to illustrate this point is the response of one mother when her daughter referred to her as "pal." To this her mother replied, "I'll give you pal in the mouth. I'm *not* your pal!" While at first glance this appears to be a rather harsh reaction, the interaction in its totality was characterized by a great deal of give-and-take, warmth, and good humor. Even in this instance, the mother's manner was an almost teasing one; both were smiling and engaged. The mother succeeded in making a point, however, which was that she was the boss and that she would not be charmed out of the position she had taken on an issue. This point seemed clear and appropriate to the African-American coders who saw this mother as warm and effective. The interpretation of this type of interaction was much less clear to the non-African-American coders.

When we statistically examined the ratings provided by the two groups of raters (ingroup versus outgroup) we found a similar pattern of differences in their perceptions (Gonzales, Cauce, & Mason, 1995a). Mean ingroup and outgroup ratings for each of the four scales are presented in Table 1 along with results from paired t tests, which were used to compare means. No differences were noted on the maternal support dimension. Consistent with the differences that were observed during training, however, the non-African-American coders rated families as significantly more conflictual (t = -2.39, p < .05) and rated mothers as somewhat more controlling of their daughters (t = -2.36, p < .05). The African-American coders, on the other hand, were significantly more likely to interpret the behavior of mothers as appropriately "firm" (t = 3.06, p < .01), rather than controlling, in addition to viewing the interactions as less conflictual. Inspection of the means in Table 1 reveal that these differences are not substantial. However, when considered in light of the hours of training that were invested in eliminating discrepancies between coders, the significant differences do suggest the presence of systematic ethnic biases. Furthermore, when outgroup and ingroup ratings were compared to mother and daughter reports, the African-American (ingroup) raters provided scores that were uniformly more consistent with the individual family members' own perceptions than those provided by non-African-American raters (outgroup).

Table 1
Differences Between Ingroup and Outgroup Ratings of Maternal Support, Maternal Restrictive Control, Maternal Firm Control, and Parent-child Conflict in African-American Families.

	Ethnicity of Raters				
	Ingroup		Outgroup		
Scale	Mean*	S.D	Mean*	S.D.	t-Test
Maternal Support	4.47	.108	4.44	.125	.30
Maternal Restrictive Control	3.05	.074	3.32	.077	-2.36[a]
Maternal Firm Control	3.39	.101	3.22	.113	3.06[b]
Parent-Child Conflict	2.18	.099	2.54	.100	-2.39[a]

[a] Significant at p < .05
[b] Significant at p < .01
* Total scale scores have been converted to original scaling units (1=Not at all, 6 = Extremely).

Seven coders (two Japanese-American, two Chinese-American, and three Anglo-American) were trained to code the Asian-American family interactions. All of the Asian-American coders were bilingual because, though uncommon, some of the less acculturated mothers began to speak in their native language during the interaction task. Typically when this occurred, the daughters responded in English. Needless to say it was not possible for our Anglo coders, none of whom spoke Japanese or Chinese, to code these portions of the tapes. Many hours were spent in training with these coders, including a substantial portion of time reviewing *amae* and the difference between *tatemae* and *honne*. Similar to our struggles with the African-American families, coders for this group also disagreed frequently about whether a family appeared "warm" and/or "controlling." By the end of training, coders had reached acceptable levels of agreement with interrater reliabilities for the final data ranging from .77 to .85. We have yet to assess whether the ethnic or cultural makeup of these coders themselves influenced their ratings.

Questions of Validity: Some Good News and Some Bad News

Additional contrasts between the Asian-American and African-American data were found when we examined convergent and concurrent validity indices for each group. Convergent validity was examined first by comparing the observational ratings with mothers' and daughters' ratings of each construct. Because our analysis of the African-American ratings revealed differences between ingroup and outgroup scores, the outgroup scores were dropped as the least valid set of observational ratings upon which to evaluate the self-report measures. As such, the following analyses are based strictly on those ratings provided by the respective ingroup raters (African-American and Asian-American).

Convergent Validity. As shown in Table 2, the correlations between the independent ratings and self-report indices are strikingly different between the African-American and Asian-American samples. Indeed, none of the correlations within the Asian-American sample are significant. Even after allowing for differences in sample size, the magnitude of the correlations are obviously much poorer for the Asian-American sample than for the African-American sample. Independent ratings of maternal support and maternal control are not related to mothers' and daughters' views of the relationship within the Asian-American families. Furthermore, independent ratings of conflict were actually negatively related to the mothers' and daughters' reports, though not significantly so. Despite the difficulties we experienced in the coding process with the Asian-American families, the complete absence of significant findings was surprising to us. These findings indicate that either the coded data is not a valid indicator of the chosen constructs, or that the self report measures are not valid, or perhaps both.

Table 2
Convergent Validity Coefficients: Correlations Between Adolescent Report, Parent Report, and Direct Observation of Maternal Support, Maternal Restrictive Control, and Parent-Adolescent Conflict.

Independent Ratings	African-American (N = 57)		Asian-American (N = 33)	
	Parent Report	Adolescent Report	Parent Report	Adolescent Report
Warmth / Support	.32[a]	.39[a]	.13	.13
Control	.03	.32[a]	.18	.12
Conflict	.26[+]	.54[c]	-.15	-.09

[+] Significant at $p < .10$.
[a] Significant at the .05 level
[b] Significant at the .01 level.
[c] Significant at the .001 level.

In contrast to the non-significant results with the Asian-American families, evidence of convergent validity was provided for each of the constructs within the African-American sample. Conflict ratings were significantly related to adolescent reports at a level indicating good convergent validity $(r = .54, p < .001)$. The correlations with adolescents' and mothers' reports of maternal support were moderate and significant (respectively, $r = .39$ and $r = .32, p < .05$), as was that with adolescent reports of maternal control $(r = .32, p < .05)$. Maternal reports of control, however, were virtually unrelated to observer ratings $(r = .03, NS)$. This finding is consistent with the argument that mothers may be unable to provide valid reports of their own parental behavior particularly with regard to the control or power dimension of family life (Feldman, Wentzel, & Gehring, 1989; Jessop, 1981) and that adolescents may be the more valid source of this information (Bengston & Kuypers, 1971; Gonzales et al., 1995a; Schwarz, Barton-Henry, & Pruzinsky, 1985).

Concurrent Validity. Concurrent validity was assessed by examining correlations between the observational ratings and three developmental outcomes that have been linked to family influences—academic achievement, problem behavior, and depressive symptomatology. These figures are presented in Table 3 along

Table 3
Concurrent Validity Coefficients: Correlations Between Family Predictor Variables and Adolescent Outcome Variables

Predictor Variables	African-American Families (N=57)			Asian-American Families (N=33)		
	Grade Point Average	Behavior Problems	Depressive Symptoms	Grade Point Average	Behavior Problems	Depressive Symptoms
Maternal Support						
Independent Ratings	**.41**[b]	**-.48**[b]	**-.28**[a]	**.27**[+]	**.06**	**.05**
Mother Report	.26[+]	-.38[a]	-.07	.21	-.23	-.26
Teen Report	.42[b]	-.32[a]	-.08	-.04	-.05	-.28[+]
Maternal Control						
Independent Ratings	**-.27**[a]	**.26**[+]	**.08**	**.17**	**-.17**	**-.04**
Mother Report	-.16	.07	-.10	.24	.19	.15
Teen Report	-.37[b]	.17	.23	-.22	.30[a]	.48[b]
Conflict						
Independent Ratings	**-.37**[b]	**.54**[d]	**.31**[a]	**-.43**[b]	**.07**	**-.03**
Mother Report	-.34[a]	.45[c]	.08	-.12	.58[c]	.14
Teen Report	-.41[b]	.35[a]	.35[a]	-.11	.54[b]	.47[b]

Figures in **bold** print represent validity coefficients for observational ratings.
+ p < .10
[a] p < .05
[b] p < .01
[c] p < .001
[d] p < .0001

with the same predictor-outcome correlations based on mothers' and daughters' reports of family variables.

For the African-American sample, each of the independent ratings predicted adolescent outcomes in the expected directions. Independent ratings of maternal support were positively related to grade point average ($r = .41$, $p < .01$), which has been used as a marker for academic achievement, and negatively related to adolescent behavior problems ($r = -.48$, $p < .01$) and symptoms of depression ($r = -.28$, $p < .05$). Independent ratings of maternal control were also negatively related to grade point average ($r = -.27$, $p < .05$), but only marginally related to behavior problems ($r = .26$, $p < .10$), and not related to depression ($r = .08$, NS). This pattern of differential influence on academic achievement is consistent with the developmental literature that suggests that intrinsic motivation, in particular, is enhanced in environments that provide ample opportunities for autonomy (Deci & Ryan, 1985; Patrick, Skinner, & Connell, 1993). The lack of a strong empirical link between self-report measures of maternal control and either behavior problems or symptoms of depression also seems to confirm the finding that maternal restrictive control may not be as significant a predictor of adolescent adjustment with this sample. Finally with regard to mother-daughter conflict, independent ratings were negatively related to grades ($r = -.37$, $p < .01$), and positively related to behavior problems ($r = .54$, $p < .0001$) and depression ($r = .31$, $p < .05$). These findings are also consistent with the available adolescent literature and the self report data.

For the Asian-American sample, a few of the expected predictions were supported. Independent ratings of conflict were negatively related to grades ($r = -.43$, $p < .01$). However, given the fact that this link was not replicated with either parent or adolescent reports, and in light of the negative correlation between the independent ratings and self reports of conflict, this finding is difficult to interpret. Independent ratings of maternal support were also marginally related to adolescent grade point average ($r = .27$, $p < .10$), a trend that was not statistically significant given the small sample size. With the exception of these two findings, however, the observational ratings failed to predict adolescent outcomes in the expected manner. This was true even when empirical links were evident with the adolescent and parent reports. For example, a clear pattern of association between parent-adolescent conflict and adolescent behavior problems was revealed when conflict was assessed by mother report ($r = .58$, $p < .001$) and adolescent report ($r = .54$, $p < .01$). Likewise, adolescent reports of maternal control were associated with behavior problems ($r = .30$, $p < .05$) and depressive symptoms ($r = .48, p < .01$). The independent ratings of these constructs, however, failed to replicate this pattern. Furthermore, additional analyses revealed that warmth and control in these families, as measured by the observational data, correlated with the family's level of acculturation. The more acculturated families scored higher in warmth and lower in control, and the less acculturated families scored lower in warmth and higher in control. This finding also suggests that the coding system may reflect something other than warmth and control as expressed within Japanese and Chinese cultures; perhaps something having to do with being more "American" in interactional style.

Discussion

The process of examining mother-daughter interactions in parallel studies with African-American and Asian-American families was as informative as it was, at times, frustrating. We have described the process in some detail in the hopes that our struggles may be helpful to others who seek to study families and individuals across ethnic groups. Though we had predicted that the process within each family might be somewhat different, it was surprising that the same approach could yield such distinct problems and outcomes.

With the African-American families we are confident that the observational ratings represent valid information about mother-daughter interactions and that this information is reasonably consistent with the self-report data (Gonzales et al., 1995a). Thus we achieved our goal of validating the survey measures. Moreover, our community consultants provided a rich knowledge base that has directly informed subsequent data analysis and interpretation.

Our observations of Asian-American mothers and daughters have led us to quite different conclusions. Given our recruitment difficulties, the inhibited reactions of our research participants, and the struggle of our coders to decipher the videotaped interactions, we do not believe that we have adequately captured Asian-American family interactions. This doubt was confirmed by the fact that we found no empirical evidence that the independent ratings were at all valid. Indeed, we believe that the observational paradigm itself may be inappropriate in that it asks families to do something that is not just potentially "artificial" in the way that laboratory research often is, but perhaps culturally prohibited. By saying this, we are not suggesting that we completely close the door on this method, or on Asian-American families, but that future researchers will need to think carefully about how to structure and code the task in a way that will produce more valid results. Furthermore, because our observational data did not provide us with the validation we were hoping for, we also feel on shakier ground in asserting that our self-report measures accurately reflect Asian-American family dynamics. Clearly more research in this area is needed.

The results of the study also indicate that direct observation of family behavior may pose problems for researchers who seek to code the behavior of cultural groups different from their own. Indeed, there are social psychological findings which bear directly on this issue, and suggest that interpersonal perception may be biased by cultural stereotypes (Sagar & Schofield, 1980), and by whether individuals are members of a particular group they are asked to judge (Islam & Hewstone, 1993; Tajfel, 1982). Our analysis of the coded data revealed systematic differences between ingroup and outgroup coders in their ratings of African-American families that persisted despite extensive training designed to reduce such biases. Though these analyses do not provide a rigorous test of ethnically linked biases, they do suggest a potential problem that may have important implications for observational family research. At the very least, these findings suggest that it is important to include ethnic individuals in the development and implementation of research with ethnic populations. Principal investigators, research assistants, and consultants who can provide an inside perspective on a cultural group can play a critical role, particularly when observational techniques will be used.

Our experience also raises interesting problems for researchers who want to conduct observations on more than one cultural group in a single study. Measurement equivalence is a central concern within cross-cultural research (Hui & Triandis, 1985), and investigators have begun to examine commonly used measures for cross-"ethnic" equivalence, including many of the most commonly employed family measures (Knight, Tein, Shell, & Roosa, 1992). The equivalence of observational measures, or even the use of observational measures across ethnic groups, however, remains largely unexplored and there are many unanswered questions. What coding systems should be employed when one seeks to make cross-ethnic comparisons? Do we need to have different theoretical frameworks when dealing with different cultures and constrain ourselves to within group analyses? Can similar coding systems be used to examine the differences that do exist between culturally distinct families?

In the present study we attempted to include identical items for the core constructs of interest, but even this presented problems. Because there were such notable cultural differences, we employed two separate groups of coders who were trained to apply quite distinct criteria in assigning ratings. Thus, it would not be appropriate to conduct direct comparisons between the scores obtained for the two groups, or to combine scores to conduct analyses on the full sample. If instead we had used one panel of coders to code all tapes, we might still be struggling to achieve an acceptable level of interrater reliability. Furthermore, even if we could agree on how to apply the same codes to both groups, it is likely that unit of scaling would not be equivalent between the two groups.

Given the long list of issues that must be addressed when ethnicity becomes a focus of study, it's little wonder that many researchers have chosen to leave Pandora's box firmly closed on ethnicity and culture. This is not, however, an appropriate response to the challenge of ethnic diversity within the social sciences. Nor are some of the more extreme responses of individuals who suggest that everything about the content and form of current research within psychology must be abandoned in service of cultural diversity—research topics, procedures, measures, as well as fundamental positivist beliefs about psychology as a science. This is certainly not the message we are trying to communicate here. We agree with those who advocate a more balanced response to the challenge, one that utilizes existing approaches, in combination with attempts to incorporate new theoretical models and culturally appropriate methods of inquiry (Berry et al., 1992; Betancourt & Lopez, 1993; Maton, 1993). How this balance will be achieved, and whether it can be made fully convincing and workable, remains to be seen.

Notes

1. This research was supported by a grant (NICHHD: HD24056) awarded to A.M. Cauce. The authors wish to thank Nydia Ordonez and Tanya Aguilar for their contributions to the project. Correspondence regarding this article should be sent to: Nancy Gonzales, Department of Psychology, Arizona State University, Tempe, AZ 85287-1104.

2. For all subsequent analyses, the total number of families in the African-American sample is 57. Three families have been dropped from analyses due to problems with the videotaped interactions that could not be coded.

3. It is also true that cultural differences exist within African-American groups, particularly where relatively new immigrants from Africa or the West Indies are represented. Thus it may be problematic that researchers frequently group these individuals together as well, and fail to distinguish between national or regional divisions that may be culturally meaningful. In the present study, the single Asian-American ethnic category proved to be more obviously problematic than the African-American category. For example, none of the African-American adolescents or their parents were immigrants, the majority of these families resided in a similar geographic area within the inner city, and they all spoke the same language. This was not true of the Asian-American families. Nevertheless, it is important to recognize the fact that there may be other cultural distinctions that we have not considered in our attempts to define an African-American cultural group.

References

Achenbach, T.M., & Edelbrock, C.S. (1983). The child behavior profile: I. Boys aged 12–16 and girls aged 6–11 and 12–16. *Journal of Consulting and Clinical Psychology*, *47*, 223–233.

Baumrind, D. (1971). Current patterns of parental authority. *Developmental Psychology Monograph*, *4*, 1–103.

Baumrind, D. (1972). An exploratory study of socialization effects on black children: Some black-white comparisons. *Child Development*, *43*, 261–267.

Bell, D.C., Bell, L.G., & Munakata, T. (1989). *Why cross-cultural research on family interaction is impossible.* Paper presented at the National Council on Family Relations: Theory Construction and Methodology Workshop, New Orleans.

Bengston, V.L., & Kuypers, J.A. (1971). Generational differences and the developmental stake. *Aging and Human Development*, *2*, 249–260.

Berry, J.W., Poortinga, Y.H., Segall, M.H., & Dasen, P.R. (1992). *Cross-cultural psychology: Research and applications.* New York: Cambridge University Press.

Betancourt, H., & Lopez, S.R. (1993). The study of culture, ethnicity, and race in American psychology. *American Psychologist*, *48*, 629–637.

Block, J.H. (1965). *The childrearing practices report: A set of parental socialization attitudes and values.* Berkeley, CA: Institute of Human Development, University of California.

Campbell, D.T., & Fiske, D.W. (1959). Convergent and discriminant validation by the multitrait-multimethod matrix. *Psychological Bulletin*, *56*, 81–105.

Cauce, A.M., Hiraga, Y., Mason, C., Aguilar, T.A., & Gonzales, N. (1992). Between a rock and a hard place: Social adjustment of biracial youth. In M.P.P. Root (Ed.), *Racially mixed people in America* (pp. 207–369). Newbury Park, CA: Sage.

Deci, E.L., & Ryan, R.M. (1985). *Intrinsic motivation and self-determination in human behavior.* New York: Plenum.

Dornbusch, S.M., Ritter, P.L., Leiderman, D.R., & Fraleigh, M.J. (1987). The relation of parenting style to adolescent school performance. *Child Development, 58,* 1244–1257.

Feldman, S.S., Wentzel, K.R., & Gehring, T.M. (1989). A comparison of the views of mothers, fathers, and pre-adolescents about family cohesion and power. *Journal of Family Psychology, 3,* 39–60.

Finch, A.J., Jr., & Conway, F.S. (1985). Children's depression inventory: Sex and grade norms for normal children. *Journal of Consulting and Clinical Psychology, 3,* 424–425.

Foster, S.L., & Robin, A.L. (1988). Family conflict and communication in adolescence. In E.J. Mash & L. Terdal (Eds.), *Behavioral assessment of childhood disorders* (pp. 717–775). New York: Guilford.

Gonzales, N.A., Cauce, A.M., & Mason, C. A. (1995a). *Interobserver agreement in assessing parental behavior and parent-child conflict among African American mothers and their adolescent daughters: Cross-informant and cross-ethnic perspectives.* Manuscript submitted for publication.

Gonzales, N.A., Cauce, A.M., Friedman, R. & Mason, C.A. (1995b). *Parent and peer support for academic achievement in high risk neighborhoods.* Manuscript submitted for publication.

Huang, L.N., & Ying, Y. (1989). Chinese American children and adolescents. In J.T. Gibbs & L.N. Huang (Eds.), *Children of color: Psychological interventions with minority youth.* San Francisco: Jossey-Bass.

Hui, C.H., & Triandis, H.C. (1985). Measurement in cross-cultural psychology: A review and comparison of strategies. *Journal of Cross-Cultural Psychology, 16,* 131–152.

Hsu, J., Tseng, W., Ashton, G., McDermott, J.F., & Char, W. (1985). Family interaction patterns among Japanese-American and Caucasian families in Hawaii. *American Journal of Psychiatry, 142,* 577–581.

Islam, M.R., & Hewstone, M. (1993). Intergroup attributions and affective consequences in majority and minority groups. *Journal of Personality and Social Psychology, 64,* 936–950.

Jessop, D.J. (1981). Family relations as viewed by parents and adolescents: A specification. *Journal of Marriage and the Family, 43,* 95–107.

Knight, G.P., Tein, J.Y., Shell, R., & Roosa, M. (1992). The cross-ethnic equivalence of parenting and family interaction measures among Hispanic and Anglo American families. *Child Development, 63,* 1392–1403.

Kovacs, M. (1981). Rating scales to assess depression in school-aged children. *Acta Paediopsychiatrica, 46,* 305–315.

Kovacs, M. (1986). A developmental perspective on methods and measurements in the assessment of depressive disorders: The clinical interview. In M. Rutter, C.E. Izard, & P.B. Read (Eds.), *Depression in young people: Developmental and clinical perspectives* (pp. 435–465). New York: Guilford.

Lebra, T.S. (1976). *Japanese patterns of behavior.* Honolulu, HI: University Press of Hawaii.

Liddle, H.A. (1987). Family psychology: The journal, the field. *Journal of Family Psychology, 1,* 5–22.

Maccoby, E.E., & Martin, J. (1983). Socialization in the context of the family. In E.M. Hetherington (Ed.) *Handbook of child psychology: Vol. 4. Socialization, personality, and social development* (pp. 1–102). New York: Wiley.

Mason, C.A., Cauce, A.M., Gonzales, N.A., & Hiraga (1994a). Problem behavior: The effect of peers and the moderating role of father absence and the mother-child relationship. *American Journal of Community Psychology,* December.

Mason, C.A., Cauce, A.M., Gonzales, N.A., Hiraga, Y., & Grove, K. (1994b). An ecological model of externalizing in African American adolescents: No family is an island. *Journal of Adolescent Research, 4,* 639–655.

Maton, K. (1993). A bridge between cultures: Linked ethnographic-empirical methodology for culture anchored research. *American Journal of Community Psychology, 21,* 747–773.

Minturn, L., & Lambert, W.W. (1964). *Mothers of six cultures.* New York: Wiley.

Patrick, B., Skinner, E., & Connell, J. (1993). What motivates children's behavior and emotion? Joint effects of perceived control and autonomy in the academic domain. *Journal of Personality and Social Psychology, 65,* 781–791.

Prinz, R.J., Rosenblum, R.S., & O'Leary, K.D. (1978). Affective communication differences between distressed and nondistressed mother-adolescent dyads. *Journal of Abnormal Child Psychology, 6,* 373–383.

Rickel, A.U., & Biasatti, L.R. (1982). Modification of the black child rearing practices report. *Journal of Clinical Psychology, 39,* 129–134.

Robin, A.L., & Foster, S.L. (1984). Problem-solving communication training: A behavioral-family systems approach to parent-adolescent conflict. In P. Karoly and J.J. Steffen (Eds.), *Adolescent behavior disorders.* Lexington, MA: Heath.

Robin, A.L., & Weiss, J. (1980). Criterion-related validity of behavioral and self-report measures of problem solving communication skills in distressed and non-distressed parent-adolescent dyads. *Behavioral Assessment, 2,* 339–352.

Sagar, H.A., & Schofield, J.W. (1980). Racial and behavioral cues in black and white children's perceptions of ambiguously aggressive acts. *Journal of Personality and Social Psychology, 39,* 590–598.

Sarason, B.R., Pierce, G.R., & Sarason, I.G. (1990). *Parent-child relationships: Social support, conflict, and sensitivity.* Unpublished manuscript.

Schaefer, E.S. (1965). Children's reports of parental behavior: An inventory. *Child Development, 36,* 413–424.

Schwarz, J.C., Barton-Henry, M.S., & Pruzinsky, T. (1985). Assessing child-rearing behaviors: A comparison of ratings made by mother, father, child, and sibling on the CRPBI. *Child Development, 56,* 462–479.

Shweder, R.A., & Sullivan, M.A. (1993). Cultural psychology: Who needs it? *Annual Review of Psychology, 44,* 497–523.

Steinberg, L. (1990). Interdependency in the family: Autonomy, conflict, and harmony in the parent-adolescent relationship. In S. Feldman & G. Elliott (Eds.), *At the threshold: The developing adolescent.* Cambridge, MA: Harvard University Press.

Steinberg, L., Mounts, N.S., Lamborn, S.D., & Dornbusch, S.M. (1991). Authoritative parenting and adolescent adjustment across varied ecological niches. *Journal of Research on Adolescence, 1,* 19–36.

Szapocznik, J., & Kurtines, W.M. (1993). Family psychology and cultural diversity: Opportunities for theory, research, and application. *American Psychologist, 48,* 400–407.

Tajfel, H. (1982). A social psychology of intergroup relations. *Annual Review of Psychology, 17,* 833–840.

Triandis, H.C. (1978). Some universals of social behavior. *Personality and Social Psychology Bulletin, 4,* 1–16.

Chapter 14

Resiliency and Coping in "At Risk" African-American Youth and Their Families[1]

*Hamilton I. McCubbin, Wm. Michael Fleming,
Anne I. Thompson, Paul Neitman,
Kelly M. Elver, and Sue Ann Savas*

Interest in resiliency in children, youth, and families has grown rapidly in the past two decades (Rutter, 1979; Garmezy, 1981; Masten, 1989; Werner, 1989; Haggerty, Sherrod, Garmezy, & Rutter, 1994; McCubbin, Thompson, Thompson, & Fromer, 1995; McCubbin, Thompson, Thompson, & Futrell, 1995). These topics are of prime interest for social and behavioral scientists because of the apparent role that resilience plays in understanding individual and family development and recovery under conditions that favor both personal and family failure or dysfunction. Knowledge about successful adaptation under stressful life conditions also strengthens the conceptual base needed to frame both treatment and preventive interventions for high-risk children and youth (Cowen, Wyman, Work, & Parker, 1990), families (Mooradian & Grasso, 1993; McCubbin & McCubbin, 1993), and ethnic minority families (McCubbin, Thompson, Thompson, McCubbin, & Kaston, 1993). Despite the acknowledged importance of understanding resilience in both families and youth, current knowledge about resilience is relatively limited, particularly for ethnic families and youth at risk. The purpose of this chapter, which is based on a longitudinal study of African-American youth at risk and their families, is to examine the relative importance of both youth coping and family coping repertoires as predictors of youth offenders' ability to recover from adversity.

Family Systems Theory and Youth at Risk

Several theoretical models have emerged that examine deviance and delinquency within the context of the family system (e.g., Patterson, Reid, & Dishion, 1992; Moffitt, 1993; Sampson & Laub, 1993; Simons, Wu, Conger, & Lorenz, 1994) and have guided therapeutic interventions serving this population (Minuchin, 1974; Henggeler, 1989). Several basic assumptions from family systems theory have influenced these theory building efforts. One central assumption is that adolescents and youth, as individual systems, are embedded in and interact with multiple interconnected systems and subsystems such as the family, school, peer group, and community. The family system, as the most proximal system to the adolescent, exerts the greatest influence on development and thus on treatment. Family systems theorists argue that as a system, adolescents and youth (elements of the larger family system) are interdependent and as a result behaviors of any one individual family member influence and affect every other member of the family. The system is therefore viewed as being greater than the sum of its parts and adolescent and youth behavior is understood only within the interpersonal context of that behavior (Henggeler & Borduin, 1990; Minuchin, 1974).

The relationship between juvenile delinquency and family system dynamics is strong, significant, direct, and also complex. Studies exploring family composition and delinquency have focused on a variety of aspects such as family size, birth order, intactness, occupation of parents, number of employed parents, economic status of the family and broader contextual systems such as neighborhoods. Youth from single-parent families are frequently more autonomous with respect to decision making, have lower amounts of parental monitoring and subsequently have been found to be more likely to engage in deviant behavior (Dornbusch, Carlsmith, Bushwall, Ritter, Leiderman, Hastorf, & Gross, 1985). Free (1991) argues that single-parent households are related to the commission of status offenses, but there is little support for its relationship to serious offenses. Parental absence can have an effect on serious offenses if it is compounded by other family related stressors (McCord, 1990).

Family affect has been shown to be related to delinquency. In general, family affect refers to the degree of emotional closeness felt among family members, the perceived degree of distancing and rejecting that occurs, and the level of conflict. Delinquent youth have been found to come from family systems that express less positive and more negative affect (Jacob, 1975). Family systems characterized by high levels of parental rejection and neglect are more likely to have youth who commit antisocial behavior (Cernkovich & Giordano, 1987; Loeber & Stouthammer-Loeber, 1986; McCord, 1983). Gray-Ray and Ray (1990) found that among lower and middle class African-American families, high levels of parental rejection were the most powerful predictor of serious and minor forms of delinquency. Other studies suggest that parental styles which rely on negativistic, power assertive techniques to control a child's behavior are most likely to give rise to abrasive, negativistic childhood behavior (Dishion, 1990; Dekovic & Janssens, 1992; Kochanska, 1992).

Studies exploring family communication patterns have found that patterns that are vague, rigid and intolerant are more likely to be found in families with youth exhibiting delinquent behavior (Cernkovich & Giordano, 1987; Jacob, 1975). In these families, disjointed and unclear family communications are most prominent regarding conflict resolution (Tolan, Cromwell, & Brasswell, 1986). Family conflict itself has also been found to be associated with delinquency (Kazdin, 1985; Rutter & Giller, 1983; Tolan & Lorion, 1988). Such conflict usually takes the form of marital discord or parent-adolescent conflict (Gove & Crutchfield, 1982; Cernkovich & Giordano, 1987; Wells & Rankin, 1991).

Tolan, Cromwell, and Brasswell (1986) argue that delinquent behavior is often found in family systems characterized by problematic structural organization, interactions, and reactions to stress. However, the specific nature of such systems and the relationship to delinquency remain unclear. Families of delinquents have been found to exist in chaotic and disorganized systems (Rodick, Henggeler, & Hanson, 1986) and rigid and inflexible systems (Blaske, Borduin, Henggeler, & Mann, 1989). Low family adaptability when paired with parental absence was found to have a direct effect on serious criminal behavior (McCord, 1986). However, Tolan (1988), examining the effects of social stress on delinquency, found no association between family adaptability and delinquency. However, three types of social stressors—daily hassles, developmental transitions, and circumscribed life events—were found to be associated with delinquency.

Mann, Borduin, Henggeler, and Blaske (1990) examined whether adolescent behavioral problems, as evidenced by delinquent behavior, were associated with cross-generational coalitions; as well as whether the treatment of these coalitions led to decreases in problem behaviors—two premises that are at the core of family system models of treatment. Results indicate that delinquents were more likely to be in a cross-generational coalition with their mothers (as evidenced by more verbal activity with the mother and disengagement from the father). These parents were also more likely to have a marital relationship characterized by higher rates of conflict and lower levels of supportiveness than parents of non-delinquents. Their results also found that decreases in conflict-hostility and increases in supportiveness in the parent dyad were significantly related to decreases in problem behavior among the delinquent adolescents.

Patterson and colleagues (Patterson & Dishion, 1985; Patterson & Stouthamer-Loeber, 1984; Loeber, Dishion, & Patterson, 1984) have examined the role of ineffective parental discipline practices and poor parental monitoring and supervision in the development of antisocial behavior among children. As a whole their work has demonstrated that punitive parental disciplinary responses to children's aggressive or aversive behavior accelerated this behavior in the child. Children who are socialized in this manner tend to develop a coercive interpersonal style that becomes generalized to other contexts and social groups including that of schools and peers. Subsequently, these children often experience rejection by their peers and ultimately drift to a social group that is tolerant, if not supportive, of such behavior. The combination of parenting practices, the use of aggressive interpersonal methods, social rejection and association with deviant peers leads to delinquent behavior. Snyder and Patterson (1987) found that ineffective discipline practices and strategies were used by families of delinquents prior to and following the commencement of delinquency. They argue that conscientious supervision permits the parents to respond more quickly and appropriately to adolescent antisocial behavior as well as association with peers who commit or advocate deviant behaviors. Several other studies have confirmed the critical role that effective parental supervision and monitoring can have in reducing the likelihood of delinquent behavior (Laub & Sampson, 1988; Cernkovich & Giordano, 1987; McCord, 1991; Loeber, Stouthamer-Loeber, Van Kammen, & Farrington, 1991).

African-American Families and Delinquency

Gibbs (1989) has described the fate of African-American adolescents as being analogous to that of endangered species, arguing that they have been, in part, mishandled by the juvenile justice system, and mislabeled by, ignored, or excluded from the mental health system. These experiences, in addition to those associated with limited social and economic resources and opportunities, suggest that African-American youth are exposed to unique risk factors that may influence their development (Rickel & Allen, 1987; Simons & Gray, 1989; Spencer, Cole, DuPree, Glymph, & Pierre, 1993; McAdoo, 1995). Although developmental pathways between minority children and youth may be similar (e.g., Rowe, Vazsonyi, & Flannery, 1994), in recent years there has been a call for empirical efforts to be directed toward the understanding of African-American children and adolescents based on African-American norms, rather than on white normative models (Barbarin, 1993; Jones, 1989; Piatt et al., 1993). For example, Myers (1989) argues that reality for urban African-American youth is quite different from the reality of other youth. These youth grow up in insidiously stressful environments. They must develop coping behaviors for a variety of stressors with limited resources. These youth often have fewer models of competent coping. Myers suggests that one approach to understanding the specific mental health needs and issues of African-American urban youth is to examine the stress and coping processes that may be unique and/or utilized by these youth.

Unfortunately, efforts directed toward understanding antisocial behavior among African-American adolescents have primarily been based on studies with Caucasian youth (e.g., Moffitt, 1993). A noticeable exception comes from the recent work of Loeber and colleagues (1993). In their initial work exploring developmental pathways in disruptive youth behavior, they looked at both Caucasian and African-American youth and found few distinctions with respect to the sequencing of disruptive behavior and the age of onset. One exception was noted, however, for youth exhibiting overt aggressive acts. African-American youth were more likely to begin their developmental pathway with aggressive behavior such as fighting and gang fighting; whereas Caucasian youth were more likely to begin the sequence earlier by exhibiting disruptive behavior such as annoying and bullying others before proceeding to fighting behavior.

Borduin, Pruitt, and Henggeler (1986) were among the first to examine differences within African-American families based on the delinquency status of the adolescent. They found that, in general, family affect and conflict were significantly correlated with the commitment of delinquent behavior by the adolescents. Fathers and adolescents in delinquent families reported less warmth and nurturance than non-delinquent families. The mother-adolescent relationships in these families were more conflictual than in non-delinquent families. Observational scores for these families, in general, supported the self-report findings.

Gray-Ray and Ray (1990) found that in contrast to models that emphasize family structure, parental rejection, and parental supervision as critical components in the development of delinquent behavior, only perceived parental rejection had a significant effect on African-American youths' involvement in delinquent activities. The authors argue that particular aspects of African-American culture may play a greater role in serving as protective factors against the development of antisocial behavior. Specifically, a greater reliance on extended family members may offset the diminished parental supervision often found in single-headed households. Furthermore, they suggest that the value placed on motherhood over other roles may also help to offset the limitations associated with single parenthood.

It has been argued that effective clinical treatment of African-American families is enhanced if specific cultural and historical factors are taken into consideration (Coates, 1990; Billson, 1988; Robinson, 1989; Boyd-Franklin, 1987, 1989; Hines & Boyd-Franklin 1982). These authors argue that in general, African-American families have had a greater reliance on extended family members; that religion often plays a significant role within the family unit; and that a history of racism and blocked opportunities often have shaped family members' perspectives on mental health services and agencies. Furthermore, these authors and others (e.g., Aponte, 1976; Mason, Cauce, Gonzales, Hiraga, & Grove, 1994) argue that a broader ecological consideration of factors that may influence family system dynamics and individual development must be considered if clinical treatment is to be effective. Given our interest in understanding what dimensions and processes of youth coping and family coping are most important to the successful treatment and rehabilitation of youth and families, this review of past studies emphasizing the deficiencies and dysfunctional aspects would best be reframed within a resiliency perspective.

Resiliency, Families, and Youth: A Conceptual Framework

The Resiliency Model of Family Adjustment and Adaptation (McCubbin & McCubbin, 1988; McCubbin, Thompson, Thompson, Elver, & McCubbin, 1994; Thompson, McCubbin, Thompson, &

Elver, 1995) was developed to guide research, prevention efforts, and clinical intervention with ethnic minority families (McCubbin, McCubbin, Thompson, & Thompson, 1995), and has been empirically tested (Lavee, McCubbin, & Patterson, 1985) and applied to guide interventions with health care populations at risk (McCubbin & McCubbin, 1993; Kosciulek, McCubbin, & McCubbin, 1993), as well as the treatment of youth at risk and their families. The basic propositions of a modified Resiliency Model in the study of African-American youth and their families in crises may be stated as follows:

> Families at risk are characterized in part by imbalance and disharmony, a condition which is fostered by the inadequacy of or the problematic nature of the family's established patterns of functioning (T) in response to stressful situations, and which places the family in a crisis situation (e.g., being vulnerable, but faced with an opportunity for constructive changes in its patterns of functioning). These families' situations are exacerbated by the concurrent pile-up of demands (AA) (e.g., other life changes and hardships). By the family's own accord and will, and possibly with crisis oriented or transitional assistance or treatment, the family and its members may take on the challenge to regenerate itself, to change and to improve upon its situation, enter into a process of change and thereby work to achieve a level of adaptation (XX). The goal of this process is the restoration of family harmony and balance in the family's interpersonal relations, the family's structure and function, the development, well-being, and spirituality of the family unit and its members, as well as the family's relationship to the community and the natural environment. The level of successful adaptation referred to as Bonadaptation (XX) is determined by the interacting influence of newly instituted patterns of functioning (T) (e.g., patterns of communication, rules, boundaries, etc.), the modification, maintenance or revitalization of already established patterns of functioning (e.g., traditions, celebrations, ethnic practices, etc.), the family's own internal resources and capabilities (BB) (e.g., hardiness, coalitions, respect, support), the family's network of social support (e.g., extended family, neighborhood, church, community, friends, kinship, etc.), and the family's situational appraisal (CC). The family's situational appraisal (CC) is influenced by the families appraisal processes: Schema (CCCCC) (e.g., values, beliefs, ethnic orientation); the family's Sense of Coherence (CCCC) (e.g., dispositional view of the family's sense of order, trust, predictability and manageability); and Paradigms (CCC) (e.g., shared expectations as to how the family will function in areas of child rearing, discipline, etc.). Finally, the instituted patterns of functioning,

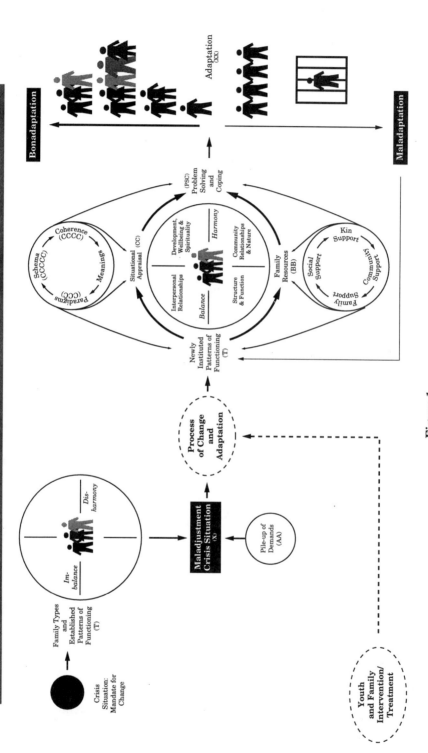

Figure 1
Youth and Family At Risk: Modification of the Adaptation
Phase of the Resiliency Model of Family Stress, Adjustment and

resources, and appraisal components of the family unit influence and are influenced by the family's problem-solving and coping abilities (PSC) (e.g., conflict resolution, family problem-solving, coping repertoires, etc.). The family engages in a dynamic relational process over time, introducing changes directed at restoring and maintaining family harmony and balance within the family system as well as in the family's relationship to the larger community and environment. The dynamic relational process involves a cyclical effort in such situations where the family's efforts at change prove to be unsuccessful and propel the family into a maladaptive outcome. In the case of youth "at risk" bonadaptation may be viewed as successfully completing a treatment program, and as living with family, with extended family, with a single parent, or even alone—in a less restrictive setting. In contrast, in a maladaptive outcome, the youth's living situation may be in a group home with other youth or being incarcerated, in a more restrictive setting.

When used to guide research and treatment of youth offenders and their families in a treatment context, the Resiliency Model underscores the importance of family coping and problem-solving as critical elements of resiliency. The resiliency framework is built upon the premise that even in the most chaotic situations where youth and family dysfunction appear to be the predictable outcome, the family unit and its members have competencies and abilities. This strength, particularly in the context of the community, albeit limited, allows the family to transcend the obvious deficiencies, seize opportunities to improve upon themselves, and fulfill their shared responsibilities to promote the development of its members.

In the context of this study of youth and families involved in residential treatment, three fundamental assumptions and basic propositions may be stated. First, families faced with the placement of a member in residential care are confronted with transitional crises demanding changes in the way the family unit behaves and adapts. The degree of success in residential treatment for both the family and the adolescent is dependent upon background characteristics of the family unit and the youth involved. The ethnicity of the family has a major bearing upon the youth's successful completion of treatment and the long term adaptation and living situation three and twelve months after the completion of treatment.

Second, families create for themselves specific and predictable styles of functioning that can be measured and identified.

These patterns have predictive power in explaining which adolescents and young adults are most likely to respond to residential care and post-treatment living situations. The family's general patterns of coping with stress and crises and the changes in these coping patterns in response to treatment will have a major bearing upon the youth's successful completion of the treatment program and the youth's long-term adaptation and living situation three and twelve months following the completion of treatment.

Third, youth develop and cultivate specific and predictable styles of functioning that can be measured and identified. These patterns have predictive power in explaining which adolescents and young adults are most likely to adapt in residential care and in post-treatment living situations. The youth's general patterns of coping with stress and crises and the changes in these coping patterns in response to treatment will have a major bearing upon the youth's successful completion of the residential program and the youth's long term adaptation, and the youth's living situation three and twelve months following the completion of treatment.

The Human Services Context: The Demand for Parsimony and Effectiveness in Treatment

As described in other publications (Patti, 1983; Whittaker, Overstreet, Grasso, Tripodi, & Boylan, 1988), the 1970s and 1980s were characterized as a conservative era of federal policy with increasing pressure on human service organizations to contain costs. Predictably, programs whose existence had historically been unquestioned found themselves being asked to justify financial expenditures in relationship to service effectiveness. The "Contract with America" orientation of the 1990s (see Gingrich et al., 1994) is accompanied by downsizing of the federal government, reduction in funding for social service programs, and a mandate to expand service delivery while reducing, or at least maintaining, costs for residential care (Cartwright, 1982). As already noted by Overstreet, Grasso, and Epstein (1993) the rising costs of residential care in the State of Michigan placed considerable strain on the Department of Social Services efforts to provide needed services to children and their families. In 1985, for example, the Michigan Department of Social Services had to accommodate approximately 1,000 new commitments. With the average cost of services reaching about $36,000 annually for each client entering residential care, the addition of 1,000 new commitments each year represents an enormous financial burden on an already beleaguered program of services for children, youth, and their families. Clearly, the emerging conservative and anti-federal government economic context of the 1990s is accompanied by a responsibility to find more cost-effective ways to have an impact on children and youth and their families through residential care, to promote their long-term adjustment and adaptation, but also to provide this service with the most parsimonious set of interventions proven to be effective.

A Mandate for Demonstrated
Effectiveness of Treatment
Interventions

Although residential treatment agencies are beginning to document treatment outcomes and establish the validity and efficacy of their interventions, few have attempted to demonstrate changes in youth and families on critical dimensions of individual and family functioning that are expected to be influenced by the residential program, nor have these changes been linked to successful outcomes. The literature remains sparse in the consideration of post-treatment success in the months and years following residential treatment. The paucity of research is glaring when we search for evidence to confirm the value of residential treatment for African-American youth and their families.

Savas, Epstein, and Grasso (1993) utilized the Boysville Management Information System to identify client characteristics and intervention patterns that are associated with successful program completion. They found that age and the number of contacts between the family worker and at least one family member were positively related to successful program completion. Other studies have also pointed to the importance of age as a predictor (Cowden & Monson, 1969; Shennum & Thomas, 1987). While others have focused on the effect of race and prior offenses on successful program completion (Gilliland-Mallo & Judd, 1986), Whittaker, Tripodi, and Grasso (1993) have attempted to carry these evaluative studies further by adding post-treatment adaptation to the list of criterion indices of success. With a sample of 239 adolescents released from the Boysville Residential Program (1984–1985), the investigators developed a profile of successful cases: Youth with a longer stay in the program, a greater number of family-worker contacts, more minutes of family work by staff members, and higher total family contacts were more likely to succeed. The investigators also emphasized the need to look at racial differences in intake characteristics and the treatment process. Furthermore, they argued that "future analyses will focus on within-race relationships to characterize more fully the typical youth and his or her own history . . . ." While instructive, these investigators did not address the critical issues of what youth and family changes occur in response to the interventions, for better or for worse, and whether these changes are related to successful program completion and post-treatment adaptation in the months and years following treatment. Yet, if we are to respond to the challenges of federal and state agencies to demonstrate efficacy and accountability, these pressing issues deserve consideration and scientifically based answers.

The Residential Treatment Setting: Design and Method

Data were obtained through the Boysville Management Information System (BOMIS) (see Grasso & Epstein, 1993), which is an integral part of the total treatment initiative. Boysville of Michigan is the State of Michigan's largest private agency serving troubled youth. The agency has grown considerably since its founding in 1948. It now serves more than 2,000 boys and girls and their families annually; 1,000 in various forms of residential care, and 1,000 in specialized foster care, in-home, and other community-based service alternatives. Residential treatment centers are located at the main campus in Clinton and other campuses in Saginaw, and Monroe, Michigan, and Toledo, Ohio. Group home sites are located in Detroit, Ecorse, Mt. Clemens, Redford, Saginaw, Mt. Morris, Frankenmuth, and Alpena, Michigan. The original treatment program was based on an adapted version of "Positive Peer Culture" in which the peer group's natural influence was enlisted to bring about changes in a youth's behavior and attitude. Over the past ten years, Boysville has emphasized family therapy as part of the treatment program (Mooradian & Grasso, 1993). While a growing number of the Boysville youth in treatment are neglected and/or abused, most are adjudicated delinquents with serious behavioral, social and educational problems (Grasso & Epstein, 1993).

Youth and Family Coping Measures: Targets for Intervention and Change

Youth Coping Index. Youth coping was assessed through the development and use of the *Youth Coping Index (YCI)* (McCubbin, Thompson, & Elver, 1995b). The YCI was developed specifically for the study of African-American youth in residential treatment. Given the importance of youth coping as a viable target for intervention, the goal was to develop a measure that would be ethnically sensitive but applicable to both Caucasian and African-American youth. The Youth Coping Index emerges from *A-COPE—Adolescent Coping Orientation for Problem Experiences* (Patterson & McCubbin, 1987) through a systematic assessment of the self-reported coping responses of African-American youth offenders, the identification of the coping repertoires and the testing of the reliability and validity of the measures through factor analysis and tests of internal consistency. The original A-COPE is a 54-item Likert scale with responses ranging from "Not at All" (1) to "Most of the Time" (5), and includes five subscales that assess the degree to which youth use these coping behaviors and strategies to manage life's stressors and strains. In contrast, the YCI is a 31-item measure and was utilized at two points in time during the treatment process: at intake and shortly before the youth completed the Boysville program. The respondents were the youth offenders who were being asked to record their typical strategies for coping with stress and distress. Common to both the original A-COPE and the current YCI is the inclusion and emphasis on coping behaviors directed at the maintenance or development of a constructive interpersonal communication in the family context. This feature is important for treatment programs that are designed in part to promote a more harmonious relationship between the youth and his or her family, and with an added emphasis on family preservation. Change scores were obtained and utilized for this study with scores derived by subtracting scores at time 1 (at intake) from scores at time 2 (before but near program completion) and adding a constant (10) to create scores that ranged upward from zero. Overall reliability for the YCI is .86. The YCI consists of three subscales:

> *The Youth Spiritual and Personal Development Subscale* is a 13-item subscale that assesses the degree to which youth engage in behaviors that would be considered constructive

activities that promote positive development and self-improvement when faced with a major hardship or crisis. This subscale emphasizes the importance of a youth's efforts to promote spiritual and personal development and includes such coping behaviors as "going to church"; "working hard on schoolwork or other school projects"; "getting involved in activities in school"; "praying"; "talking to a teacher or counselor at school about what bothers you"; "saying nice things to others"; "doing things with the family"; and "work on a hobby"; "read"; "try to improve yourself (get better grades, etc.)"; "get professional counseling (not from a school teacher or school counselor)"; "do a strenuous physical activity (jogging, biking, etc.)"; and "play video games." The overall Cronbach Alpha reliability for the Youth Spiritual and Personal Development Subscale is .84.

The Youth Positive Appraisal and Problem Solving Subscale is a 10-item subscale that assesses the degree to which youth adopt a coping repertoire that emphasizes the importance of a positive self-directed outlook, world view and approach to problem solving. The coping repertoire includes: "trying to see the good things in difficult situations"; "trying to figure out how to deal with problems or tension on their own"; "trying to reason with family and talk things out, compromise"; "organize your life and what you have to do"; "apologize to people"; "try to make your own decisions"; "try to help other people solve their problems"; "try to keep up friendships or make new friends"; "try to think of the good things in your life"; and "talk to a friend about how you feel." The overall Cronbach Alpha reliability for the Youth Positive Appraisal and Problem Solving Subscale is .79.

The Youth Incendiary Communication and Tension Management is an 8-item subscale that assesses the degree to which youth adopt coping strategies that exacerbate interpersonal tensions and conflicts and by adopting cognitive appraisal strategies that minimize the significance of the problem or makes the issue larger than it is. The subscale includes the coping behaviors of: "saying mean things to people or to be sarcastic"; "blaming others for what's going wrong"; "get angry and yell at people"; "let off steam by complaining to your friends"; "swear"; "going along with family's requests and rules"; "tell yourself the problem is not important"; and "daydream about how you would like things to be." The overall Cronbach Alpha reliability for the Interpersonal Conflict Resolution and Tension Management subscale is .70.

Family Coping Index. For this study, family problem-solving and coping efforts were assessed using the *Family Coping Index (FAMCI)*

(McCubbin, Thompson, & Elver, 1995a), which was derived from the *Family Crisis Oriented Personal Evaluation Scales (F-COPES)* (McCubbin, Olson, & Larsen, 1987). The original F-COPES is a 30-item inventory that asks the adult members, usually the parent(s), to record on a 5-point Likert scale the degree to which they agree or disagree with the coping behavior listed that describes how their family unit as a group typically responds to and copes with problems or difficulties. The FAMCI was administered to the parent(s) at their son's or daughter's intake and shortly before his or her departure from the Boysville program. Change scores were utilized for analysis and were created by subtracting scores at time 1 (intake) from scores at time 2 (before but near completion of the program) and adding a constant (10) to a range of scores beginning with 0 or higher. The overall reliability of the FAMCI was .85. Through factor analysis three subscales were identified.

> *The Seeking Professional and Spiritual Guidance Subscale* is a 7-item measure that assesses the degree to which the family unit, faced with a hardship or a cluster of difficulties, will seek the support of professional service providers and support systems including the church and the ministry. The family's coping repertoire includes: "participating in church activities"; "attending church"; "seeking advice from a minister"; "seeking professional counseling and help"; "seeking assistance from community agencies and programs"; "doing things with relatives"; and "seeking information and advice from the family doctor." The overall reliability for the Seeking Professional and Spiritual Guidance subscale is .80.

> *The Seeking Family and Neighbor Support* is a 9-item subscale directed at recording the family's efforts to solicit support and guidance from relatives and friends as part of their coping repertoire. The family's coping efforts include: "sharing our difficulties with relatives"; "asking relatives how they feel about problems we face"; "seeking advice from relatives"; "seeking encouragement and support from friends"; "seeking information and advice from persons in other families who face the same or similar problems"; "receiving gifts and favors from neighbors"; "asking neighbors for help and assistance"; "sharing concerns with close friends"; and "sharing problems with neighbors." The overall Cronbach Alpha reliability for the Seeking Family and Neighbor Support subscale is .78.

> *The Affirming the Family's Confidence Subscale* is an 8-item subscale that solicits self-appraisal of the family's

confidence in its ability to handle, solve, or withstand major problems and issues that may arise. This subscale includes the coping repertoire of: "knowing we have the power to solve major problems"; "knowing we have the strength within our family to solve our problems"; "facing the problems head on"; "showing we are strong"; "believing we can handle our own problems"; "accepting difficulties occur unexpectedly"; "defining the family problem in a more positive way"; "having faith in God"; and "showing that we are strong." The overall Cronbach Alpha for the Affirming the Family's Confidence subscale is .70

The Criterion of Success: Program Completion and Post-Treatment Adaptation

Two classic writings point to the importance of defining the success in residential youth care and treatment (Matsushima, 1965; Gershenson, 1956). In spite of these earlier statements of concern, the delineation of what would be viewed as measures of successful residential treatment continues to plague the field of residential treatment research (Whittaker, 1979; Whittaker & Pecora, 1984). Embedded in their valuable critique of current studies and their charge to adopt a multiple indicators of success approach to the assessment of residential treatment, Whittaker, Overstreet, Grasso, Tripodi, and Boylan (1988, pp. 143–144) also called attention to the basic issues and needs of the field, which included: (a) the need to obtain baselines on target behavior; (b) the need for control or contrast groups; (c) the need for measurement point and restricted indicators of success; and (d) the need for in-program tracking and monitoring and community follow-up. To this list, and of importance to this investigation, we would add (e) the need for greater specification of youth and family changes expected to be influenced by the treatment program; (f) the need to specify both short- and long-term outcomes expected of the program and the clients served; and (g) the need for clear articulation of what specific changes are expected of youth and family, and how they will relate, either predictively or causally to both short- and long-term goals of the treatment program.

Two criterion indices of success were adopted for this investigation: (a) program completion and (b) post-treatment (3- and 12-month) living situation. "Successful" completion is operationalized as a classification given to youth who finish the Boysville treatment program or who, in the staff's judgment met the staff's expectation for progress and achieved an acceptable level of improvement to be released earlier. Successful post-program adaptation is defined and operationalized as a classification given to youth who leave the Boysville program and who upon follow-up (3 or 12 months later) are found to be in less restrictive living situations (e.g., with family, in a foster home, group home, or independent living situation). Conversely, failure is defined as youth living in more restrictive settings (e.g., jail, youth home, shelter, private care facility, state institution, or mental health facility).

For this investigation, the target behaviors and expected changes are related to both the youth offenders in residential treatment and the families who participate in the concomitant family-oriented therapies. While a comparison group is included in the overall investigation, for this chapter, their analysis is set aside for a future report. Data on youth and family coping, as already noted in the measurement section of the chapter, were collected at intake and near completion of the program, with the intention of measuring changes in these targeted dimensions of the treatment program. From the outset it was hypothesized that changes in youth and family coping would be observable and recordable objectives of the treatment program and these changes would be positively related to successful program completion (short-term objective) and to both 3-month post-treatment adaptation (long-term) as measured by the degree to which youth are living in less restrictive settings (e.g., at home, in adoptive home, in foster home) or in more restrictive settings (e.g., incarceration, police custody, etc.) and 12-month adaptation (long term) (see Figure 1). Following these guidelines we expect to be able to answer the fundamental questions of residential treatment: whether changes in youth and family coping were recorded and whether these changes are related to both short- and long-term indices of treatment success.

Results

Profile of Youth and Families

During the period of study, a total of 821 African-American youth were treated in the Boysville program. The population averaged 15 years of age. The majority (60.4%) of the youth offenders at Boysville came from single-parent family units, while the remaining minority (39.6%) were from either nuclear, reconstituted, foster, or adoptive families. Over two thirds (68.2%) of the youth were either enrolled in school or had graduated from high school. The grade levels were fairly evenly distributed, with 59.8% in grade school or middle school, and 40.2% in high school. Over half of the youth (53.5%) had experienced two or more previous placements (i.e., in delinquent, dependent-neglect settings, etc.), nearly one fourth (23.9%) had one previous placement, while nearly another one fourth (22.6%) had no prior placements before coming to Boysville. The vast majority of the youth offenders at Boysville (71.0%) had two or less adjudications before treatment at Boysville, while a notable percentage (20.0%) had three or four adjudications. Nearly one tenth (9.0%) had five or more adjudications.

Subsample A: Family and Youth Coping and Program Completion

From the total population of African-American youth at Boysville, a subsample of 91 African-American youth offenders treated in the Boysville program was identified. This cluster of youth, referred to as Subsample A, consisted of youth offenders for whom intake data, youth and family coping information recorded at intake and at a point near the completion of the program, as well as program completion information were available. The subsample averaged 15 years of age. The majority (68.1%) of these youth offenders at Boysville came from single-parent family units, while the remaining minority (31.9%) were from either nuclear, reconstituted, foster, or adoptive families. Nearly two thirds (65.9%) of the youth were either enrolled in school or had graduated from high school. The grade levels were evenly distributed, with 51.7% in grade or middle school and 48.3% in high school. Close to half of the youth (41.8%) had experienced two or more previous placements (i.e., in delinquent, dependent-neglect settings, etc.), slightly over one fourth (29.7%) had one previous placement, while slightly over one fourth (28.6%) had no prior placements before coming to Boysville. The majority of the youth offenders at Boysville (63.7%) had two or less adjudications before treatment at Boysville, while nearly one fourth (22.0%) had three or four adjudications. A notable percentage (14.3%) of the youth in Subsample A had five or more adjudications.

Subsample B: Family and Youth Coping, Program Completion, and 3-Month Post-Treatment Living

From Subsample A another subsample of 76 African-American youth offenders treated in the Boysville program was identified. This subsample consisted of youth offenders for whom intake data, youth and family coping information obtained at intake and a point near the completion of the Boysville program, information on program completion and 3-month post-treatment living situation were available. This group of youth, referred to as Subsample B, also averaged 15 years of age. The majority (66.5%) of these youth offenders came from single-parent family units, while the remaining minority (34.2%) were from either nuclear, reconstituted, foster, or adoptive families. Nearly three fourths (73.7%) of the youth were either enrolled in school or had graduated from high school. The grade levels were evenly distributed, with 54.1% in grade or middle school and 45.9% in high school. Close to half of the youth (43.4%) had experienced two or more previous placements (i.e., in delinquent, dependent-neglect settings, etc.), slightly over one fourth (27.6%) had one previous placement, while over one fourth (28.9%) had no prior placements before coming to Boysville. Nearly two thirds of the youth offenders at Boysville (60.5%) had two or less adjudications before treatment at Boysville, while over one fourth (25.0%) had three or four adjudications, and a notable percentage (14.5%) had five or more adjudications.

Subsample C: Family and Youth Coping, Program Completion, and 12-Month Post-Treatment Living

From Subsample B another subsample of 56 African-American youth offenders treated in the Boysville program was identified. This subsample consisted of youth offenders for whom intake data, youth and family coping information obtained at intake and at a point near completion of the Boysville program, program completion information, 3-month post-treatment living information, and 12-month post-treatment living information were available. This group of youth offenders, referred to as Subsample C, also averaged 15 years of age. Nearly two thirds (64.3%) of these youth offenders came from single-parent family units, while the remaining minority (35.7%) were from either nuclear, reconstituted, foster, or adoptive families. Nearly three fourths (71.4%) of the youth were either enrolled in school or had graduated from high school. The grade levels were evenly distributed, with 57.1% in grade or middle school and 42.9% in high school. Close to half of the youth (42.9%) had experienced two or more previous placements (i.e., in delinquent, dependent-neglect settings, etc.), nearly one fourth (23.2%) had one previous placement, while one third (33.9%) had no prior placements before coming to Boysville. The majority of the youth offenders at Boysville (55.4%) had two or less adjudications before treatment, slightly over one fourth (28.6%) had three or four adjudications, and a notable percentage (16.1%) had five or more adjudications.

African-American Youth: A Comparative Analysis on Demographic Information

The basic question to be answered is: To what degree are the three subsamples of African-American youth different from each other and from the total group of African-American youth offenders who were provided treatment at Boysville? In other words, are the subsamples representative of the total group, or because of the data collected at time of program completion, 3-month and 12-month post-treatment, are they unique groups, distinctly different from the original population and from each other? To answer these questions we compared all the subsamples, A, B, and C with each other and with the total population of African-American youth treated at Boysville. An analysis of variance (on continuous variables) and Chi-square analysis (on categorical data) is presented in Tables 1 and 2. Briefly, the analysis of the youth's age at intake, number of prior adjudications, number of prior placements, family structure and education, reveals no differences, with one single exception. Significant differences were observed between the subsamples and the total group on the variable of the number of prior adjudications. Specifically, the African-American youth on whom 12-month follow-up living situation was recorded, Subsample C, had a significantly ($p=.01$) greater number of prior adjudications (mean=1.61). The findings take on relative importance when compared to the total group (mean=1.38) of African-American youth offenders who received treatment at Boysville. One could have hypothesized that if there were to be observed differences the youth with the greatest number of adjudications would be found in the general population and not be overrepresented in the 12-month follow-up group. In general, it is reasonable to conclude on the basis of available data that the subgroups are minimally different from each other and similar in profile to that of the total group of youth offenders at Boysville. There is little evidence to support the concern of a skewed distribution of youth and their families in any of the three subsamples.

Table 1
Comparative Analysis of the Demographics of the Three Subsamples, A,B,C and the
Total Population of African-American Youth Offenders Treated in the Boysville Program

Demographic Data	All African-American Youth N=821 Means	Subsample A African-American Youth N=91 Means	Subsample B African-American Youth N=76 Means	Subsample C African-American Youth N=56 Means	F=	P	Notation
Youth Age at Intake	14.98	15.11	15.04	15.14	0.63	0.59	Not Significant
Youth Education Level at Intake	8.04	8.37	8.28	8.29	1.90	0.13	Not Significant
Youth number of prior adjudications	1.38	1.51	1.54	1.61	3.78	0.01	Significant
Youth number of prior placements (e.g., foster homes, treatment centers etc.)	1.77	1.55	1.58	1.66	1.66	0.17	Not Significant

Table 2
Comparative Analysis of the Demographics of the Three Subsamples, A,B,C and the Total Population of African-American Youth Offenders Treated in the Boysville Program

Demographic Data	All African-American Youth N=821 Percentage	Subsample A African-American Youth N=91 Percentage	Subsample B African-American Youth N=76 Percentage	Subsample C African-American Youth N=56 Percentage	χ^2	P
Youth Family structure						
Single Parent Unit	60.4%	68.1%	65.8%	64.3%		
Nuclear, reconstituted, foster and adoptive family unit	39.6%	31.9%	34.2%	35.7%	20.86	.14
Youth Education Level at Intake						
Grade School or Middle School	59.8%	51.7%	54.1%	57.1%		
High School	40.2%	48.3%	45.9%	42.9%	2.92	.40

Significant Changes in and Intercorrelation of Changes in Youth and Family Coping

Before presenting the prediction findings for coping and the three criterion indices, a brief analysis of changes (between intake and program completion and the relationship of these changes between youth and family coping) are in order. Two related questions may be answered: (1) while this study focuses on the prediction of program completion and post-treatment adaptation, the question remains—what areas of youth and family coping are most likely to change and (2) to what degree are changes in youth coping and family coping related to each other?

The analysis reveals that while changes were observed in all six dimensions of coping, statistically significant changes were observed in only two areas of coping. Specifically, between the intake data and the near program completion data significant changes ($t=2.55$, $p=.01$) were observed for youth positive appraisal and problem solving. Additionally, significant ($t=2.89$, $p=.05$) changes were observed in family coping to improve family confidence.

Changes in youth coping appeared to be moderately related to changes in family coping. Specifically, changes in youth spiritual and personal development were significantly ($r=.21$, $p=.05$) and positively related to changes in family coping by seeking professional and spiritual guidance. Additionally, changes (reduction) in youth incendiary communication were negatively related to positive changes in family coping to improve family confidence. The less the youth's emphasis on incendiary communication, the greater the degree of family confidence and vice versa. A family systems view of coping appears to be supported with a moderate but significant relationship between changes in youth and family coping.

Efficacy of Residential Treatment: Predicting Success

The importance of youth coping and family coping as predictors of successful or unsuccessful Boysville program completion, and successful or unsuccessful post-treatment adaptation 3 and 12 months after completing the Boysville program was tested in this investigation. Specifically, to determine the efficacy of youth and family coping, three analyses were conducted, each designed to shed light on the relative importance of coping in explaining the outcome of the Boysville interventions. The first set of discriminant analyses (*SPSS, Professional Statistics 6.1*, 1994) were conducted to determine: (a) whether the six coping strategies (three for youth and three for family) were predictive of successful or unsuccessful program completion; (b) which of the six coping strategies are predictive of less or more restrictive living situations 3 months following treatment—this set of discriminant analyses included a stepwise algorithm with both forward selection and backward elimination procedures with the Mahalanobis distance method (at each step, the variable that maximizes the smallest F ratio for pairs of groups is entered); and (c) which of the six coping strategies are predictive of less or more restrictive living situations 12 months following treatment. The stepwise algorithm and Mahalanobis distance method were applied in this set of discriminant analyses.

The second and third clusters of discriminant analyses were introduced to achieve greater parsimony by isolating the most important youth and family coping strategies, and through discriminant analysis, to determine how accurate our predictions would be for successful program completion and post-treatment adaptation if we only considered these "best predictors (coping)." Finally, by comparing this "parsimonious" best set of predictors to our predictions based on changes in all six coping strategies, we can determine whether our interventions could or should focus on all aspects of youth and family coping or whether we can narrow our focus to those aspects of youth and/or family coping found to be equally predictive of both short and long term outcomes.

Predictors of Successful
Program Completion

The discriminant analysis of youth and family coping with the criterion of successful or unsuccessful completion of the Boysville program revealed the importance of both sets of youth and family coping. Specifically, when changes (difference between data taken at intake and near completion of the Boysville program) in all six coping repertoires are taken into account and used as predictors of program completion (see Table 3), the value of youth and family coping is confirmed. The statistics presented in Table 3 reveal that a 75% level of accuracy is achieved in predicting successful program completion when changes in youth and family coping are taken into consideration. It is of equal importance to note that an even higher level of accuracy, 90.9%, is achieved in the prediction of unsuccessful program completion. Given our specific interest in predicting successful program completion or unsuccessful program

Table 3
Classification Summary for African-American Youth
on their Successful Program Completion Based on a
Discriminant Analysis with A Stepwise Entry of All Indices
of Youth Coping and Family Coping as Predictors

Youth and Family Coping as Predictors of Successful Program Completion	Percent Accuracy of Prediction for Successful Program Completion	Percent Accuracy of Prediction for Unsuccessful Program Completion	Overall Accuracy of Successful Program Completion
Youth Coping: Change (Reduction) in Youth in Incendiary Communication and Tension Management Coping	68.8%	72.7%	69.2%
Family Coping: Change (Improvement) in Family Coping by Affirming the Family Confidence	68.8%	72.7%	69.2%
Youth Coping: Change (Improvement) in Youth Spiritual and Personal Development Coping	76.2%	63.6%	74.7%
Family Coping: Change (Improvement) in Family Coping by Seeking Professional and Spiritual Guidance	75.0%	72.7%	74.7%
Family Coping: Change (Improvement) in Family Coping by Seeking Family and Neighbor Support	76.2%	81.8%	79.9%
Youth Coping: Change (Improvement) in Positive Apparaisal and Problem Solving Coping	75.0%	90.9%	76.9%

completion, the statistics on overall prediction (76.9%) are of less salience in interpreting our results.

In an effort to achieve parsimony, that is to find the smallest set of predictors (changes in youth and family coping) for successful and unsuccessful program completion, the second set of discriminant analysis, summarized in Table 4, confirms the importance of two indices of youth coping. Specifically, the analysis affirms the importance of changes (reduction) in Youth Incendiary Communication and Tension Management, and the importance of changes (improvement) in Youth's Spiritual and Personal Development as viable predictors of program completion. When changes in these two youth coping repertoires are considered in the analysis as predictors of program completion, a significant level of accuracy (see Table 5) is achieved. Specifically, when changes in these two youth coping repertoires are considered alone, a 76.2% level of accuracy is achieved in predicting successful program completion;

Table 4
Summary Table of Discriminant Analysis Isolating the Critical
Predictors for Explaining Successful Boysville Program Completion

Predictors	Wilks' Lambda	Sig.	Minimum D Squared	Sig.	Correlations with Discriminant Functions
1 Changes (Reduction) in Youth Incendiary Communication and Tension Management Coping	.91149	.0042	.89374	.0042	.72873
2 Changes (improvement) in Youth Spiritual and Personal Development Coping	.84541	.0006	1.68296	.0006	-.28506

χ^2= 14.779, p=.0006

and a 72.7% level of accuracy is achieved in predicting unsuccessful program completion. Overall, the accuracy rate is 75.8%.

It is important to emphasize the power of changes in all dimensions of both youth and family coping for predicting successful program completion (75.0%) and unsuccessful program completion (90.9%). The more parsimonious predictors of considering changes in two youth coping repertoires appear to be beneficial in the case of predicting successful program completion (76.2% versus 75.0%) and less beneficial in predicting unsuccessful program

Table 5
Classification Results for African-American Youth
Based on Discriminant Analysis for Predicting
Boysville Program Completion

Actual Group	Actual Outcome for African-American youth	Predicted Classification of African-American youth	
		0	1
Group 0 Released from Boysville for reasons unrelated to treatment or treatment goals	11	8 72.7%	3 27.3%
Group 1 Completion of Boysville Program or achievement of treatment goals	80	19 23.8%	61 76.2%

Percent of "Grouped" cases correctly classified: 75.82%

completion (72.7% versus 90.9%). Based on the parsimonious findings, it is compelling to look for ways to make the residential program more efficient emphasizing a reduction in incendiary communication and an improvement of spiritual and personal development. However, the findings indicate that by considering changes in both youth and family coping we can produce a higher level of accuracy, particularly in predicting unsuccessful program completion.

Predictors of 3-Month Post-Treatment Adjustment and Adaptation

The discriminant analysis of changes in youth and family coping with the criterion of successful or unsuccessful 3-month post-treatment adaptation (i.e., successful adaptation equals a less restrictive living situation) revealed the importance of both sets of youth and family coping. Specifically, when changes (difference between data taken at intake and near completion of the Boysville program) in all six coping repertoires are taken into account and used as predictors of 3-month post-treatment adaptation (see Table 6), the value of youth and family coping is confirmed. The statistics presented in Table 6 reveal that a 73% level of accuracy is achieved in predicting successful 3-month post-treatment adaptation (i.e., less restrictive living situation) when changes in youth and family coping are taken into consideration. A slightly lower level of accuracy, 69.2%, is achieved in the prediction of unsuccessful 3-month post-treatment adaptation (i.e., more restrictive living situation). Given our specific interest in predicting successful post-treatment, less restrictive living situations for youth offenders at Boysville, the overall accuracy of 72.4% takes on importance.

In an effort to achieve parsimony, that is to find the smallest set of predictors (changes in youth and family coping) for successful and unsuccessful 3-month post-treatment adaptation, the second set of discriminant analysis, summarized in Table 7, confirms the importance of two indices of youth coping. Specifically, the analysis affirms the importance of changes (reduction) in Youth Incendiary Communication and Tension Management, and the importance of changes (improvement) in Youth's Positive Appraisal and Problem Solving as predictors of 3-month post-treatment adaptation. When changes in these two youth coping repertoires are considered in the analysis as predictors of 3-month post-treatment adaptation (e.g., less or more restrictive living situa-

Table 6
Classification Summary for African-American Youth on Their
3-Month Successful Adaptation in Less Restrictive Living
Situation Based on a Discriminant Analysis with A Stepwise Entry
of All Indices of Youth Coping and Family Coping as Predictors

Youth and Family Coping as Predictors of 3-Month Follow-up of Youth Living Situation	Percent Accuracy of Prediction for 3-Month Success in Less Restrictive Living Situation	Percent Accuracy of Prediction for 3-Month More Restrictive Living Situation	Overall Accuracy of Prediction for 3-Month Living Situation
Youth Coping: Change (Reduction) in Youth Incendiary Communication and Tension Management Coping	63.5%	69.2%	64.5%
Family Coping: Change (Improvement) in Family Coping by Seeking Professional and Spiritual Guidance	68.3%	69.2%	68.4%
Family Coping: Change (Improvement) in Family Coping by Seeking Family and Neighbor Support	66.7%	76.9%	68.4%
Youth Coping: Change (Improvement) in Positive Appraisal and Problem Solving Coping	74.6%	69.2%	73.7%
Youth Coping: Change (Improvement) in Youth Spiritual and Personal Development Coping	74.6%	69.2%	73.7%
Family Coping: Change (Improvement) in Family Coping by Affirming the Family Confidence	73.0%	69.2%	72.4%

tion), a statistically significant but modest level of accuracy (see Table 8) is achieved. Specifically, when changes in these two youth coping repertoires are considered alone, a 69.8% accuracy is achieved in predicting a successful 3-month post-treatment adaptation; and a 61.5% accuracy is achieved in predicting unsuccessful 3-month post-treatment adaptation. Overall, the accuracy rate is a modest 68.4%.

It is important to emphasize the power of changes in all dimensions of both youth and family coping for predicting successful post-treatment adaptation (less restrictive living situation) (73.0%) and unsuccessful 3-month post-treatment adaptation (more restrictive living situation) (69.2%). The more parsimonious predictors of considering changes in two youth coping repertoires,

Table 7
Summary Table of Discriminant Analysis Isolating the Critical
Predictors for Explaining 3-Month Post Treatment Adaptation
and Living in Less Restrictive Situations

Predictors	Wilks' Lambda	Sig.	Minimum D Squared	Sig.	Correlations with Discriminant Functions
1 Changes (Reduction) in Youth Incendiary Communication and Tension Management Coping	.92918	.0201	.52335	.0201	.77532
2 Changes (Improvement) in Youth Positive Appraisal and Problem Solving Coping	.88748	.0128	.87063	.0128	-.35523

$\chi^2 = 8.714, p = .0128$

appear to be less beneficial in the case of predicting successful 3-month post-treatment adaptation (69.8% versus 73.0%) and less beneficial in predicting unsuccessful post-treatment adaptation (61.5% versus 69.2%). Based on the findings, it is compelling to look for ways to make the residential program more efficient by emphasizing a reduction in incendiary communication and an improvement of youth positive appraisal and problem solving. However, the findings suggest that a focus on changes in all youth and family coping repertoires can produce a higher level of accuracy, particularly in predicting both unsuccessful and successful 3-month post-treatment adaptation.

Table 8
Classification Results for African-American Youth Based
on Discriminant Analysis for Predicting Post Boysville
Program Living Situation 3 Months After Treatment

Actual Group	Actual Outcome for African-American youth	Predicted Classification of African-American youth	
		0	1
Group 0 More Restrictive Living Situation	13	8 61.5%	5 38.5%
Group 1 Less Restrictive Living Situation	63	19 30.2%	44 69.8%

Percent of "Grouped" cases correctly classified: 68.42%

Predictors of 12-Month Post-Treatment Adjustment and Adaptation

The discriminant analysis of changes in youth and family coping with the criterion of successful (less restrictive living situation) or unsuccessful (more restrictive living situation) 12-month post-treatment adaptation revealed the importance of both sets of youth and family coping. Specifically, when changes (difference between data taken at intake and near completion of the Boysville program) in all six coping repertoires are taken into account and used as predictors of 12-month post-treatment adaptation (see Table 9), the value of youth and family coping is confirmed. The statistics presented in Table 9 reveal that a 76.2% level of accuracy is achieved in predicting successful 12-month post-treatment adaptation (i.e., less restrictive living situation) when changes in youth and family

Table 9
Classification Summary for African-American Youth on Their 12-Month Successful Adaptation in Less Restrictive Living Situation Based on a Discriminant Analysis with A Stepwise Entry of All Indices of Youth Coping and Family Coping as Predictors

Youth and Family Coping as Predictors of 12-Month Follow-up of Youth Living Situation	Percent Accuracy of Prediction for 12-Month Success in Less Restrictive Living Situation	Percent Accuracy of Prediction for 12-Month More Restrictive Living Situation	Overall Accuracy of Prediction for 12-Month Living Situation
Youth Coping: Change (Improvement) in Youth Spiritual and Personal Development Coping	66.7%	50.0%	62.5%
Youth Coping: Change (Reduction) in Youth Incendiary Communication and Tension Management Coping	71.4%	64.3%	69.6%
Youth Coping: Change (Improvement) in Positive Appraisal and Problem Solving Coping	69.0%	71.4%	69.6%
Family Coping: Change (Improvement) in Family Coping by Seeking Family and Neighbor Support	71.4%	71.4%	71.4%
Family Coping: Change (Improvement in Family Coping by Affirming the Family Confidence	76.2%	71.4%	75.0%
Family Coping: Change (Improvement) in Family Coping by Seeking Professional and Spiritual Guidance	76.2%	71.4%	75.0%

coping are taken into consideration. It is of equal importance to note that a slightly lower level of accuracy, 75.0%, is achieved in the prediction of unsuccessful 12-month post-treatment adaptation (i.e., more restrictive living situation). Given our specific interest in predicting successful post-treatment (less restrictive living situation) for youth offenders at Boysville, the overall accuracy of 71.4% takes on less importance.

In an effort to achieve parsimony, that is to find the smallest set of predictors (changes in youth and family coping) for successful and unsuccessful 12-month post-treatment adaptation, the second set of discriminant analyses, summarized in Table 10, confirms the importance of two indices of youth coping. Specifically, the analysis affirms the importance of changes (improvement) in Youth's Spiritual and Personal Development, and the importance of changes (reduction) in Youth Incendiary Communication and Tension Management as predictors of 12-month post-treatment, adaptation. When changes in these two youth coping repertoires are considered in the analysis as predictors of 12-month post-treatment adaptation (e.g., less or more restrictive living situation), a statistically significant level of accuracy (see Table 11) is achieved. Specifically, when changes in these two youth coping repertoires are considered alone, a 71.4% accuracy is achieved in predicting a successful 12-month post-treatment adaptation; and a modest 64.3% accuracy is achieved in predicting unsuccessful 12-month post-treatment adaptation. Overall, the accuracy rate is a modest 69.6%.

It is important to emphasize the power of changes in all dimensions of both youth and family coping for predicting success-

Table 10
Summary Table of Discriminant Analysis Isolating the Critical Predictors for Explaining 12-Month Post-Treatment Adaptation and Living in Less Restrictive Situations

Predictors	Wilks' Lambda	Sig.	Minimum D Squared	Sig.	Correlations with Discriminant Functions
1 Changes (improvement) in Youth Spiritual and Personal Development Coping	.94337	.0774	.30872	.0774	.79877
2 Changes (Reduction) in Youth Incendiary Communication and Tension Management Coping	.83080	.0074	1.04743	.0074	-.39867

χ^2= 9.825, p=.0074

Table 11
Classification Results for African-American Youth Based
on Discriminant Analysis for Predicting Post Boysville
Program Living Situation 12 Months After Treatment

Actual Group	Actual Outcome for African-American youth	Predicted Classification of African-American youth	
		0	1
Group 0 More Restrictive Living Situation	14	9 64.3%	5 35.7%
Group 1 Less Restrictive Living Situation	42	12 28.6%	30 71.4%

Percent of "Grouped" cases correctly classified: 69.64%

ful post-treatment adaptation (i.e., less restrictive living situation) (76.2%) and unsuccessful 12-month post-treatment adaptation (i.e., more restrictive living situation) (71.4%). The more parsimonious predictors of considering changes in two youth coping repertoires appear to be less beneficial in the case of predicting successful 12-month post-treatment adaptation (71.4% versus 76.2%) and less beneficial for predicting unsuccessful 12-month post-treatment adaptation (64.3% versus 71.4%). It is compelling to look for ways to make the residential program more efficient through an emphasis on improving youth spiritual and personal development, and reducing incendiary communication. However, the findings indicate that a focus on changes in all youth and family coping repertoires can produce a higher level of accuracy, particularly in predicting both unsuccessful and successful 12-month post-treatment adaptation.

Discussion

The concept of resiliency appears to have relevance for studies directed at understanding the impact of family and youth oriented residential treatment upon both the short-term and long-term adaptation of youth at risk. Specifically, this prospective investigation of youth and families reveals the relative importance of changes in both youth and family coping during, and in response to, the treatment process. It is striking to note that positive changes in youth coping efforts directed at spiritual and personal development and negative changes (reduction) in youth coping efforts directed at incendiary communication play an important part in predicting successful completion of the Boysville program and successful post-treatment adaptation 12 months later. In slight contrast, successful 3-month post-treatment adaptation is explained by an improvement in the youth's positive appraisal and problem-solving coping accompanied by negative changes in the youth's incendiary communication. With changes (reduction) in incendiary communication emerging as the single common youth coping strategy predicting program completion and post-treatment adaptation, we affirm the findings of Tolan, Cromwell, and Brasswell (1986), who pointed to family conflict, exacerbated in part by the youth's own contributions to family conflict, as a key factor distinguishing delinquent families from nondelinquent families. As already noted, incendiary communication is a key factor in marital discord and parent-adolescent or youth conflict (Gove & Crutchfield, 1982; Cernkovich & Giordano, 1987; Wells & Rankin, 1991), all of which were found to be associated with juvenile delinquency.

The salience of resiliency in families as a concept in residential treatment improves when we consider the central finding that changes in youth *and* family coping, a family systems perspective, provides the strongest set of predictions in explaining successful program completion and successful adaptation 3 and 12 months following treatment. When increases in youth spiritual and personal development, positive appraisal and problem solving, as well as decreases in incendiary communication occur, in conjunction with increases in the family coping efforts of seeking professional and spiritual guidance, family and neighborhood support and affirming the family confidence during the period of residential treatment, the strongest prediction of the relative success of the Boysville program is possible. When both changes in youth and family coping are considered, we observe the highest accuracy in predicting successful and unsuccessful program completion (75.0% successful; 90.9% unsuccessful); post-program adaptation at 3 months (73.0% less restrictive living situation; 69.2% more restrictive living situation); and post-program adaptation at 12 months (76.2% less restrictive living situation; 71.4% more restrictive living situation).

These findings affirm the relative importance of a family systems perspective for understanding and predicting treatment outcomes: As a system, youth and the family unit are interdependent and, as a result, behavior of any one individual family member influences and affects every other member of the family. Therefore, youth behavior is best understood, and some would argue, best treated, within the interpersonal or family context of the behavior (Henggeler & Borduin, 1990). The family's coping strategies directed at seeking professional and spiritual assistance, neighborhood and kin support, and improving family confidence in itself affirm earlier findings that point to the importance of extended family members and family "kin" as well as religion in the family's adaptation to stressful situations (Coates, 1990; Billson, 1988; Robinson, 1989). It is striking to note that increases in African-American families' use of professional assistance is related to successful program completion. The findings point to the value of family involvement in residential treatment programs that facilitate the family unit's use of both professional and spiritual assistance. The findings also confirm other research that argues for a more ecological approach when treating juvenile offenders and their families (e.g., Henggeler & Borduin, 1990). These findings gain importance in light of prior research that argues that with a history of racism and blocked opportunities, African-American youth and families tend to share a cautious, if not pejorative, view of professional assistance and particularly mental health services and agencies (Boyd-Franklin, 1987, 1989; Hines & Boyd-Franklin, 1982; Robinson, 1989).

These findings contribute to our ever-increasing need to validate the importance of treatment interventions, particularly those programs supported by public funds that are constantly under scrutiny. The findings point to the importance of empowering and strengthening the coping repertoires of both African-American youth at risk and their families with the goal of creating mutually supportive relationships, which will foster the development and independence of both the adolescent and his or her family. This focus on empowering families and individuals is more realistic than the idealistic goal of these families becoming reunited and marching into the future "hand in hand." The follow-up assessments of youths' living situations (less restrictive versus more restrictive) and their relationship to youth and family coping may be viewed as offering partial support for this line of reasoning; one of the goals of youth and family treatment is to foster the independent living of youth at risk. This investigation offers some confirmatory evidence that an investment in the treatment of families contributes to the well-being of youth following treatment.

These findings only skim the surface of our continuous need to understand African-American youth and their families. Despite the need for such information, and the national mandate for federally funded research to include persons of color, we lack knowledge about racial and ethnic minority families. The findings of this investigation press us to further examine the ethnic identification of African-American youth at risk and their families and to determine what role ethnic identification plays in adaptation and responses to treatment. Further examination of the dynamics of youth and family interactions after treatment that promote or undermine post-treatment adaptation are needed. We have only touched upon one dimension in the resiliency framework used to guide this research. Youth and family coping are important in this investigation, but whether these dimensions of the resiliency model will remain important when all factors are considered remains to be tested empirically. Future investigations might question whether coping remains prominent when considered along with other factors such as family functioning (including family flexibility and bonding) and levels of stress. Further, one might also question whether coping will remain prominent when family functioning, stress, and coping are considered simultaneously in predicting program completion and post-treatment adaptation.

These findings raise questions about residential treatment programs which choose to focus exclusively on the reduction and elimination of dysfunctional behaviors and strategies as their primary goal. This investigation suggests that coping as part of both youth and family resiliency may be an appropriate target for intervention; a means of empowering youth and families to manage a host of future stressors and strains rather than focusing on the unique hardships of life in residential treatment or the vissitudes of being a delinquent or troubled family unit. The findings suggest that strengthening the family coping repertoire to include the use of professional assistance, to build confidence, and to build social support, which may be enhanced by the propensity of African-American families to seek such forms of aid and assistance, may assist the youth member in his or her future adaptations. These same general observations may be cited in the case of youth coping—personal and spiritual development, positive appraisal and problem-solving, and communication may have an impact upon the future development of the adolescent members. Residential treatment appears to do well in shaping the scope, depth, and quality of the youth's coping repertoire to be employed in a range of real and unavoidable future life changes and circumstances. While the treatment of deviance and dysfunction is important, preparing the family and youth by enhancing their basic repertoire of coping strategies appears to have merit in this investigation.

While this investigation has drawn from and used research measures which are relevant to African-American families and youth, the investigators do not claim to offer definitive answers or measures which capture the unique aspects of treating and evaluating families of color. Rather, when stated in more modest and realistic terms, this investigation suggests that in addition to developing more ethnically sensitive measures, there is also value in including and developing measures which may apply to all families independent of color or ethnic heritage. Important to this investigation, however, is the belief that applying standard measures to families of color has numerous limitations, just as there are limitations in taking African-American family and youth measures and applying them to other racial or ethnic groups. This study suggests the need for a planful effort to develop measures which include ethnic considerations, but which are directed at common features of youth and family coping common across groups. Although we remain at an embryonic stage in the development and use of these measures, this investigation offers an alternative approach to the study and assessment of African-American youth and families in residential treatment.

Note

1.   This project was supported by the Graduate School, the Agricultural Experiment Station, the Center for Excellence in Family Studies, the Institute for the Study of Resiliency in Families, University of Wisconsin–Madison and Boysville of Michigan.   The authors would like to thank the Boysville of Michigan National Research Advisory Council, who encouraged and supported this effort, and particularly: Drs. Irwin Epstein, Sheldon Rose, James Whittaker, Tony Tripodi, Oscar Barbarin, Bogart Leashore, Paula Allen-Meares, and Rev. Thomas Harvey. The authors also thank Dr. Anthony Grasso and extend their deepest appreciation to Brother Francis Boylan and Edward Overstreet, whose vision of and commitment to Boysville and the serving of youth at risk and their families made this project possible.

References

Aponte, H. (1976). The family school interview: An eco-structural approach. *Family Process, 15*, 303–311.

Barbarin, O.A. (1993). Coping and resilience: Exploring the inner lives of African American children. *Journal of Black Psychology, 19*, 478–492.

Billson, J. M. (1988). Fostering nondeviant lifestyles against the odds: Toward a clinical sociological model of intervention strategies. *Adolescence, 23,* 517–532.

Blaske, D.M., Borduin, C.M., Henggeler, S.W., & Mann, B.J. (1989). Individual, family, and peer characteristics of adolescent sex offenders and assaultive offenders. *Developmental Psychology, 25,* 846–855.

Borduin, C.M., Pruitt, J.A., & Henggeler, S.W. (1986). Family interactions in black, lower class families with delinquent and nondelinquent adolescent boys. *Journal of Genetic Psychology, 147,* 333–342.

Boyd-Franklin, N. (1987). The contribution of family therapy models to the treatment of black families. *Psychotherapy, 24,* 621–629.

Boyd-Franklin, N. (1989). *Black families in therapy.* New York: Guilford.

Cartwright, P. (1982). *Children's residential services in Michigan: A study of outcomes and costs.* Unpublished manuscript.

Cernkovich, S.A., & Giordano, P.C. (1987). Family relationships and delinquency. *Criminology, 25,* 295–321.

Coates, D. L. (1990). Social network analysis as mental health intervention with African American adolescents. In F. C. Serafica et al. (Eds.), *Mental health of ethnic minorities* (pp. 5–37). New York: Praeger.

Cowden, J., & Monson, L. (1969). An analysis of some relationships between personality adjustment, placement, and post-release adjustment of delinquent boys. *Journal of Research in Crime and Delinquency, 6,* 63–70.

Cowen, E., Wyman, P., Work, W., & Parker, G. (1990). The Rochester Child Resiliency Project: Overview and summary of first year findings. *Development and Psychopathology, 2,* 193–212.

Dekovic, M., & Janssens, J. (1992). Parent's child rearing style and child's sociometric status. *Developmental Psychology, 28,* 925–932.

Dishion, T. (1990). The family ecology of boy's peer relations in middle childhood. *Child Development, 61,* 874–892.

Dornbusch, S.M., Carlsmith, J.M., Bushwall, S.J., Ritter, P.L., Leiderman, H., Hastorf, A.H., & Gross, R.T. (1985). Single parents, extended households and the control of adolescents. *Child Development, 56,* 326–341.

Free, M.D. (1991). Clarifying the relationship between the broken home and juvenile delinquency: A critique of the current literature. *Deviant Behavior, 12,* 109–167.

Garmezy, N. (1981). Children under stress: Perspectives on antecedents and correlates of vulnerability and resistance to psychopathology. In A.I. Rubin, J. Arnoff, A.M. Barclay, & R.A. Zucker (Eds.), *Further explorations in personality* (pp. 196–269). New York: Wiley.

Gershenson, C. (1956). Residential treatment of children: Research problems and possibilities. *Social Service Review, 30,* 268–275.

Gibbs, J. T. (1989). Black adolescents and youth: An update on an endangered species. In R. J. Jones (Ed.), *Black adolescents* (pp. 3–28). Berkeley, CA: Cobb & Henry.

Gilliland-Mallo, D., & Judd, P. (1986). The effectiveness of residential care facilities for adolescent boys. *Adolescence, 21,* 310–321.

Gingrich, N., Armey, D., & the House Republicans to Change the Nation. (1994). *Contract with America.* New York: Times Books.

Gove, W.R., & Crutchfield, R.D. (1982). The family and juvenile delinquency. *Sociological Quarterly, 23,* 301–319.

Grasso, A., & Epstein, I. (1993). Introduction: The need for a new model of information utilization in human service agencies. *Child and Youth Services, 16,* 1–16.

Gray-Ray, P., & Ray, M.C. (1990). Juvenile delinquency in the black community. *Youth & Society, 22,* 67–84.

Haggerty, R., Sherrod, L., Garmezy, N., & Rutter, M. (1994). *Stress, risk, and resilience in children and adolescents: Processes, mechanisms, and interventions.* Cambridge: Cambridge University Press.

Henggeler, S. W. (1989). *Delinquency in adolescence.* Newbury Park, CA: Sage.

Henggeler, S.W., & Borduin, C.M. (1990). Treatment of delinquent behavior. In S.W. Henggeler & C.M. Borduin (Eds.), *Family therapy and beyond: A multisystemic approach to treating the behavior problems of children and adolescents.* Pacific Grove, CA: Brooks/Cole.

Hines, P., & Boyd-Franklin, N. (1982). Black families. In M. McGoldrick, J. K. Pearce, & J. Giordano (Eds.), *Ethnicity and family therapy* (pp. 84–107). New York: Guilford.

Jacob, T. (1975). Family interaction in disturbed and normal families: A methodological and substantive review. *Psychological Bulletin, 82,* 33–65.

Jones, R. L. (1989). *Black adolescents.* Berkeley, CA: Cobb & Henry.

Kazdin, A. (1985). *Treatment of antisocial behavior in children and adolescents.* Homeward, IL: The Dorsey Press.

Kochanska, G. (1992). Children's interpersonal influence with mothers and peers. *Developmental Psychology, 28,* 491–499.

Kosciulek, J., McCubbin, M., & McCubbin, H. (1993). A theoretical framework for family adaptation to head injury. *Journal of Rehabilitation, 59,* 40–45.

Laub, J., & Sampson, R. (1988). Unraveling families and delinquency: A reanalysis of the Gluecks' data. *Criminology, 26,* 355–380.

Lavee, Y., McCubbin, H.I., & Patterson, J.M. (1985). The double ABCX model of family stress and adaptation: An empirical test by analysis of structural equations with latent variables. *Journal of Marriage and the Family, 47,* 811–825.

Loeber, R., Dishion, T.J., & Patterson, G.R. (1984). Multiple gating: A multistage assessment procedure for identifying youths at risk for delinquency. *Journal of Research in Crime and Delinquency, 21,* 7–32.

Loeber, R., & Stouthamer-Loeber, M. (1986). Family factors as correlates and predictors of juvenile conduct problems and delinquency. In M. Tonry & N. Morris (Eds.), *Crime and justice* (Vol. 7, pp. 29–150). Chicago: University of Chicago Press.

Loeber, R., Stouthamer-Loeber, M., Van Kammen, W., & Farrington, D. (1991). Initiation, escalation and desistence in juvenile offending and their correlates. *The Journal of Criminal Law and Criminology, 82,* 36–49.

Loeber, R., Wung, P., Keenan, K., Giroux, B., Stouthamer-Loeber, M., Van Kammen, W., & Maughan, B. (1993). Developmental pathways in disruptive child behavior. *Development and Psychopathology, 5,* 103–133.

Mann, B.J., Borduin, C.M., Henggeler, S. W., & Blaske, D. M. (1990). An investigation of systemic conceptualizations of parent-child coalitions and symptom change. *Journal of Consulting and Clinical Psychology, 58,* 336–344.

Mason, C.A., Cauce, A.M., Gonzales, N., Hiraga, Y., & Grove, K. (1994). An ecological model of externalizing behaviors in African American adolescents: No family is an island. *Journal of Research on Adolescence, 4,* 639–655.

Masten, A. S. (1989). Resiliency in development: Implications of the study of successful adaptation for developmental psychopathology. In D. Cicchetti (Ed.). *Rochester symposium on developmental psychopathology* (Vol 1., pp. 261–294). Hillsdale, NJ: Erlbaum Associates.

Matsushima, J. (1965). Some aspects of defining "success" in residential treatment. *Child Welfare, 44,* 272–277.

McAdoo, H.P. (1995). African-American families: Strengths and realities. In H.I. McCubbin, E.A. Thompson, A.I. Thompson, & J.A. Futrell (Eds.). *Resiliency in ethnic minority families: African-American families (Vol. 2).* Madison, WI: University of Wisconsin System.

McCord, J. (1983). A forty year perspective on the effects of child abuse and neglect. *Child Abuse and Neglect, 7,* 265–270.

McCord, J. (1986). Instigation and insulation: How families affect antisocial aggression. In J. Block, D. Olweus, & M.R. Yanow (Eds.), *Development of antisocial and prosocial behavior* (pp. 343–358). New York: Academic Press.

McCord, J. (1990). Long term effects of parental absence. In L. Robins & M. Rutter (Eds.), *Straight and devious pathways from childhood to adulthood* (pp. 116–134). New York: Cambridge University Press.

McCord, J. (1991). Family relationships, juvenile delinquency, and adult criminality. *Criminology, 29,* 397–417.

McCubbin, H.I., & McCubbin, M.A. (1988). Typologies of resilient families: Emerging roles of social class and ethnicity. *Family Relations, 37,* 245–254.

McCubbin, H.I., McCubbin, M.A., Thompson, A.I., & Thompson E.A. (1995). Resiliency in ethnic families: A conceptual model for predicting family adjustment and adaptation. In H.I. McCubbin, E.A. Thompson, A.I. Thompson, & J.E. Fromer. (Eds.), *Resiliency in ethnic minority families: Native and immigrant American families* (Vol. 1, pp. 3–48). Madison, WI: University of Wisconsin System.

McCubbin, H.I., Olson, D., & Larsen, A. (1987). F-COPES: Family crisis oriented coping evaluation scales. In H.I. McCubbin & A.I. Thompson (Eds.), *Family assessment inventories for research and practice* (pp. 203–216). Madison, WI: University of Wisconsin.

McCubbin, H.I., Thompson, A.I., & Elver, K.M. (1995a). *Family Coping Index (FAMCI).* Madison, WI: University of Wisconsin–Madison.

McCubbin, H.I., Thompson, A.I., & Elver, K.M. (1995b). *Youth Coping Index (YCI).* Madison, WI: University of Wisconsin–Madison.

McCubbin, H.I., Thompson, A.I., Thompson, E.A., Elver, K.M., & McCubbin, M.A. (1994). Ethnicity, schema, and coherence: Appraisal processes for families in crisis. In H.I. McCubbin, E.A. Thompson, A.I. Thompson, & J.E. Fromer (Eds.), *Sense of coherence and resiliency: Stress, coping, and health* (pp. 41–67). Madison, WI: University of Wisconsin System.

McCubbin, H.I., Thompson, E.A., Thompson, A.I., & Fromer, J.E. (1995). *Resiliency in ethnic minority families: Native and immigrant American families* (Vol. 1). Madison, WI: University of Wisconsin System.

McCubbin, H.I., Thompson, E.A., Thompson, A.I., & Futrell, J.A. (1995). *Resiliency in ethnic minority families: African-American families* (Vol. 2). Madison, WI: University of Wisconsin System.

McCubbin, H.I., Thompson, E.A., Thompson, A.I., McCubbin, M.A., & Kaston, A. (1993). Culture, ethnicity and the family: Critical factors in childhood chronic illness and disabilities. *Journal of Pediatrics, 91,* 1063–1070.

McCubbin, M.A., & McCubbin, H.I. (1993). Families coping with illness: The resiliency model of family stress, adjustment and adaptation. In C. Danielson, B. Hamel-Bissell, & P. Winstead-Fry (Eds.). *Families, health and illness* (pp. 21–63). New York: Mosby.

Minuchin, S. (1974). *Families and family therapy.* Cambridge, MA: Harvard University Press.

Moffitt, T. (1993). Adolescence limited and life course persistent antisocial behavior: A developmental taxonomy. *Psychological Review, 100,* 674–701.

Mooradian, J., & Grasso, A. (1993). The use of an agency-based information system in structural family therapy treatment. *Child and Youth Services, 16,* 49–74.

Myers, H. F. (1989). Urban stress and mental health in black youth: An epidemiologic and conceptual update. In R. J. Jones (Ed), *Black adolescents* (pp. 123–154). Berkeley, CA: Cobb & Henry.

Overstreet, E., Grasso, A., & Epstein, I. (1993). Management information systems and external policy advocacy: The Boysville lengths of stay study. *Child and Youth Services, 16,* 107–122.

Patterson, G.R., & Dishion, T.J. (1985). Contributions of families and peers to delinquency. *Criminology, 23,* 63–79.

Patterson, G.R., Reid, J.B., & Dishion, T.J. (1992). *Antisocial boys.* Eugene, OR: Castalia.

Patterson, G.R., & Stouthamer-Loeber, M. (1984). The correlation of family management practices and delinquency. *Child Development, 55,* 1299–1307.

Patterson, J., & McCubbin, H. (1987). A-COPE: Adolescent crisis oriented coping evaluation scales. In H. McCubbin & A. Thompson (Eds.), *Family assessment inventories for research and practice* (pp. 203–216). Madison: University of Wisconsin.

Patti, R. (1983). *Social welfare administration.* Englewood Cliffs, NJ: Prentice Hall.

Piatt, A.L., Ketterson, T.U., Skitka, L.J., Searight, H.R. Rogers, B.J., Reuterman, N.A., & Manley, C.M. (1993). The relationship of psychological adjustment to perceived family functioning among African American adolescents. *Adolescence, 28,* 673–684.

Rickel, A., & Allen, L. (1987). Preventing maladjustment from infancy through adolescence. In A. Kazdin (Ed.), *Developmental clinical psychology and psychiatry* (pp. 217–232). Newbury Park, CA: Sage.

Robinson, J.B. (1989). Clinical treatment of black families: Issues and strategies. *Social Work, 34,* 323–329.

Rodick, J.D., Henggeler, S.W., & Hanson, C.L. (1986). An evaluation of the family adaptability and cohesion evaluation scales and the circumplex model. *Journal of Abnormal Child Psychology, 14*, 77–87.

Rowe, D.C., Vazsonyi, A.T., & Flannery, D.J. (1994). No more than skin deep: Ethnic and racial similarity in developmental process. *Psychological Review, 101*, 398–413.

Rutter, M. (1979). Protective factors in children's responses to stress and disadvantage. In M.W. Kent & J. E. Rolf (Eds.), *Primary prevention of psychopathology: Social competence in children* (Vol. 3, pp. 49–74). Hanover, NH: University Press of New England.

Rutter, M., & Giller, H. (1983). *Juvenile delinquency: Trends and perspectives*. New York: Penguin.

Sampson, R.J., & Laub, J.H. (1993). The family context of juvenile delinquency. In R.J. Sampson & J.H. Laub. (Eds.), *Crime in the making: Pathways and turning points through life*. Cambridge, MA: Harvard University Press.

Savas, S., Epstein, I., & Grasso, A. (1993). Client characteristics, family contacts, and treatment outcomes. *Child and Youth Services, 16*, 125–137.

Shennum, W., & Thomas, C. (1987). A computer-based system for processing client behavior data in a residential treatment program. *Residential Treatment for Children & Youth, 5*, 83–93.

Simons, R. L., & Gray, P. A. (1989). Perceived blocked opportunity as an explanation of delinquency among lower class black males: A research note. *Journal of Research in Crime and Delinquency, 26*, 90–101.

Simons, R.L., Wu, C.I., Conger, R.D., & Lorenz, F.O. (1994). Two routes to delinquency: Differences between early and later starters in the impact of parenting and deviant peers. *Criminology, 32*, 247–276.

Snyder, J., & Patterson, G. (1987). Family interaction and delinquency. In H. C. Quay (Ed.), *Handbook of juvenile delinquency* (pp. 216–243). New York: John Wiley.

Spencer, M.B., Cole, S.P., DuPree, D., Glymph, A., & Pierre, P. (1993). Self efficacy among urban African American early adolescents: Exploring issues of risk, vulnerability, and resilience. *Development and Psychopathology, 5*, 719–739.

SPSS: Professional Statistics 6.1, (1994). SPSS: Chicago, IL.

Thompson, E.A., McCubbin, H.I., Thompson, A.I., & Elver, K.M. (1995). Vulnerability and resiliency in Native Hawaiian families under stress. In H.I. McCubbin, E.A. Thompson, A.I. Thompson, & J.E. Fromer (Eds.), *Resiliency in ethnic minority families: Native and immigrant American families* (Vol. 1, pp. 115–131). Madison, WI: University of Wisconsin System.

Tolan, P.H. (1988). Delinquent behavior and male adolescent development: A preliminary study. *Journal of Youth and Adolescence, 17*, 413–427.

Tolan, P.H., Cromwell, R.E., & Brasswell, M. (1986). Family therapy with delinquents: A critical review of the literature. *Family Process, 25*, 619–649.

Tolan, P.H., & Lorion, R.P. (1988). Multivariate approaches to the identification of delinquency proneness in adolescent males. *American Journal of Community Psychology, 16*, 547–561.

Wells, L.K., & Rankin, J.H. (1991). Families and delinquency: A meta-analysis of the impact of broken homes. *Social Problems, 38,* 71–93.

Werner, E. (1989). High-risk children in youth adulthood: A longitudinal study from birth to 32 years. *American Journal of Orthopsychiatry, 59,* 72–81.

Whittaker, J. (1979). *Caring for troubled children: Residential treatment in a community context.* San Francisco: Jossey-Bass.

Whittaker, J., Overstreet, E., Grasso, A., Tripodi, T., & Boylan, F. (1988). Multiple indicators of success in residential youth care and treatment. *American Journal of Orthopsychiatry, 58,* 143–147.

Whittaker, J., & Pecora, P. (1984). A research agenda for residential care. In T. Philpot (Ed.), *Group care practice* (pp. 71–87). Sutton, Surrey, UK: Community Care Business Press International.

Whittaker, J., Tripodi, T., & Grasso, A. (1993). Youth and family characteristics, treatment histories, and service outcomes: Some preliminary findings from the Boysville Research Program. *Child and Youth Services, 16,* 139–153.

Chapter 15

Resilient Families in an Ethnic and Cultural Context[1]

Hamilton I. McCubbin, Jo A. Futrell,
Elizabeth A. Thompson, and Anne I. Thompson

Considering the wealth of research on resiliency in children (Werner & Smith, 1982, 1992; Haggerty, Sherrod, Garmezy, & Rutter, 1994), and the paucity of research on resiliency in families (McCubbin & McCubbin, 1988; McCubbin, Thompson, Thompson, McCubbin, & Kasten, 1993) a family scholar would be startled to read Emery and Forehand's (1994) conclusion that "more attention has been devoted to family [in the parental divorce literature] than to individual child factors that lead to risk or resiliency in children's coping." This unexpected statement is best understood when placed in the overall context of resiliency research. The study of resiliency has traditionally focused on children with family factors considered as influential. This line of inquiry has flourished in the past two decades, calling attention to family factors that lead to risk such as parental conflict, poor communication, poor problem solving, and little involvement with the child (Capaldi & Patterson, 1991; Forehand, Thomas, Wierson, Brody, & Fauber, 1990). A second line of inquiry focuses on family factors that foster resiliency in children such as a trusting relationship between a child and an adult (Gelman, 1991) and positive sibling relationships (Kempton, Armistead, Wierson, & Forehand, 1991).

In contrast, resiliency research on families has focused upon what factors come into play in the family system's ability to endure and survive in the face of adversity, and secondarily, how the family's own resiliency factors come to shape the vulnerability and resiliency in children and other members of the family. This focus on the family system and its survival and endurance in the face of adversity makes the family unit, not the child, the central focus and primary unit of analysis. When we add ethnicity and culture to this already complex arena of resiliency studies we begin to appreciate and understand more fully the value of this line of scientific inquiry. In contrast to our typical approach to the study of ethnic groups and families of color, the focus on resiliency presses family scholars to look beyond the obvious mandates that ethnicity and culture be studied as complex independent variables that have depth and meaning far beyond the "categorical" or "dummy variable" classifications typically employed by demography. We are pressed to examine the important aspects of culture and ethnicity such as family ethnic identification, family schemas in a mixed-race family unit, customs and traditions of family systems, and how they all come to shape the family's patterns of functioning, particularly in the face of adversity. The demographer's standard tool of treating ethnicity as a classification variable falls short as a viable instrument for the study of resiliency in families of color. We are compelled to examine the complexity of ethnicity in the family context and determine, as best possible, how ethnicity is defined, developed, cultivated, and treated in the family system. We have only begun to advance this line of scientific inquiry. This chapter is designed to bring together the observations, findings, and conceptualizations from two volumes of writings on *Resiliency in Ethnic Minority Families: Native and Immigrant American Families* (Volume 1) *and Resiliency in African-American Families* (Volume 2), with the purpose of highlighting some major themes and emergent dimensions of research that shed light on resiliency in general, and resiliency as the concept applies to the study of ethnic families.

**Family Resiliency: A
Relational Perspective**

Resiliency is traditionally viewed as an attribute of individuals rather than a relational concept that occurs within a family system or within an ethnic and cultural context. Psychology has laid the foundation for the study of resiliency, and consequently, the research has been influenced by a Western perspective, which emphasized individuals, their traits, attributes, and competencies. An interpersonal and relational perspective emerged only recently, and the relational focus of family science literature provided a natural forum for the further development of the concept of resiliency. The relational perspective, characterized by four factors, an emphasis on harmony and interdependence of relationships, mind, body, and spirit, places the resilience of families within a balanced system (Cross, 1995; Marsella et al., 1995; McCubbin, McCubbin, Thompson, & Thompson, 1995). Cultures provide mechanisms to help maintain balance as the four factors interact and change. This relational perspective is central to the advancement of research on and provision of services to Native American, Native Hawaiian, Asian-American, African-American, and Hispanic/Latino families, as well as families from many other cultural traditions. In human services provision from a relational perspective, balance is considered vital to family stability, development, and the well-being of the family's members:

> When I look for the origins of family resilience within families of color I am not looking for linear cause and effect relationships to isolate the causal factors. Rather I am asking, 'What are the holistic and complex interrelationships that come into harmony and allow a family to not only survive but also to grow strong?' The nature of our strengths and challenges becomes evident as we examine family resilience from the relational perspective (Cross, 1995).

Other family scientists take a relational perspective on the survival of traditional culture in the face of "the demands of contemporary Western life." In an analysis of the Native Hawaiian culture and community, Marsella and colleagues (1995) asserted that:

> Native Hawaiian views on health and well-being are very holistic in that they emanate from the basic assumption that there is a felt sense of psychic unity that emerges from the harmonious interdependency of person, family, nature, and spiritual forces via the life force and power called *mana*. For the Native Hawaiian, any or all actions, intentional or unintentional, that result in the destruction of harmony among the different levels of being can result in illness, misfortune, or death. Behavior is supposed to preserve harmony in the social, natural and spiritual orders (Marsella, Oliveira, Plummer, & Crabbe, 1995).

Within the relational perspective we can ask what specific aspects of culture are important to families. An observational study of Navajo families with autistic or mentally retarded members illustrates how family life and the relational world view come into balance. This study examined how Navajo traditional culture legitimates and affirms acceptance and flexibility when a family is faced with disability. The accommodation of a disabled family member helps maintain family unity. The acceptance of disability is supported by traditional views of competence and wholeness; all are seen as contributing family members and an individual strives to be in harmony with his or her own condition, to integrate the mind, body, and spirit, regardless of disability (Connors & Donnellan, 1995).

This relational perspective, exemplified in the insightful relational world views of Native Americans and Native Hawaiians, are placed in a broader conceptual framework referred to in these volumes (I and II) as the Resiliency Model of Family Adjustment and Adaptation (McCubbin, McCubbin, Thompson, & Thompson, 1995). In this framework, the relational perspective is central with harmony, balance, and adaptation as the major themes. This framework emphasizes the complex interplay among a host of factors that not only shape the course of resiliency and adaptation, but also help to identify the specific components of family resiliency (e.g., schema, meanings, coping, supports, etc.) and the four underlying and dynamic processes:

(1) The relational process of family system changes in and integration of patterns of functioning,

(2) The relational process of family appraisal and development of meaning,

(3) The relational process of family community resource development and use,

(4) The relational process of family problem solving and coping.

These relational processes operate within the family system and its transactions with the community as the family faces adversities and vulnerabilities and works to maintain its integrity and achieve a new level of harmony and balance.

> The Resiliency Model . . . emphasizes the family's relational process of adaptation and the family's appraisal processes involving ethnicity and culture which facilitate the family's ability to institute new patterns of functioning and achieve harmony while promoting the well-being and development of its members (McCubbin, McCubbin, Thompson, & Thompson, 1995).

Family Resiliency: Ethnic
Identity and Values

Family scientists have also focused on the adaptation of cultural values. In a study of Asian-American college students, researchers examined how traditional cultural values may evolve to promote success in mainstream society. In this study, an Asian ethnic identity was positively related to educational achievement for these students (Ngo & Malz, 1995). In another study of Native American youth, cultural values emerged as protective mechanisms. Factors such as the strength of ethnic identity and participation in cultural activities promoted self-esteem, pride, and well-being, thereby acting as protective factors for youth at risk (Zimmerman, Ramirez, Washienko, Walter, & Dyer, 1995). The process of identifying with one's ethnic culture and involvement in cultural traditions, known as enculturation, appears to strengthen resiliency in individuals and families. These findings at the individual and family levels reinforce what anthropologists have long argued or suggested, that resiliency is a characteristic of the survivor found in cultures struggling to adapt and endure in the face of domination. Resilience in these circumstances grows out of a shared cultural identity, history and collective action (Elsass, 1992). The preservation of cultural values serves as a vital means of human and community survival.

Family Resiliency: Cultural
and Ethnic Preservation

Some scholars have pushed the cultural perspective to assert that the preservation of cultural values depends upon returning Native Americans and Native Hawaiians to their land and to sovereignty. They believe the only way to rebuild family life for native peoples and ensure their resiliency is to return these families to their lands of origin (Trask, 1995). While provocative, the thesis that cultural preservation and the affirmation of ethnic and cultural identity are central to family adaptation in the future cannot be set aside or dismissed.

> At present, the only policy that can begin to reverse this alarming reality [emigration, high infant mortality, low life expectancy] is Federal recognition of our nationhood, the transfer of lands, monies, and resources to a Native government, and the rebuilding of our people's lives on their indigenous lands . . . returning Hawaiians to their

familial origins—that is, to their land—is the only way to ensure the resiliency of the Hawaiian 'ohana [family]. . . .

We are children of *Paphanaumoku*—Earth Mother—and *Wakea*—Sky Father. Hawai'i is our mother; rejoining her completes our family circle. In modern terms, then, we must be returned to the lands of our birth. Our ability to survive as a people depends upon it (Trask, 1995).

Family Resiliency: The Community Context and Social Milieu

The entire concept of resiliency is also viewed in terms of the family within both the cultural context and the socioeconomic/ environmental context of which culture is a part. In fact, one may look at children at the greatest risk, those living in the ghettos, to see a different kind of culture emerging, one characterized by violence, abuse, despair, and a vision of little hope. Distinguished journalists such as Alex Kotlowitz (1995) have argued that a commitment to understanding resiliency in families must be accompanied by a commitment to understanding and changing the environment in which these families are called upon to survive.

In his discussion of African-American families living in the housing projects of Chicago, Kotlowitz described children who have developed a sense of hope in spite of their environment. He views this hopefulness as a sign of resilience and a resource and basis for rebuilding community for these families. Three major targets for intervention in changing the social milieu emerge: the school as an important target for improvement; the development of a broader sense of community; and the family as an integral and vital part of the social milieu.

Although listening is the first step, what we need to do ultimately is to find a way to rebuild a sense of community, both physically and spiritually. I feel very strongly about this. If we are to strengthen the family, if we are to provide a sense of future for these children, the first thing we must do is provide a sense of community.

I have become convinced over time that the place we must begin is in the schools. . . . It will make no difference in the lives of the children if we don't also rebuild community, if we don't address the other forces at work on the lives of the children.

> I want to challenge you to rethink what we mean by family. To rethink how we approach helping families in distress. Family, in its broadest sense, is more than just those we live with. It is the person next door, the person upstairs, the teacher, the local beat cop. It is, in short, community (Kotlowitz, 1995).

In general, the concept of resiliency moves beyond the ethnocentric cultural perspective that has been underscored in the literature and takes into account the physical and social environment in which families and children live and develop. It is the combination of culture and community, many would argue, that will shape the process and determine the level of resiliency of families.

Family Resiliency: Family Relationships, Community Reciprocal Help, and Social Support

The largest body of research that encompasses the community and deals with resiliency focuses on what is more commonly known as social support. Communities foster a variety of support systems, both formal and informal. The support systems for African-American families have been characterized as deeply rooted in the church and other healing forces in the community (Bagley & Carroll, 1995). In addition, and predictably, social support is also viewed as consisting of formal services that families can call upon to promote family resiliency. For example, researchers have looked at housing and neighborhood resources as sources of resiliency for single parent mothers and grandmothers (Cantwell & Jenkins, 1995), and studied the experiences of poor women who lack prenatal care to determine how community resources can be improved and made more available to these women (Holtz, 1995).

Community resources can provide support to families and children in need. In an investigation of low-income Latino/Hispanic families, family scientists explored a family-focused approach to needs assessment and intervention. Specifically, these researchers found that:

> . . . resiliency is developed in children by enhancing the likelihood that they experience positive and nurturing family environments. In other word, resiliency is developed in families through the provision of an appropriate combination of formal and informal support thereby enhancing the

resiliency of the children of those family units as well (San Miguel, Morrison, & Weissglass, 1995).

The importance of the family system and its influence on children's educational attainment cannot be overstated. One national study indicated that African-American, Hispanic, and Native American sophomores were disadvantaged relative to white sophomores in that their parents were less educated, less likely to live in a two-parent family, and were more likely to live in larger families (Sandefur, 1995). In addition, Native American, African-American, and Hispanic sophomores were significantly less likely than white sophomores to have their school work monitored by their parents. Furthermore, Native American and Hispanic sophomores talked with their parents significantly less than their white counterparts, and had parents whose aspirations were lower than those of parents of white sophomores. Clearly, lower high school graduation rates and college attendance rates of Native American, African American, and Hispanics were in part due to differences in family background (Sandefur, 1995). The resulting recommendation is that:

> We must work to insure that the barriers to educational success created by these [family and parental] traits are erased by providing encouragement, support, and financial assistance to children from disadvantaged backgrounds to allow them to take advantage of the educational opportunities available in American society (Sandefur, 1995).

Some studies have found that although children may be disadvantaged by factors such as discrimination, they can overcome these "barriers" with social support and these barriers need not be roadblocks to educational success. In fact, researchers have recommended that the educational system and the support that it can provide, such as promoting the value of education, striving toward ethnic sensitivity in schools, and increased hiring of ethnic minority teachers, can make a qualitative if not a quantitative difference in the lives of children and families (Fennelly, Mulkeen, & Giusti, 1995).

Family scientists have also examined the use of community resources in counseling with families at risk, and some social scientists call for a degree of cultural competence and sensitivity among professionals.

Healing forces are defined as factors contributing to the physical, mental, or spiritual health of the individual or family. When African Americans have a problem they generally first look within their indigenous support systems; the family, the church, black organizations and businesses. . . . Those who counsel with African-American families should have an awareness of the forces that promote healing. There should be a recognition that an African-American individual's heritage differs from a person of Eurocentric background. Recognition would involve a therapist's knowledge of the culture, an awareness of African retentions such as the concept of oral tradition, and knowledge of the impact of values, religion, and oppression in the client's life (Bagley & Carroll, 1995).

Access to community resources and formal support services has been shown to be a significant factor in promoting resilience in ethnic minority families. Studies have shown that adolescents who have access to these kinds of resources can prove resilient in dealing with risks of pregnancy or the challenge of a disruptive home environment. In one study of adolescent girls, factors were identified that decrease vulnerability to early pregnancy (McBride Murry, 1995). Poverty and adolescent pregnancy are viewed as disruptions of the traditional pathways to achieving adulthood, and the avoidance of early pregnancy may provide clues to adolescent strategies of resilience.

This study attempted to enhance our understanding of factors that decrease sexually active adolescents' vulnerability to early pregnancy and childbearing. . . . One of the most important conclusions from this study is that sexually active adolescents are more likely to avoid pregnancy when they have access to resources that provide opportunities for youth to obtain adulthood status through more traditional pathways, as well as avenues to prevent unplanned pregnancies and 'off-time' motherhood (McBride Murry, 1995).

Another study, focusing on Hispanic adolescents, found that access to resources was key to the resilience these youth demonstrated in spite of family conflict and parental alcoholism (Barrera, Li, & Chassin, 1995). Community resources can help reduce family conflict and a better understanding of ethnic minority families can lead to more effective preventive interventions for this conflict. This particular study concluded that:

> . . . some individuals have access to resources of resiliency
> that appear to protect them from harsh consequences while
> others have vulnerabilities (diatheses) that render them
> susceptible to negative outcomes. Both the epidemiology
> of psychological disorders and the development of inter-
> ventions to prevent or treat the consequences of stressful
> events are informed by a keener explication of resiliency
> and vulnerability (Barrera, Li, & Chassin, 1995).

Resources of resiliency are also found in the informal support systems within communities. Community building relies on
this informal support. In reviewing the initial findings from an
experimental community-based study of African-American women,
Genero (1995) examined the development of mutual relationships
as a vital though relatively unstudied aspect of resiliency. Mutual
relationships provide validation, ethnic identity and a sense of
community, all of which help ethnic minority families in coping
with a negative social environment. By testing the value of mutuality in relationships in ethnic families, Genero (1995) adds to the
growing body of work underscoring the importance of viewing resiliency in families as a relational process. Her work points to the
importance of understanding the processes of developing and maintaining relationships as critical to adaptation. She points out that:

> Families may develop and maintain a sense of resiliency
> by engaging in . . . diverse modes of social interaction that
> facilitate participation in and growth through relationships.
> Consequently, a relational rather than an individualistic
> mode of adaptation is key to understanding resiliency. . . .
> A relational perspective assumes the centrality of relation-
> ships in human development (Genero, 1995).

In a study of Navajo adolescent mothers, researchers found
that mothers take primary responsibility for caregiving, but family
support provides help as they adjust to the parenting role (Dalla &
Gamble, 1995). Researchers found that the social networks of
young Navajo mothers are often comprised of rich, extended networks of informal supports. These support systems may serve as
"buffering mechanisms," thus easing the transition to motherhood
and promoting positive adjustment to the maternal role:

> It is also noteworthy that these women do not appear to
> bestow child-related tasks upon other individuals, even
> when others are available and apparently willing to help.
> Rather, these young mothers assume the greatest amount
> of responsibility in caring for their young children. Pro-

grams offering child development training classes, for not only the mother but the entire family, including the male partner, may yield the most successful results in terms of increased program participation and decreased attenuation (Dalla & Gamble, 1995).

One family scientist looked at family support of the elderly and the socialization of children in African-American families in order to illustrate the mutual aid strategies of a community, and the strengths found in ethnic identity and resistance. In his review of resiliency studies in African-American communities, Thornton (1995) asserts that:

> Like many emerging works, this chapter begins with the assumption that communities and families possess resources that, while remaining unappreciated, contribute immensely to survival, to the abilities to counteract oppressive forces. These resources are left unexplored because they are often manifest in day-to-day activities. These mundane struggles of life that form the foundation of the overall effort of resistance are unspectacular, they are average. Nevertheless, placing these average life events at the center of analysis reveals empowered individuals within structures of domination (Thornton, 1995).

Both community and family support are important in the study of the long-term impact of residential treatment for African-American youth offenders and their families. In a longitudinal study of youth at risk, in particular, juvenile offenders who were mandated to receive residential treatment, family scientists focused on determining the relative importance of improvement in youth and family coping skills as predictors of successful program completion and positive (i.e., less restrictive) living situations 3 months and 12 months after completing treatment. The study, reflecting a family systems perspective, points to the value of changes in both youth and family coping as predictors of long- and short-term outcomes for African-American youth and their families.

> . . . it is when changes in youth spiritual and personal development (increase), youth positive appraisal and problem solving (increase), youth incendiary communication (reduction) as well as changes in family seeking professional and spiritual guidance (increase), seeking family and neighborhood support (increase) and affirming the family's confidence (increase) during the period of residential treatment are considered together as predictors, that we gain the

strongest prediction of the relative success of the Boysville program [treatment] (McCubbin, Fleming, Neitman, Thompson, Elver, & Savas, 1995).

The family is seen as part of a larger community. The community provides resources that enable ethnic minority family members to maintain their identities and to support one another. An important aspect of this research involves the concept of agency, when individuals intervene, make choices and act to change their world (Thornton, 1995). These choices are reflected in everyday resilience; the functioning of families in seeking out resources to meet the needs of family members, the preservation of ethnic identity against the pressures of a dominant society, as well as the adaptation that is required day to day to maintain balance as a family and within a community.

In a study of Native Hawaiian single-parent households, researchers explored the resilient effects of ethnic identity and support networks (Thompson et al., 1995). They found that single mothers draw upon these resources for family stability and survival.

> The single parents in this study demonstrated a creative and resilient approach to buffering the impact of family pressures through their use of community social support. Single-parent households faced a significantly greater impact of family pressures on their families, however, they were able to mobilize community resources to face those pressures (Thompson, McCubbin, Thompson, & Elver, 1995).

Family Resiliency: Flexibility and Adaptability to Change

Much of family science research on resiliency focuses on successful functioning in the face of adversity, the process of overcoming disadvantages in ordinary family life. But it is in the face of adversity that we find the values, practices, and norms that serve as a foundation for resiliency. One study cites poverty as the greatest challenge to resiliency for African-American families (McAdoo, 1995). Cultural resources have proven successful in maintaining resilient families in spite of the challenges of poverty and discrimination.

> It is very tempting to move into a problem oriented focus when one looks at African-American families, for the problems that we face are life threatening and overwhelming.

Yet one must avoid this orientation as much as possible, for it will force us to focus on the disproportionate representation of families who are in trouble. We need to examine families who are resilient and who have overcome many of the hurdles present in their environment. We will otherwise overlook the families who are making it everyday, although under less than ideal conditions.

The common cultural patterns that have contributed to the resiliency of African-American families are: supportive social networks; flexible relationships within the family unit; a strong sense of religiosity; extensive use of extended family helping arrangements; the adoption of fictive kin who become as family; and strong identification with their racial group (McAdoo, 1995).

A study of Korean immigrant couples describes how families accommodate a dual work and family role for women (Kim & Kim, 1995). The family's resiliency centers on this dual role, which serves as an adaptation to American culture and helps maintain family unity in the new environment. While this dual role may be adaptive for the family unit, it may not be a positive factor for individual women in those families.

In Korean immigrant families, the wife's employment signifies the addition of a new role to her traditional family role. Employed wives, therefore, bear a heavy burden of double roles. Furthermore, they do so regardless of length of residence in the United States.

This pattern of resilient adaptation is likely to continue through the personal sacrifice of the mother/wife in Korean immigrant families, unless some conscious effort is made for an equitable distribution of the family roles among family members (Kim & Kim, 1995).

A different approach to women's dual roles is taken in a qualitative study of Puerto Rican migrant families (Toro-Morn, 1995). The researcher concludes that this dual role provides family stability and goes further to explore the adaptive strategies of female-headed households; these households are seen as resourceful and adaptive, as well as a source of resistance to the dominant culture and the expectations of traditional family roles.

To what extent do the strategies families develop in the process of adapting to life in the city challenge the traditional division of labor within the household? Interviews suggest that husbands may have accommodated to their wives' temporary employment, but that did not change the traditional division of labor within the household. Instead, women developed strategies to accommodate their roles as working wives (Toro-Morn, 1995).

In many cultures, families accommodate their members with illnesses or disabilities to maintain family stability. A study of minority families who give home care to the mentally ill demonstrates the resilience of families responsible for continuous care in spite of limited resources. The caregivers in this study focused on the strengths of the mentally ill member and relied on cultural traditions and religious beliefs for help in confronting and resolving problems (Parra & Guarnaccia, 1995).

A study of the multigenerational family system of Chinese-Americans focused on the perceptions of middle generation parents toward grandparents as a resource in childrearing (Tam & Detzner, 1995). The researchers examined the resiliency afforded by an expansion of the definitions we give of the family, and concluded that,

> As revealed in this study, the experiences of immigration and their ethnic cultural background have immense influence on the family dynamics and interactions of the families studied. To understand the experiences of Chinese-American families fully, analysis should be expanded from focusing on the notion of a nuclear family to the idea of a multigenerational family system in which family members live in separate households spanning thousands of miles while still exerting influence or extending assistance to one another (Tam & Detzner, 1995).

Family Resiliency: Parenting, Marital Relationships, and Family Meanings

Relationships appeared to be a resiliency factor in Mexican-American and African-American homeless families. While relationship disruption often leads to homelessness, caregivers in these families continued to strive to maintain family stability, to be good parents despite their circumstances. Resiliency was reflected in these caregiving relationships, a resiliency factor, characterized by persistence in adapting to the environment and the available resources, and by consistent contributions to family stability (Torquati & Gamble, 1995).

Other researchers have taken this focus on parenting as a primary resource for resiliency. In an empirical study of the relationship between home and school environments, and their influence on the school achievement of Mexican-American children, researchers identified parental support as a resilient factor and concluded that,

> In our view, parents of successful children are better consumers of the school system and are better able to access the resources the school system has for families. Finally, it also seems that in successful or resilient families, the parents are more confident that their children will not encounter barriers to their success in life because of their ethnicity (Okagaki & Frensch, 1995).

Family scientists conducted an observational study of parenting dynamics in African-American and Asian-American families in which they examined the interactions between mothers and daughters. They found significant cultural differences in parent-to-child issues such as support, conflict, and control (Gonzales, Hiraga, & Cauce, 1995). The observational ratings and self-report data were consistent for African-American families, but not for Asian-American families. The researchers were challenged by the task of coding the behavior of a cultural group other than their own and they questioned the validity of measurement equivalence in cross-cultural studies, noting that the equivalence of observational measures has been largely unexplored. This study speaks to the importance of developing research methods and measures that adequately reflect the realities of racial and ethnic minority families and that are essential to the advancement of our understanding of the role of culture and ethnicity in resiliency research.

The resilient strategies of single parents were also explored as a resource for resiliency. Single parents may have inadequate resources, but they compensate by adjusting to their circumstances and seeking support (Gamble & Dalla, 1995). In an empirical study of parenting in Euro- and Mexican-American families, comparisons were made between single- and two-parent households. Researchers found that single-parent women adapt to a new role as head of household with competence, positive adaptation, and social support (Gamble & Dalla, 1995).

Other family scientists have studied African-American adolescent fathers and their perceptions of their role as parents. In one empirical study the fathers expressed a commitment to parenting that may serve as a resource, a starting point for building a sense of responsibility for remaining involved with their children (Allen & Doherty, 1995). Researchers hope to explore ways around the developmental and structural obstacles to that involvement.

> The majority of the adolescent fathers in this study appeared truly dedicated to being involved with their children and performing their roles as fathers, as they understood that role. Regardless of the empirical evidence suggesting less involvement by adolescent fathers over time, it is important not to lose sight of this group of fathers' sense of commitment. Therein might lie the key to ensuring a continuing commitment to their children over time, and perhaps even to their natal partners (Allen & Doherty, 1995).

Other family science researchers find the marriage relationship to be a central resource for resiliency. In a study of interracial couples, researchers found the marriage relationship itself to be a source of strength for these couples (Chan & Wethington, 1995). Their discussion of resilience and marital stability demonstrates how the resilience perspective can focus on strengths and successful coping to find answers to the challenges interracial couples face. These researchers found that:

> A resilience perspective on interracial marriages differs from more traditional approaches by paying as much attention to positive resources brought by individuals to these marriages as to the social and personal circumstances which may threaten marital stability. It also redefines the outcome of interest, shifting the focus from negative emotional adjustment and unhappiness to "competence" and good coping (Luthar, 1993) . . . the resilience approach elaborates not only circumstances under which a marriage is likely to be a failure, but also the circumstances that produce success . . . . Most importantly, the resilience perspective views the intimate marital relationship in an interracial marriage as a resource to the couple, rather than as a basis for conflict (Chan & Wethington, 1995).

Similarly, in a qualitative study, African-American couples dealing with infertility demonstrated that their relationship was a resource for resiliency; the challenge of infertility strengthened their relationship and led to improved communication and support for one another (Phipps, 1995).

Some family scientists propose the study of successful, lasting marriages as a key to understanding marital issues. In a study of marital satisfaction for African-American couples, the researcher emphasized how successful couples work through conflicts and deal with discrimination (Connor, 1995). Again, the marriage relationship was seen as a resource for resiliency. In critiquing previous research on marital issues, the author of this study asserted that:

> None of these tools seem to include input from couples who have experienced conflict and 'worked through' it. Additionally, none of them seem pertinent to the assessment of marital or relationship strengths. Each seems to imply that by somehow determining the areas of stress, conflict, and problems, marital issues can be resolved. Given the clinical orientation of the assessment devices, this approach is not surprising. One wonders, however, if the approach is somewhat lacking. That is, there may be more value in assessing couples who remain together after many years of marriage, who are reasonably satisfied with their marital relationship and who acknowledge problematic areas—both past and present (Connor, 1995).

While family research in the military has flourished in the past two decades, we remain pressed to find penetrating studies on ethnic families of enlisted personnel. Reporting on one investigation conducted on a representative sample of African-American families of enlisted Army personnel, family scholars report on the critical resiliency factors that promote family adaptation (McCubbin, 1995). The study revealed the importance of spouse's employment, spouse's self-reliance, and family time together as vital to the adaptation of families relocated to Europe. Of equal importance is the family's sense of coherence or goodness of fit between the family and the community, in this case the Army and its lifestyle. The researcher concluded:

> African-American families appear to have a stronger sense of coherence, or fit, if they feel they belong, have some say about their future, have some degree of predictability in their lives, and feel their families will be cared for should a crisis emerge (McCubbin, 1995).

In most of the investigations reviewed, the family is not viewed as an isolated unit, but is seen as a vital element in a larger social and economic context. Therefore, resiliency is not defined as the internal capacities of a family, as psychology has focused on the personality traits of an individual. Rather, the concept that emerges is that of a family's ability to change itself, capability to adapt to a situation, and the ability to change its circumstances and environment. In all cases, the family is resilient by virtue of its proactive responses to circumstances.

These observations by family scholars focusing on ethnic families and resiliency, gleaned from family research and theory building efforts, call into question the casual and potentially misleading argument that adaptation is merely a process of being absorbed into the majority culture and thus compromising ethnic identity and worth. It is apparent that adaptation is not a passive process dictated by a powerful majority. Adaptation for racial and ethnic minority families is an active and proactive process in which families of color are able to maintain, affirm, and assert their ethnic heritage and identity, respond to conditions as they are, and work to change the environment to be more supportive and respectful of diverse cultures.

Note

1. This project was supported by the Agricultural Experiment Station, the Center for Excellence in Family Studies, and the Institute for the Study of Resiliency in Families, School of Family Resources and Consumer Sciences, University of Wisconsin–Madison, Madison, Wisconsin. The authors would like to thank Mr. Wade Masshardt for his outstanding support of and contributions to this effort.

References

Allen, W.D. & Doherty, W.J. (1995). Being there: The perception of fatherhood among a group of African-American adolescent fathers. In H.I. McCubbin, E.A. Thompson, A.I. Thompson, & J.A. Futrell (Eds.), *Resiliency in ethnic minority families: African-American families* (Vol. 2, pp. 207–244). Madison, WI: University of Wisconsin System.

Bagley, C.A. & Carroll, J. (1995). Healing forces in African-American families. In H.I. McCubbin, E.A. Thompson, A.I. Thompson, & J.A. Futrell (Eds.), *Resiliency in ethnic minority families: African-American families* (Vol. 2, pp. 117–142). Madison, WI: University of Wisconsin System.

Barrera, M., Jr., Li, S.A., & Chassin, L. (1995). Exploring adolescents' vulnerability to life stress and parental alcoholism: The role of ethnicity and family conflict. In H.I. McCubbin, E.A. Thompson, A.I. Thompson, & J.E. Fromer (Eds.), *Resiliency in ethnic minority families: Native and immigrant American families* (Vol. 1, pp. 295–324). Madison, WI: University of Wisconsin System.

Cantwell, M.L. & Jenkins, D.I. (1995). Housing and neighborhood satisfaction of single-parent mothers and grandmothers. In H.I. McCubbin, E.A. Thompson, A.I. Thompson, & J.A. Futrell (Eds.), *Resiliency in ethnic minority families: African-American families* (Vol. 2, pp. 99–115). Madison, WI: University of Wisconsin System.

Capaldi, D. M. & Patterson, G.R. (1991). Relation of parental transitions to boys' adjustment problems: I. A linear hypothesis. II. Mothers at risk for transitions and unskilled parenting. *Developmental Psychology, 3,* 489–504.

Chan, A.Y. & Wethington, E. (1995). Factors promoting marital resilience among interracial couples. In H.I. McCubbin, E.A. Thompson, A.I. Thompson, & J.E. Fromer (Eds.), *Resiliency in ethnic minority families: Native and immigrant American families* (Vol. 1, pp. 71–87). Madison, WI: University of Wisconsin System.

Connor, M.E. (1995). Level of satisfaction in African-American marriages: A preliminary investigation. In H.I. McCubbin, E.A. Thompson, A.I. Thompson, & J.A. Futrell (Eds.), *Resiliency in ethnic minority families: African-American families* (Vol. 2, pp. 159–177). Madison, WI: University of Wisconsin System.

Connors, J.L. & Donnellan, A.M. (1995). Walk in beauty: Western perspectives on disability and Navajo family/cultural resistance. In H.I. McCubbin, E.A. Thompson, A.I. Thompson, & J.E. Fromer (Eds.), *Resiliency in ethnic minority families: Native and immigrant American families* (Vol. 1, pp. 159–182). Madison, WI: University of Wisconsin System.

Cross, T.L. (1995). Understanding family resiliency from a relational world view. In H.I. McCubbin, E.A. Thompson, A.I. Thompson, & J.E. Fromer (Eds.), *Resiliency in ethnic minority families: Native and immigrant American families* (Vol. 1, pp. 143–157). Madison, WI: University of Wisconsin System.

Dalla, R.L. & Gamble, W.C. (1995). Social networks and systems of support among American Indian Navajo adolescent mothers. In H.I. McCubbin, E.A. Thompson, A.I. Thompson, & J.E. Fromer (Eds.), *Resiliency in ethnic minority families: Native and immigrant American families* (Vol. 1, pp. 183–198). Madison, WI: University of Wisconsin System.

Dubos, R. (1978). *The resiliency of ecosystems.* Boulder: Colorado Associated University Press.

Elsass, P. (1992). *Strategies for survival: The psychology of cultural resilience in ethnic minorities.* New York: New York University Press.

Emery, R. & Forehand, R. (1994). Parental divorce and children's well-being: A focus on resiliency. In R. Haggerty, L. Sherrod, N. Garmezy, & M. Rutter. (Eds.), *Stress, risk, and resiliency in children and adolescents* (pp. 63–99). New York: Cambridge University Press.

Fennelly, K., Mulkeen, P., & Giusti, C. (1995). Coping with racism and discrimination: The experience of young Latino adolescents. In H.I. McCubbin, E.A. Thompson, A.I. Thompson, & J.E. Fromer (Eds.), *Resiliency in ethnic minority families: Native and immigrant American families* (Vol. 1, pp. 367–383). Madison, WI: University of Wisconsin System.

Forehand, R., Thomas, A., Wierson, M., Brody, G., & Fauber, R. (1990). Role of maternal functioning and parenting skills in adolescent functioning following parental divorce. *Journal of Abnormal Psychology, 99*, 278–283.

Gamble, W.C. & Dalla, R.L. (1995). Parenting and child adjustment in single- and two-parent, Euro- and Mexican-American families. In H.I. McCubbin, E.A. Thompson, A.I. Thompson, & J.E. Fromer (Eds.), *Resiliency in ethnic minority families: Native and immigrant American families* (Vol. 1, pp. 343–365). Madison, WI: University of Wisconsin System.

Gelman, D. (1991). The miracle of resiliency. *Newsweek, 117*(26), 44–47.

Genero, N.P. (1995). Culture, resiliency, and mutual psychological development. In H.I. McCubbin, E.A. Thompson, A.I. Thompson, & J.A. Futrell (Eds.), *Resiliency in ethnic minority families: African-American families* (Vol. 2, pp. 31–48). Madison, WI: University of Wisconsin System.

Gonzales, N.A., Hiraga, Y., & Cauce, A.M. (1995). Observing mother-daughter interaction in African-American and Asian-American families. In H.I. McCubbin, E.A. Thompson, A.I. Thompson, & J.A. Futrell (Eds.), *Resiliency in ethnic minority families: African-American families* (Vol. 2, pp. 259–286). Madison, WI: University of Wisconsin System.

Haggerty, R., Sherrod, L., Garmezy, N., & Rutter, M. (1994). *Stress, risk, and resiliency in children and adolescents*. New York: Cambridge University Press.

Holtz, C.S. (1995). The lack of prenatal care in poor urban African-American postpartal women: A phenomenological study. In H.I. McCubbin, E.A. Thompson, A.I. Thompson, & J.A. Futrell (Eds.), *Resiliency in ethnic minority families: African-American families* (Vol. 2, pp. 143–156). Madison, WI: University of Wisconsin System.

Kempton, T., Armistead, L., Wierson, M., & Forehand, R. (1991). Presence of a sibling as a potential buffer following parent divorce: An examination of young adolescents. *Journal of Clinical Child Psychology, 20*, 434–438.

Kim, K.C. & Kim, S. (1995). Family and work roles of Korean immigrants in the United States. In H.I. McCubbin, E.A. Thompson, A.I. Thompson, & J.E. Fromer (Eds.), *Resiliency in ethnic minority families: Native and immigrant American families* (Vol. 1, pp. 225–242). Madison, WI: University of Wisconsin System.

Kotlowitz, A. (1995). Breaking the silence: Growing up in today's inner city. In H.I. McCubbin, E.A. Thompson, A.I. Thompson, & J.A. Futrell (Eds.), *Resiliency in ethnic minority families: African-American families* (Vol. 2, pp. 3–15). Madison, WI: University of Wisconsin System.

Marsella, A.J., Oliveira, J.M., Plummer, C.M., & Crabbe, K.M. (1995). Native Hawaiian (Kanaka Maoli) culture, mind, and well-being. In H.I. McCubbin, E.A. Thompson, A.I. Thompson, & J.E. Fromer (Eds.), *Resiliency in ethnic minority families: Native and immigrant American families* (Vol. 1, pp. 93–113). Madison, WI: University of Wisconsin System.

McAdoo, H.P. (1995). African-American families: Strengths and realities. In H.I. McCubbin, E.A. Thompson, A.I. Thompson, & J.A. Futrell (Eds.), *Resiliency in ethnic minority families: African-American families* (Vol. 2, pp. 17–30). Madison, WI: University of Wisconsin System.

McBride Murry, V. (1995). Variation in adolescent pregnancy status: A national tri-ethnic study. In H.I. McCubbin, E.A. Thompson, A.I. Thompson, & J.A. Futrell (Eds.), *Resiliency in ethnic minority families: African-American families* (Vol. 2, pp. 179–205). Madison, WI: University of Wisconsin System.

McCubbin, H. (1995). Resiliency in African-American families: Military families in foreign environments. In H.I. McCubbin, E.A. Thompson, A.I. Thompson, & J.A. Futrell (Eds.), *Resiliency in ethnic minority families: African-American families* (Vol. 2, pp. 67–97). Madison, WI: University of Wisconsin System.

McCubbin, H. & McCubbin, M. (1988). Typology of resilient families: Emerging roles of social class and ethnicity. *Family Relations, 37,* 247–254.

McCubbin, H., McCubbin, M., Thompson, A., & Thompson, E. (1995). Resiliency in ethnic families: A conceptual model for predicting family adjustment and adaptation. In H.I. McCubbin, E.A. Thompson, A.I. Thompson, & J.E. Fromer (Eds.), *Resiliency in ethnic minority families: Native and immigrant American families* (Vol. 1, pp. 3–48). Madison, WI: University of Wisconsin System.

McCubbin, H., Fleming, W.M, Neitman, P., Thompson, A., Elver, K., & Savas, S. (1995). Resiliency and coping in "at risk" African-American youth and families. In H.I. McCubbin, E.A. Thompson, A.I. Thompson, & J.A. Futrell (Eds.), *Resiliency in ethnic minority families: African-American families* (Vol. 2, pp. 287–328). Madison, WI: University of Wisconsin System.

McCubbin, H., Thompson, A., Thompson, E., McCubbin, M., & Kasten, A. (1993). Culture, ethnicity and the family: Critical factors in childhood chronic illness and disabilities. *Journal of Pediatrics, 91,* 1063–1070.

Ngo, P.Y.L. & Malz, T.A. (1995). Cross-cultural and cross-generational differences in Asian Americans' cultural and familial systems and their impact on academic striving. In H.I. McCubbin, E.A. Thompson, A.I. Thompson, & J.E. Fromer (Eds.), *Resiliency in ethnic minority families: Native and immigrant American families* (Vol. 1, pp. 265–274). Madison, WI: University of Wisconsin System.

Okagaki, L. & Frensch, P.A. (1995). Parental support for Mexican-American children's school achievement. In H.I. McCubbin, E.A. Thompson, A.I. Thompson, & J.E. Fromer (Eds.), *Resiliency in ethnic minority families: Native and immigrant American families* (Vol. 1, pp. 325–342). Madison, WI: University of Wisconsin System.

Parra, P.A. & Guarnaccia, P. (1995). Ethnicity, culture, and resiliency in caregivers of a seriously mentally ill family member. In H.I. McCubbin, E.A. Thompson, A.I. Thompson, & J.E. Fromer (Eds.), *Resiliency in ethnic minority families: Native and immigrant American families* (Vol. 1, pp. 431–450). Madison, WI: University of Wisconsin System.

Phipps, S.A. Arnn (1995). African-American couples' lived experience of infertility. In H.I. McCubbin, E.A. Thompson, A.I. Thompson, & J.A. Futrell (Eds.), *Resiliency in ethnic minority families: African-American families* (Vol. 2, pp. 245–258). Madison,WI: University of Wisconsin System.

San Miguel, S.K., Morrison, G.M., Weissglass, T. (1995). The relationship of sources of support and service needs: Resilience patterns in low-income Latino/Hispanic families. In H.I. McCubbin, E.A. Thompson, A.I. Thompson, & J.E. Fromer (Eds.), *Resiliency in ethnic minority families: Native and immigrant American families* (Vol. 1, pp. 385–400). Madison, WI: University of Wisconsin System.

Sandefur, G.D. (1995). Race, ethnicity, families and education. In H.I. McCubbin, E.A. Thompson, A.I. Thompson, & J.E. Fromer (Eds.), *Resiliency in ethnic minority families: Native and immigrant American families* (Vol. 1, pp. 49–70). Madison, WI: University of Wisconsin System.

Tam, V.C. & Detzner, D.F. (1995). Grandparents as a family resource in Chinese-American families: Perceptions of the middle generation. In H.I. McCubbin, E.A. Thompson, A.I. Thompson, & J.E. Fromer (Eds.), *Resiliency in ethnic minority families: Native and immigrant American families* (Vol. 1, pp. 243–263). Madison, WI: University of Wisconsin System.

Thompson, E.A., McCubbin, H.I., Thompson, A.I., & Elver, K.M. (1995). Vulnerability and resiliency in Native Hawaiian families under stress. In H.I. McCubbin, E.A. Thompson, A.I. Thompson, & J.E. Fromer (Eds.), *Resiliency in ethnic minority families: Native and immigrant American families* (Vol. 1, pp. 115–131). Madison, WI: University of Wisconsin System.

Thornton, M.C. (1995). Indigenous resources and strategies of resistance: Informal caregiving and racial socialization in black communities. In H.I. McCubbin, E.A. Thompson, A.I. Thompson, & J.A. Futrell (Eds.), *Resiliency in ethnic minority families: African-American families* (Vol. 2, pp. 49–66). Madison, WI: University of Wisconsin System.

Toro-Morn, M.I. (1995). The family and work experience of Puerto Rican women migrants in Chicago. In H.I. McCubbin, E.A. Thompson, A.I. Thompson, & J.E. Fromer (Eds.), *Resiliency in ethnic minority families: Native and immigrant American families* (Vol. 1, pp. 277–294). Madison, WI: University of Wisconsin System.

Torquati, J.C., & Gamble, W.C. (1995). Continuity of caregiving in Mexican-American and African-American homeless families. In H.I. McCubbin, E.A. Thompson, A.I. Thompson, & J.E. Fromer (Eds.), *Resiliency in ethnic minority families: Native and immigrant American families* (Vol. 1, pp. 401–429). Madison, WI: University of Wisconsin System.

Trask, H.K. (1995). Native sovereignty: A strategy for Hawaiian family survival. In H.I. McCubbin, E. A. Thompson, A.I. Thompson, & J.E. Fromer (Eds.), *Resiliency in ethnic minority families: Native and immigrant American families* (Vol. 1, pp. 133–139). Madison, WI: University of Wisconsin System.

Werner, E. & Smith, R. (1982). *Vulnerable but invincible.* New York: McGraw-Hill.

Werner, E. & Smith, R. (1992). *Overcoming the odds.* Ithaca, NY: Cornell University Press.

Zimmerman, M.A., Ramirez, J., Washienko, K.M., Walter, B., & Dyer, S. (1995). Enculturation hypothesis: Exploring direct and protective effects among Native American youth. In H.I. McCubbin, E.A. Thompson, A.I. Thompson, & J.E. Fromer (Eds.), *Resiliency in ethnic minority families: Native and immigrant American families* (Vol. 1, pp. 199–220). Madison, WI: University of Wisconsin System.

Index

About the Editors

Hamilton I. McCubbin is Dean of the School of Human Ecology; Professor of Child and Family Studies and Social Work; and Director of the Center for Excellence in Family Studies, the Institute for the Study of Resiliency in Families, and the Family Stress, Coping and Health Project at the University of Wisconsin—Madison. He holds academic degrees from the University of Wisconsin–Madison (BS, MS, PhD). He undertook postdoctoral studies at Yale University, University of Minnesota, and Stanford University. He has authored, edited, and coedited 18 books and maintains scholarly research on families over the life cycle and families under stress, with particular emphasis on family postcrisis responses and resiliency.

Elizabeth A. Thompson is Research Associate and Postdoctoral Scholar at the Center for Excellence in Family Studies and the Institute for the Study of Resiliency in Families at the University of Wisconsin—Madison. She holds academic degrees from St. Olaf College (BA) and the University of Wisconsin—Madison (MA, PhD). She is the author or coeditor of six books and maintains scholarly research in the advancement of qualitative methods with families faced with stigmatized hardships and adversities.

Anne I. Thompson is Assistant Dean at the School of Human Ecology and Associate Director of the Center for Excellence in Family Studies, the Institute for the Study of Resiliency in Families, and the Family Stress, Coping and Health Project, University of Wisconsin—Madison. She holds academic degrees from the University of Wisconsin—Madison (BS, MS, PhD) and undertook postdoctoral studies at Bryn Mawr College. She is the author, editor, and coeditor of eight books and maintains scholarly research on families, the workplace, and health.

Jo A. Futrell is Editor at the Center for Excellence in Family Studies and the Institute for the Study of Resiliency in Families at the University of Wisconsin—Madison. She holds academic degrees (BA, MA) from Iowa State University, Ames, Iowa.

DATE DUE

#47-0108 Peel Off Pressure Sensitive